INU✕BOKU SS

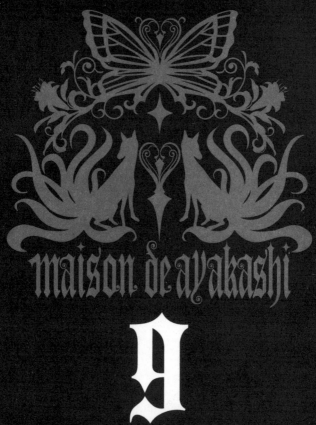

maison de ayakashi

9

Welcome to Maison de Ayakashi.
The exclusive Secret Service of
this Mansion guarantees
your mental and physical
safety by providing
superior escorts.

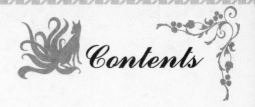

Contents

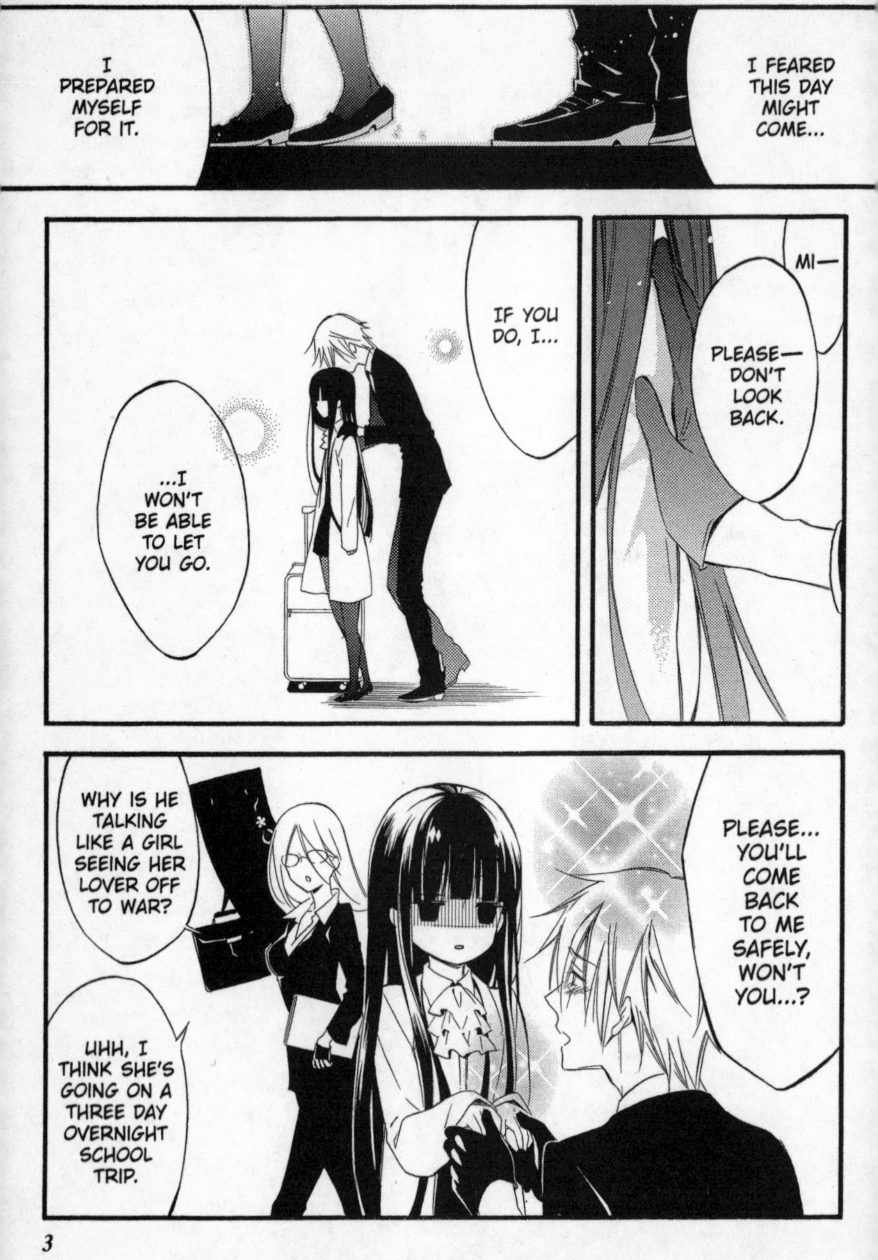
I FEARED THIS DAY MIGHT COME...
I PREPARED MYSELF FOR IT.
MI—
PLEASE— DON'T LOOK BACK.
IF YOU DO, I...
...I WON'T BE ABLE TO LET YOU GO.
PLEASE... YOU'LL COME BACK TO ME SAFELY, WON'T YOU...?
WHY IS HE TALKING LIKE A GIRL SEEING HER LOVER OFF TO WAR?
UHH, I THINK SHE'S GOING ON A THREE DAY OVERNIGHT SCHOOL TRIP.

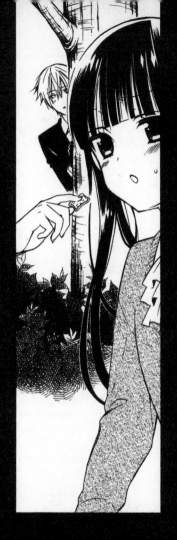

INTERLUDE 3: DISTANCE

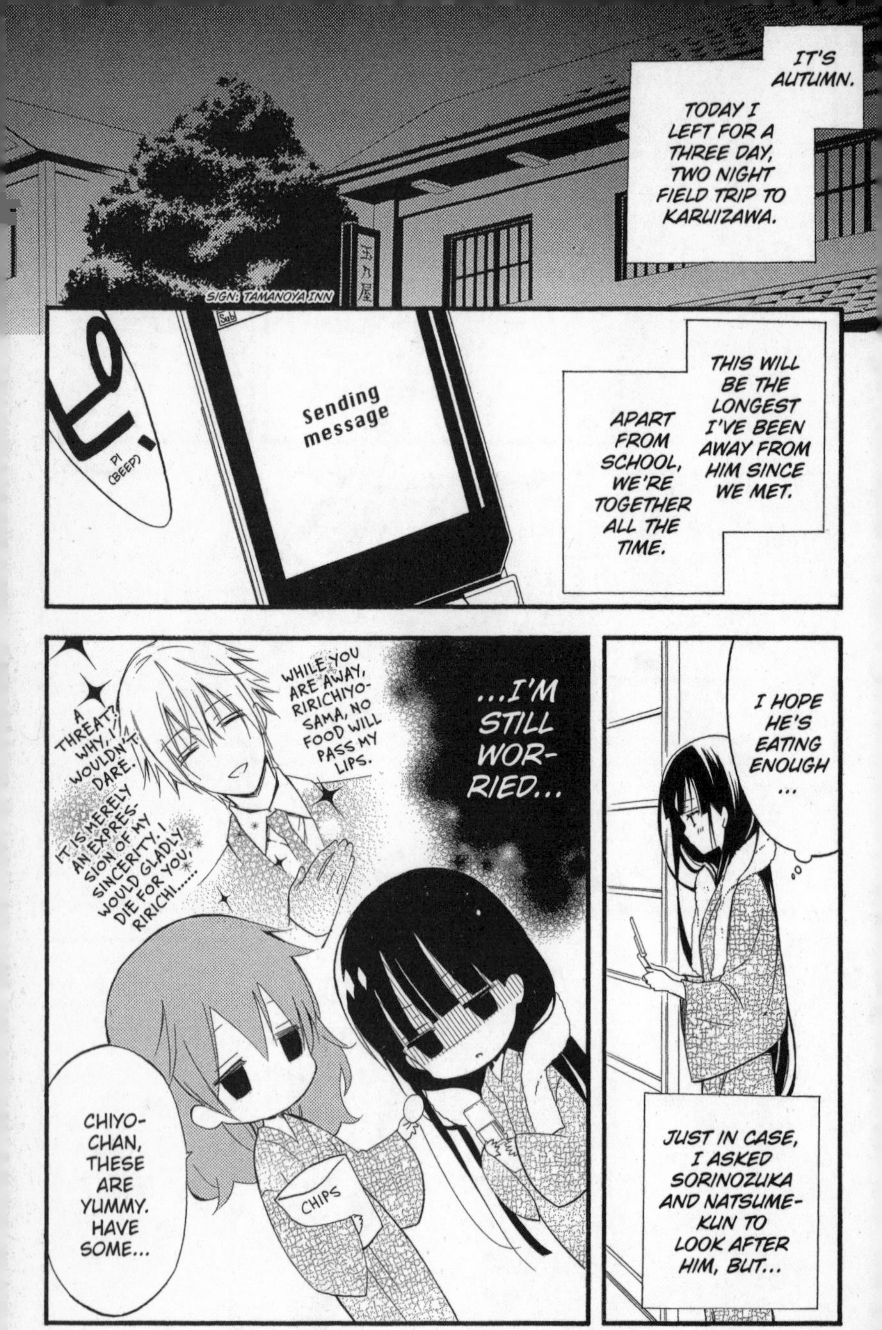
IT'S AUTUMN.
TODAY I LEFT FOR A THREE DAY, TWO NIGHT FIELD TRIP TO KARUIZAWA.
SIGN: TAMANOYA INN
THIS WILL BE THE LONGEST I'VE BEEN AWAY FROM HIM SINCE WE MET.
APART FROM SCHOOL, WE'RE TOGETHER ALL THE TIME.
Sending message
PI (BEEP)
I HOPE HE'S EATING ENOUGH...
JUST IN CASE, I ASKED SORINOZUKA AND NATSUME-KUN TO LOOK AFTER HIM, BUT...
...I'M STILL WORRIED...
WHILE YOU ARE AWAY, RIRICHIYO-SAMA, NO FOOD WILL PASS MY LIPS.
A THREAT? WHY, I WOULDN'T DARE.
IT IS MERELY AN EXPRESSION OF MY SINCERITY. I WOULD GLADLY DIE FOR YOU, RIRICHI......
CHIYO-CHAN, THESE ARE YUMMY. HAVE SOME...
CHIPS

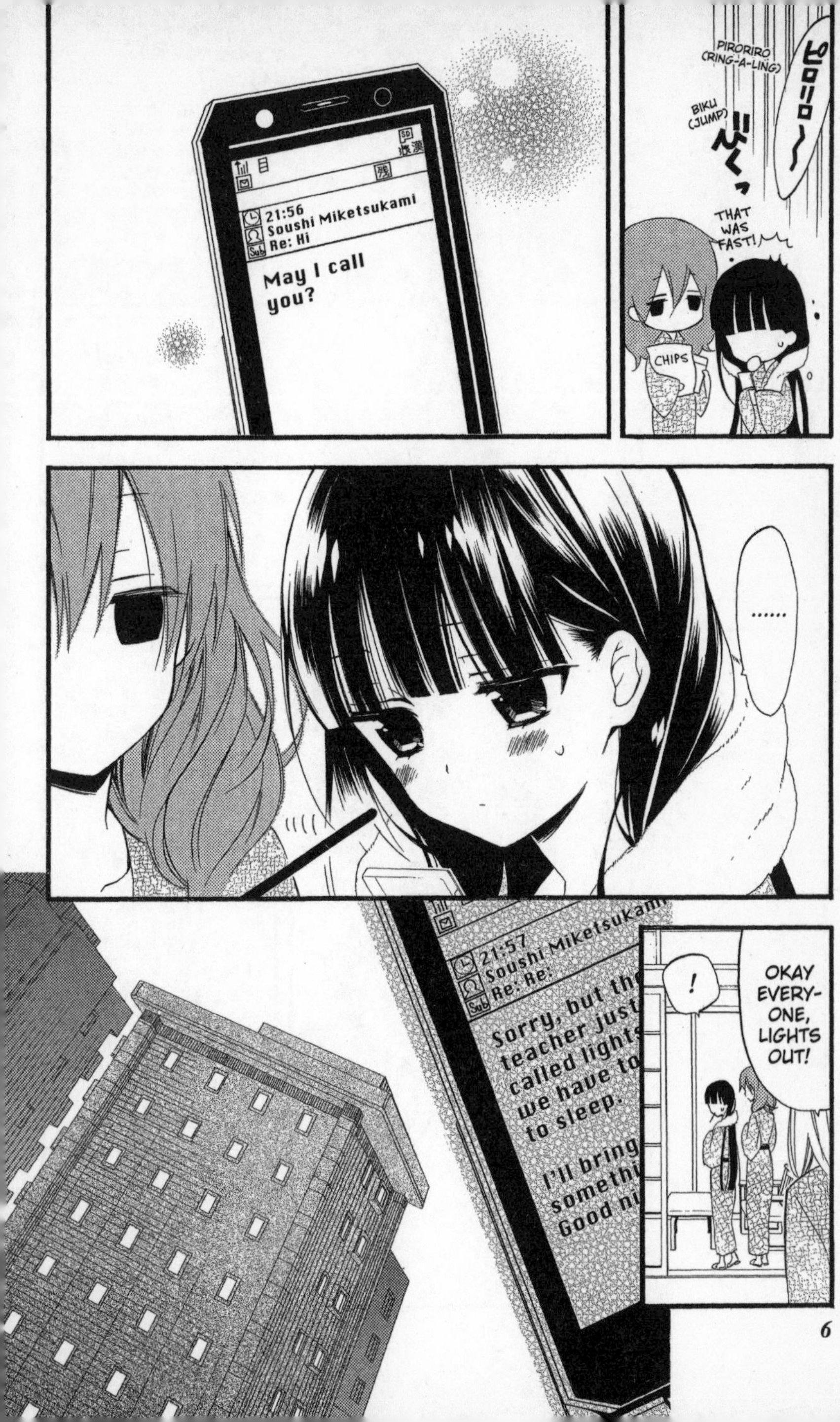
PIRORIRO (RING-A-LING)
ピロリロ～
BIKU (JUMP)
びくっ
THAT WAS FAST!
CHIPS
21:56
Soushi Miketsukami
Re: Hi
May I call you?
......
!
OKAY EVERY-ONE, LIGHTS OUT!
21:57
Soushi Miketsukami
Re: Re:
Sorry, but th
teacher just
called light
we have to
to sleep.
I'll bring
somethi
Good ni

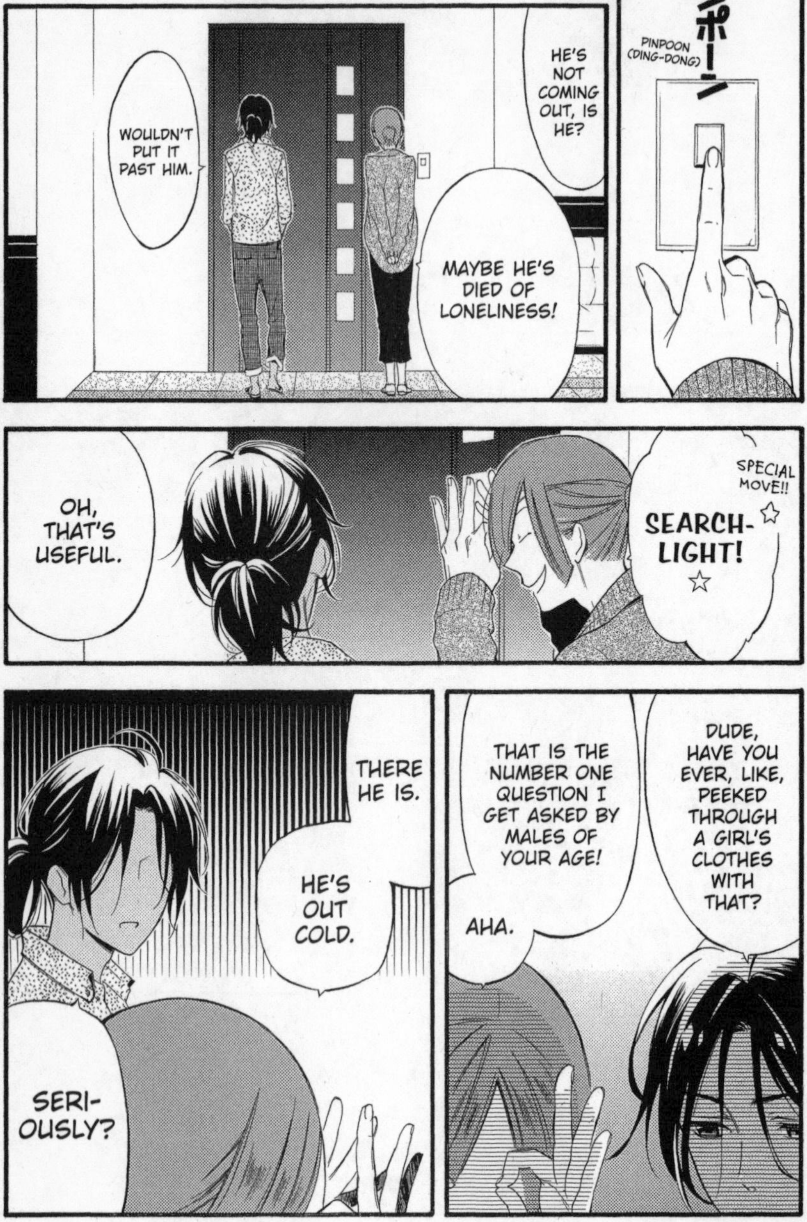
ピンポーン
PINPOON (DING-DONG)
HE'S NOT COMING OUT, IS HE?
MAYBE HE'S DIED OF LONELINESS!
WOULDN'T PUT IT PAST HIM.
SPECIAL MOVE!!
SEARCH-LIGHT! ☆
OH, THAT'S USEFUL.
DUDE, HAVE YOU EVER, LIKE, PEEKED THROUGH A GIRL'S CLOTHES WITH THAT?
THAT IS THE NUMBER ONE QUESTION I GET ASKED BY MALES OF YOUR AGE!
AHA.
THERE HE IS.
HE'S OUT COLD.
SERI-OUSLY?

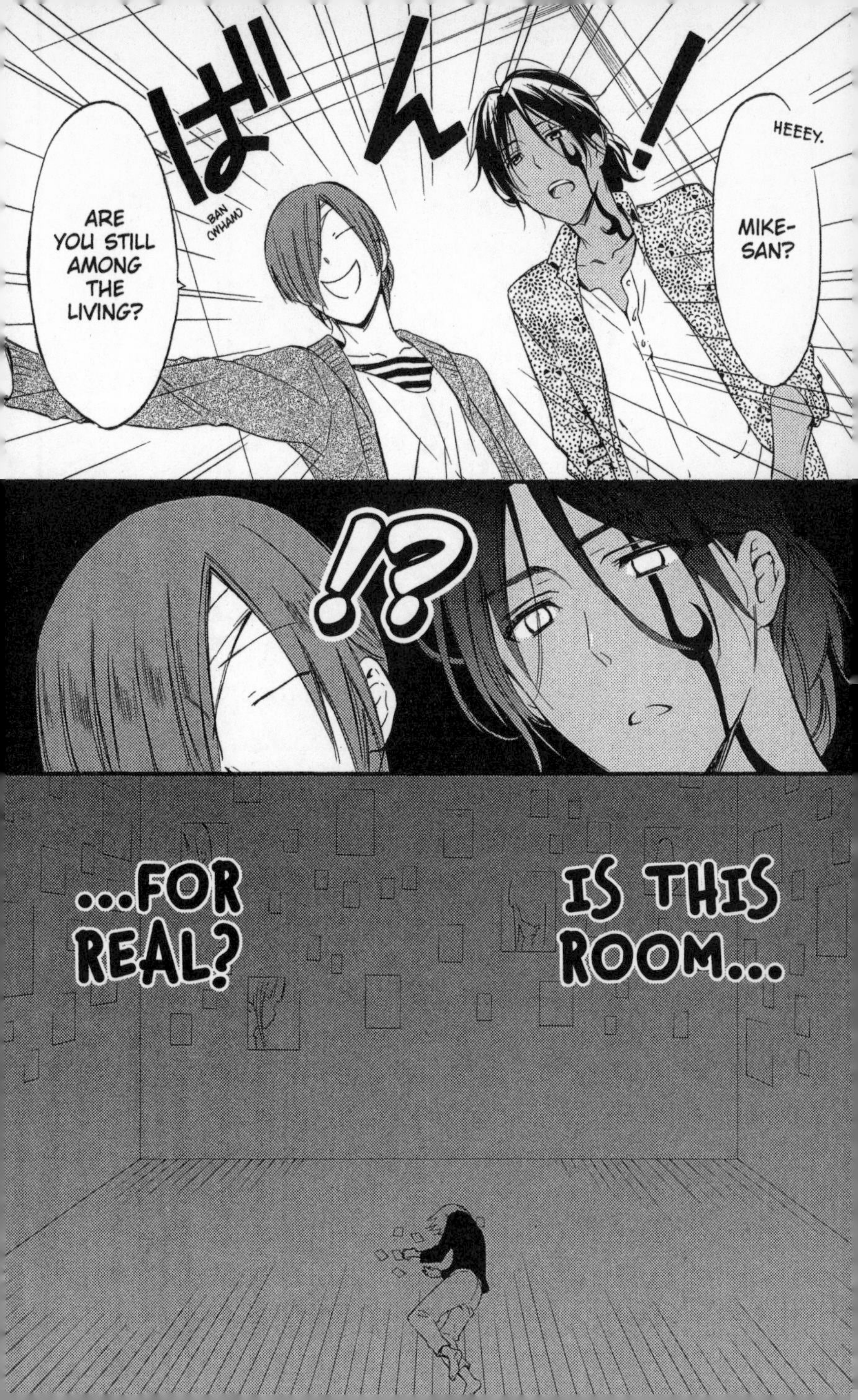
HEEEY.
MIKE-SAN?
ばん!
BAN (WHAM)
ARE YOU STILL AMONG THE LIVING?
!?
IS THIS ROOM...
...FOR REAL?

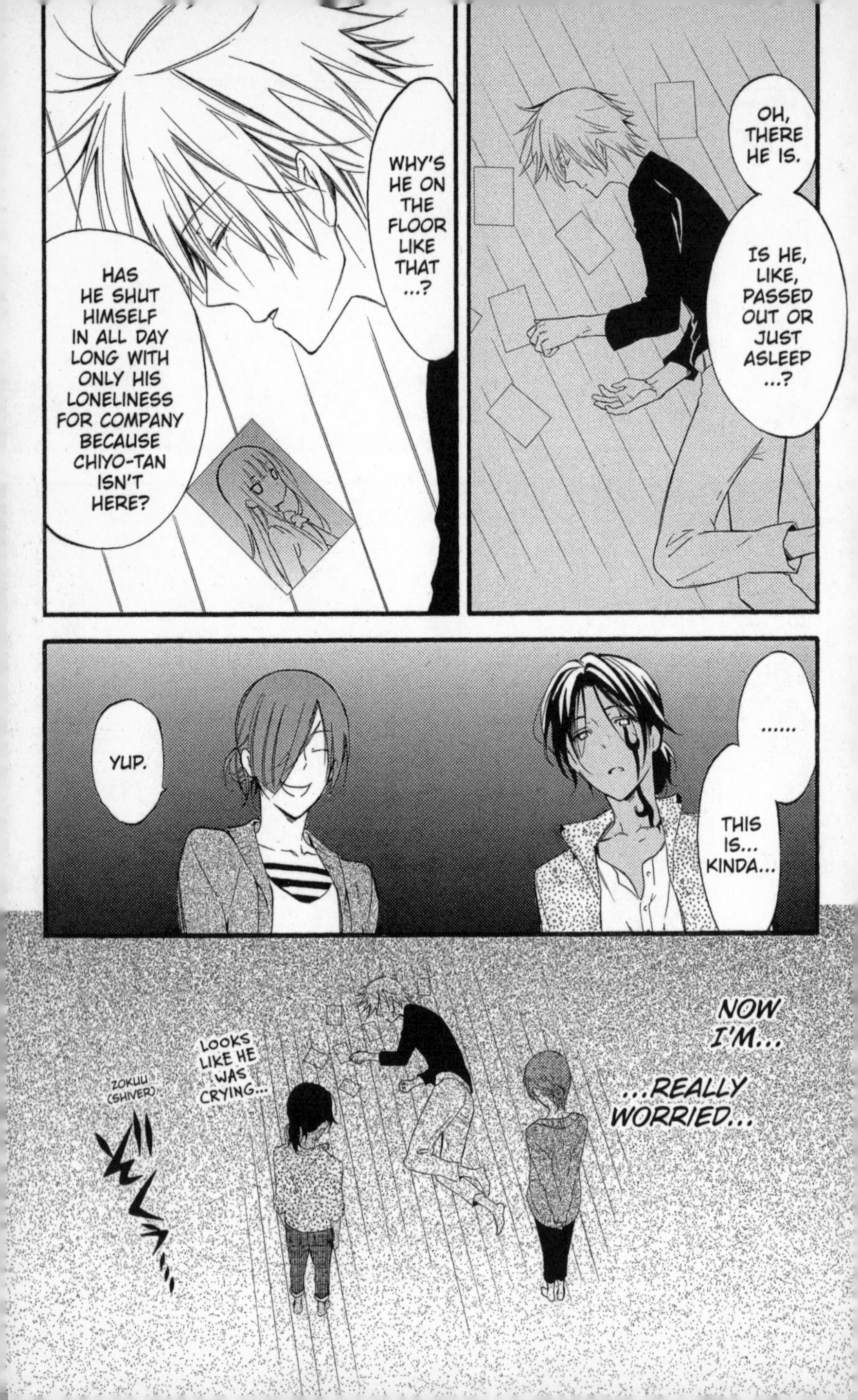
OH, THERE HE IS.
IS HE, LIKE, PASSED OUT OR JUST ASLEEP ...?
WHY'S HE ON THE FLOOR LIKE THAT ...?
HAS HE SHUT HIMSELF IN ALL DAY LONG WITH ONLY HIS LONELINESS FOR COMPANY BECAUSE CHIYO-TAN ISN'T HERE?
......
THIS IS... KINDA...
YUP.
NOW I'M...
...REALLY WORRIED...
LOOKS LIKE HE WAS CRYING...
ZOKUU (SHIVER)

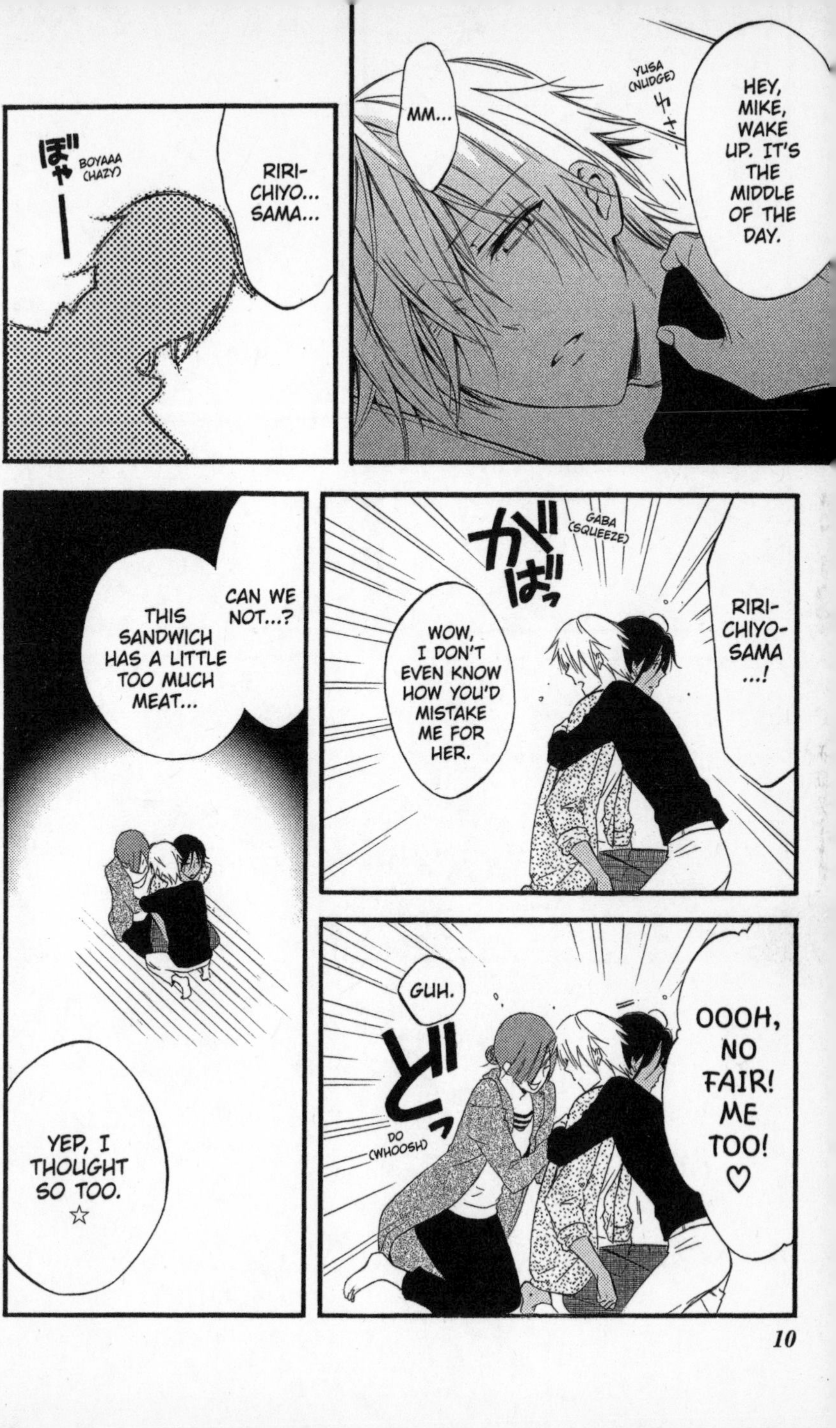
HEY, MIKE, WAKE UP. IT'S THE MIDDLE OF THE DAY.
ゆさ
YUSA (NUDGE)
MM...
RIRI-CHIYO... SAMA...
ぼやー
BOYAAA (HAZY)
RIRI-CHIYO-SAMA ...!
がばっ
GABA (SQUEEZE)
WOW, I DON'T EVEN KNOW HOW YOU'D MISTAKE ME FOR HER.
OOOH, NO FAIR! ME TOO! ♡
GUH.
どっ
DO (WHOOSH)
CAN WE NOT...?
THIS SANDWICH HAS A LITTLE TOO MUCH MEAT...
YEP, I THOUGHT SO TOO. ☆

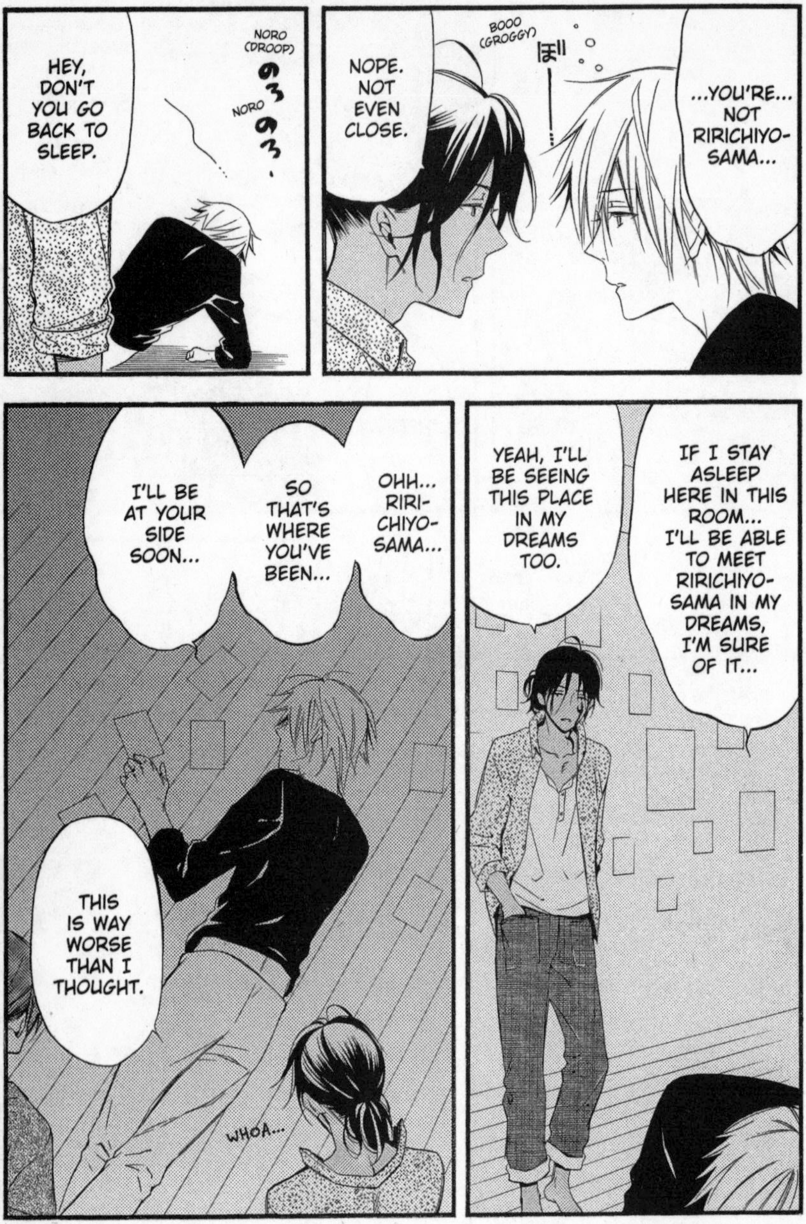
...YOU'RE... NOT RIRICHIYO-SAMA...
BOOO (GROGGY)
ぼー
NOPE. NOT EVEN CLOSE.
NORO (DROOP)
のろ
NORO
のろ
HEY, DON'T YOU GO BACK TO SLEEP.
IF I STAY ASLEEP HERE IN THIS ROOM... I'LL BE ABLE TO MEET RIRICHIYO-SAMA IN MY DREAMS, I'M SURE OF IT...
YEAH, I'LL BE SEEING THIS PLACE IN MY DREAMS TOO.
OHH... RIRI-CHIYO-SAMA...
SO THAT'S WHERE YOU'VE BEEN...
I'LL BE AT YOUR SIDE SOON...
THIS IS WAY WORSE THAN I THOUGHT.
WHOA...

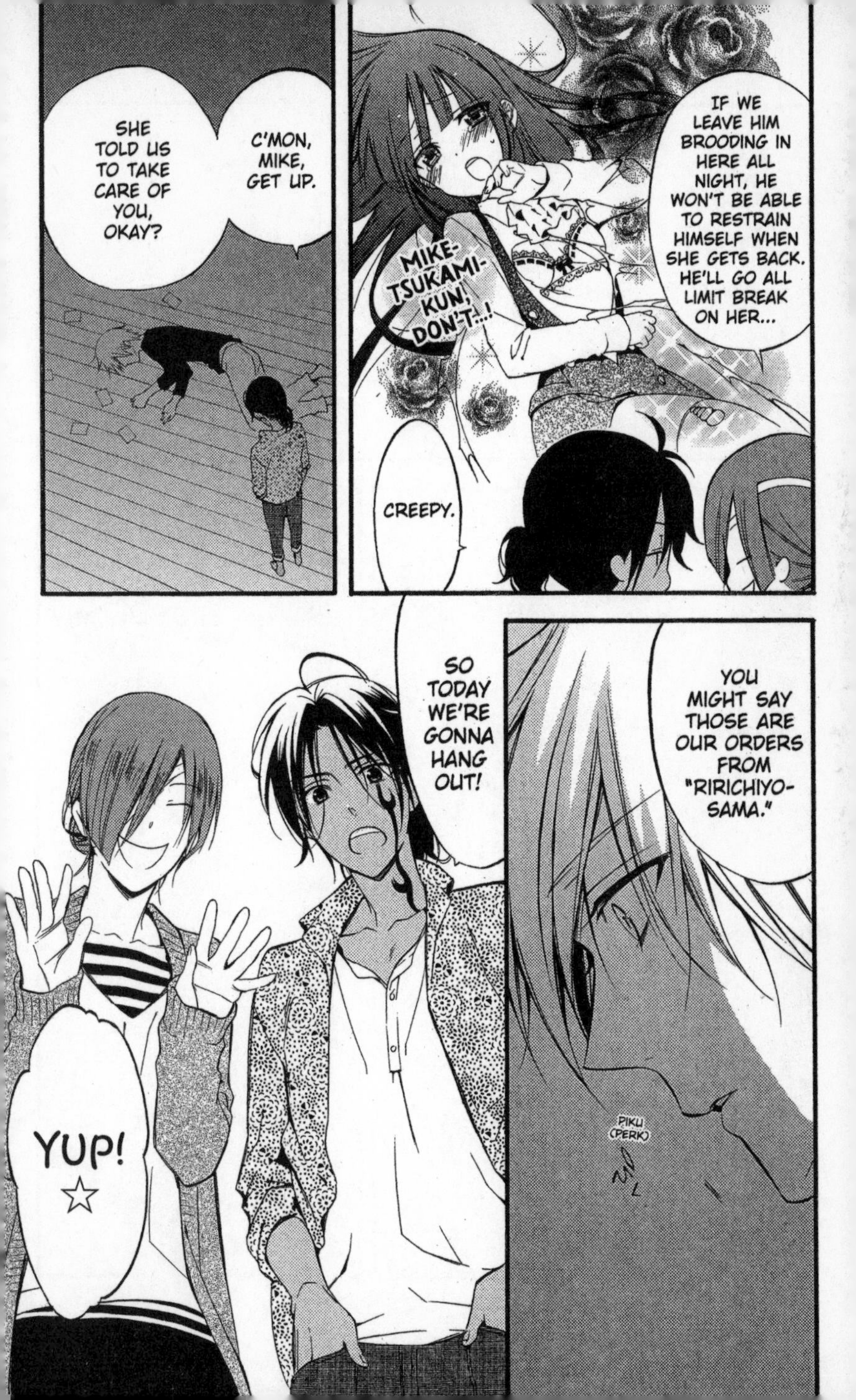
IF WE LEAVE HIM BROODING IN HERE ALL NIGHT, HE WON'T BE ABLE TO RESTRAIN HIMSELF WHEN SHE GETS BACK. HE'LL GO ALL LIMIT BREAK ON HER...
MIKE-TSUKAMI-KUN, DON'T...!
CREEPY.
C'MON, MIKE, GET UP.
SHE TOLD US TO TAKE CARE OF YOU, OKAY?
YOU MIGHT SAY THOSE ARE OUR ORDERS FROM "RIRICHIYO-SAMA."
PIKU (PERK)
SO TODAY WE'RE GONNA HANG OUT!
YUP! ☆

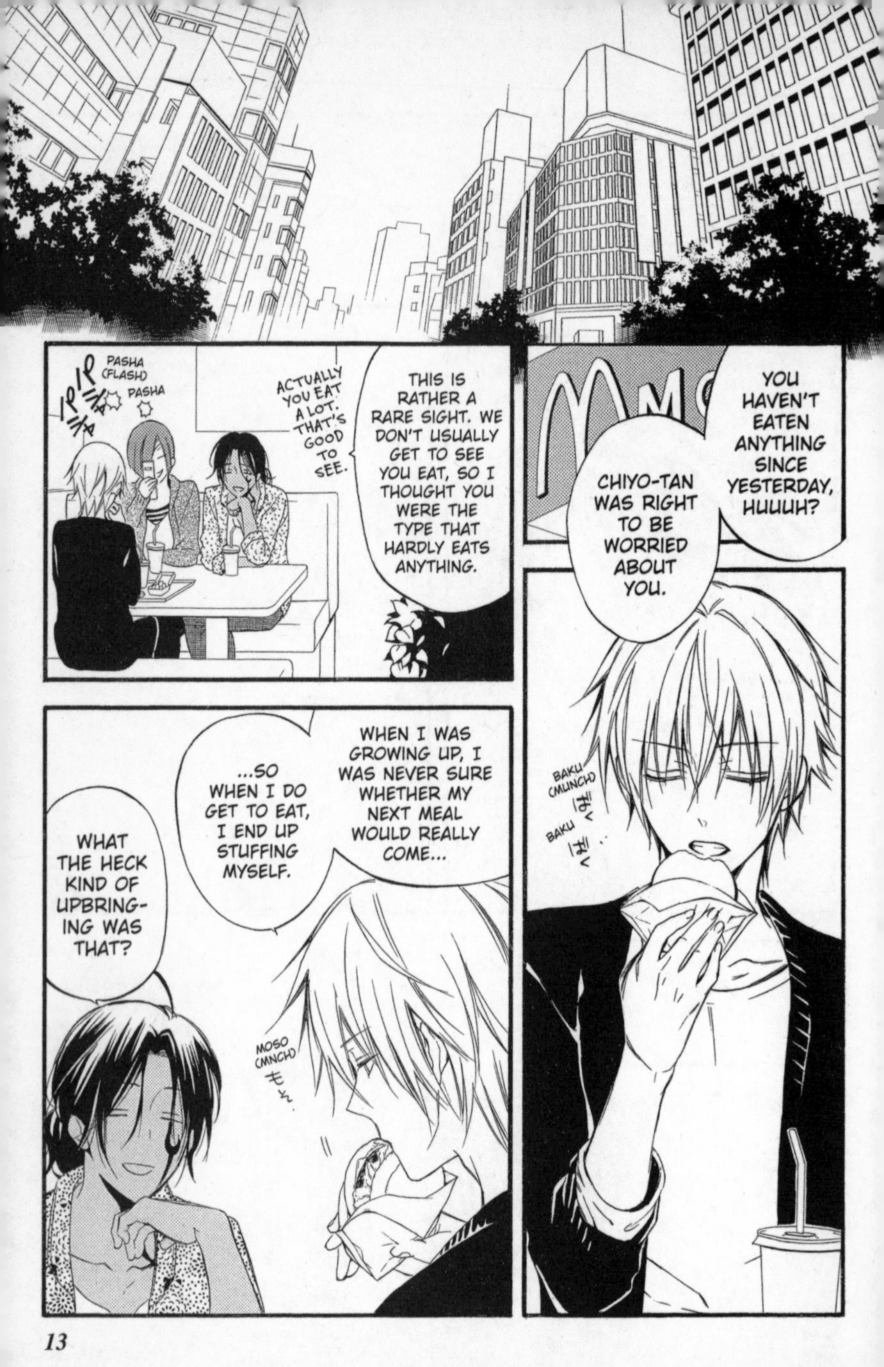

YOU HAVEN'T EATEN ANYTHING SINCE YESTERDAY, HUUUH?
CHIYO-TAN WAS RIGHT TO BE WORRIED ABOUT YOU.
BAKU (MUNCH)
BAKU
THIS IS RATHER A RARE SIGHT. WE DON'T USUALLY GET TO SEE YOU EAT, SO I THOUGHT YOU WERE THE TYPE THAT HARDLY EATS ANYTHING.
ACTUALLY YOU EAT A LOT. THAT'S GOOD TO SEE.
PASHA (FLASH)
PASHA
WHEN I WAS GROWING UP, I WAS NEVER SURE WHETHER MY NEXT MEAL WOULD REALLY COME...
...SO WHEN I DO GET TO EAT, I END UP STUFFING MYSELF.
WHAT THE HECK KIND OF UPBRING-ING WAS THAT?
MOSO (MNCH)

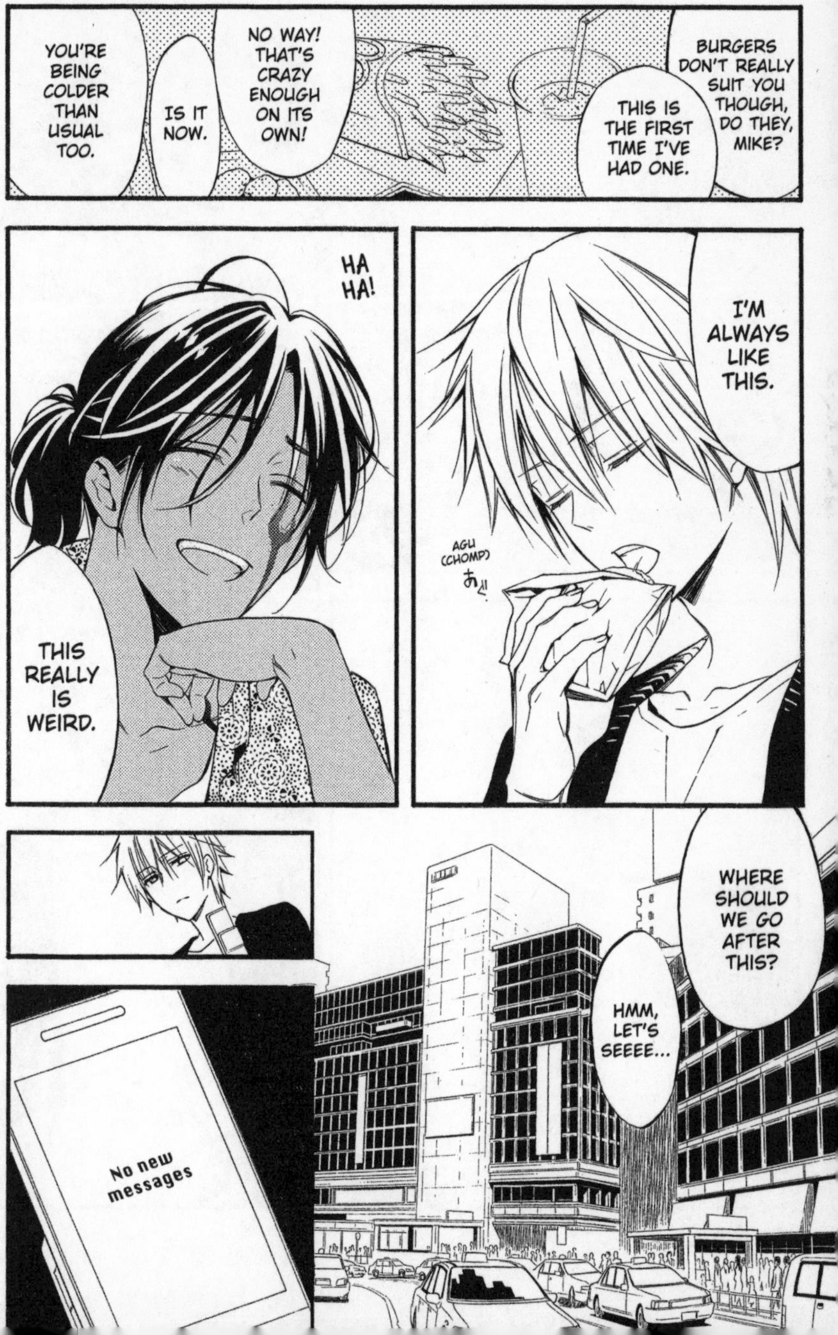
BURGERS DON'T REALLY SUIT YOU THOUGH, DO THEY, MIKE?
THIS IS THE FIRST TIME I'VE HAD ONE.
NO WAY! THAT'S CRAZY ENOUGH ON ITS OWN!
IS IT NOW.
YOU'RE BEING COLDER THAN USUAL TOO.
I'M ALWAYS LIKE THIS.
AGU (CHOMP)
あぐ
HA HA!
THIS REALLY IS WEIRD.
WHERE SHOULD WE GO AFTER THIS?
HMM, LET'S SEEEE...
No new messages

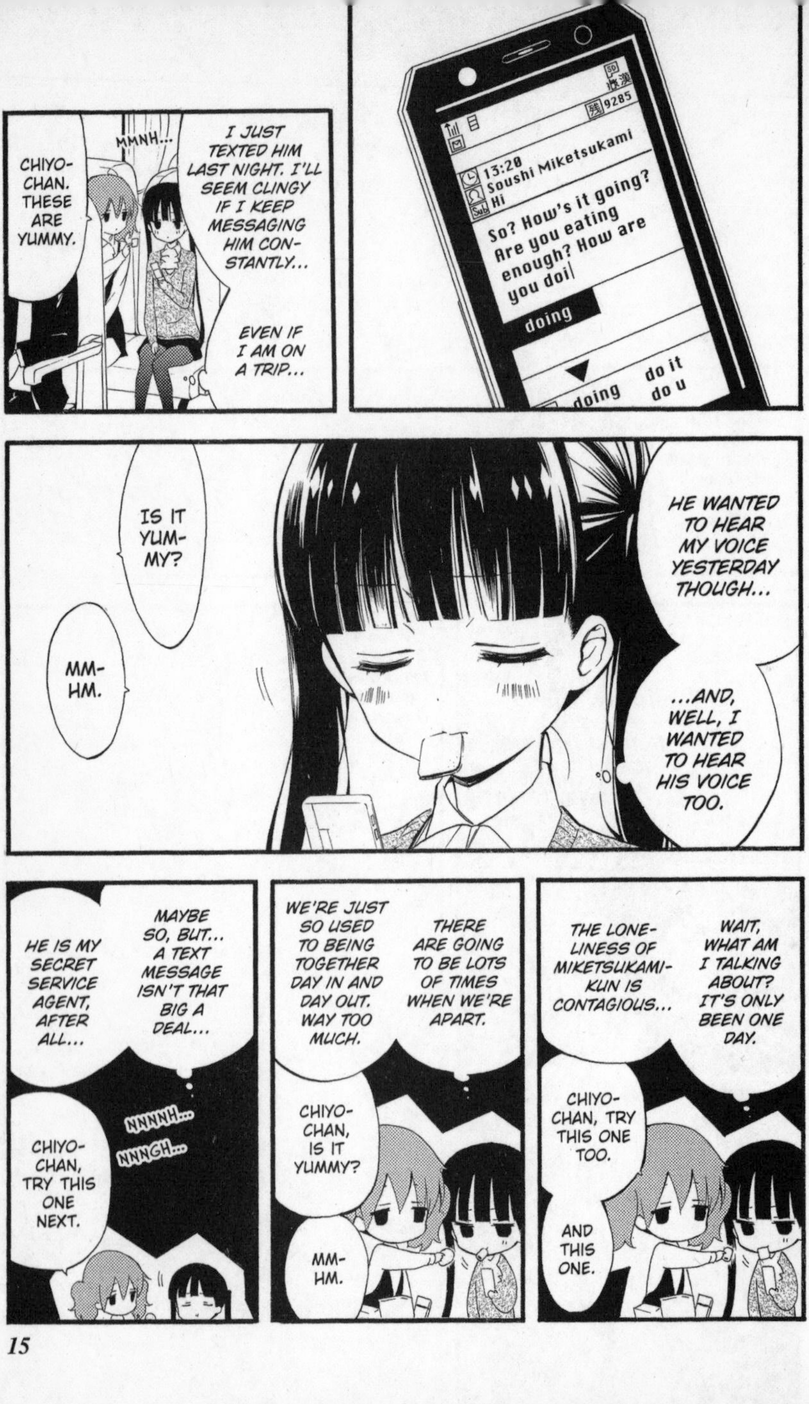

13:20
Soushi Miketsukami
Hi
So? How's it going? Are you eating enough? How are you doi
doing
doing
do it
do u
I JUST TEXTED HIM LAST NIGHT. I'LL SEEM CLINGY IF I KEEP MESSAGING HIM CONSTANTLY...
EVEN IF I AM ON A TRIP...
MMNH...
CHIYO-CHAN. THESE ARE YUMMY.
HE WANTED TO HEAR MY VOICE YESTERDAY THOUGH...
...AND, WELL, I WANTED TO HEAR HIS VOICE TOO.
IS IT YUMMY?
MM-HM.
WAIT, WHAT AM I TALKING ABOUT? IT'S ONLY BEEN ONE DAY.
THE LONELINESS OF MIKETSUKAMI-KUN IS CONTAGIOUS...
CHIYO-CHAN, TRY THIS ONE TOO.
AND THIS ONE.
THERE ARE GOING TO BE LOTS OF TIMES WHEN WE'RE APART.
WE'RE JUST SO USED TO BEING TOGETHER DAY IN AND DAY OUT. WAY TOO MUCH.
CHIYO-CHAN, IS IT YUMMY?
MM-HM.
MAYBE SO, BUT... A TEXT MESSAGE ISN'T THAT BIG A DEAL...
HE IS MY SECRET SERVICE AGENT, AFTER ALL...
NNNNH...
NNNGH...
CHIYO-CHAN, TRY THIS ONE NEXT.

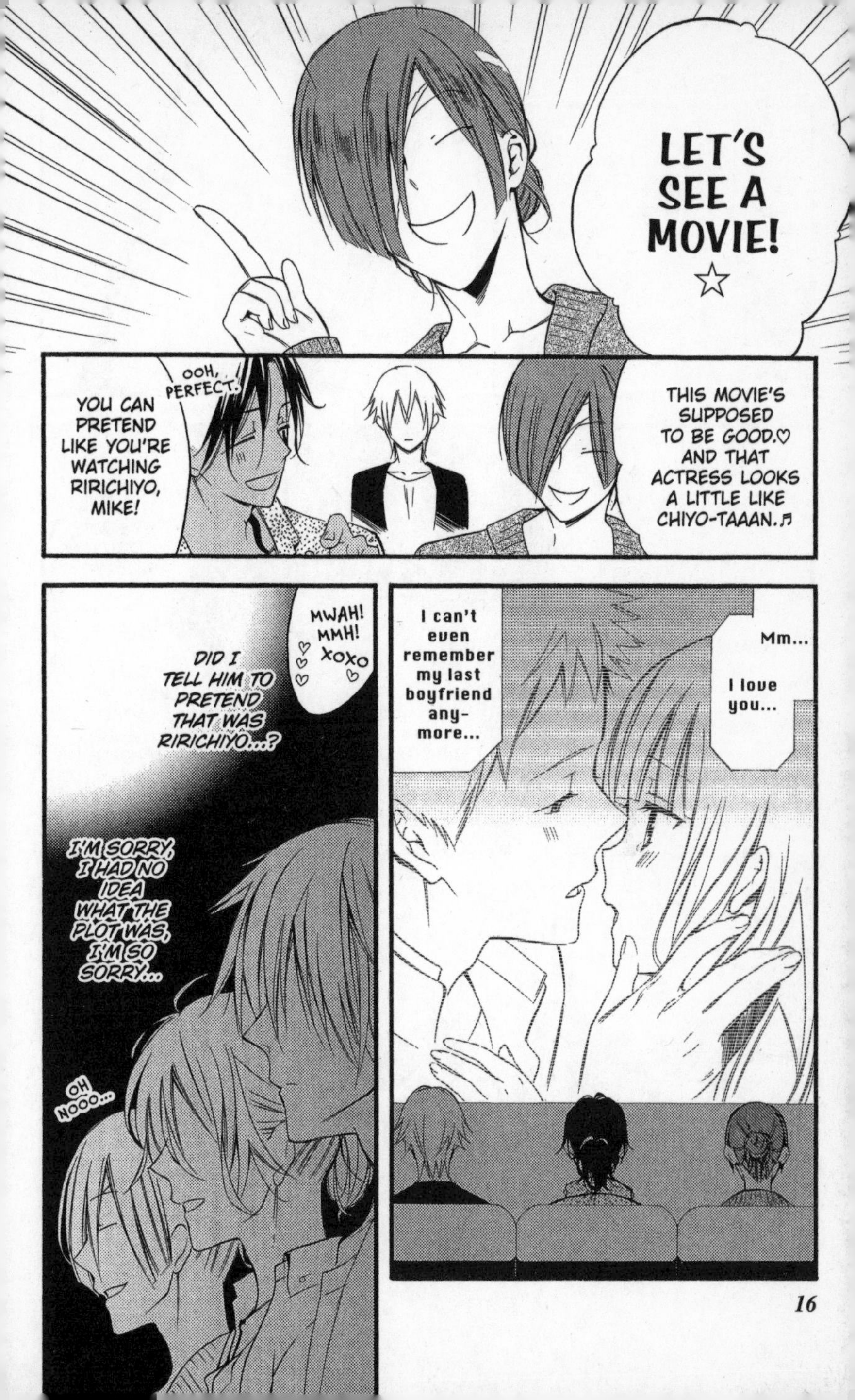
LET'S SEE A MOVIE! ☆
THIS MOVIE'S SUPPOSED TO BE GOOD.♡ AND THAT ACTRESS LOOKS A LITTLE LIKE CHIYO-TAAAN.♬
OOH, PERFECT.
YOU CAN PRETEND LIKE YOU'RE WATCHING RIRICHIYO, MIKE!
Mm...
I love you...
I can't even remember my last boyfriend any-more...
MWAH! MMH! ♡ XOXO ♡
DID I TELL HIM TO PRETEND THAT WAS RIRICHIYO...?
I'M SORRY, I HAD NO IDEA WHAT THE PLOT WAS, I'M SO SORRY...
OH NOOO...

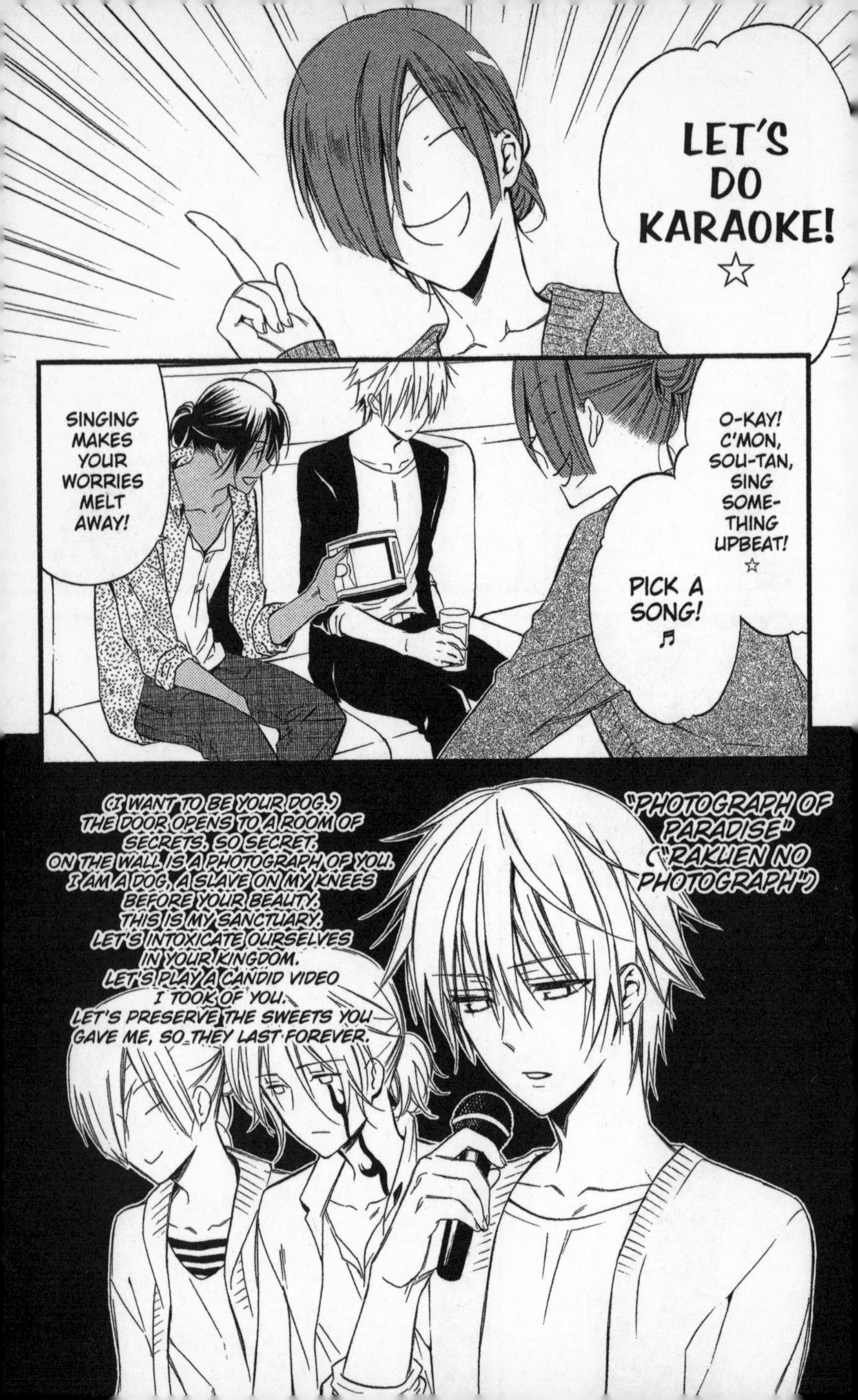
LET'S DO KARAOKE! ☆
O-KAY! C'MON, SOU-TAN, SING SOME-THING UPBEAT! ☆
PICK A SONG! ♬
SINGING MAKES YOUR WORRIES MELT AWAY!
"PHOTOGRAPH OF PARADISE" ("RAKUEN NO PHOTOGRAPH")
(I WANT TO BE YOUR DOG.) THE DOOR OPENS TO A ROOM OF SECRETS, SO SECRET. ON THE WALL IS A PHOTOGRAPH OF YOU. I AM A DOG, A SLAVE ON MY KNEES BEFORE YOUR BEAUTY. THIS IS MY SANCTUARY. LET'S INTOXICATE OURSELVES IN YOUR KINGDOM. LET'S PLAY A CANDID VIDEO I TOOK OF YOU. LET'S PRESERVE THE SWEETS YOU GAVE ME, SO THEY LAST FOREVER.

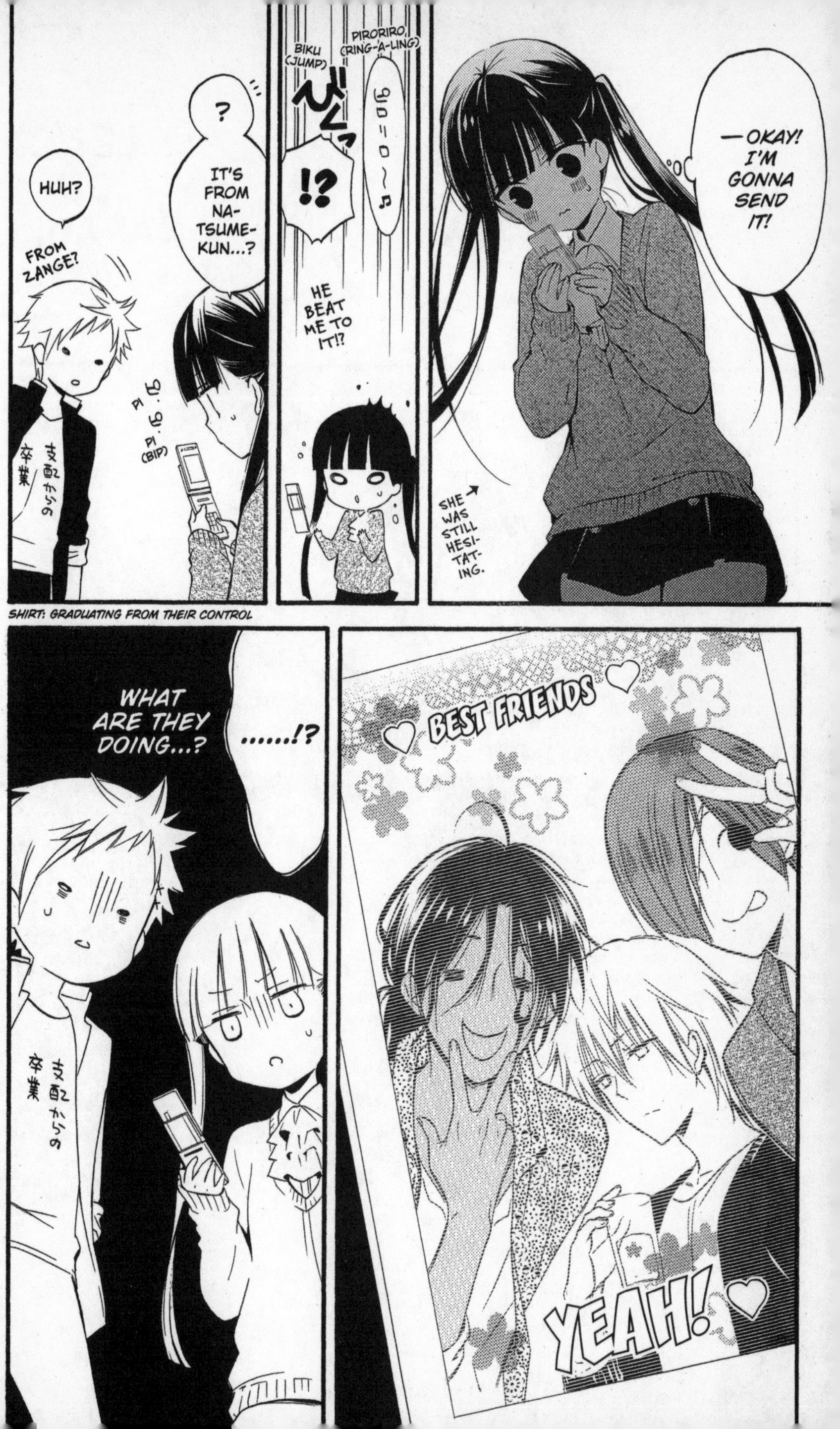
—OKAY! I'M GONNA SEND IT!
SHE WAS STILL HESITATING.
PIRORIRO (RING-A-LING)
ぴろりろ～♪
BIKU (JUMP)
びくっ
!?
HE BEAT ME TO IT!?
?
IT'S FROM NATSUME-KUN...?
HUH?
FROM ZANGE?
PI PI PI (BIP)
支配からの卒業
SHIRT: GRADUATING FROM THEIR CONTROL
BEST FRIENDS
YEAH!
......!?
WHAT ARE THEY DOING...?
支配からの卒業

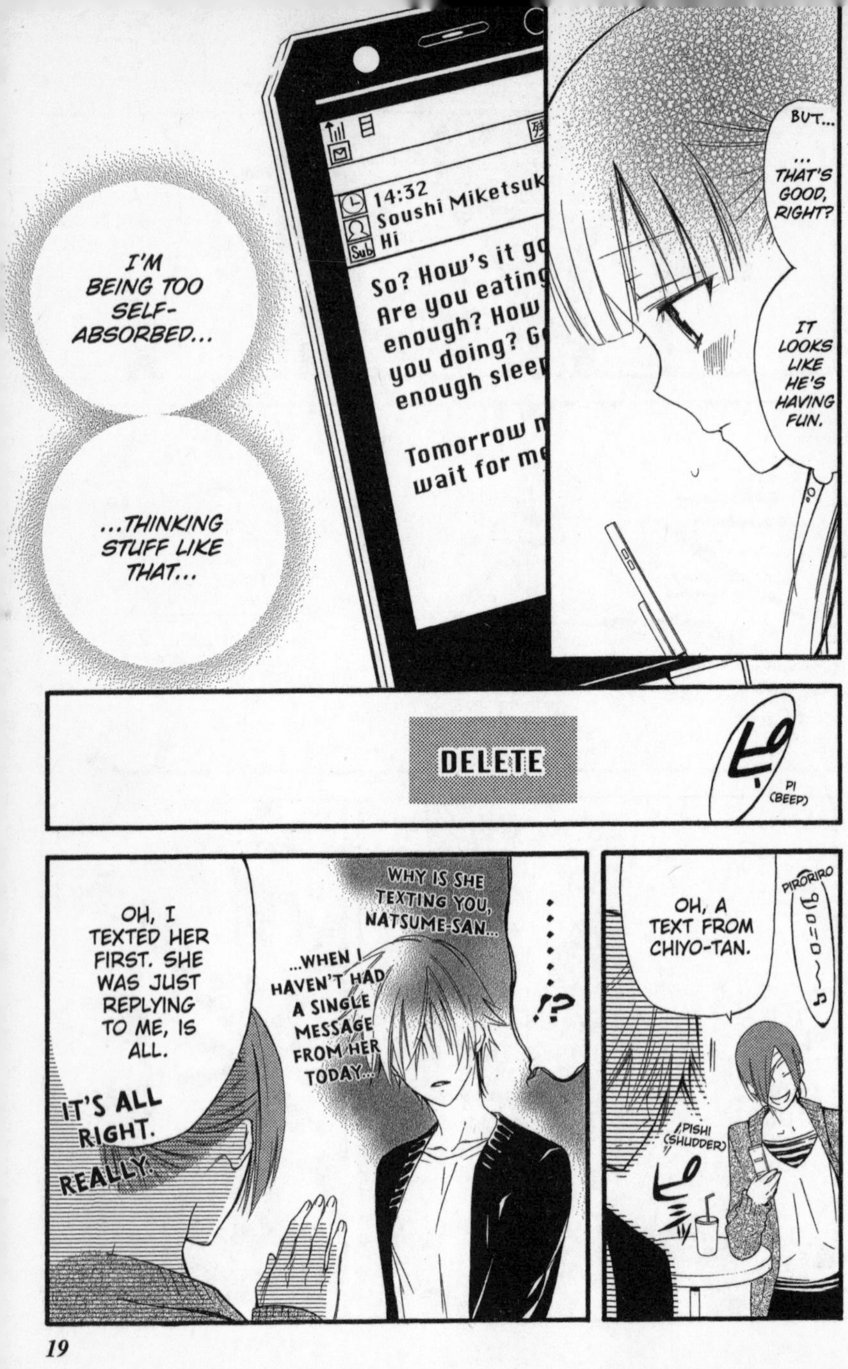

BUT...
...THAT'S GOOD, RIGHT?
IT LOOKS LIKE HE'S HAVING FUN.
14:32
Soushi Miketsuk
Hi
So? How's it go
Are you eating
enough? How
you doing? G
enough sleep
Tomorrow n
wait for me
I'M BEING TOO SELF-ABSORBED...
...THINKING STUFF LIKE THAT...
PI (BEEP)
DELETE
PIRORIRO
OH, A TEXT FROM CHIYO-TAN.
PISHI (SHUDDER)
!?
WHY IS SHE TEXTING YOU, NATSUME-SAN...
...WHEN I HAVEN'T HAD A SINGLE MESSAGE FROM HER TODAY...!
OH, I TEXTED HER FIRST. SHE WAS JUST REPLYING TO ME, IS ALL.
IT'S ALL RIGHT. REALLY.

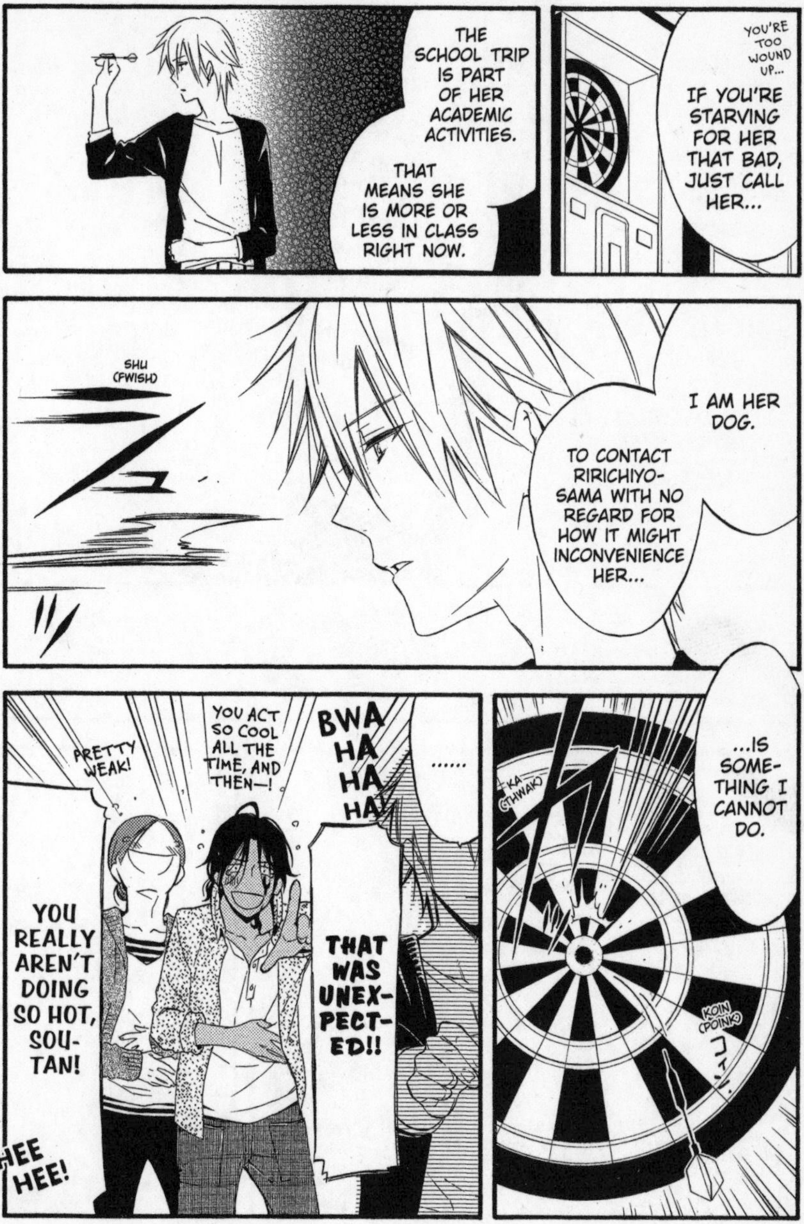
YOU'RE TOO WOUND UP...
IF YOU'RE STARVING FOR HER THAT BAD, JUST CALL HER...
THE SCHOOL TRIP IS PART OF HER ACADEMIC ACTIVITIES.
THAT MEANS SHE IS MORE OR LESS IN CLASS RIGHT NOW.
I AM HER DOG.
TO CONTACT RIRICHIYO-SAMA WITH NO REGARD FOR HOW IT MIGHT INCONVENIENCE HER...
SHU (FWISH)
...IS SOME-THING I CANNOT DO.
KA (THWAK)
KOIN (POINK)
......
BWA HA HA HA
THAT WAS UNEX-PECT-ED!!
YOU ACT SO COOL ALL THE TIME, AND THEN—!
PRETTY WEAK!
YOU REALLY AREN'T DOING SO HOT, SOU-TAN!
HEE HEE!

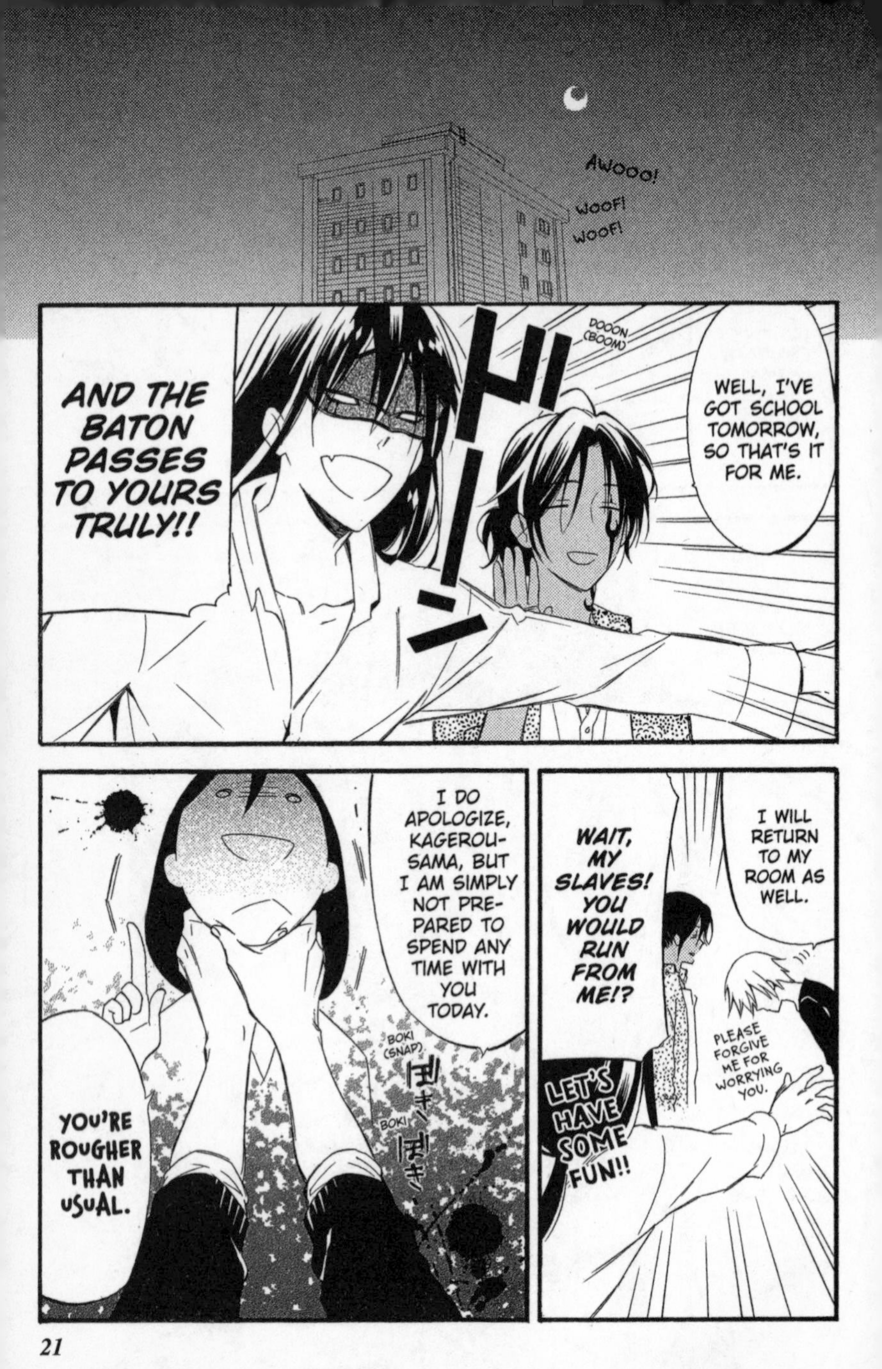
AWOOO!
WOOF! WOOF!
WELL, I'VE GOT SCHOOL TOMORROW, SO THAT'S IT FOR ME.
DOOON (BOOM)
AND THE BATON PASSES TO YOURS TRULY!!
I WILL RETURN TO MY ROOM AS WELL.
WAIT, MY SLAVES! YOU WOULD RUN FROM ME!?
PLEASE FORGIVE ME FOR WORRYING YOU.
LET'S HAVE SOME FUN!!
I DO APOLOGIZE, KAGEROU-SAMA, BUT I AM SIMPLY NOT PRE-PARED TO SPEND ANY TIME WITH YOU TODAY.
BOKI (SNAP)
BOKI
YOU'RE ROUGHER THAN USUAL.

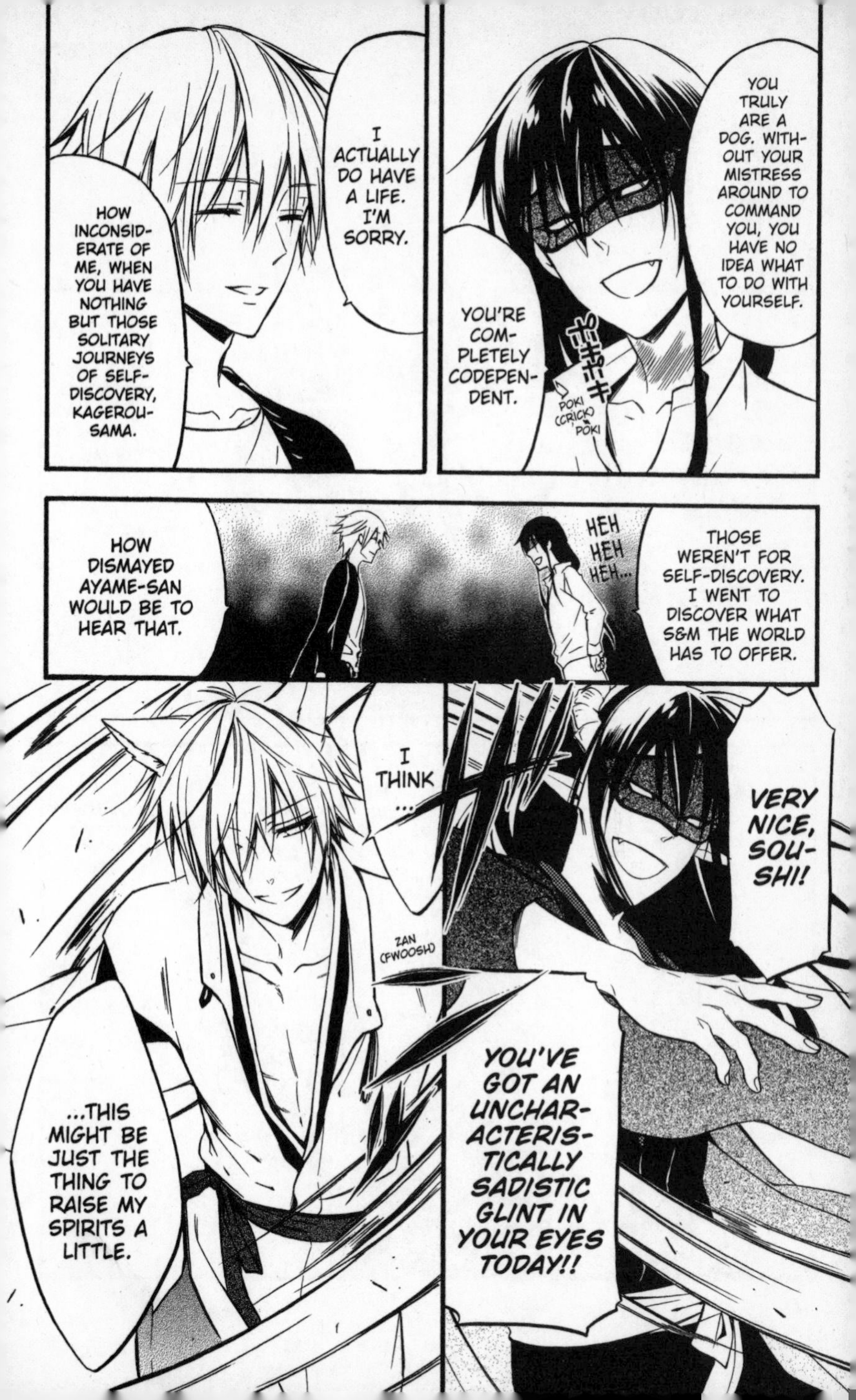

YOU TRULY ARE A DOG. WITHOUT YOUR MISTRESS AROUND TO COMMAND YOU, YOU HAVE NO IDEA WHAT TO DO WITH YOURSELF.
YOU'RE COMPLETELY CODEPENDENT.
ポキポキ
POKI (CRICK) POKI
I ACTUALLY DO HAVE A LIFE. I'M SORRY.
HOW INCONSIDERATE OF ME, WHEN YOU HAVE NOTHING BUT THOSE SOLITARY JOURNEYS OF SELF-DISCOVERY, KAGEROU-SAMA.
THOSE WEREN'T FOR SELF-DISCOVERY. I WENT TO DISCOVER WHAT S&M THE WORLD HAS TO OFFER.
HEH HEH HEH...
HOW DISMAYED AYAME-SAN WOULD BE TO HEAR THAT.
VERY NICE, SOUSHI!
YOU'VE GOT AN UNCHARACTERISTICALLY SADISTIC GLINT IN YOUR EYES TODAY!!
I THINK...
ZAN (FWOOSH)
...THIS MIGHT BE JUST THE THING TO RAISE MY SPIRITS A LITTLE.

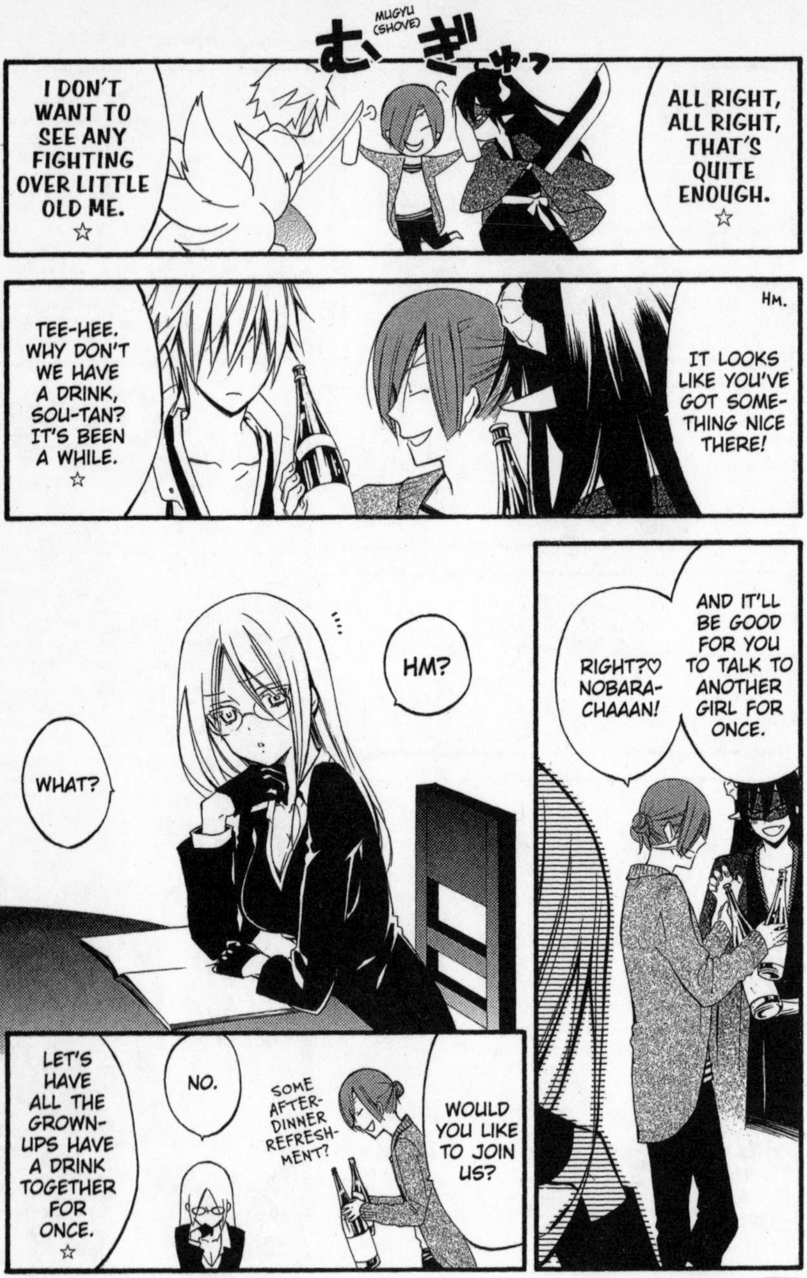
MUGYU (SHOVE)
ALL RIGHT, ALL RIGHT, THAT'S QUITE ENOUGH. ☆
I DON'T WANT TO SEE ANY FIGHTING OVER LITTLE OLD ME. ☆
HM.
IT LOOKS LIKE YOU'VE GOT SOME-THING NICE THERE!
TEE-HEE. WHY DON'T WE HAVE A DRINK, SOU-TAN? IT'S BEEN A WHILE. ☆
AND IT'LL BE GOOD FOR YOU TO TALK TO ANOTHER GIRL FOR ONCE.
RIGHT?♡ NOBARA-CHAAAN!
HM?
WHAT?
WOULD YOU LIKE TO JOIN US?
SOME AFTER-DINNER REFRESH-MENT?
NO.
LET'S HAVE ALL THE GROWN-UPS HAVE A DRINK TOGETHER FOR ONCE. ☆

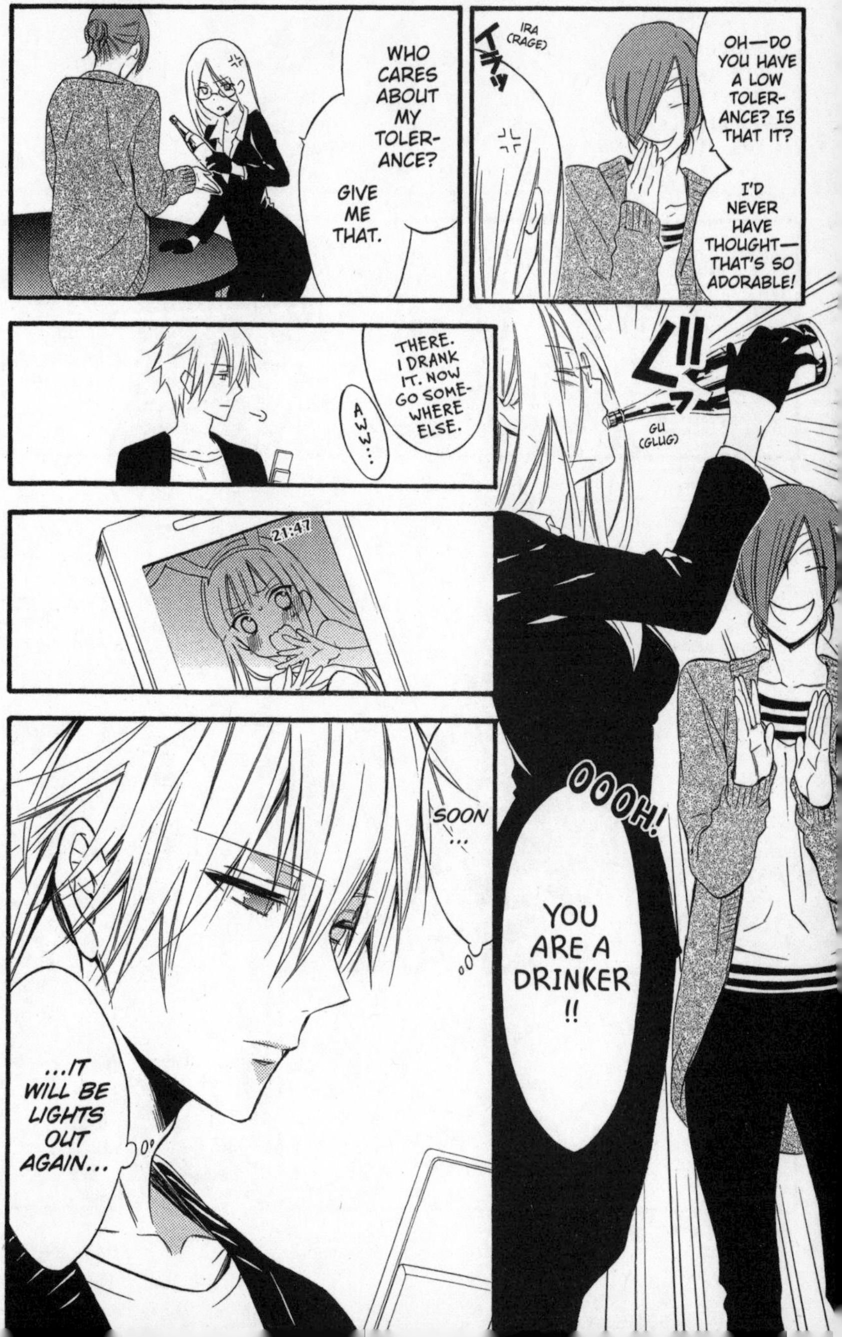
IRA (RAGE)
OH—DO YOU HAVE A LOW TOLER-ANCE? IS THAT IT?
I'D NEVER HAVE THOUGHT—THAT'S SO ADORABLE!
WHO CARES ABOUT MY TOLER-ANCE?
GIVE ME THAT.
GU (GLUG)
OOOH!
YOU ARE A DRINKER !!
THERE. I DRANK IT. NOW GO SOME-WHERE ELSE.
AWW...
21:47
SOON ...
...IT WILL BE LIGHTS OUT AGAIN...

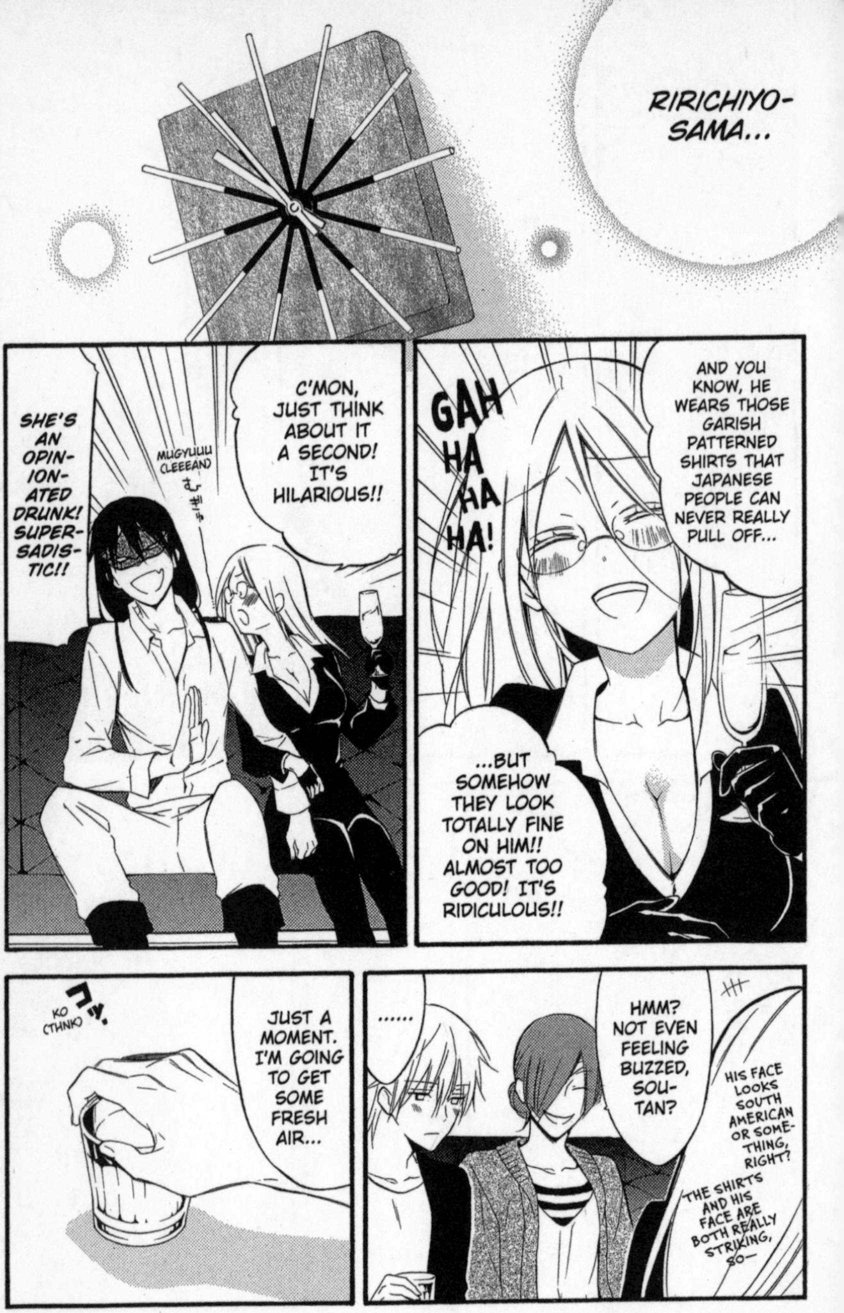
RIRICHIYO-SAMA...
GAH HA HA HA!
AND YOU KNOW, HE WEARS THOSE GARISH PATTERNED SHIRTS THAT JAPANESE PEOPLE CAN NEVER REALLY PULL OFF...
...BUT SOMEHOW THEY LOOK TOTALLY FINE ON HIM!! ALMOST TOO GOOD! IT'S RIDICULOUS!!
C'MON, JUST THINK ABOUT IT A SECOND! IT'S HILARIOUS!!
MUGYUUU (CLEEEAN)
SHE'S AN OPINIONATED DRUNK! SUPER-SADISTIC!!
HMM? NOT EVEN FEELING BUZZED, SOU-TAN?
......
HIS FACE LOOKS SOUTH AMERICAN OR SOMETHING, RIGHT?
THE SHIRTS AND HIS FACE ARE BOTH REALLY STRIKING, SO—
KO (THNK)
JUST A MOMENT. I'M GOING TO GET SOME FRESH AIR...

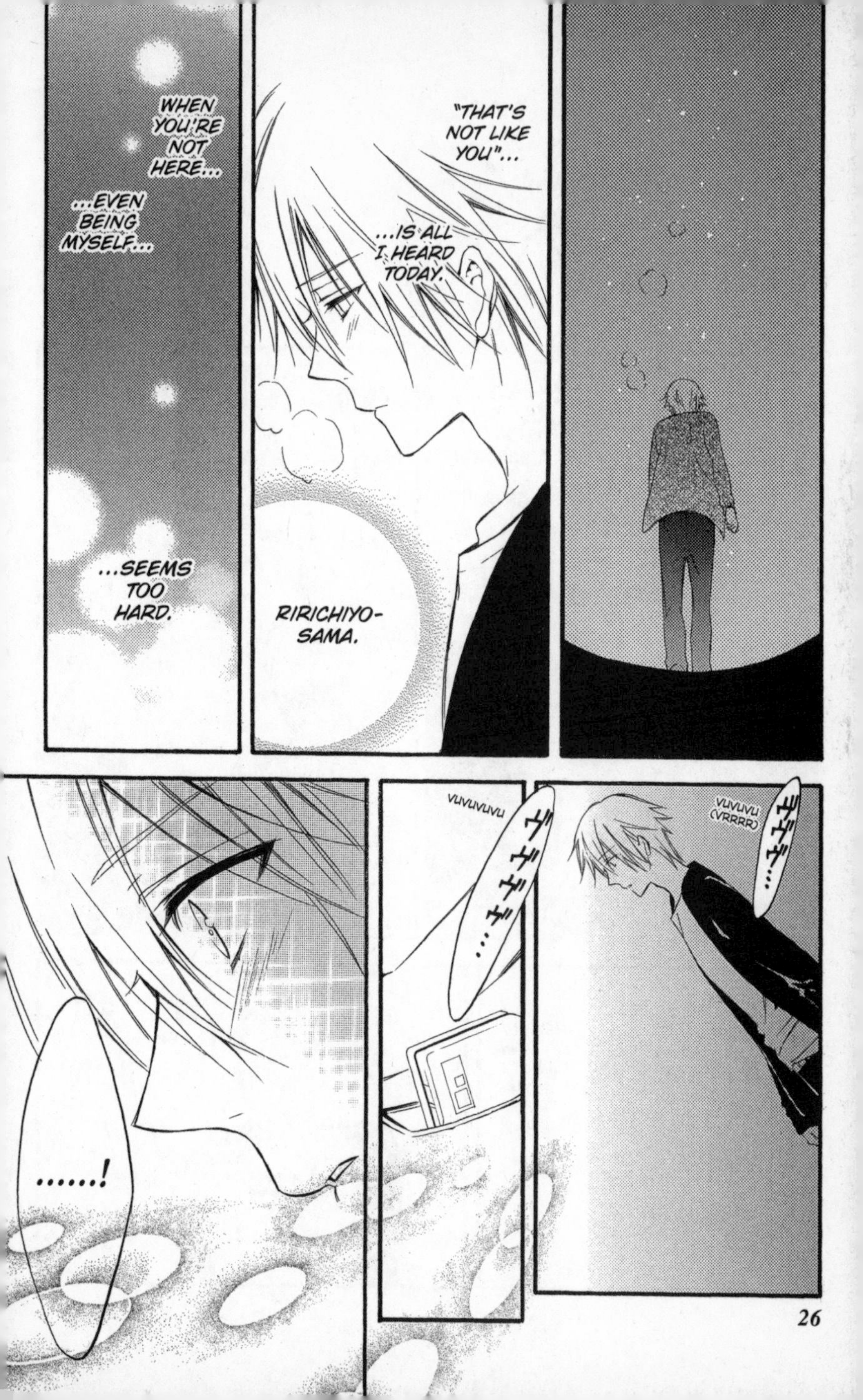
"THAT'S NOT LIKE YOU"...
...IS ALL I HEARD TODAY.
RIRICHIYO-SAMA.
WHEN YOU'RE NOT HERE...
...EVEN BEING MYSELF...
...SEEMS TOO HARD.
ヴヴヴ…
VUVUVU (VRRRR)
ヴヴヴヴ…
VUVUVUVU
......!

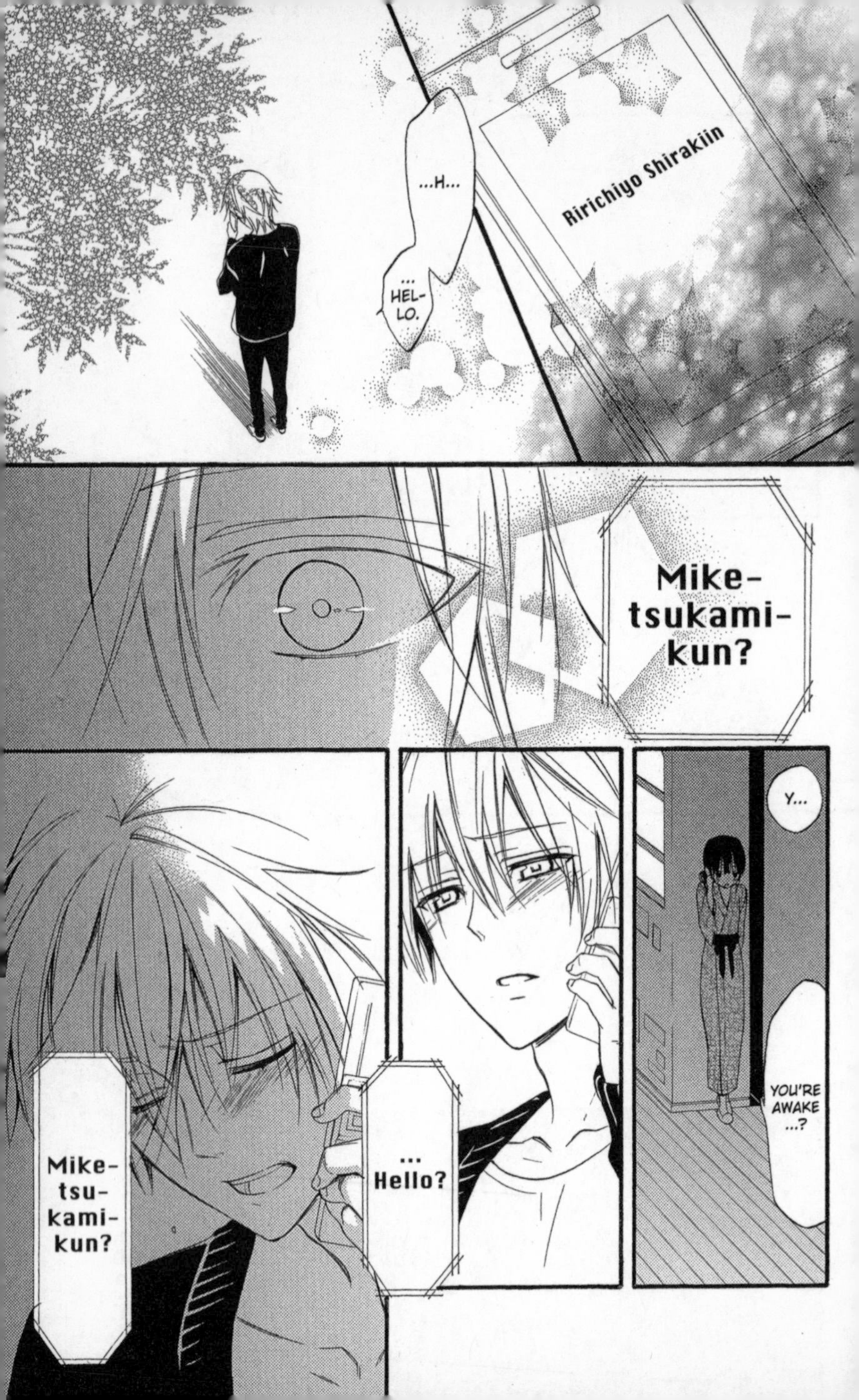
Ririchiyo Shirakiin
...H...
...HEL-LO.
Mike-tsukami-kun?
Y...
YOU'RE AWAKE ...?
... Hello?
Mike-tsu-kami-kun?

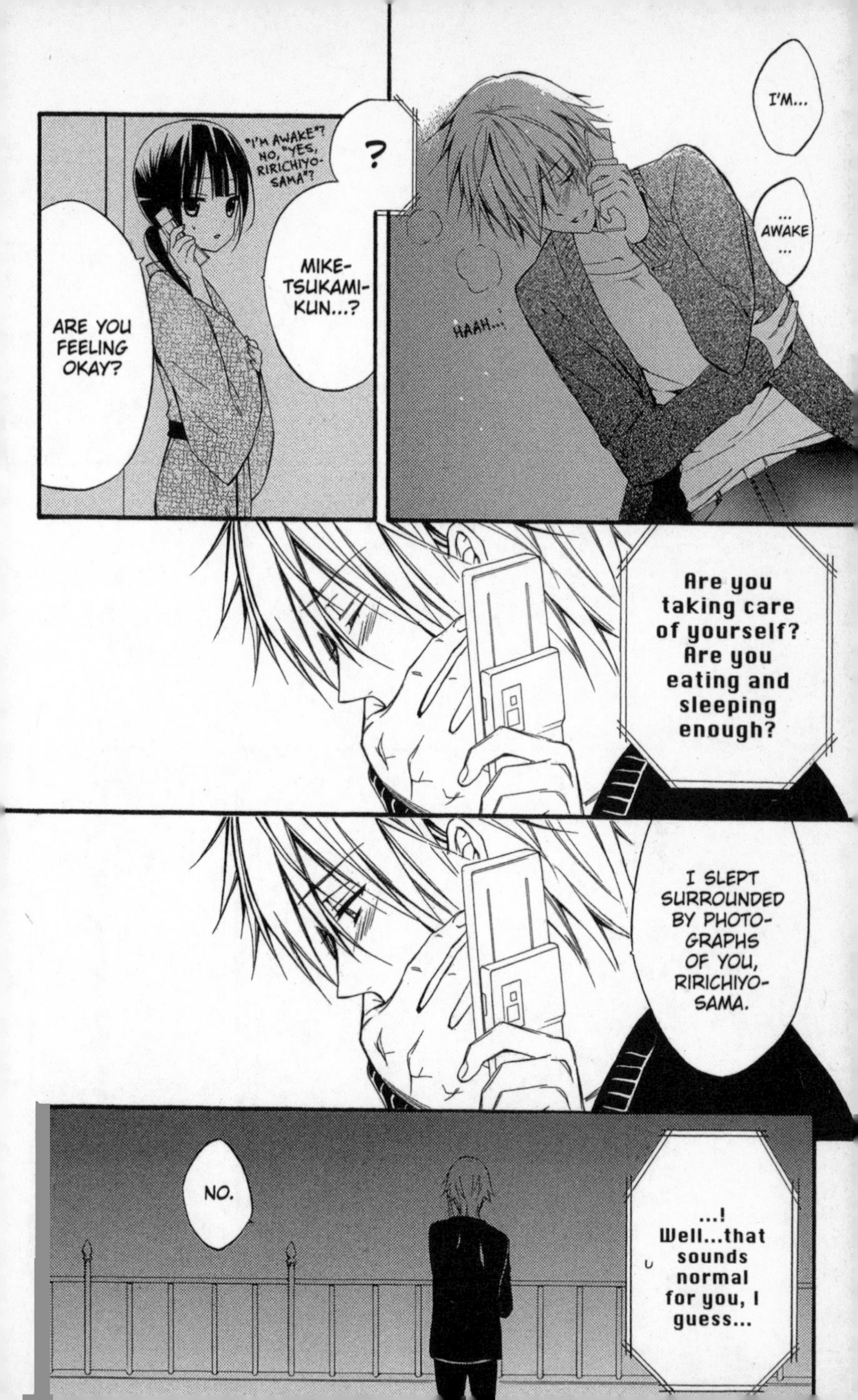
I'M...
...AWAKE...
HAAH...
?
"I'M AWAKE"? NO, "YES, RIRICHIYO-SAMA"?
MIKE-TSUKAMI-KUN...?
ARE YOU FEELING OKAY?
Are you taking care of yourself? Are you eating and sleeping enough?
I SLEPT SURROUNDED BY PHOTOGRAPHS OF YOU, RIRICHIYO-SAMA.
...! Well...that sounds normal for you, I guess...
NO.

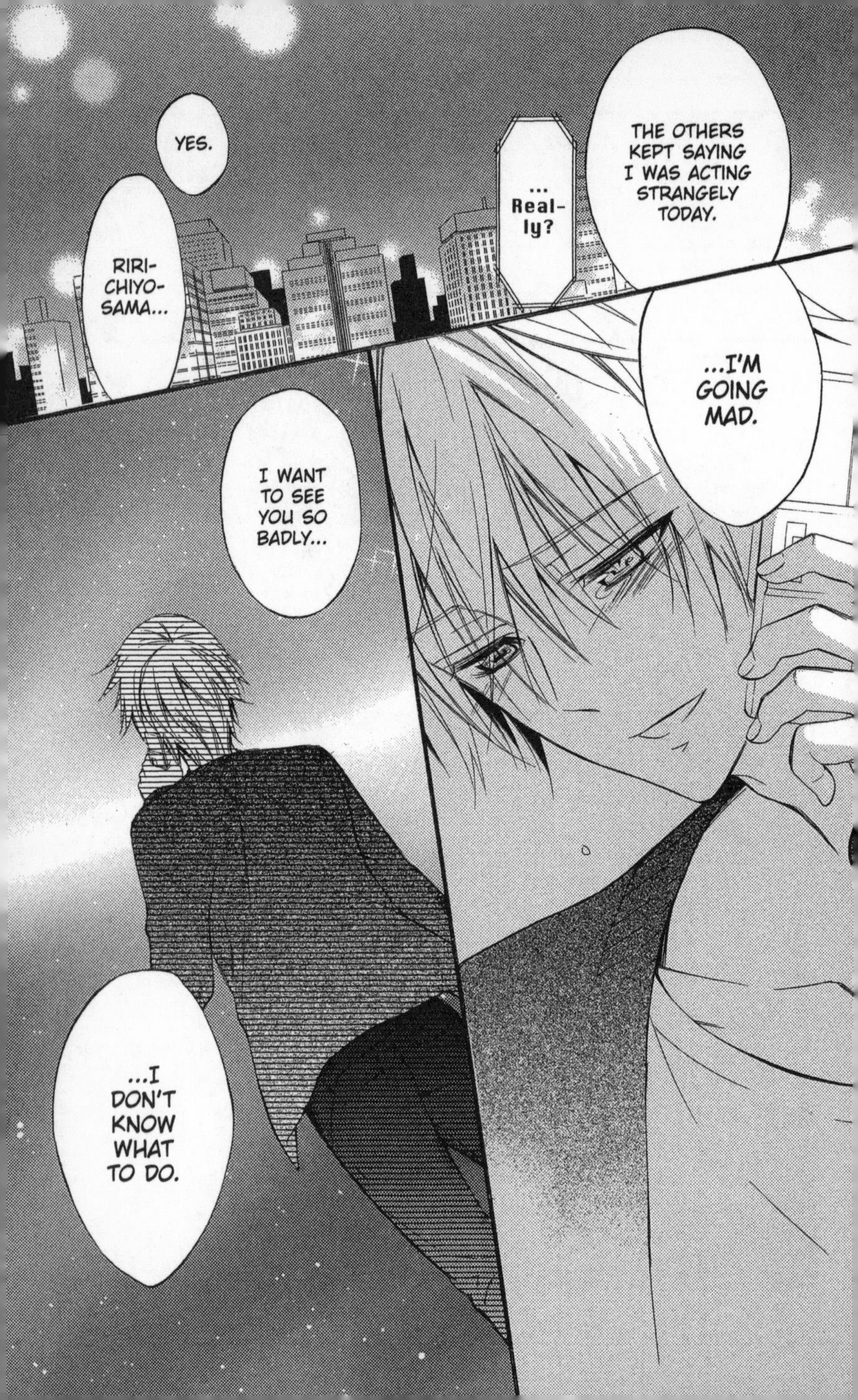
THE OTHERS KEPT SAYING I WAS ACTING STRANGELY TODAY.
...Real-ly?
YES.
RIRI-CHIYO-SAMA...
...I'M GOING MAD.
I WANT TO SEE YOU SO BADLY...
...I DON'T KNOW WHAT TO DO.

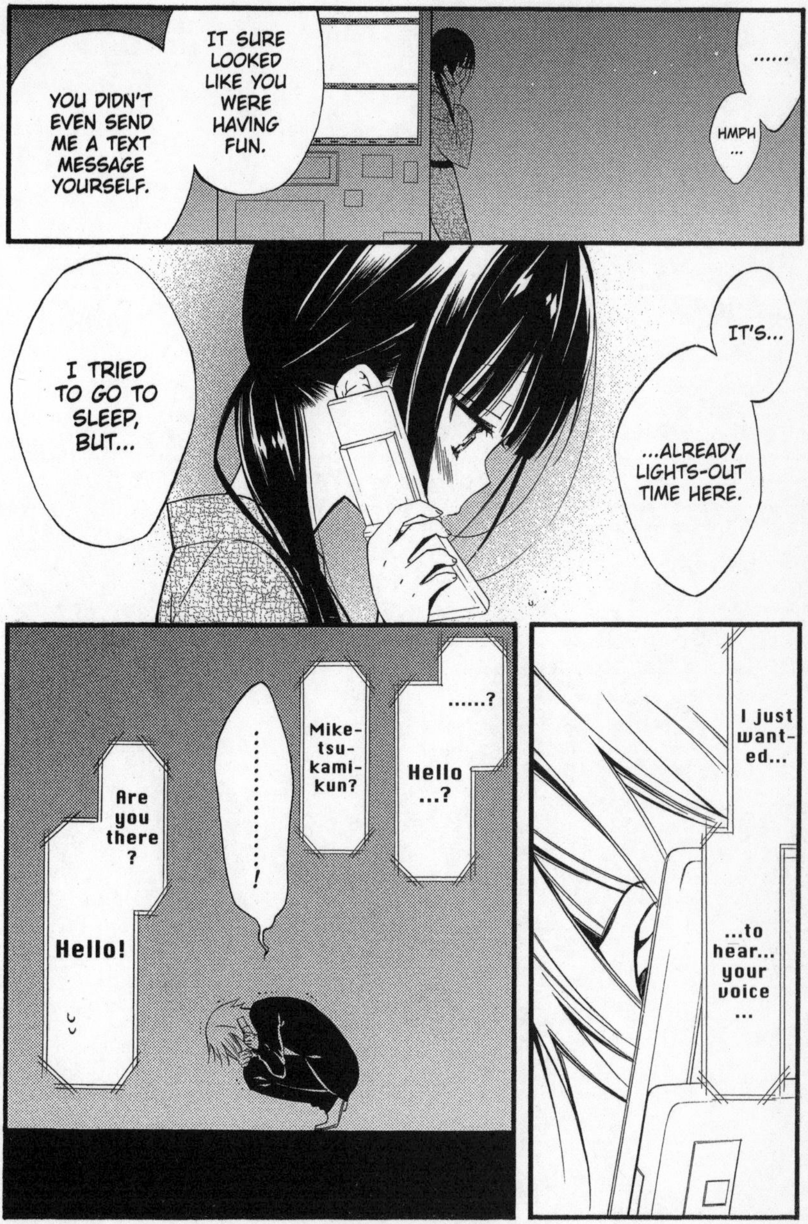
......
HMPH...
IT SURE LOOKED LIKE YOU WERE HAVING FUN.
YOU DIDN'T EVEN SEND ME A TEXT MESSAGE YOURSELF.
IT'S...
...ALREADY LIGHTS-OUT TIME HERE.
I TRIED TO GO TO SLEEP, BUT...
I just wanted...
...to hear... your voice...
......?
Hello...?
Mike-tsukami-kun?
..............!
Are you there?
Hello!

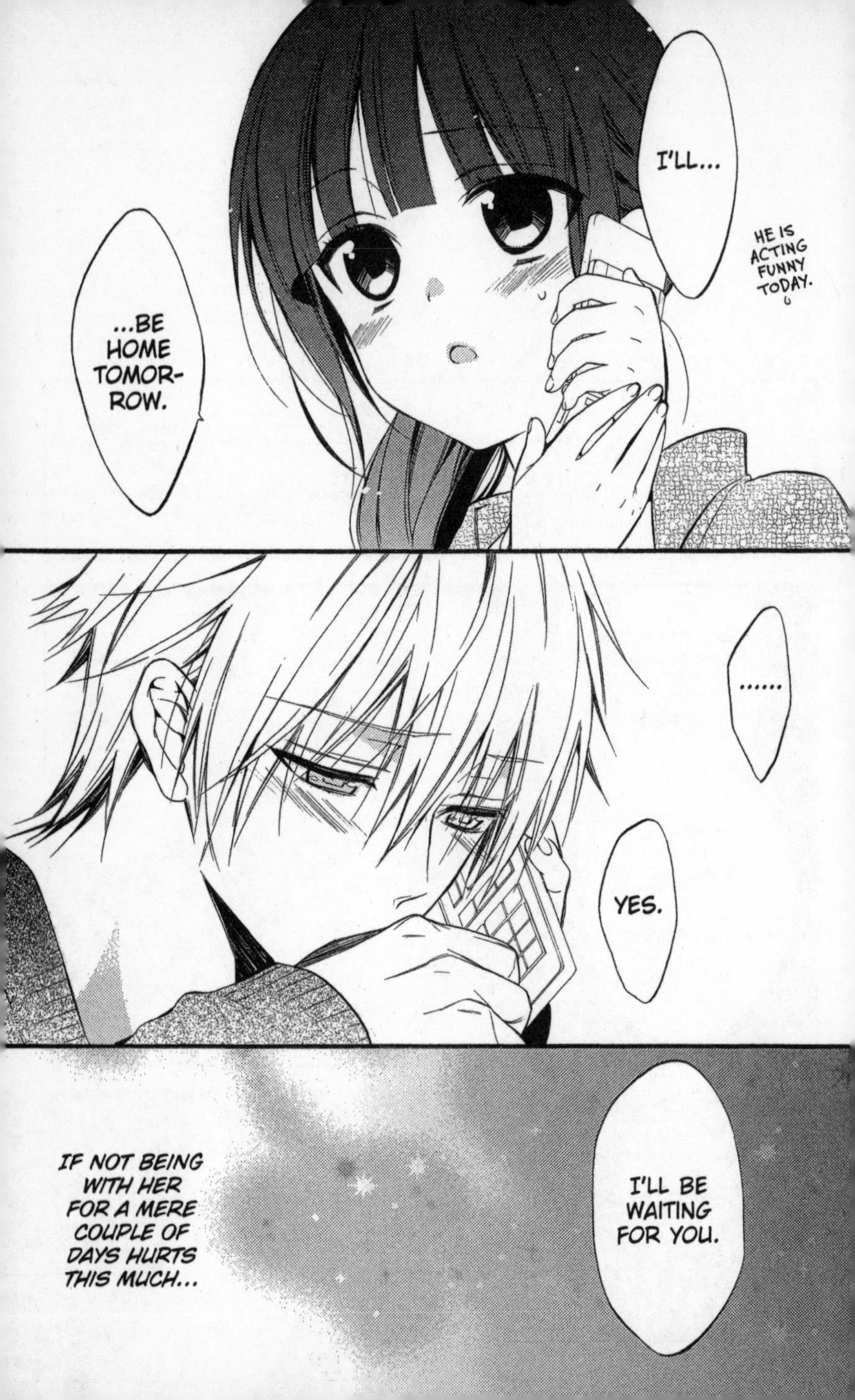
I'LL...
HE IS ACTING FUNNY TODAY.
...BE HOME TOMOR-ROW.
......
YES.
I'LL BE WAITING FOR YOU.
IF NOT BEING WITH HER FOR A MERE COUPLE OF DAYS HURTS THIS MUCH...

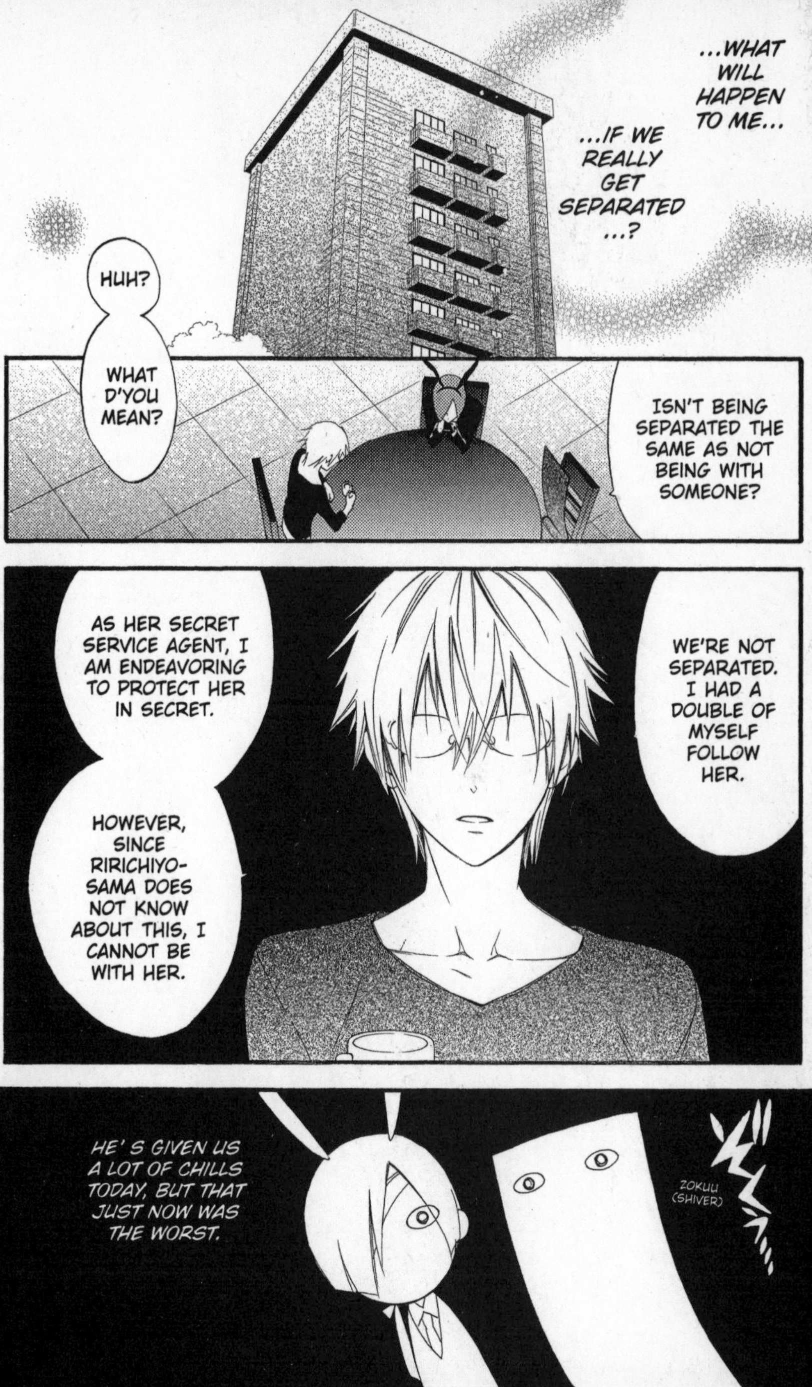
...WHAT WILL HAPPEN TO ME...
...IF WE REALLY GET SEPARATED ...?
HUH?
WHAT D'YOU MEAN?
ISN'T BEING SEPARATED THE SAME AS NOT BEING WITH SOMEONE?
WE'RE NOT SEPARATED. I HAD A DOUBLE OF MYSELF FOLLOW HER.
AS HER SECRET SERVICE AGENT, I AM ENDEAVORING TO PROTECT HER IN SECRET.
HOWEVER, SINCE RIRICHIYO-SAMA DOES NOT KNOW ABOUT THIS, I CANNOT BE WITH HER.
ZOKUU (SHIVER)
HE'S GIVEN US A LOT OF CHILLS TODAY, BUT THAT JUST NOW WAS THE WORST.

INU×BOKU SS

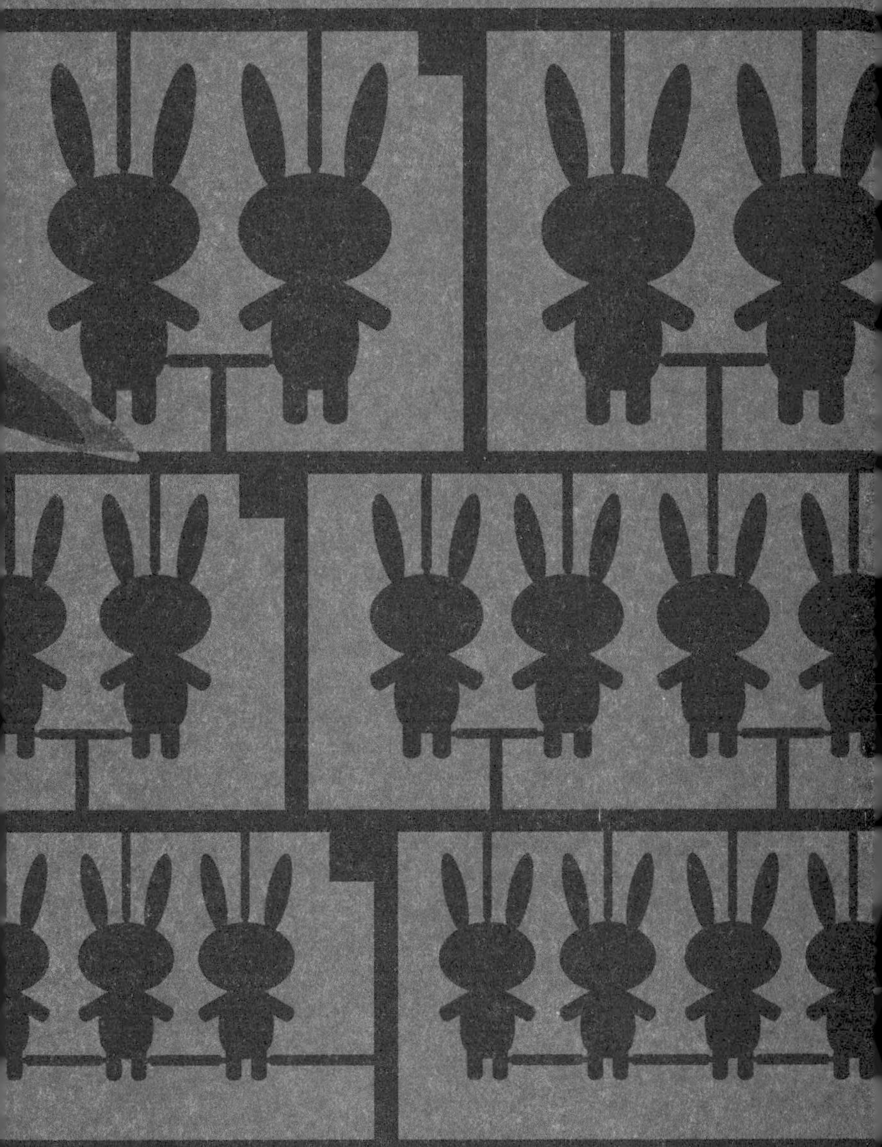

Interlude 4: Many-Colored Glasses

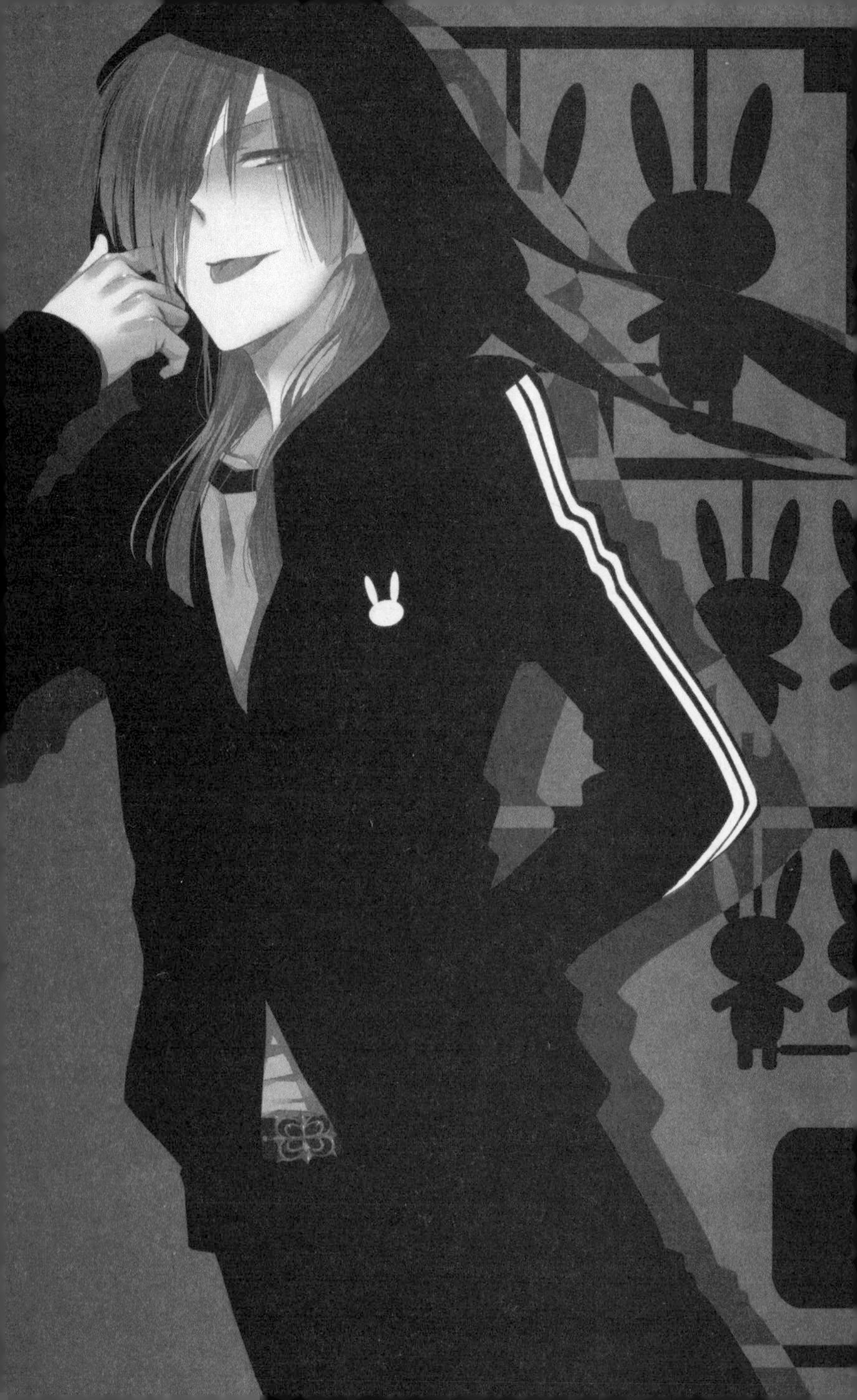

INU×BOKU SS

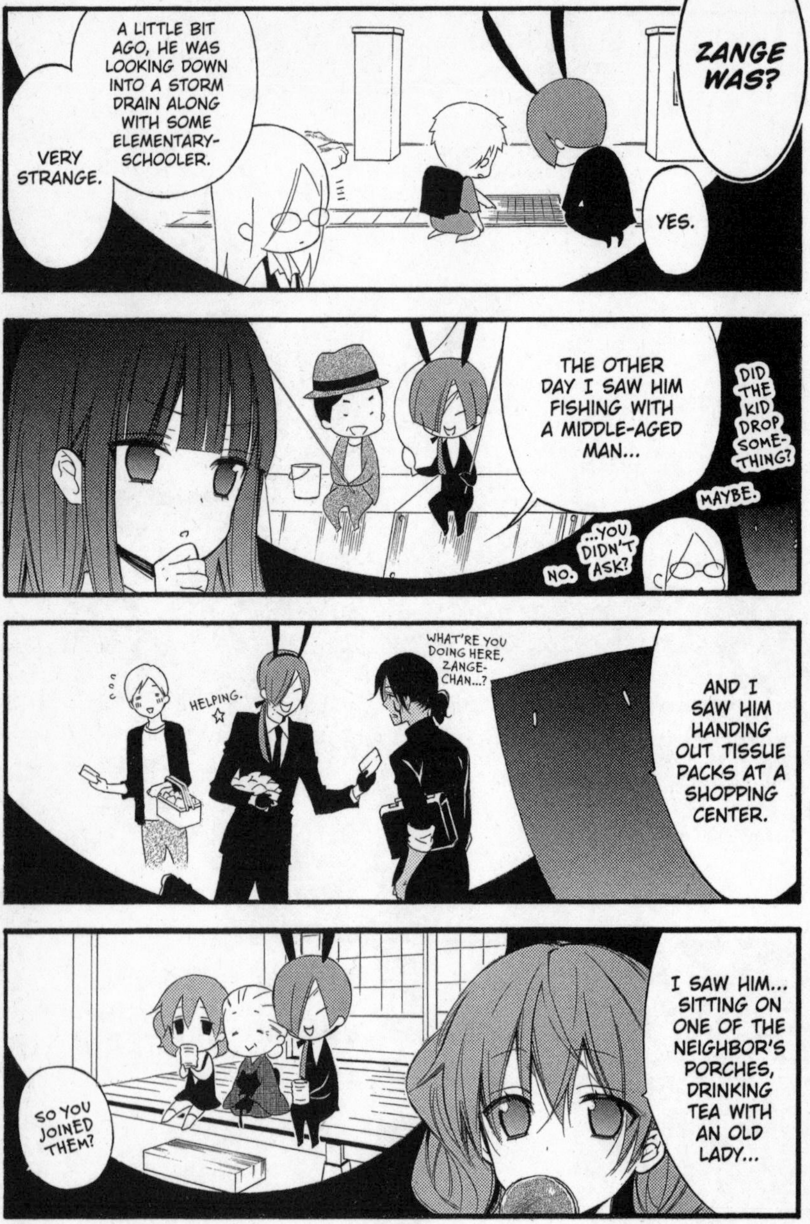
ZANGE WAS?
YES.
A LITTLE BIT AGO, HE WAS LOOKING DOWN INTO A STORM DRAIN ALONG WITH SOME ELEMENTARY-SCHOOLER.
VERY STRANGE.
DID THE KID DROP SOME-THING?
MAYBE.
...YOU DIDN'T ASK?
NO.
THE OTHER DAY I SAW HIM FISHING WITH A MIDDLE-AGED MAN...
AND I SAW HIM HANDING OUT TISSUE PACKS AT A SHOPPING CENTER.
WHAT'RE YOU DOING HERE, ZANGE-CHAN...?
HELPING.
I SAW HIM... SITTING ON ONE OF THE NEIGHBOR'S PORCHES, DRINKING TEA WITH AN OLD LADY...
SO YOU JOINED THEM?

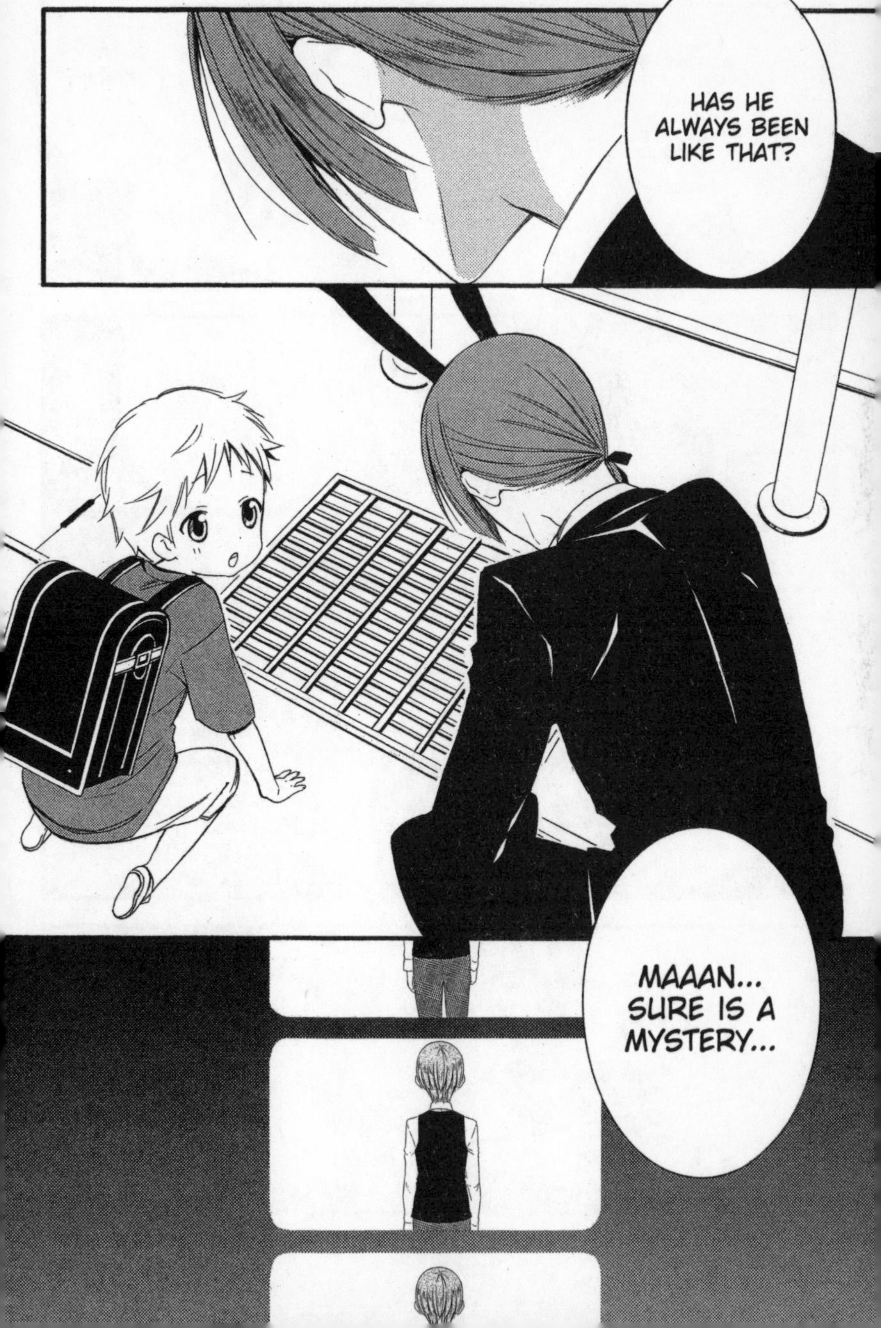
HAS HE ALWAYS BEEN LIKE THAT?
MAAAN... SURE IS A MYSTERY...

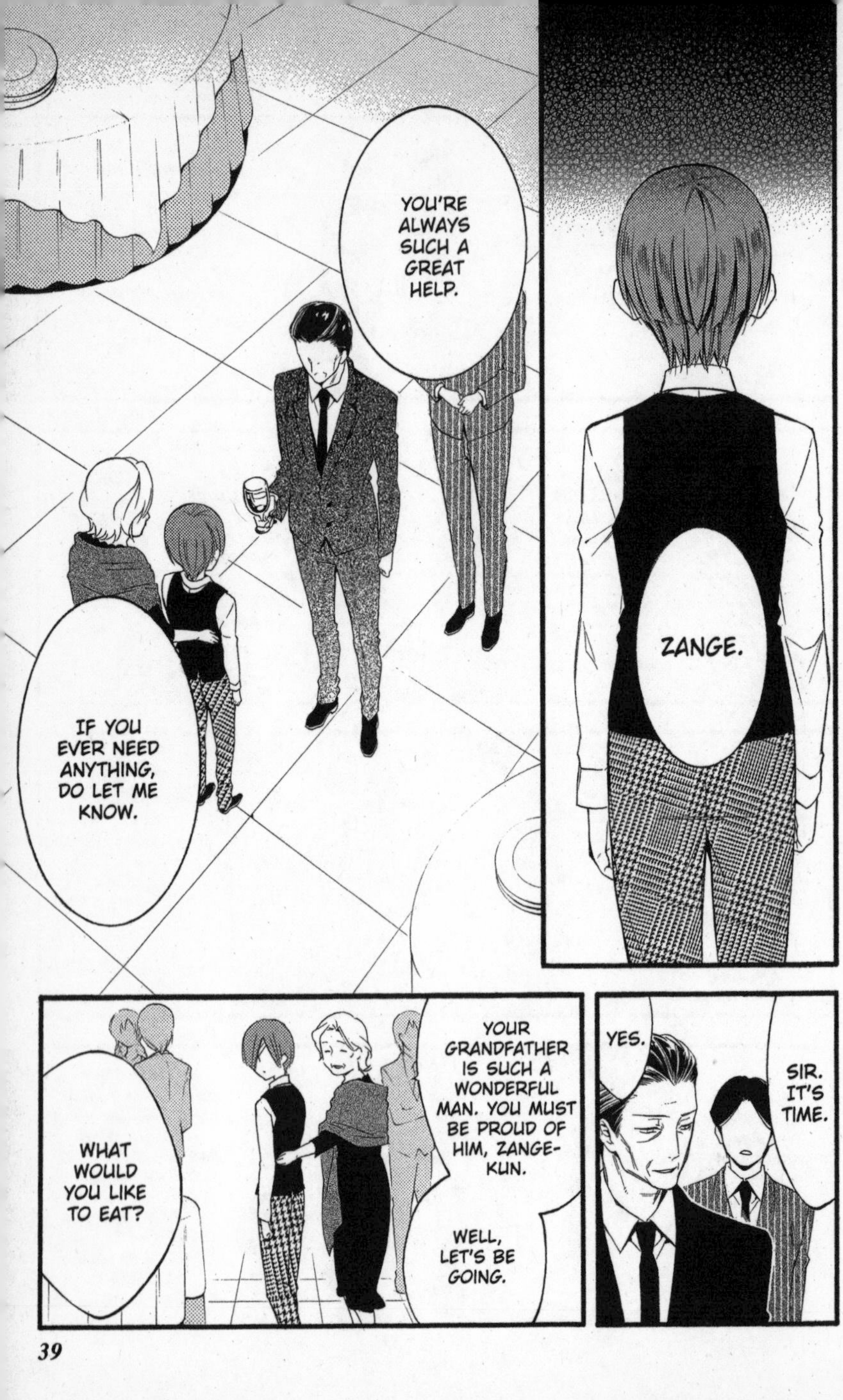
ZANGE.
YOU'RE ALWAYS SUCH A GREAT HELP.
IF YOU EVER NEED ANYTHING, DO LET ME KNOW.
SIR. IT'S TIME.
YES.
YOUR GRANDFATHER IS SUCH A WONDERFUL MAN. YOU MUST BE PROUD OF HIM, ZANGE-KUN.
WELL, LET'S BE GOING.
WHAT WOULD YOU LIKE TO EAT?

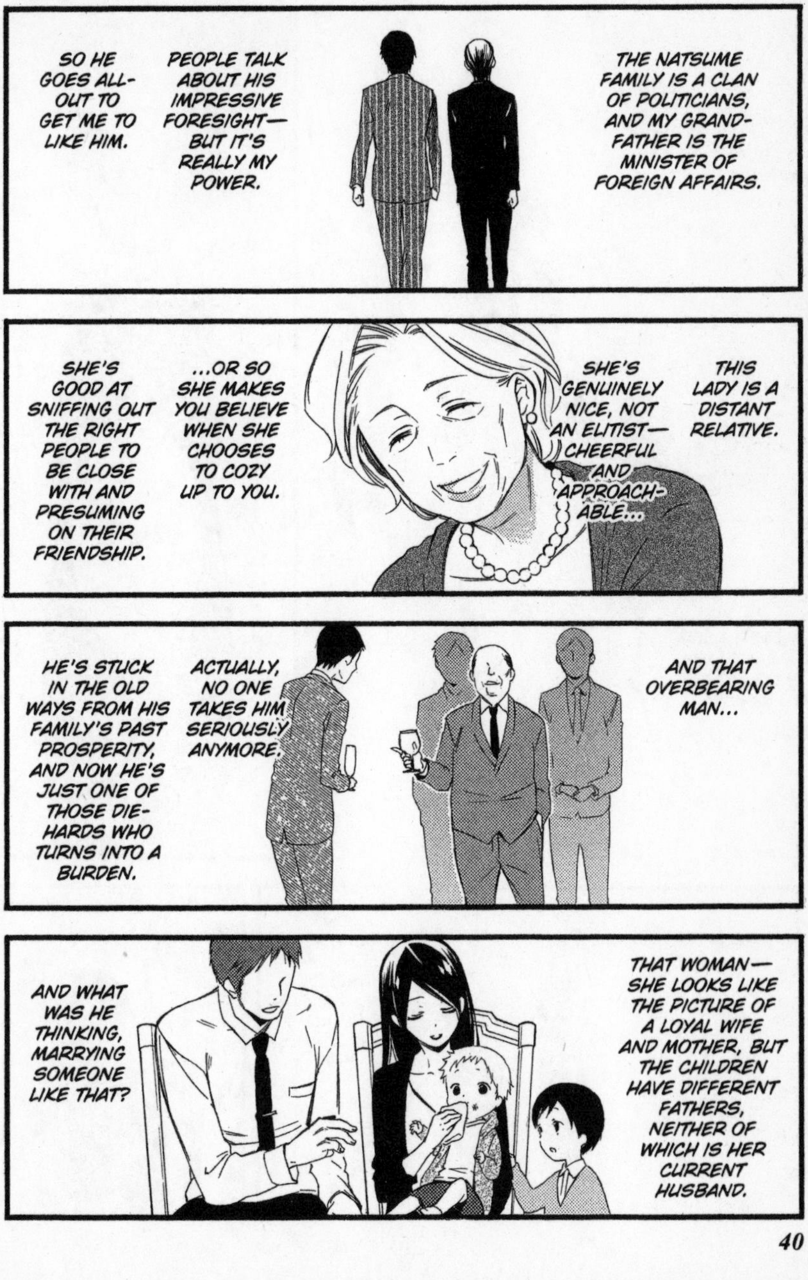
THE NATSUME FAMILY IS A CLAN OF POLITICIANS, AND MY GRANDFATHER IS THE MINISTER OF FOREIGN AFFAIRS.
PEOPLE TALK ABOUT HIS IMPRESSIVE FORESIGHT—BUT IT'S REALLY MY POWER.
SO HE GOES ALL-OUT TO GET ME TO LIKE HIM.
THIS LADY IS A DISTANT RELATIVE.
SHE'S GENUINELY NICE, NOT AN ELITIST—CHEERFUL AND APPROACHABLE...
...OR SO SHE MAKES YOU BELIEVE WHEN SHE CHOOSES TO COZY UP TO YOU.
SHE'S GOOD AT SNIFFING OUT THE RIGHT PEOPLE TO BE CLOSE WITH AND PRESUMING ON THEIR FRIENDSHIP.
AND THAT OVERBEARING MAN...
ACTUALLY, NO ONE TAKES HIM SERIOUSLY ANYMORE.
HE'S STUCK IN THE OLD WAYS FROM HIS FAMILY'S PAST PROSPERITY, AND NOW HE'S JUST ONE OF THOSE DIE-HARDS WHO TURNS INTO A BURDEN.
THAT WOMAN—SHE LOOKS LIKE THE PICTURE OF A LOYAL WIFE AND MOTHER, BUT THE CHILDREN HAVE DIFFERENT FATHERS, NEITHER OF WHICH IS HER CURRENT HUSBAND.
AND WHAT WAS HE THINKING, MARRYING SOMEONE LIKE THAT?

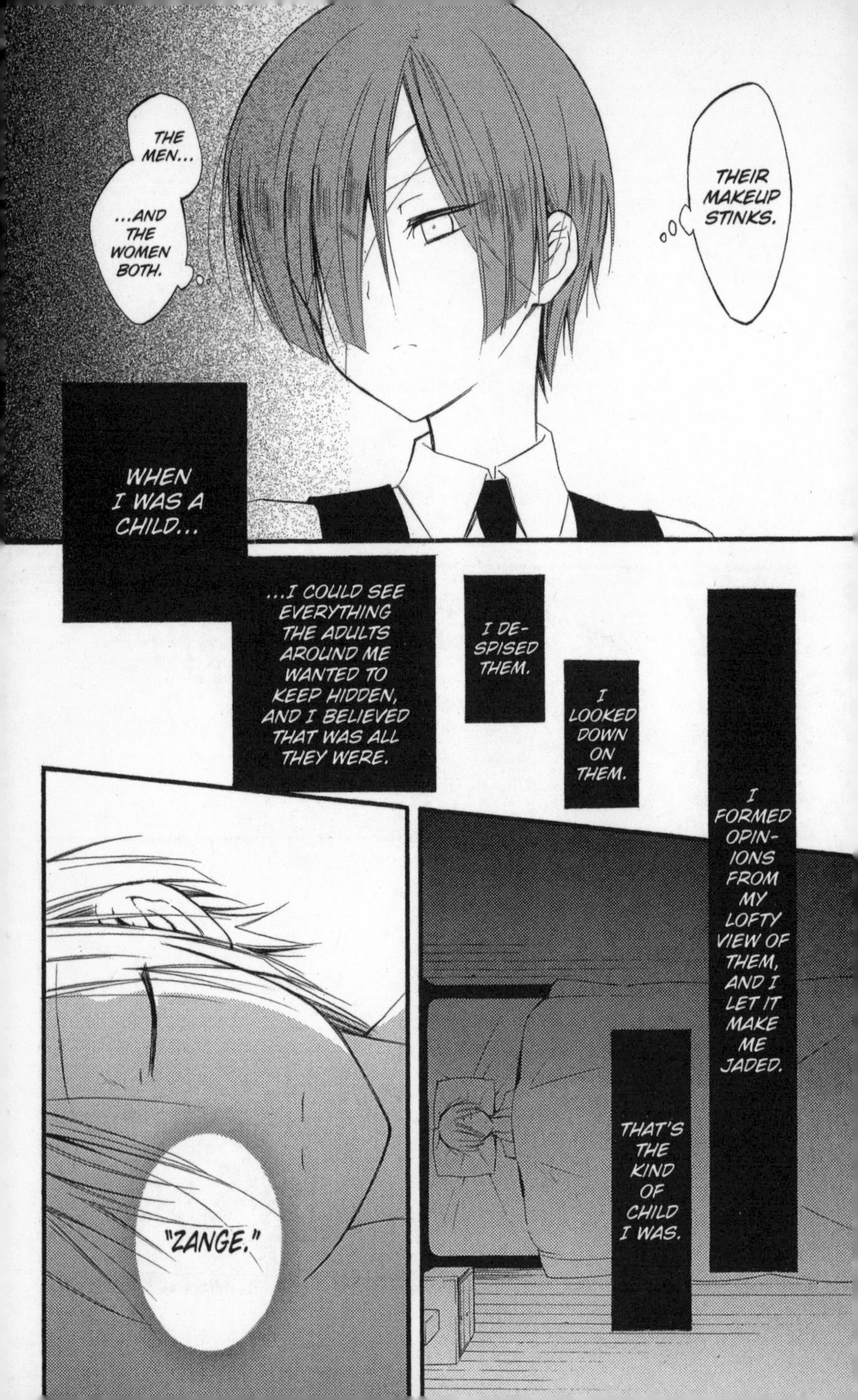
THEIR MAKEUP STINKS.
THE MEN...
...AND THE WOMEN BOTH.
WHEN I WAS A CHILD...
...I COULD SEE EVERYTHING THE ADULTS AROUND ME WANTED TO KEEP HIDDEN, AND I BELIEVED THAT WAS ALL THEY WERE.
I DE-SPISED THEM.
I LOOKED DOWN ON THEM.
I FORMED OPIN-IONS FROM MY LOFTY VIEW OF THEM, AND I LET IT MAKE ME JADED.
THAT'S THE KIND OF CHILD I WAS.
"ZANGE."

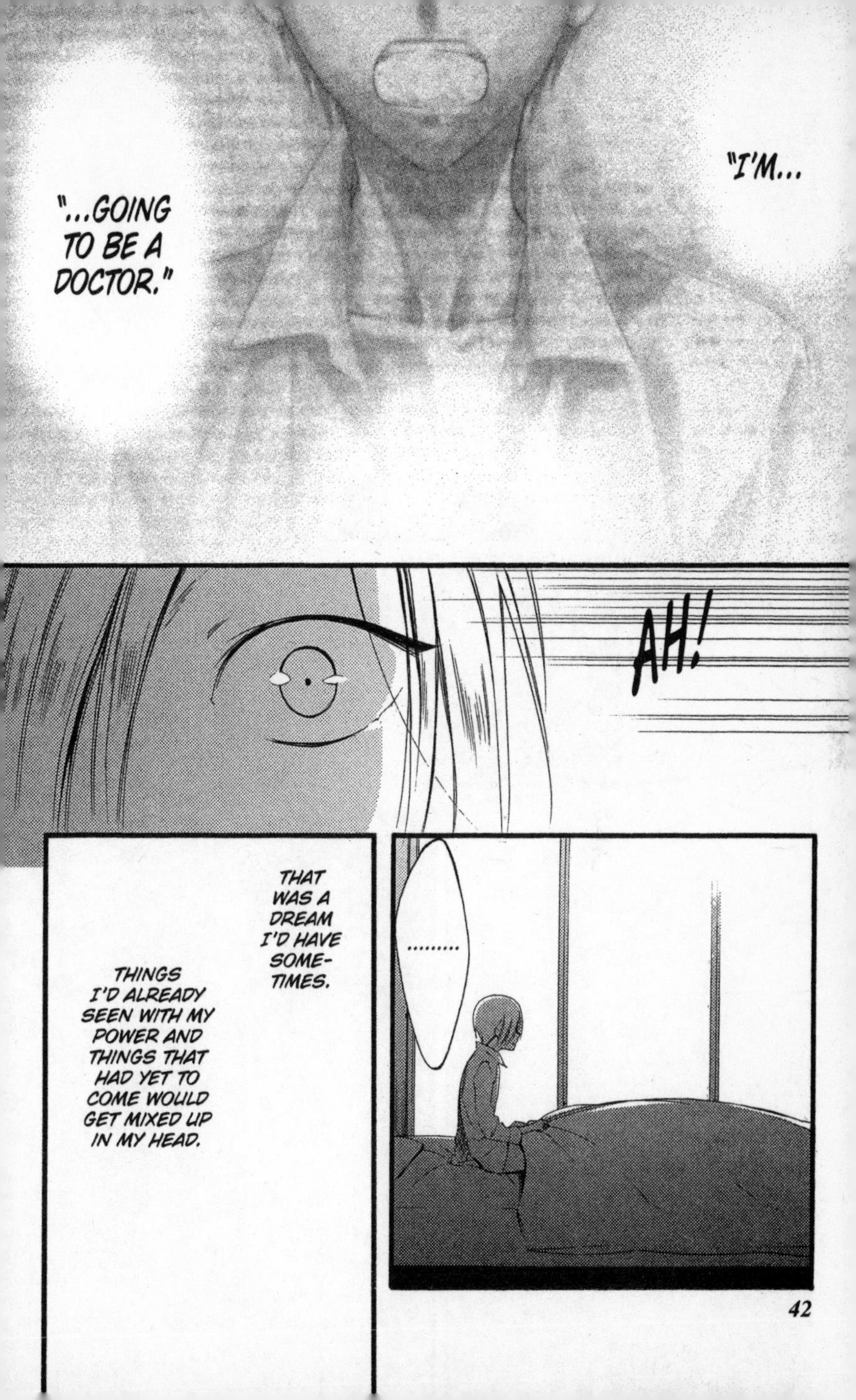
"I'M...
"...GOING TO BE A DOCTOR."
AH!
....
THAT WAS A DREAM I'D HAVE SOME-TIMES.
THINGS I'D ALREADY SEEN WITH MY POWER AND THINGS THAT HAD YET TO COME WOULD GET MIXED UP IN MY HEAD.

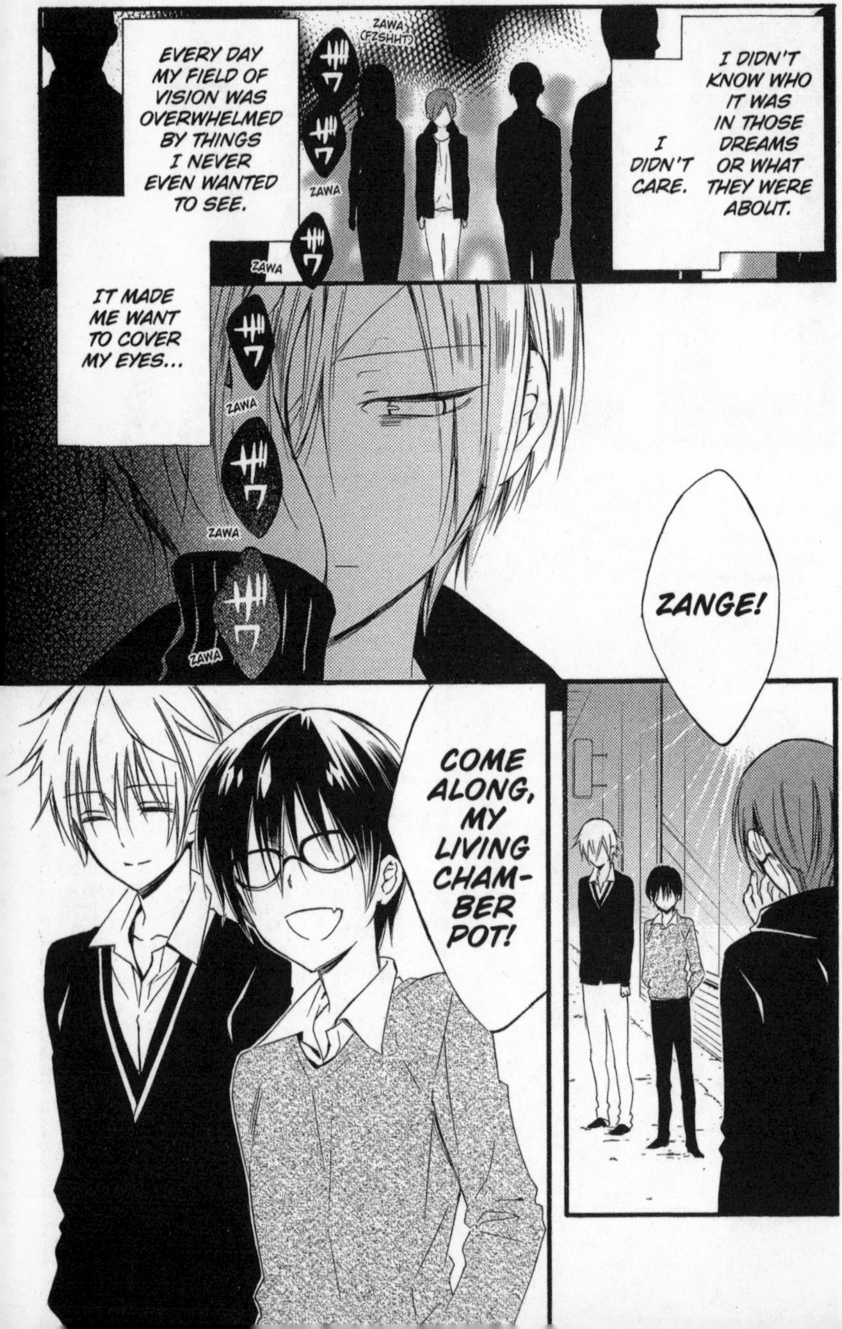
I DIDN'T KNOW WHO IT WAS IN THOSE DREAMS OR WHAT THEY WERE ABOUT.
I DIDN'T CARE.
ZAWA (FZSHHT)
EVERY DAY MY FIELD OF VISION WAS OVERWHELMED BY THINGS I NEVER EVEN WANTED TO SEE.
ZAWA
ZAWA
IT MADE ME WANT TO COVER MY EYES...
ZAWA
ZAWA
ZAWA
ZANGE!
COME ALONG, MY LIVING CHAM-BER POT!

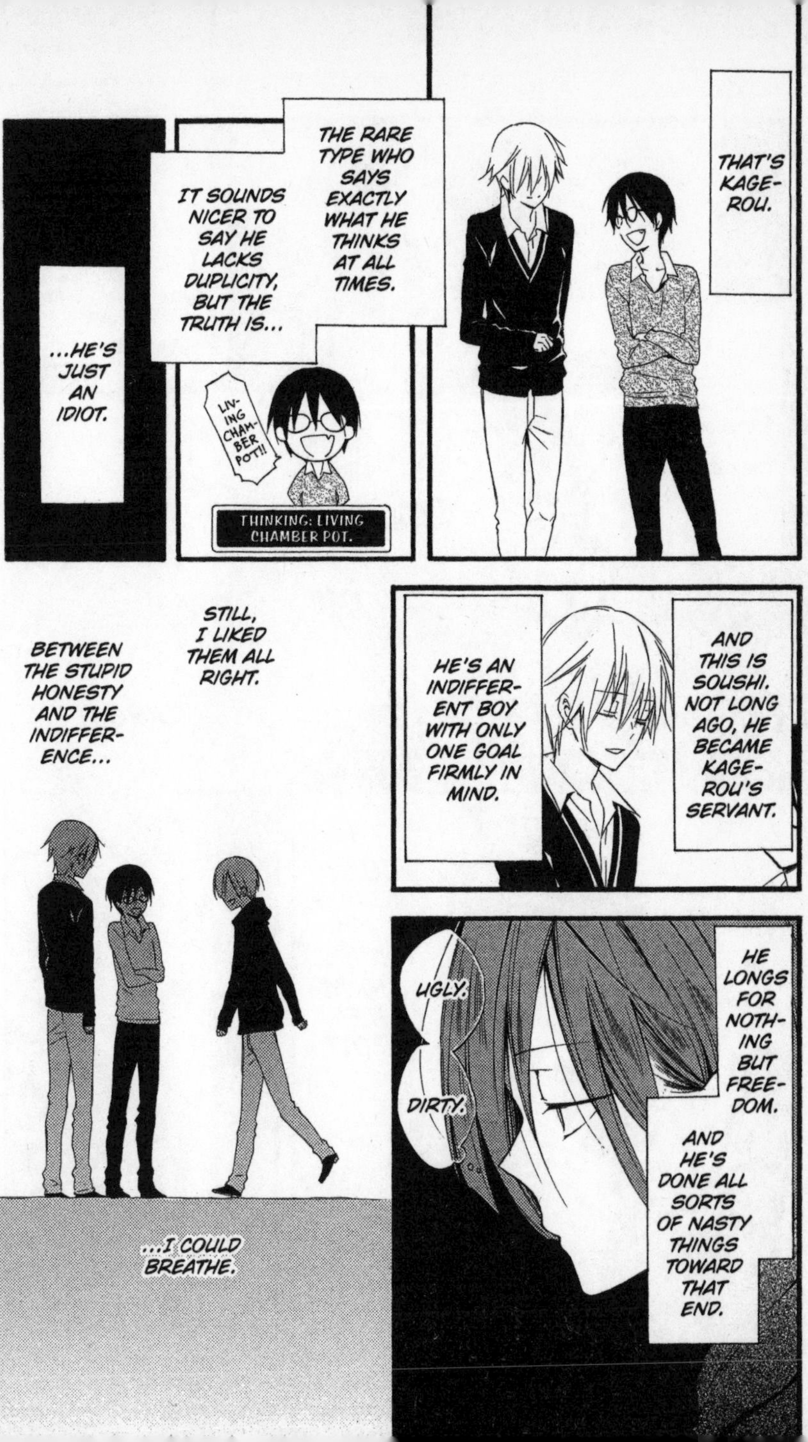
THAT'S KAGE-ROU.
THE RARE TYPE WHO SAYS EXACTLY WHAT HE THINKS AT ALL TIMES.
IT SOUNDS NICER TO SAY HE LACKS DUPLICITY, BUT THE TRUTH IS...
LIV-ING CHAM-BER POT!!
THINKING: LIVING CHAMBER POT.
...HE'S JUST AN IDIOT.
AND THIS IS SOUSHI. NOT LONG AGO, HE BECAME KAGE-ROU'S SERVANT.
HE'S AN INDIFFER-ENT BOY WITH ONLY ONE GOAL FIRMLY IN MIND.
HE LONGS FOR NOTH-ING BUT FREE-DOM.
UGLY.
DIRTY.
AND HE'S DONE ALL SORTS OF NASTY THINGS TOWARD THAT END.
STILL, I LIKED THEM ALL RIGHT.
BETWEEN THE STUPID HONESTY AND THE INDIFFER-ENCE...
...I COULD BREATHE.

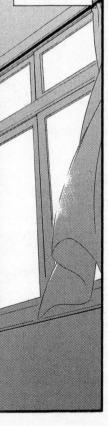

IT'S TRUE.

EVEN I HAD A FEW PEOPLE I LIKED.

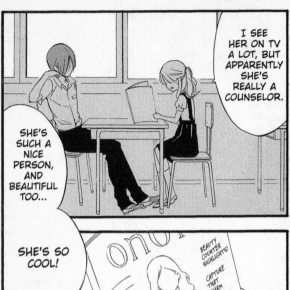

I SEE HER ON TV A LOT, BUT APPARENTLY SHE'S REALLY A COUNSELOR.

SHE'S SUCH A NICE PERSON, AND BEAUTIFUL TOO...

SHE'S SO COOL!

BEAUTY COUNTER HIGHLIGHTS!

CAPTURE THAT CHARM

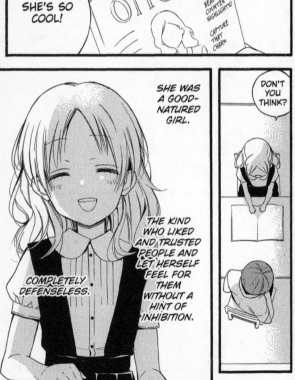

DON'T YOU THINK?

SHE WAS A GOOD-NATURED GIRL.

THE KIND WHO LIKED AND TRUSTED PEOPLE AND LET HERSELF FEEL FOR THEM WITHOUT A HINT OF INHIBITION.

COMPLETELY DEFENSELESS.

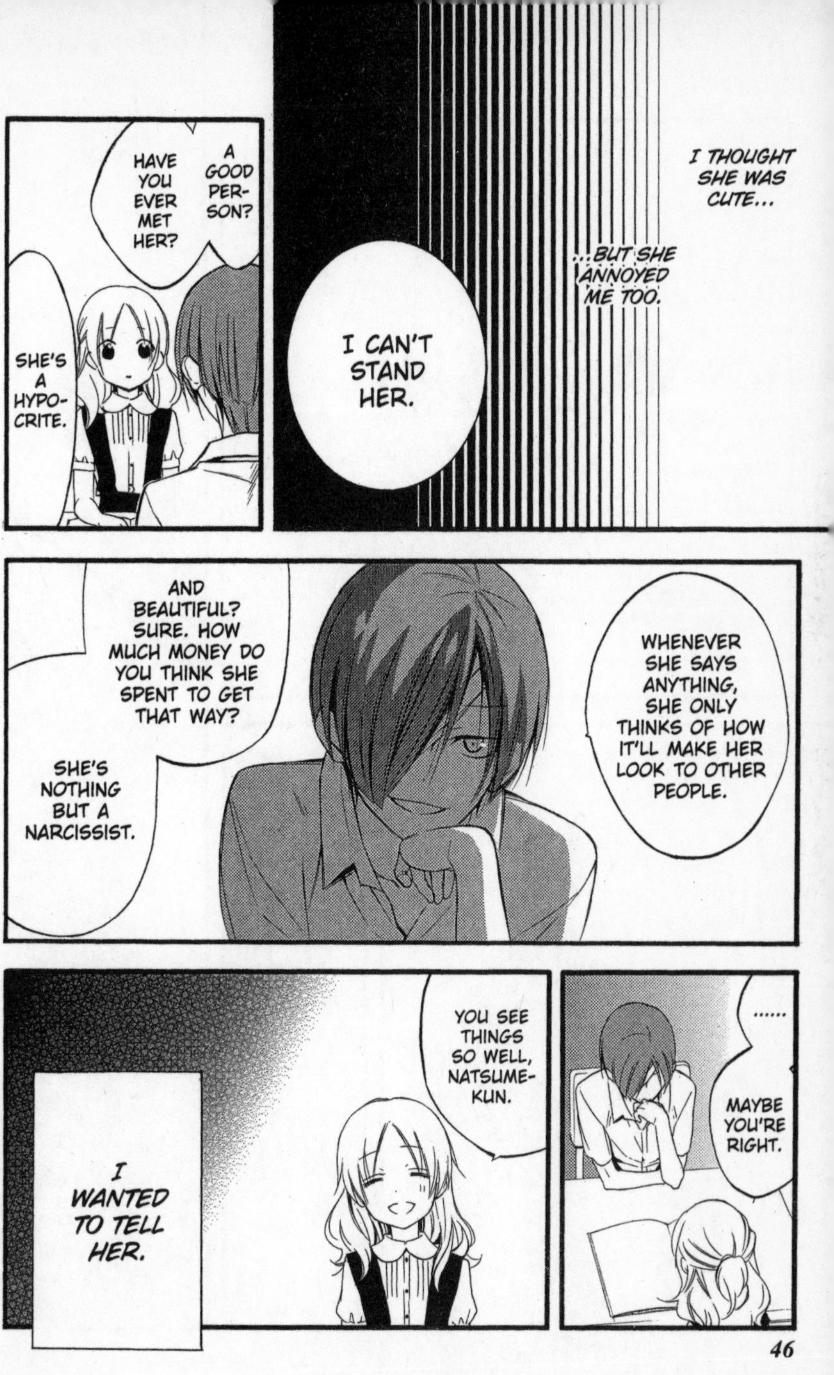
I THOUGHT SHE WAS CUTE...
...BUT SHE ANNOYED ME TOO.
I CAN'T STAND HER.
A GOOD PERSON?
HAVE YOU EVER MET HER?
SHE'S A HYPOCRITE.
WHENEVER SHE SAYS ANYTHING, SHE ONLY THINKS OF HOW IT'LL MAKE HER LOOK TO OTHER PEOPLE.
AND BEAUTIFUL? SURE. HOW MUCH MONEY DO YOU THINK SHE SPENT TO GET THAT WAY?
SHE'S NOTHING BUT A NARCISSIST.
......
MAYBE YOU'RE RIGHT.
YOU SEE THINGS SO WELL, NATSUME-KUN.
I WANTED TO TELL HER.

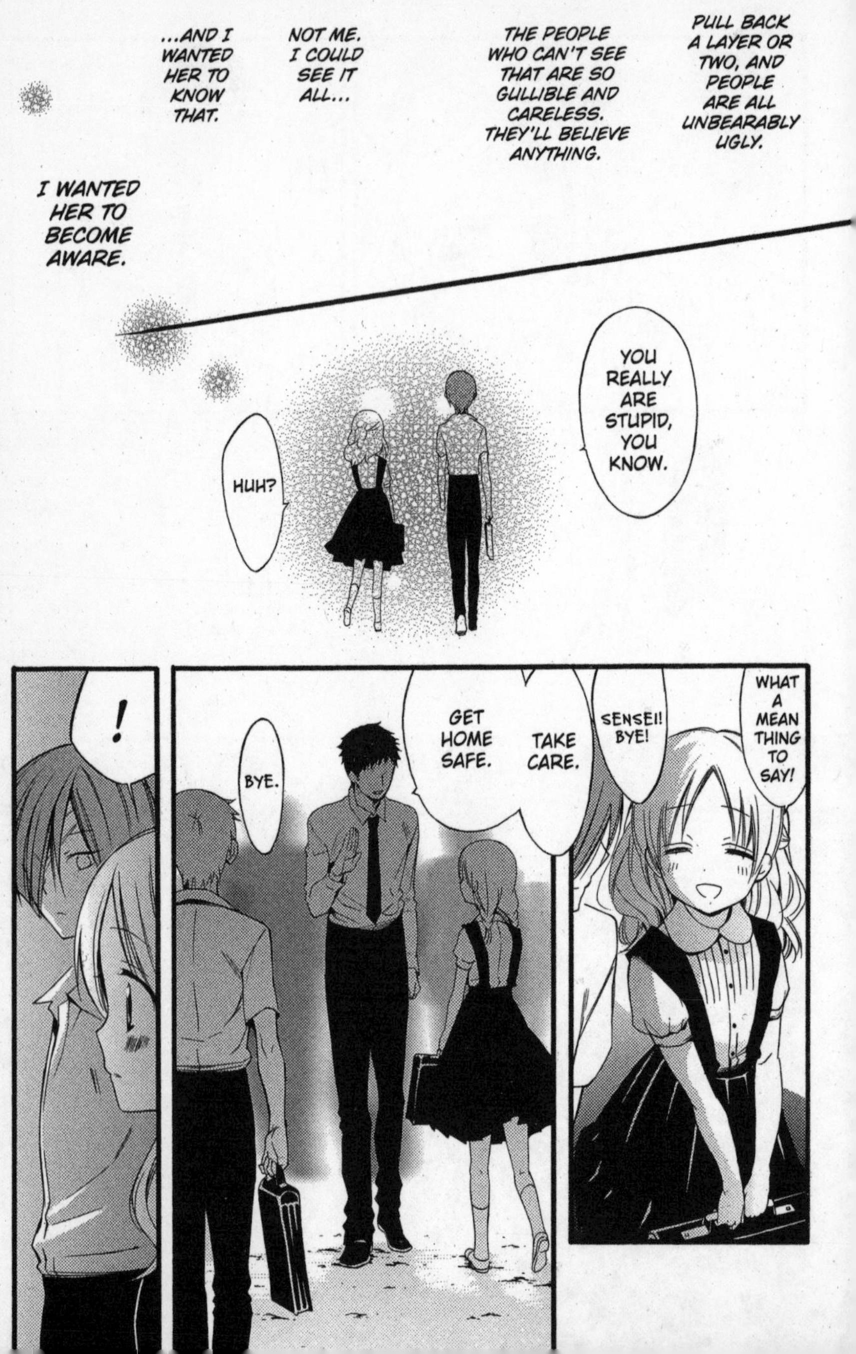
PULL BACK A LAYER OR TWO, AND PEOPLE ARE ALL UNBEARABLY UGLY.
THE PEOPLE WHO CAN'T SEE THAT ARE SO GULLIBLE AND CARELESS. THEY'LL BELIEVE ANYTHING.
NOT ME. I COULD SEE IT ALL...
...AND I WANTED HER TO KNOW THAT.
I WANTED HER TO BECOME AWARE.
YOU REALLY ARE STUPID, YOU KNOW.
HUH?
WHAT A MEAN THING TO SAY!
SENSEI! BYE!
TAKE CARE.
GET HOME SAFE.
BYE.
!

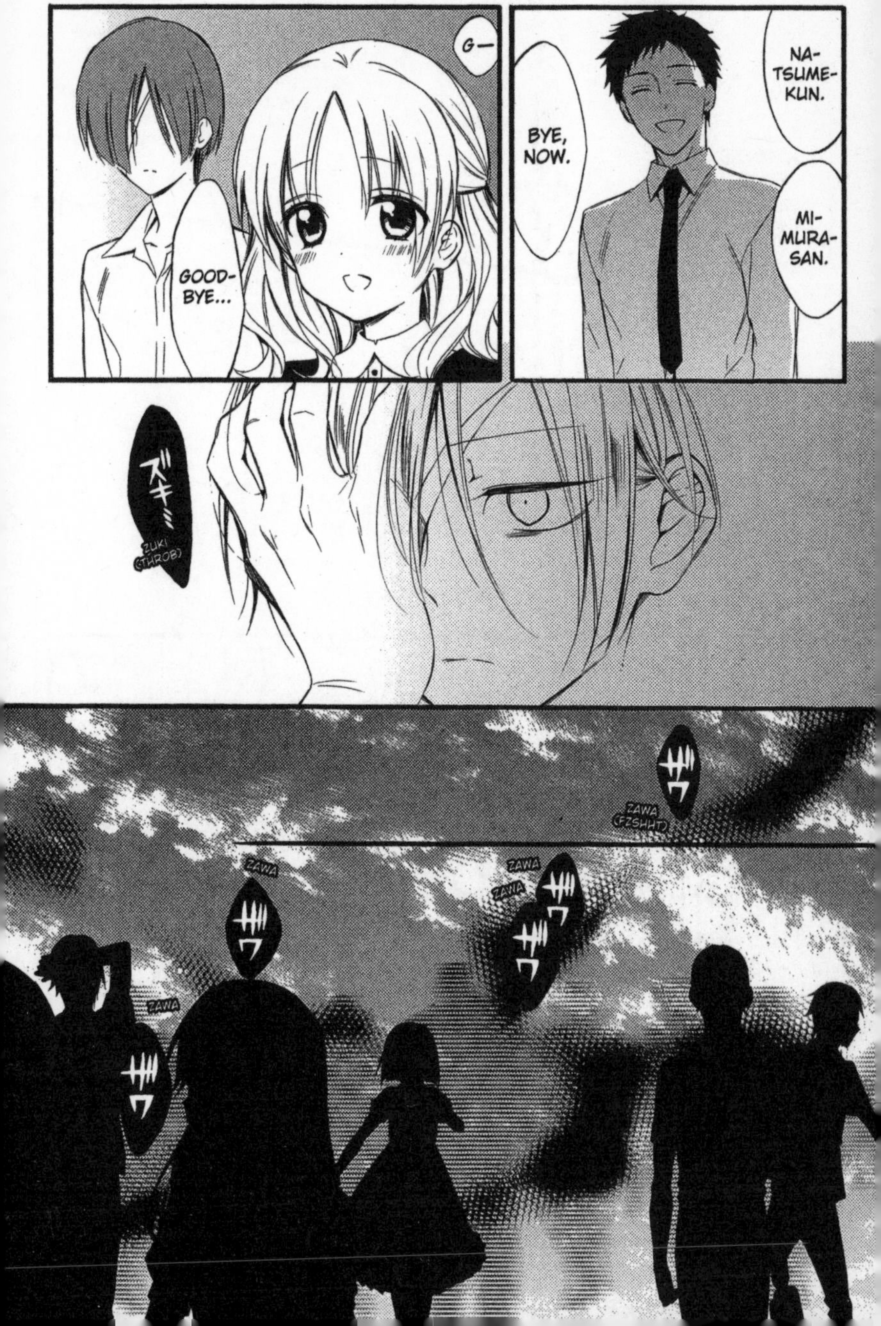
NATSUME-KUN.
MIMURA-SAN.
BYE, NOW.
G—
GOOD-BYE...
ズキ
ZUKI (THROB)
ザワ
ZAWA (FZSHHT)
ZAWA
ZAWA
ZAWA
ZAWA

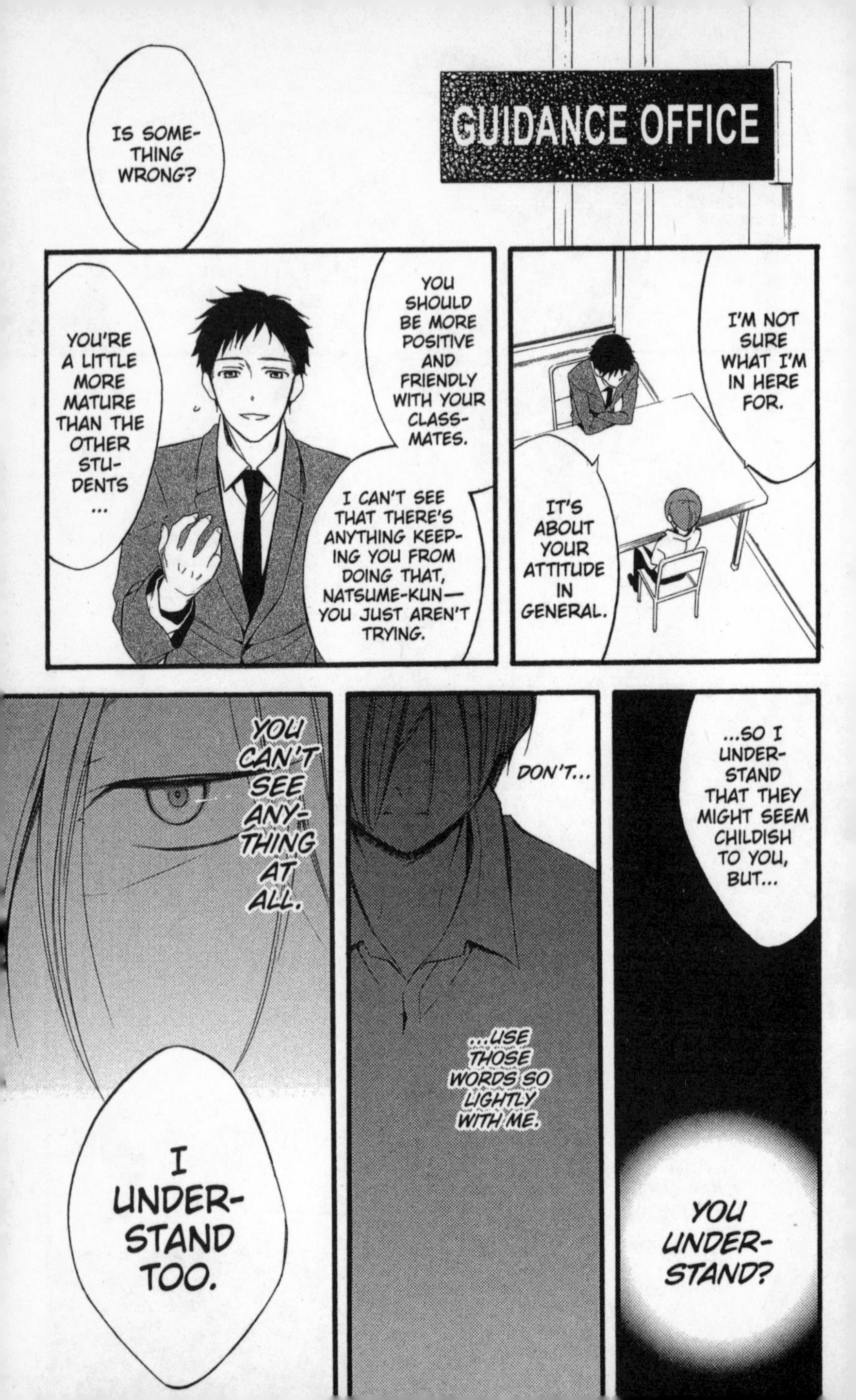
GUIDANCE OFFICE
IS SOMETHING WRONG?
I'M NOT SURE WHAT I'M IN HERE FOR.
IT'S ABOUT YOUR ATTITUDE IN GENERAL.
YOU SHOULD BE MORE POSITIVE AND FRIENDLY WITH YOUR CLASSMATES.
YOU'RE A LITTLE MORE MATURE THAN THE OTHER STUDENTS...
I CAN'T SEE THAT THERE'S ANYTHING KEEPING YOU FROM DOING THAT, NATSUME-KUN—YOU JUST AREN'T TRYING.
...SO I UNDERSTAND THAT THEY MIGHT SEEM CHILDISH TO YOU, BUT...
YOU UNDERSTAND?
DON'T...
...USE THOSE WORDS SO LIGHTLY WITH ME.
YOU CAN'T SEE ANYTHING AT ALL.
I UNDERSTAND TOO.

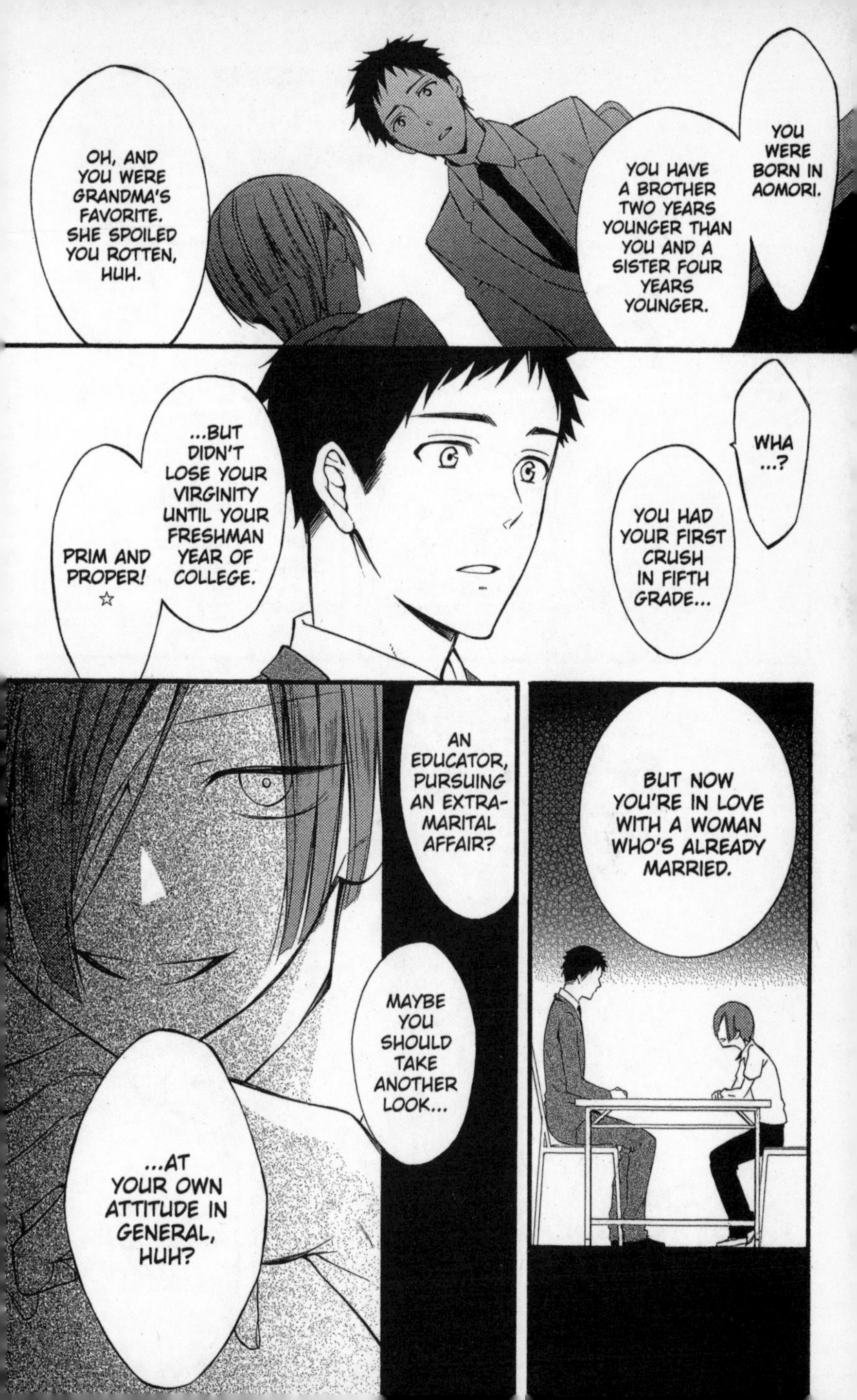
YOU WERE BORN IN AOMORI.
YOU HAVE A BROTHER TWO YEARS YOUNGER THAN YOU AND A SISTER FOUR YEARS YOUNGER.
OH, AND YOU WERE GRANDMA'S FAVORITE. SHE SPOILED YOU ROTTEN, HUH.
WHA ...?
YOU HAD YOUR FIRST CRUSH IN FIFTH GRADE...
...BUT DIDN'T LOSE YOUR VIRGINITY UNTIL YOUR FRESHMAN YEAR OF COLLEGE.
PRIM AND PROPER! ☆
BUT NOW YOU'RE IN LOVE WITH A WOMAN WHO'S ALREADY MARRIED.
AN EDUCATOR, PURSUING AN EXTRA-MARITAL AFFAIR?
MAYBE YOU SHOULD TAKE ANOTHER LOOK...
...AT YOUR OWN ATTITUDE IN GENERAL, HUH?

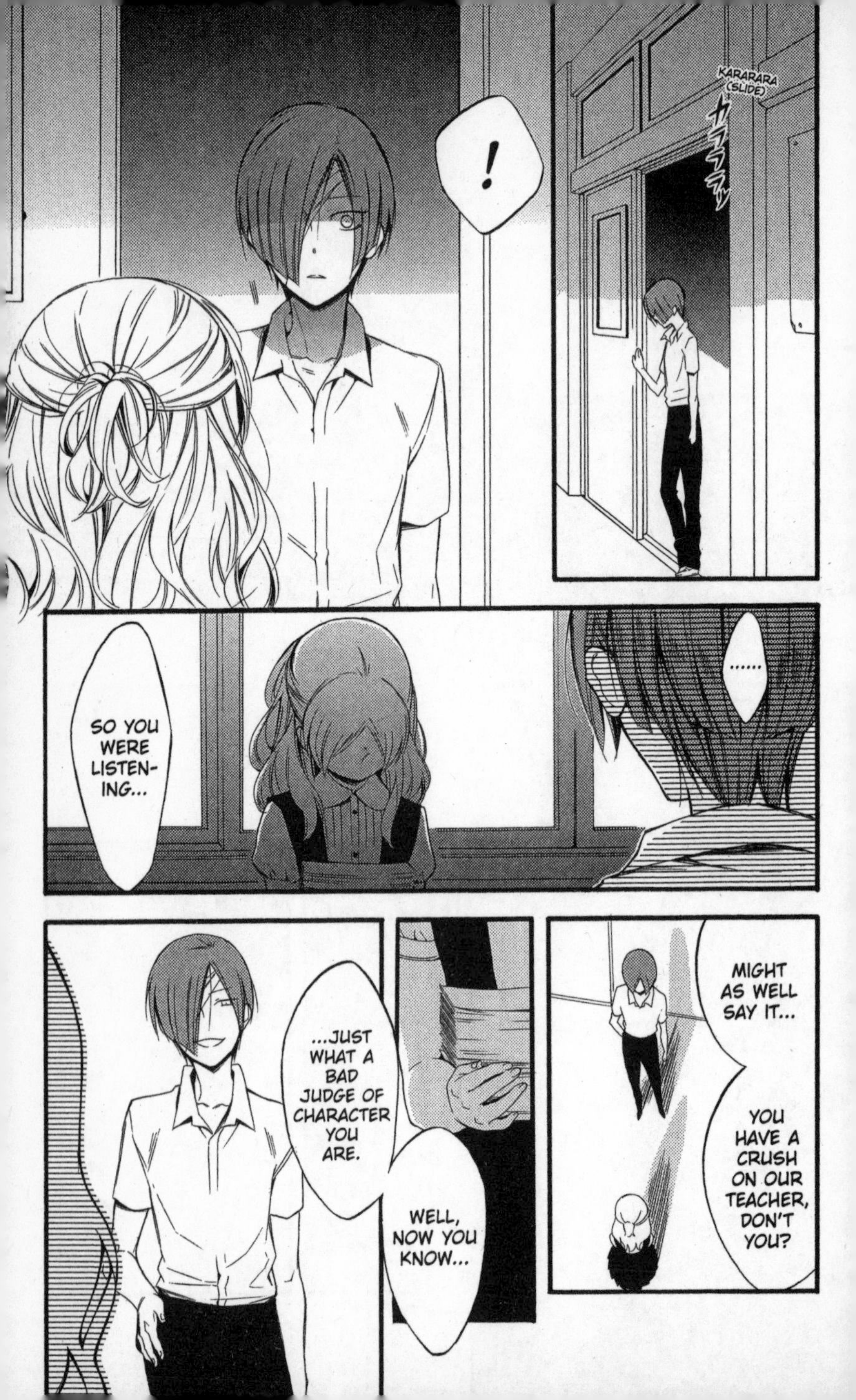
KARARARA (SLIDE)
!
......
SO YOU WERE LISTENING...
MIGHT AS WELL SAY IT...
YOU HAVE A CRUSH ON OUR TEACHER, DON'T YOU?
WELL, NOW YOU KNOW...
...JUST WHAT A BAD JUDGE OF CHARACTER YOU ARE.

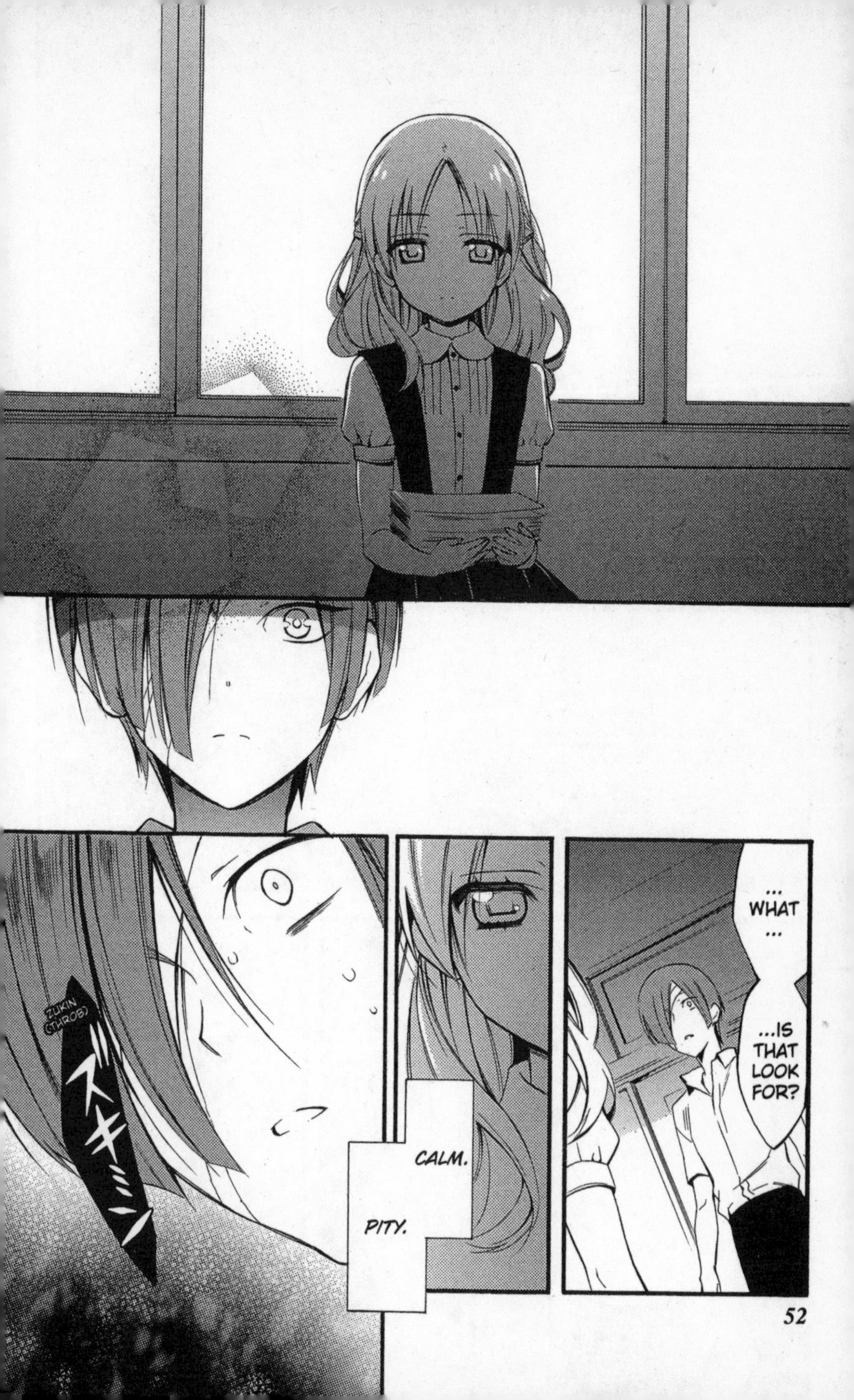
...WHAT...
...IS THAT LOOK FOR?
CALM.
PITY.
ZUKIN (THROB)

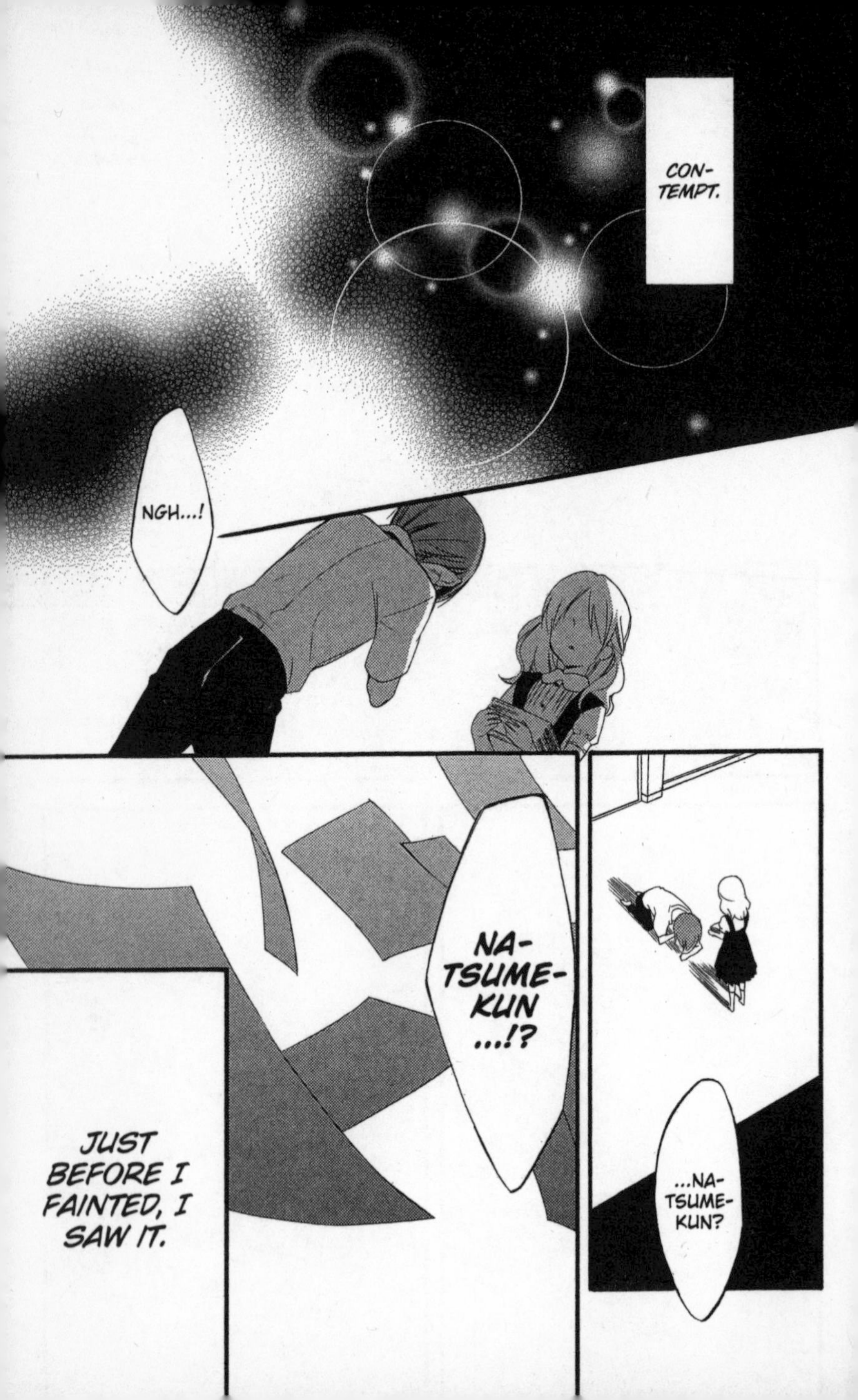
CON-TEMPT.
NGH...!
...NA-TSUME-KUN?
NA-TSUME-KUN...!?
JUST BEFORE I FAINTED, I SAW IT.

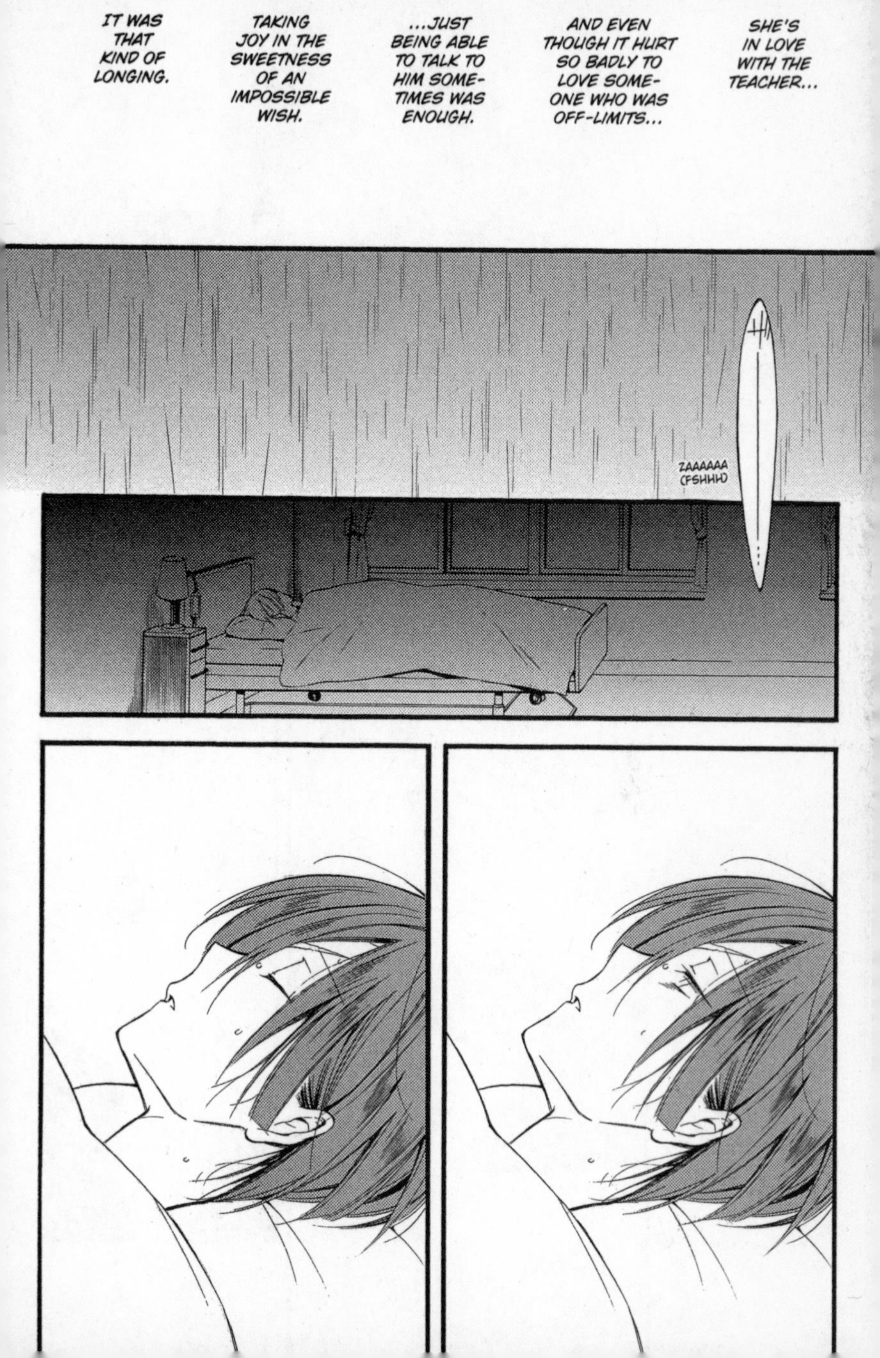
SHE'S IN LOVE WITH THE TEACHER...
AND EVEN THOUGH IT HURT SO BADLY TO LOVE SOMEONE WHO WAS OFF-LIMITS...
...JUST BEING ABLE TO TALK TO HIM SOMETIMES WAS ENOUGH.
TAKING JOY IN THE SWEETNESS OF AN IMPOSSIBLE WISH.
IT WAS THAT KIND OF LONGING.
ZAAAAAA (FSHHH)

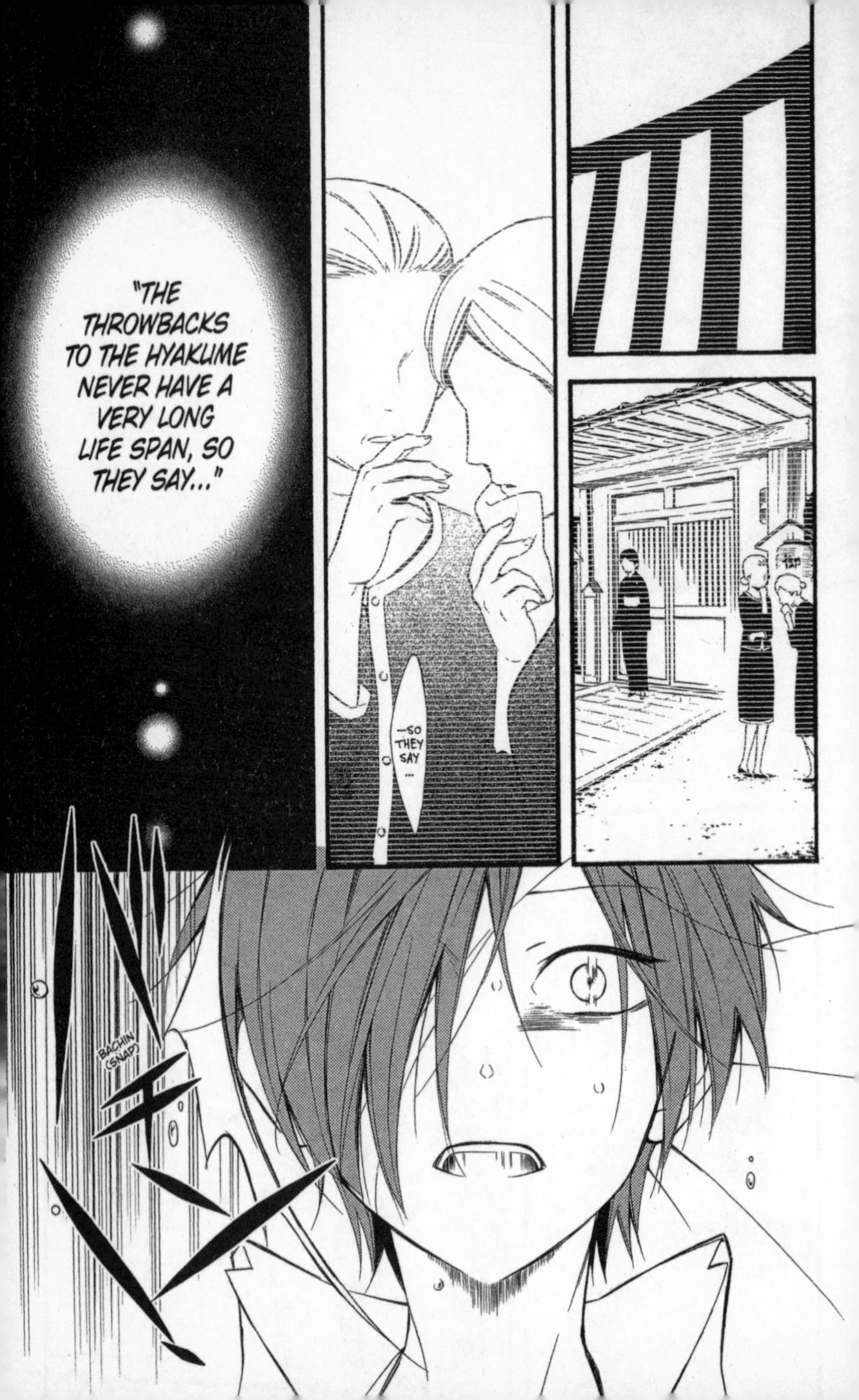
—SO THEY SAY...
"THE THROWBACKS TO THE HYAKUME NEVER HAVE A VERY LONG LIFE SPAN, SO THEY SAY..."
BACHIN (SNAP)

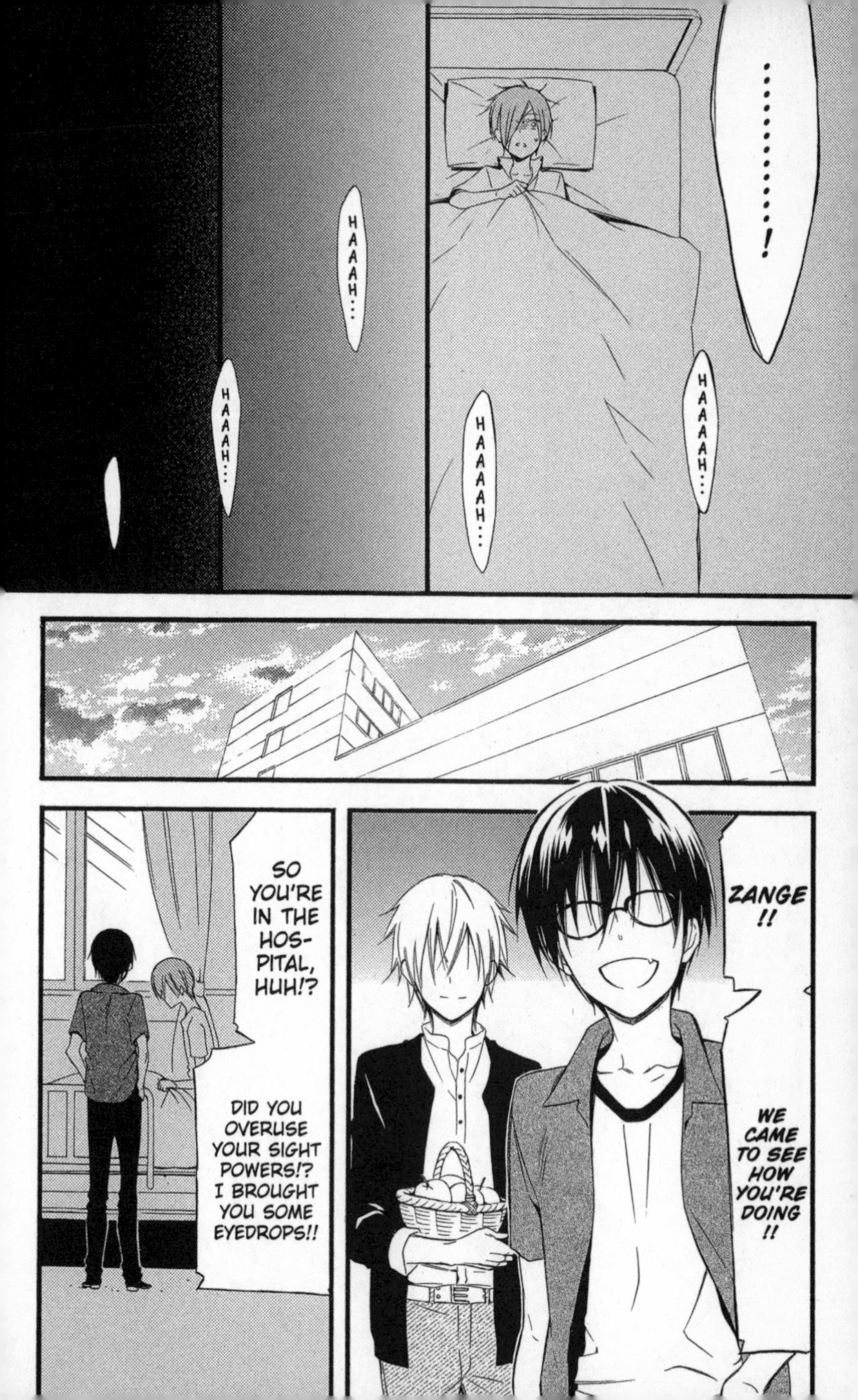
......!
HAAAAAH...
HAAAAAH...
HAAAAH...
HAAAAH...
ZANGE!!
WE CAME TO SEE HOW YOU'RE DOING!!
SO YOU'RE IN THE HOS-PITAL, HUH!?
DID YOU OVERUSE YOUR SIGHT POWERS!? I BROUGHT YOU SOME EYEDROPS!!

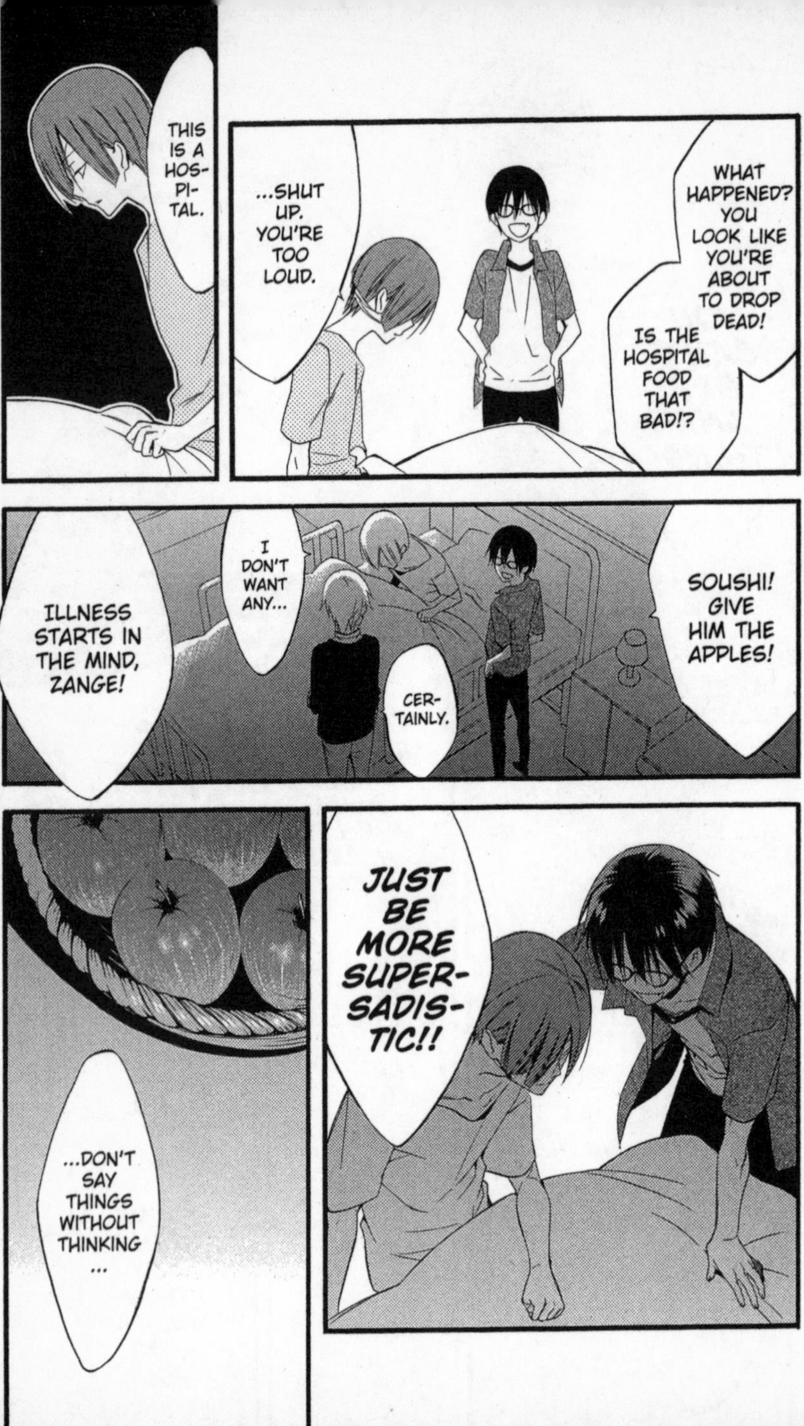
WHAT HAPPENED? YOU LOOK LIKE YOU'RE ABOUT TO DROP DEAD!
IS THE HOSPITAL FOOD THAT BAD!?
...SHUT UP. YOU'RE TOO LOUD.
THIS IS A HOS-PI-TAL.
SOUSHI! GIVE HIM THE APPLES!
CER-TAINLY.
I DON'T WANT ANY...
ILLNESS STARTS IN THE MIND, ZANGE!
JUST BE MORE SUPER-SADIS-TIC!!
...DON'T SAY THINGS WITHOUT THINKING...

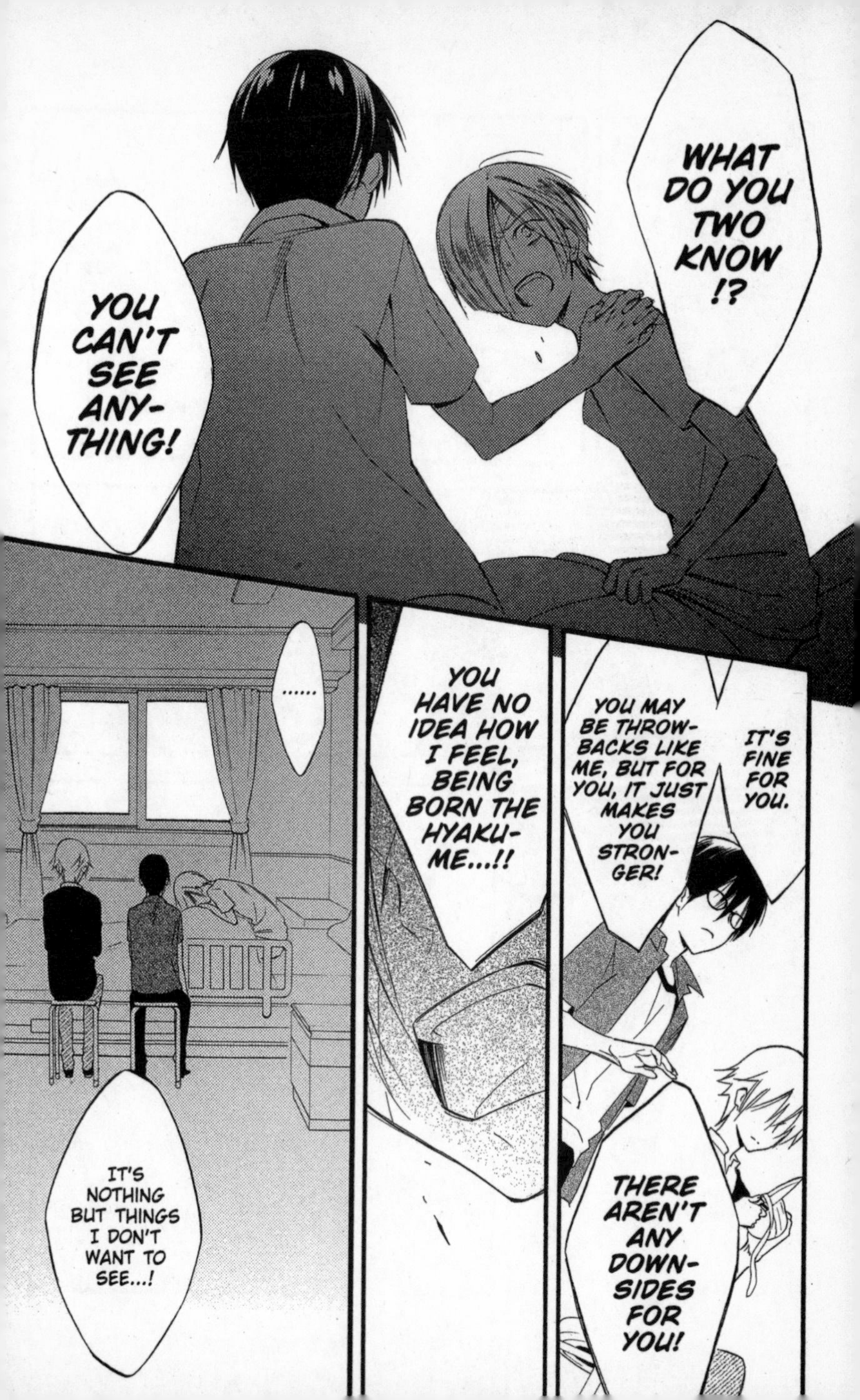
WHAT DO YOU TWO KNOW !?
YOU CAN'T SEE ANYTHING!
IT'S FINE FOR YOU.
YOU MAY BE THROWBACKS LIKE ME, BUT FOR YOU, IT JUST MAKES YOU STRONGER!
THERE AREN'T ANY DOWNSIDES FOR YOU!
YOU HAVE NO IDEA HOW I FEEL, BEING BORN THE HYAKUME...!!
......
IT'S NOTHING BUT THINGS I DON'T WANT TO SEE...!

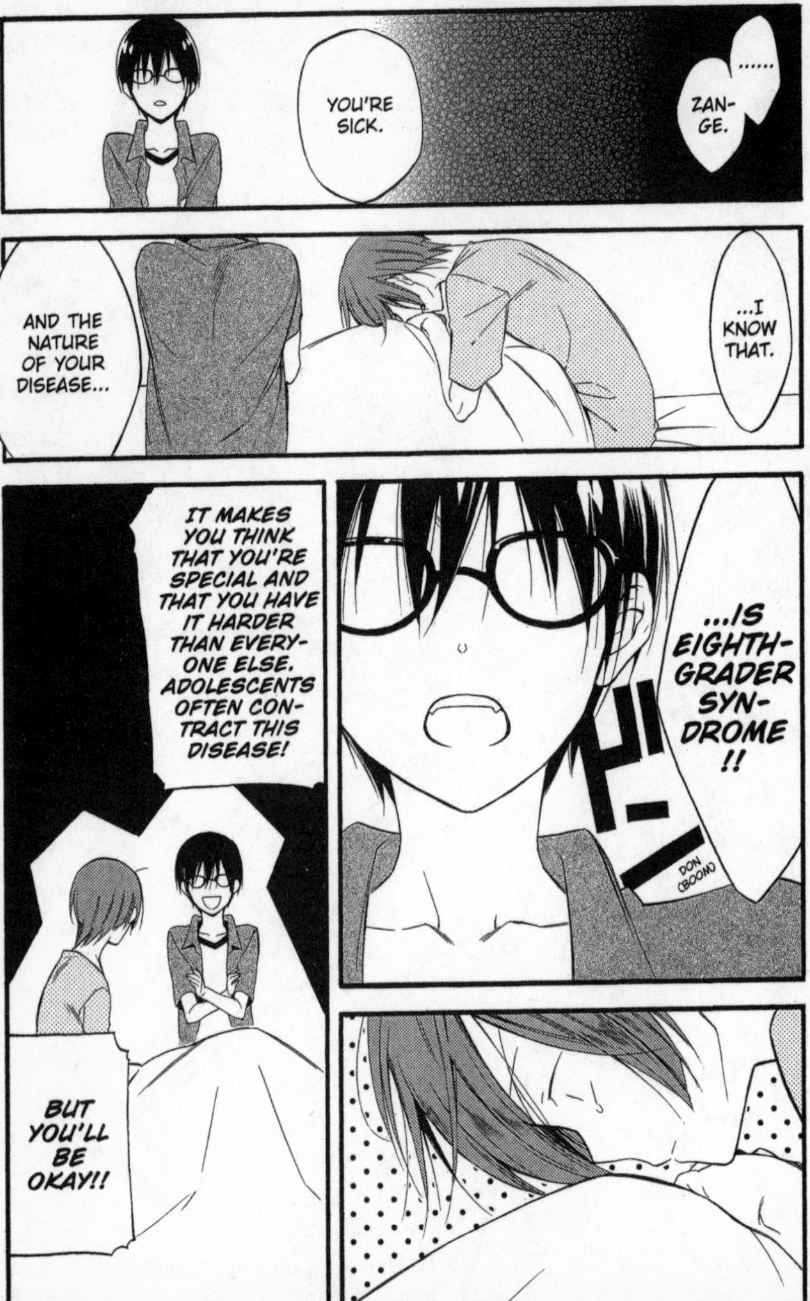
......
ZAN-GE.
YOU'RE SICK.
...I KNOW THAT.
AND THE NATURE OF YOUR DISEASE...
...IS EIGHTH-GRADER SYNDROME!!
DON (BOOM)
IT MAKES YOU THINK THAT YOU'RE SPECIAL AND THAT YOU HAVE IT HARDER THAN EVERY-ONE ELSE. ADOLESCENTS OFTEN CON-TRACT THIS DISEASE!
BUT YOU'LL BE OKAY!!

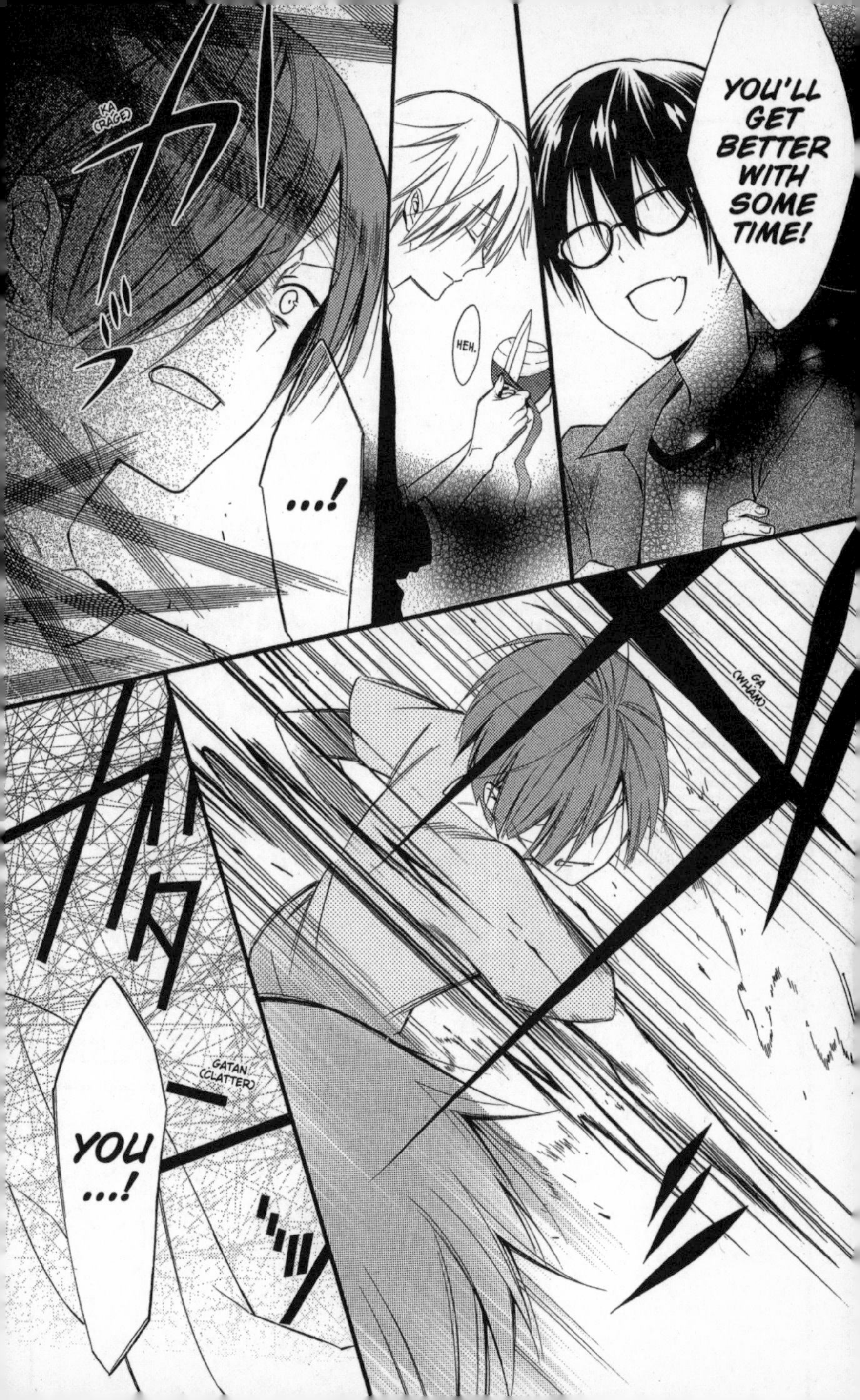
YOU'LL GET BETTER WITH SOME TIME!
HEH.
KA (RAGE)
...!
GA (WHAM)
GATAN (CLATTER)
YOU ...!

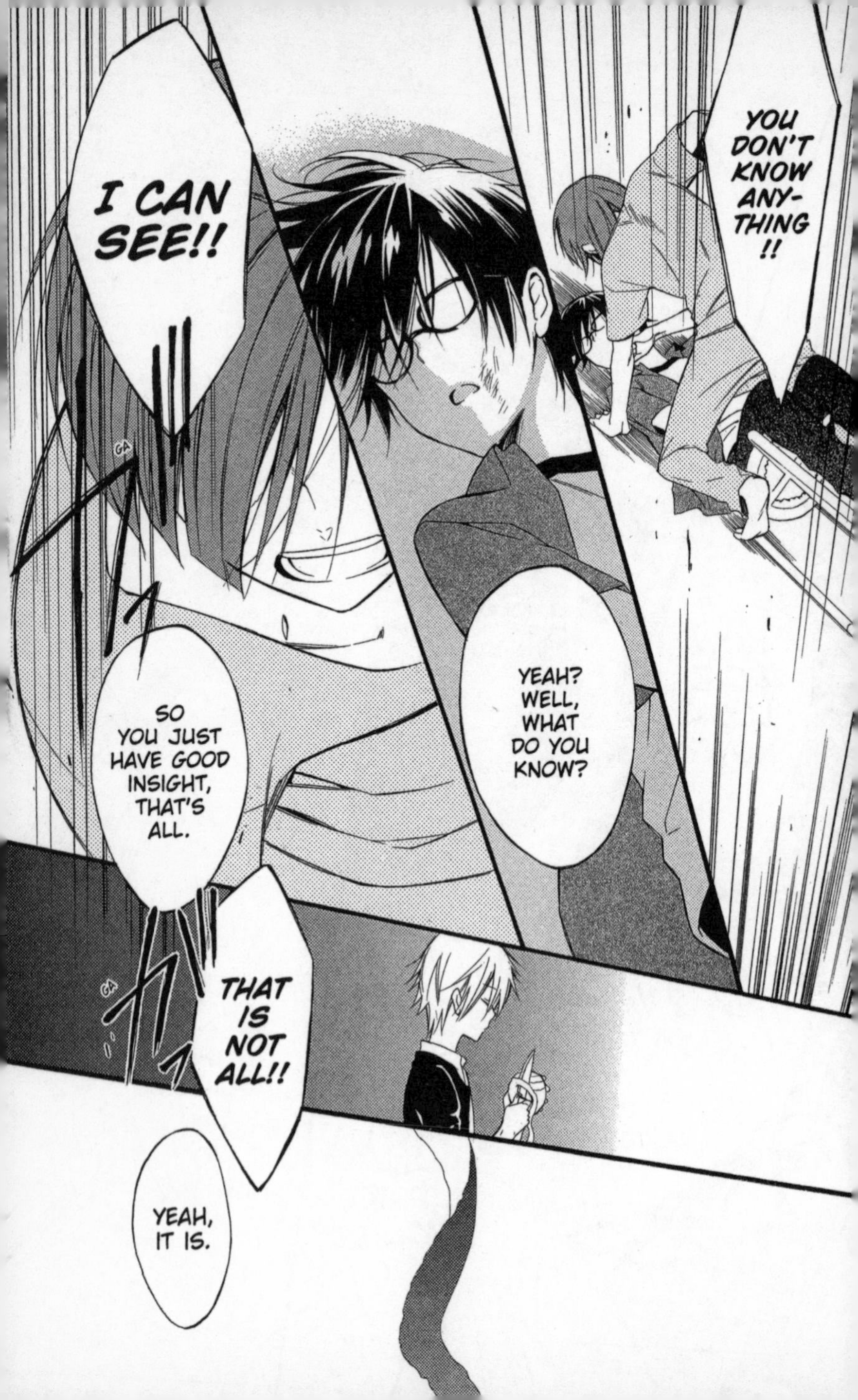
YOU DON'T KNOW ANYTHING!!
YEAH? WELL, WHAT DO YOU KNOW?
I CAN SEE!!
GA
SO YOU JUST HAVE GOOD INSIGHT, THAT'S ALL.
THAT IS NOT ALL!!
GA
YEAH, IT IS.

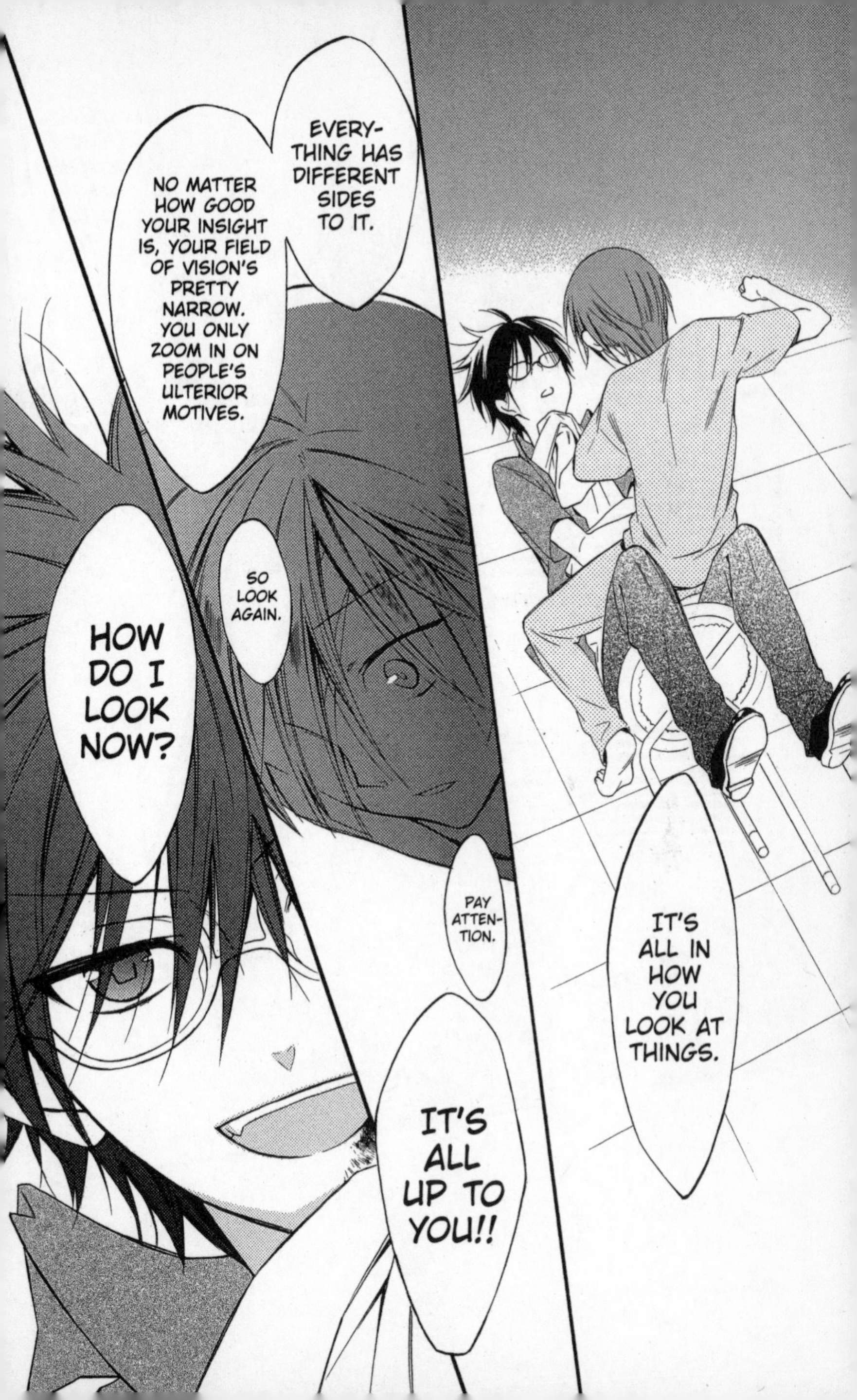
EVERYTHING HAS DIFFERENT SIDES TO IT.
NO MATTER HOW GOOD YOUR INSIGHT IS, YOUR FIELD OF VISION'S PRETTY NARROW. YOU ONLY ZOOM IN ON PEOPLE'S ULTERIOR MOTIVES.
SO LOOK AGAIN.
HOW DO I LOOK NOW?
IT'S ALL IN HOW YOU LOOK AT THINGS.
PAY ATTENTION.
IT'S ALL UP TO YOU!!

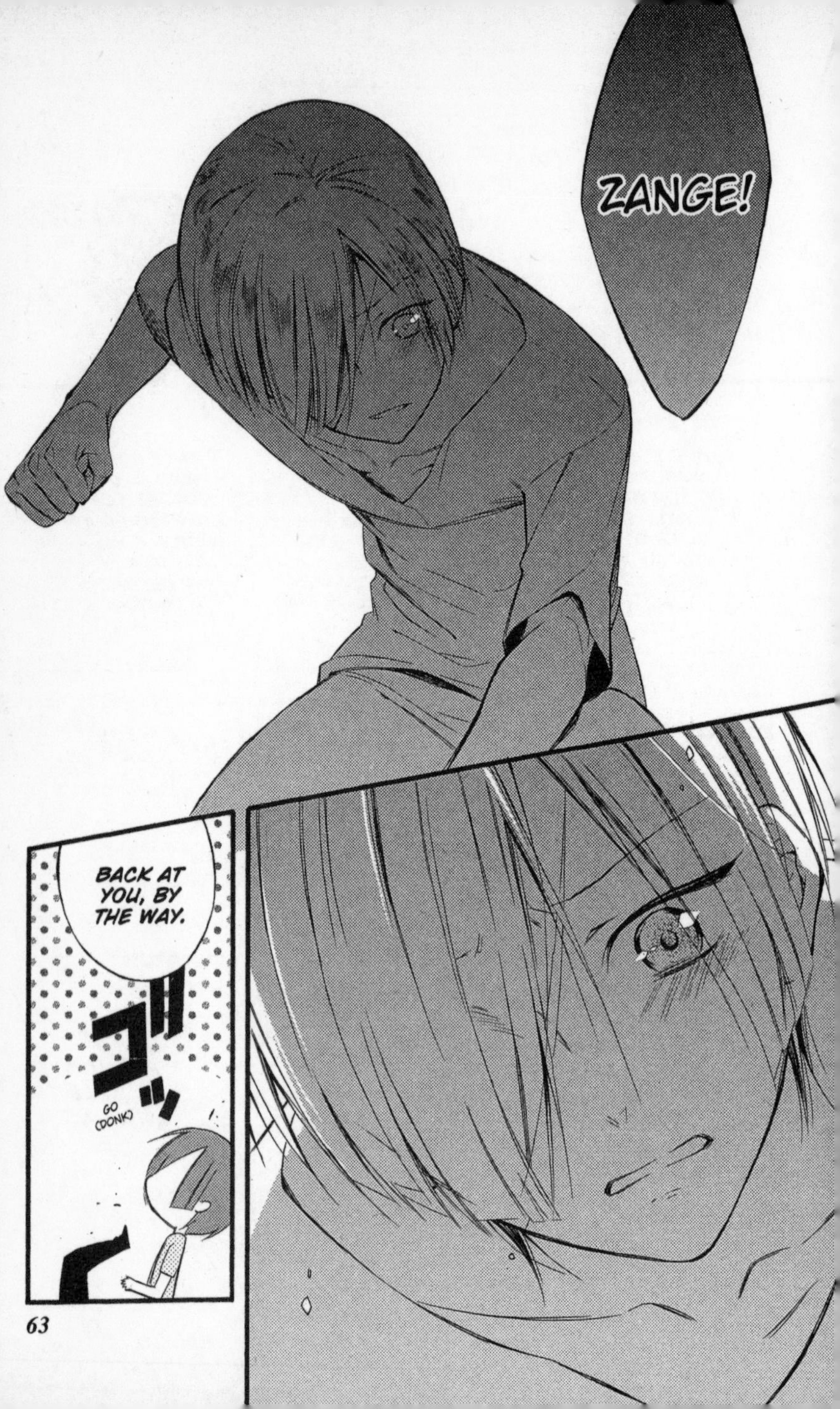
ZANGE!
BACK AT YOU, BY THE WAY.
ゴッ
GO (DONK)

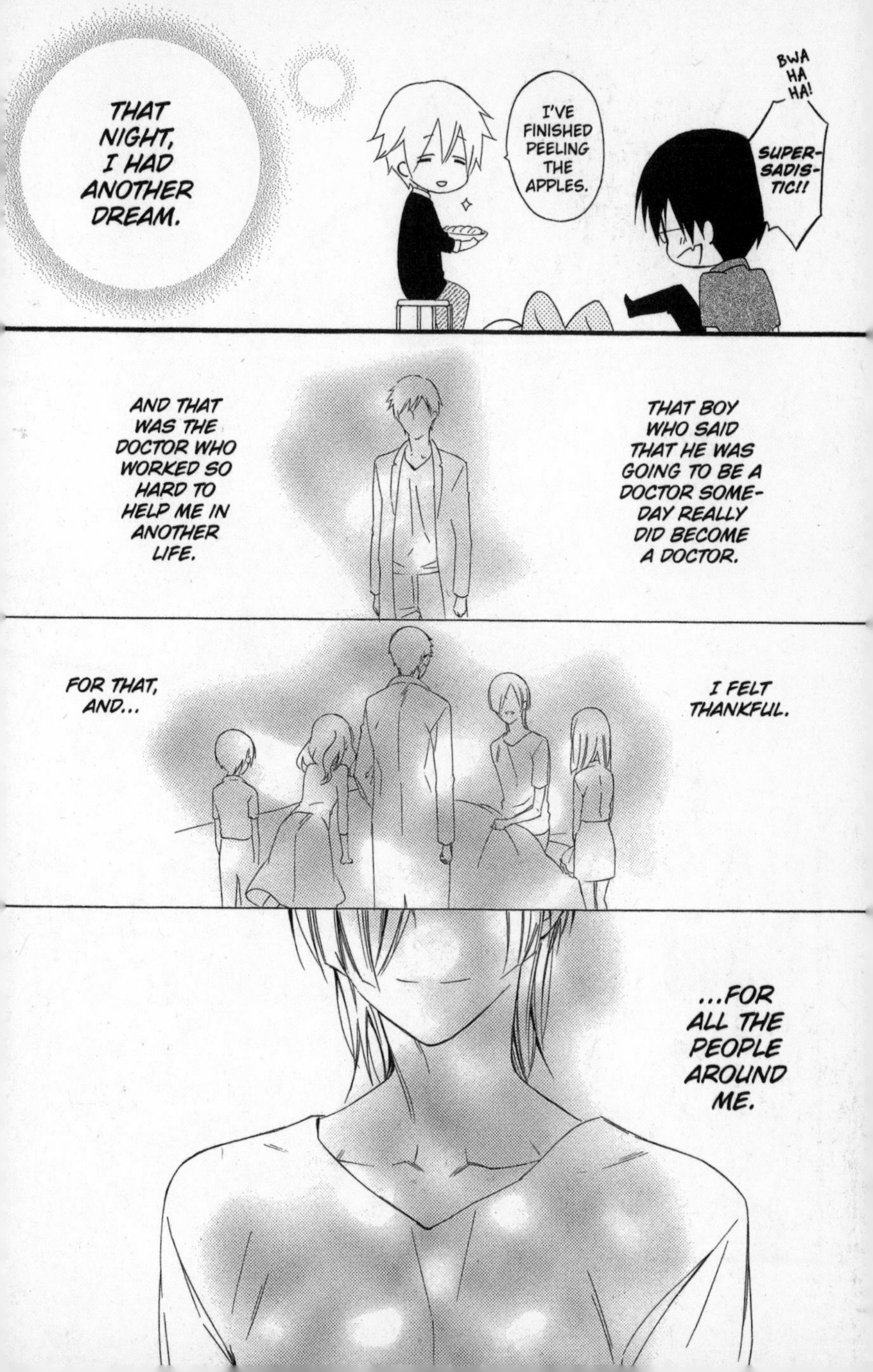
BWA HA HA!
SUPER-SADISTIC!!
I'VE FINISHED PEELING THE APPLES.
THAT NIGHT, I HAD ANOTHER DREAM.
THAT BOY WHO SAID THAT HE WAS GOING TO BE A DOCTOR SOMEDAY REALLY DID BECOME A DOCTOR.
AND THAT WAS THE DOCTOR WHO WORKED SO HARD TO HELP ME IN ANOTHER LIFE.
I FELT THANKFUL.
FOR THAT, AND...
...FOR ALL THE PEOPLE AROUND ME.

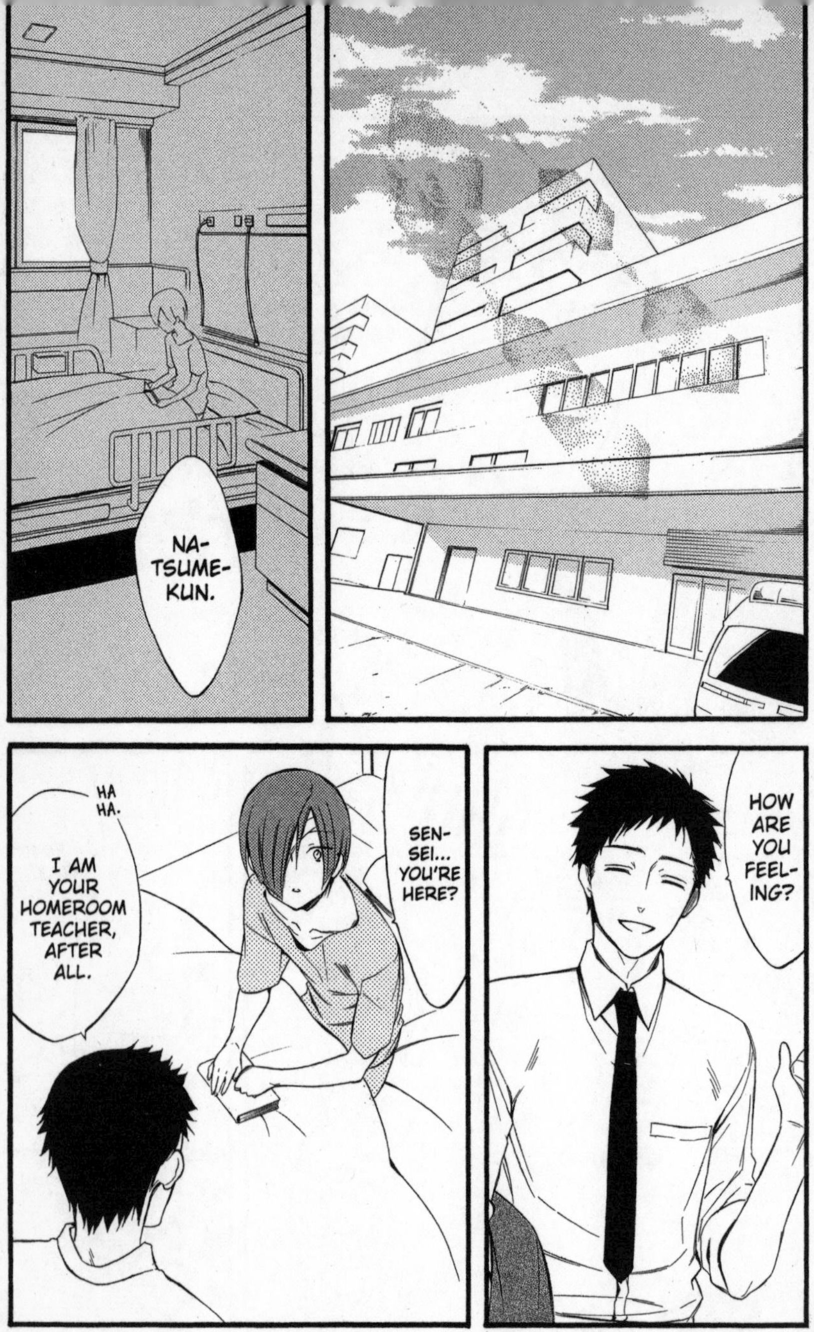
NA-TSUME-KUN.
HOW ARE YOU FEEL-ING?
SEN-SEI... YOU'RE HERE?
HA HA.
I AM YOUR HOMEROOM TEACHER, AFTER ALL.

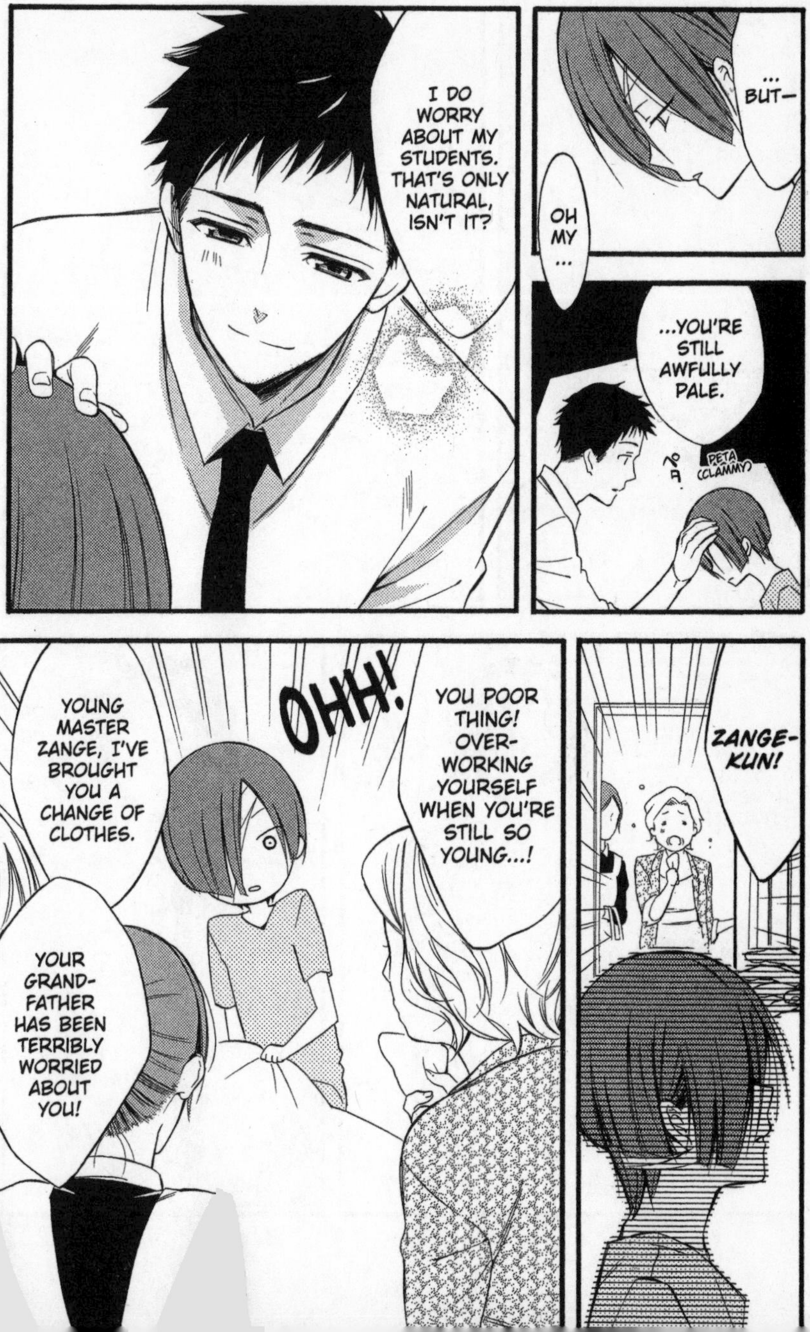
...BUT—
OH MY...
...YOU'RE STILL AWFULLY PALE.
PETA (CLAMMY)
I DO WORRY ABOUT MY STUDENTS. THAT'S ONLY NATURAL, ISN'T IT?
ZANGE-KUN!
OHH!
YOU POOR THING! OVER-WORKING YOURSELF WHEN YOU'RE STILL SO YOUNG...!
YOUNG MASTER ZANGE, I'VE BROUGHT YOU A CHANGE OF CLOTHES.
YOUR GRAND-FATHER HAS BEEN TERRIBLY WORRIED ABOUT YOU!

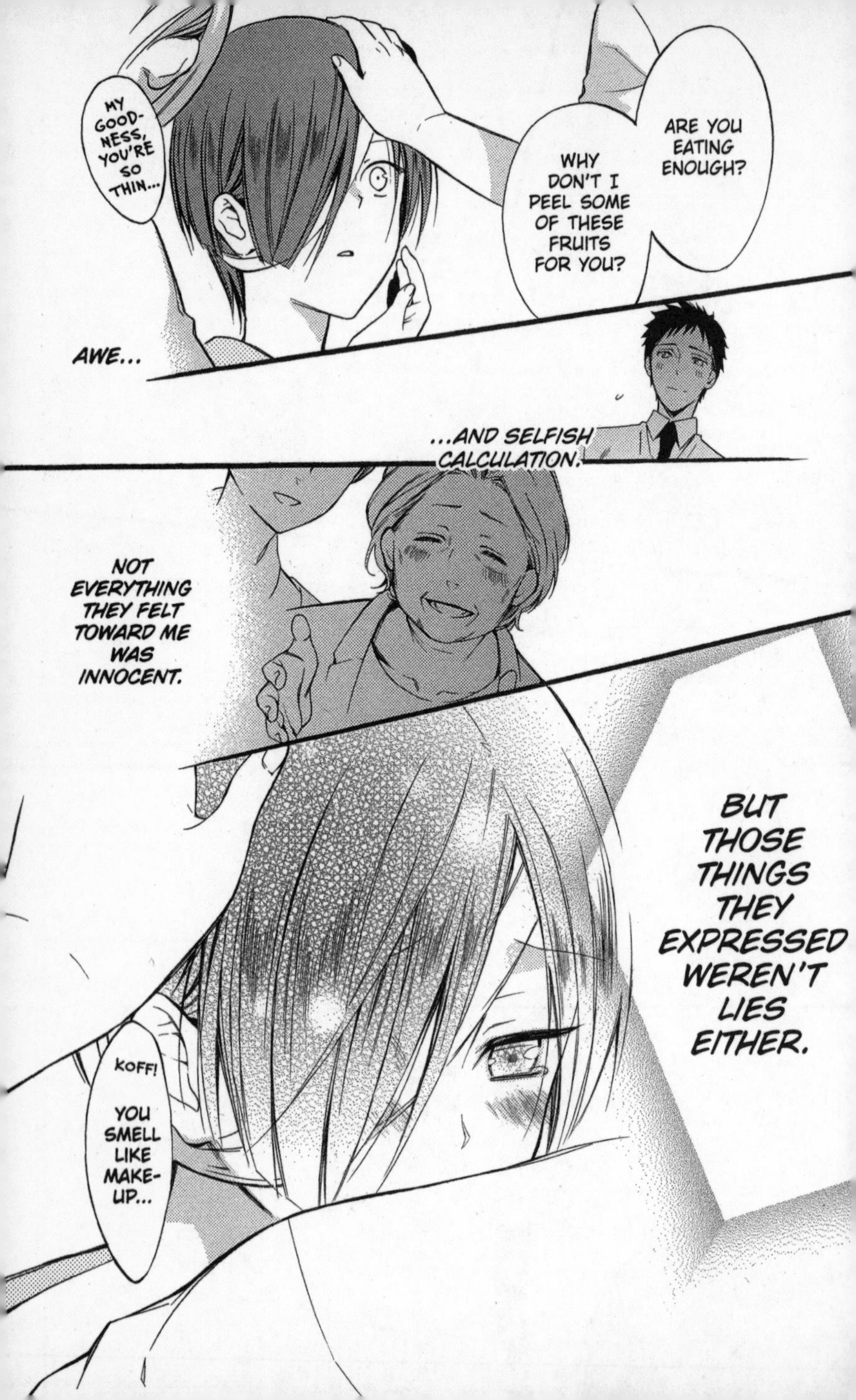
ARE YOU EATING ENOUGH?
WHY DON'T I PEEL SOME OF THESE FRUITS FOR YOU?
MY GOODNESS, YOU'RE SO THIN...
AWE...
...AND SELFISH CALCULATION.
NOT EVERYTHING THEY FELT TOWARD ME WAS INNOCENT.
BUT THOSE THINGS THEY EXPRESSED WEREN'T LIES EITHER.
KOFF!
YOU SMELL LIKE MAKE-UP...

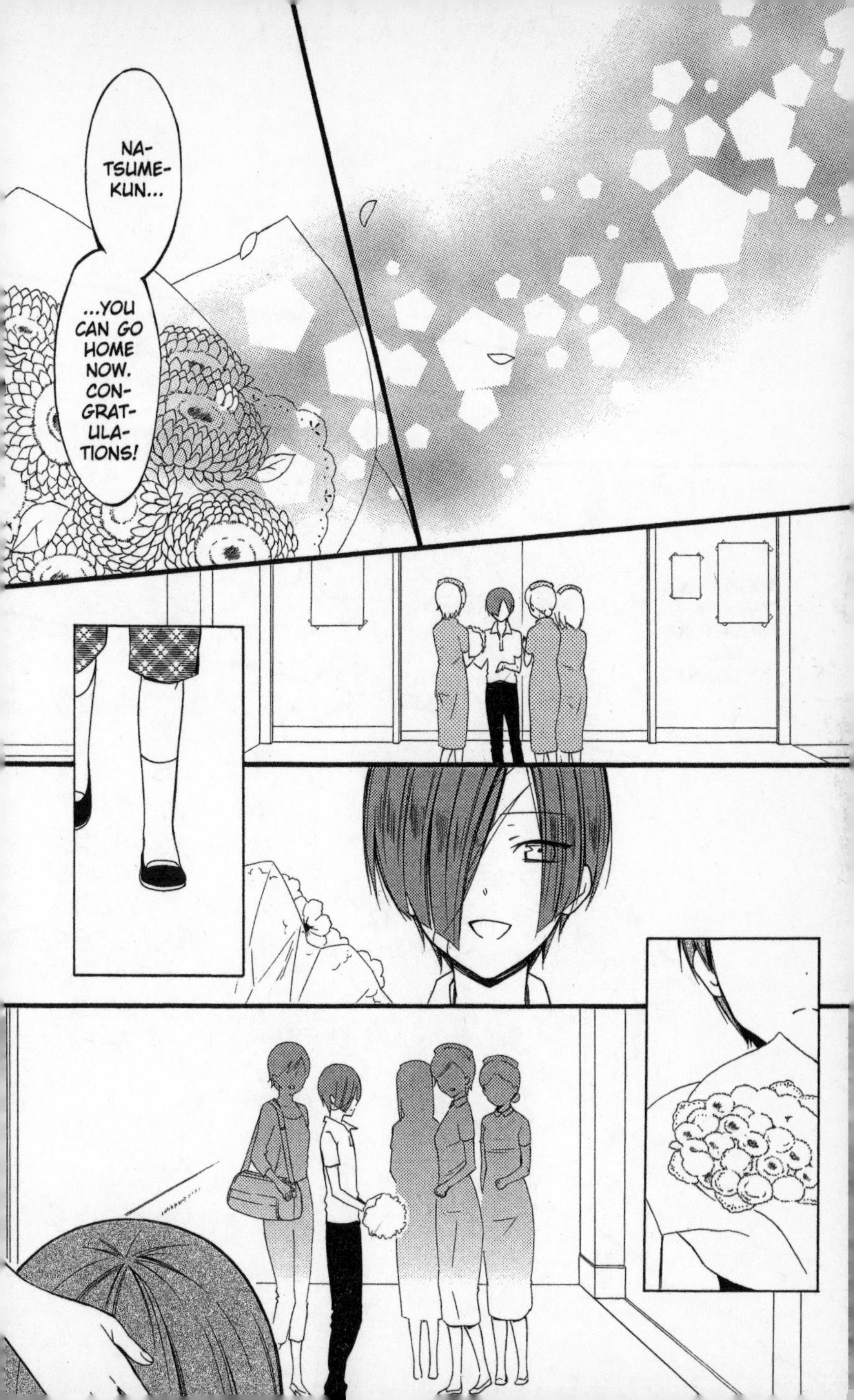
NA-TSUME-KUN...
...YOU CAN GO HOME NOW. CON-GRAT-ULA-TIONS!

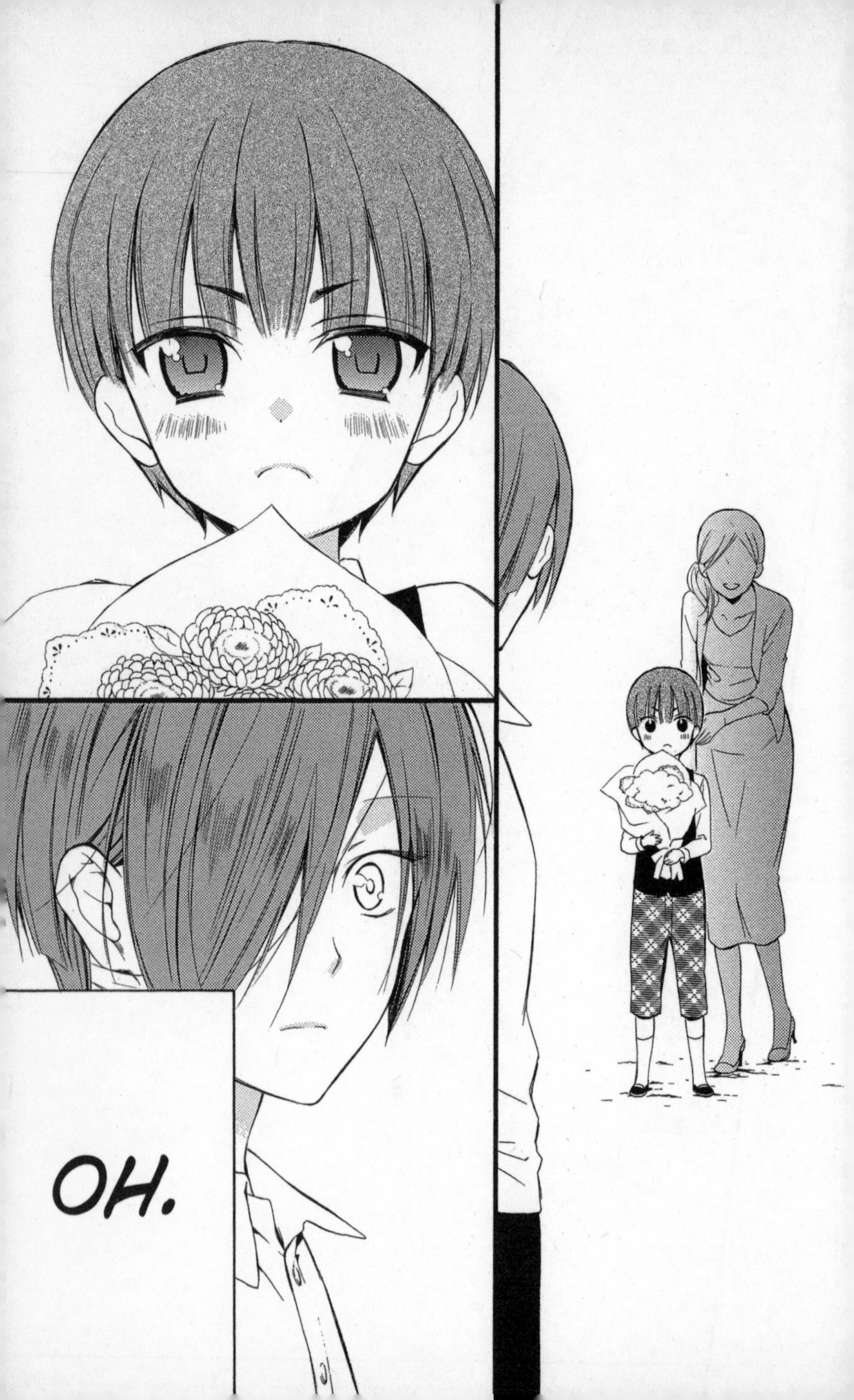
OH.

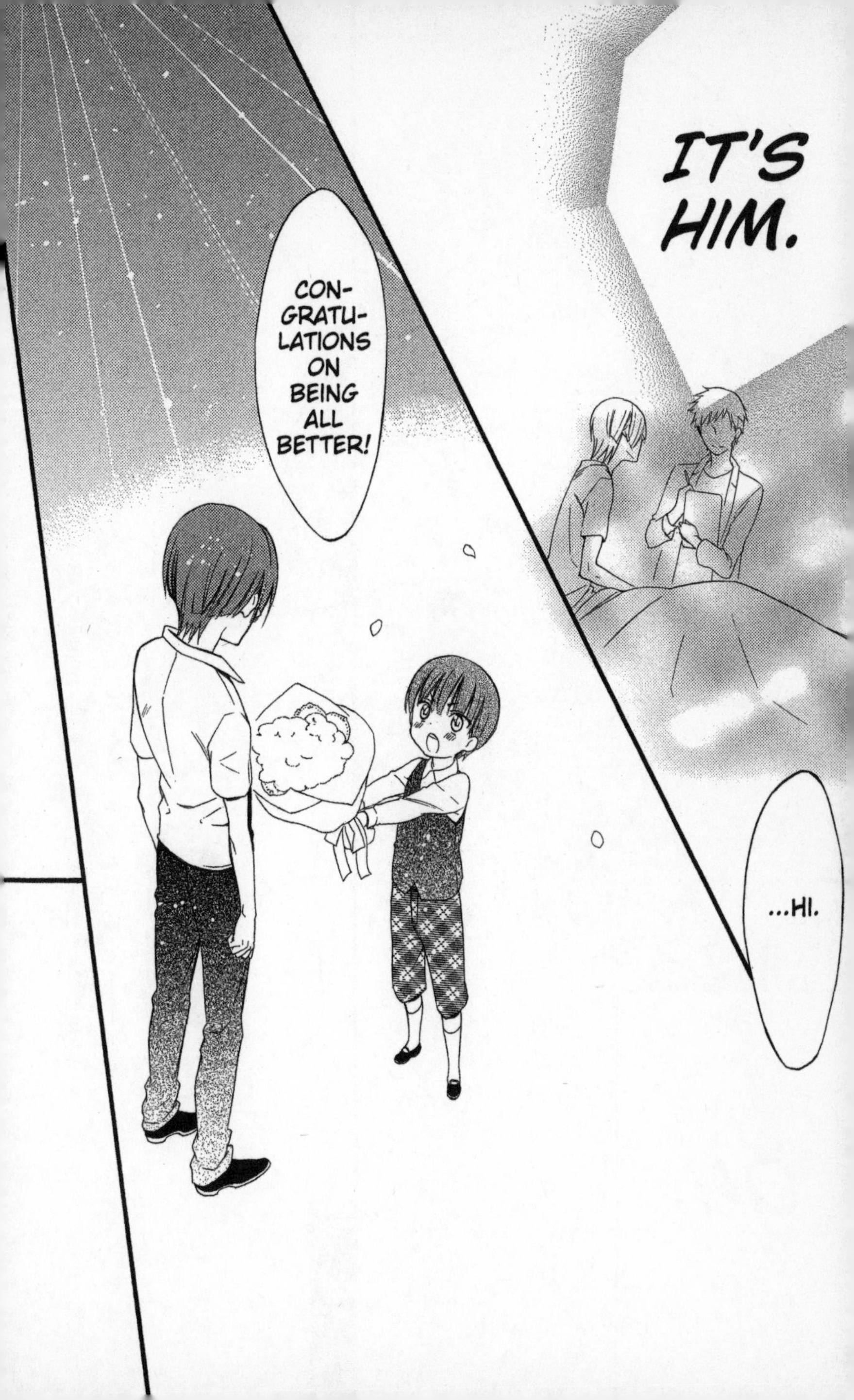
IT'S HIM.
...HI.
CON-GRATULATIONS ON BEING ALL BETTER!

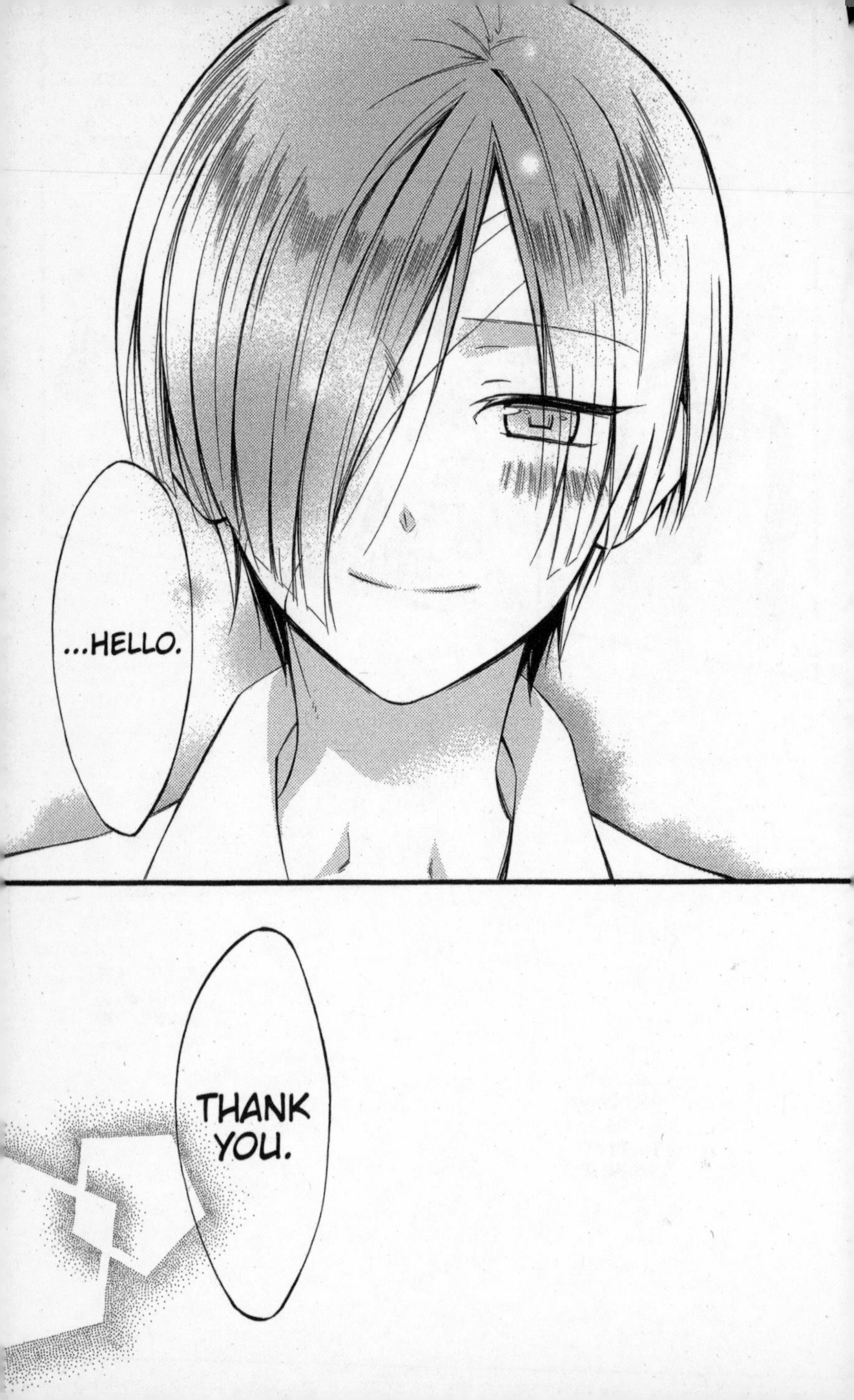
...HELLO.
THANK YOU.

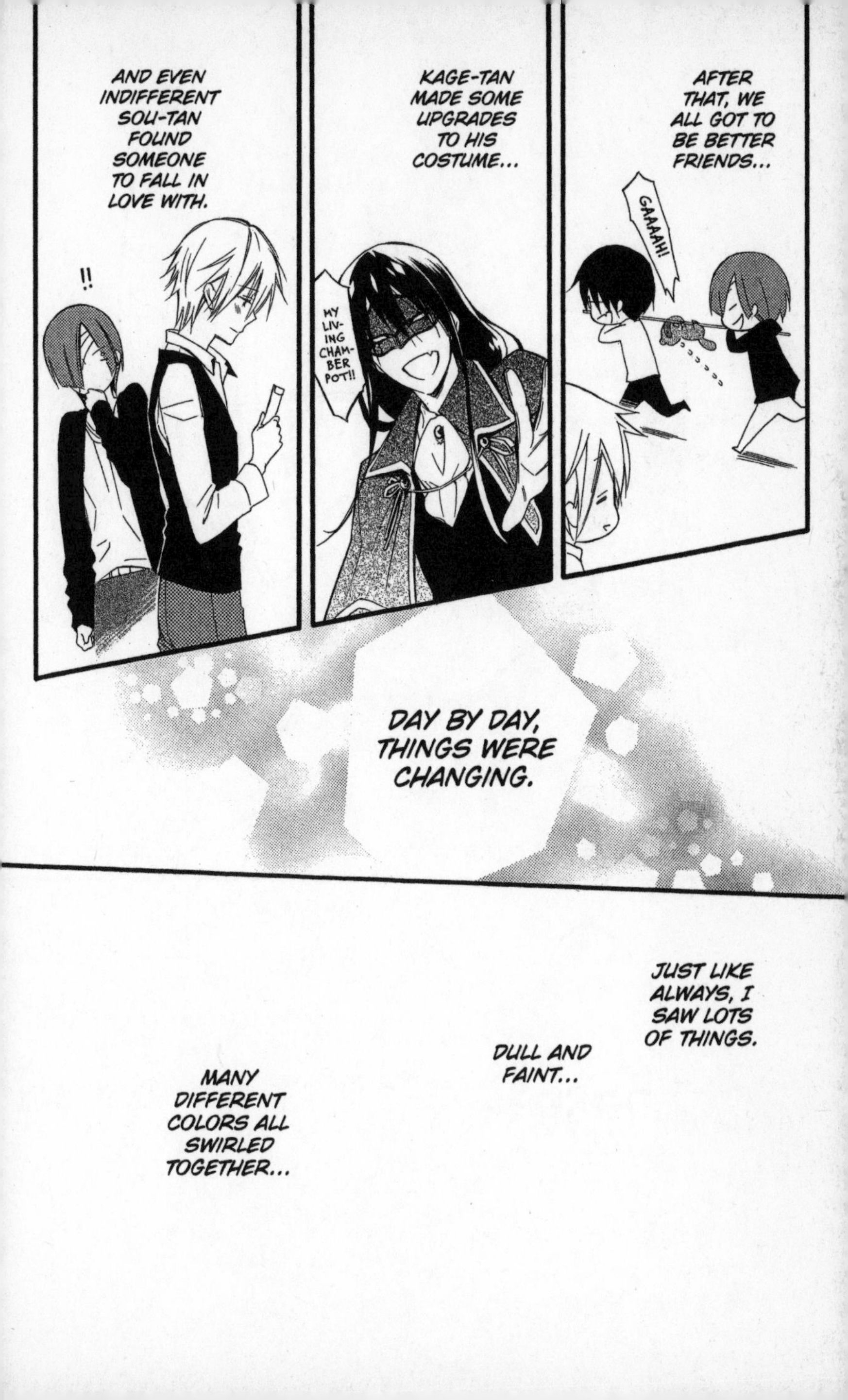
AFTER THAT, WE ALL GOT TO BE BETTER FRIENDS...
GAAAAH!
KAGE-TAN MADE SOME UPGRADES TO HIS COSTUME...
MY LIVING CHAMBER POT!!
AND EVEN INDIFFERENT SOU-TAN FOUND SOMEONE TO FALL IN LOVE WITH.
!!
DAY BY DAY, THINGS WERE CHANGING.
JUST LIKE ALWAYS, I SAW LOTS OF THINGS.
DULL AND FAINT...
MANY DIFFERENT COLORS ALL SWIRLED TOGETHER...

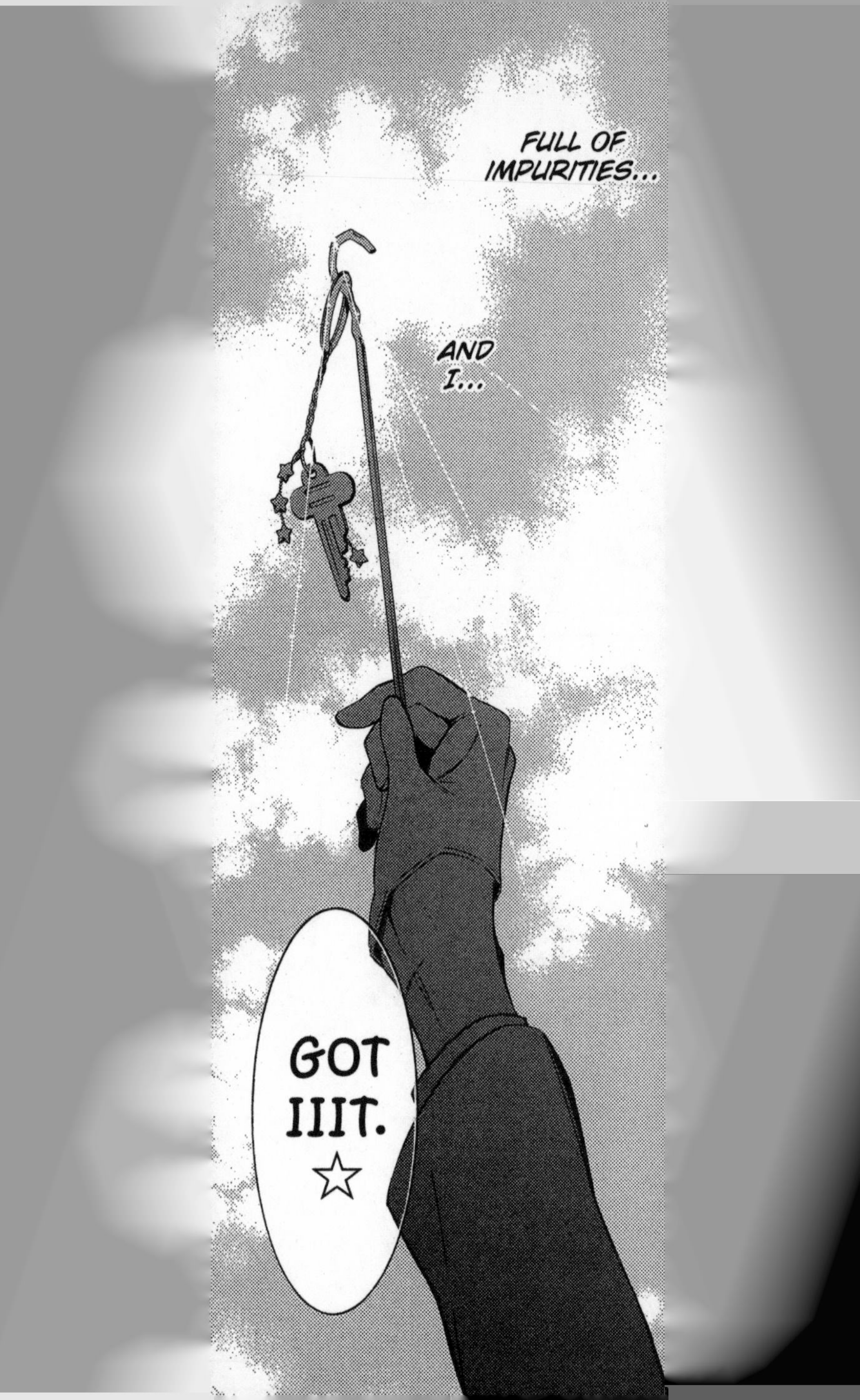
FULL OF IMPURITIES...
AND I...
GOT IIIT. ☆

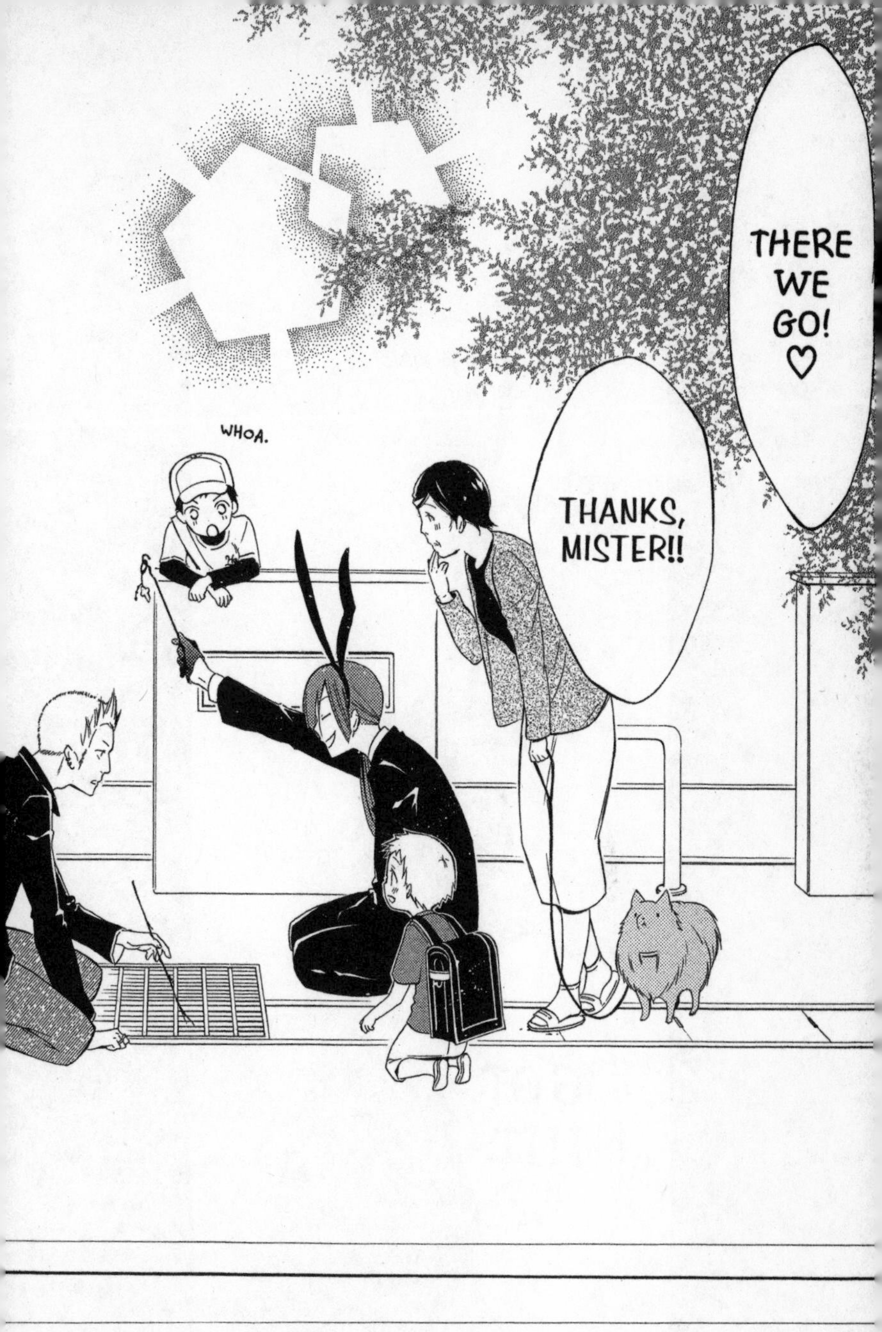
THERE WE GO! ♡
THANKS, MISTER!!
WHOA.

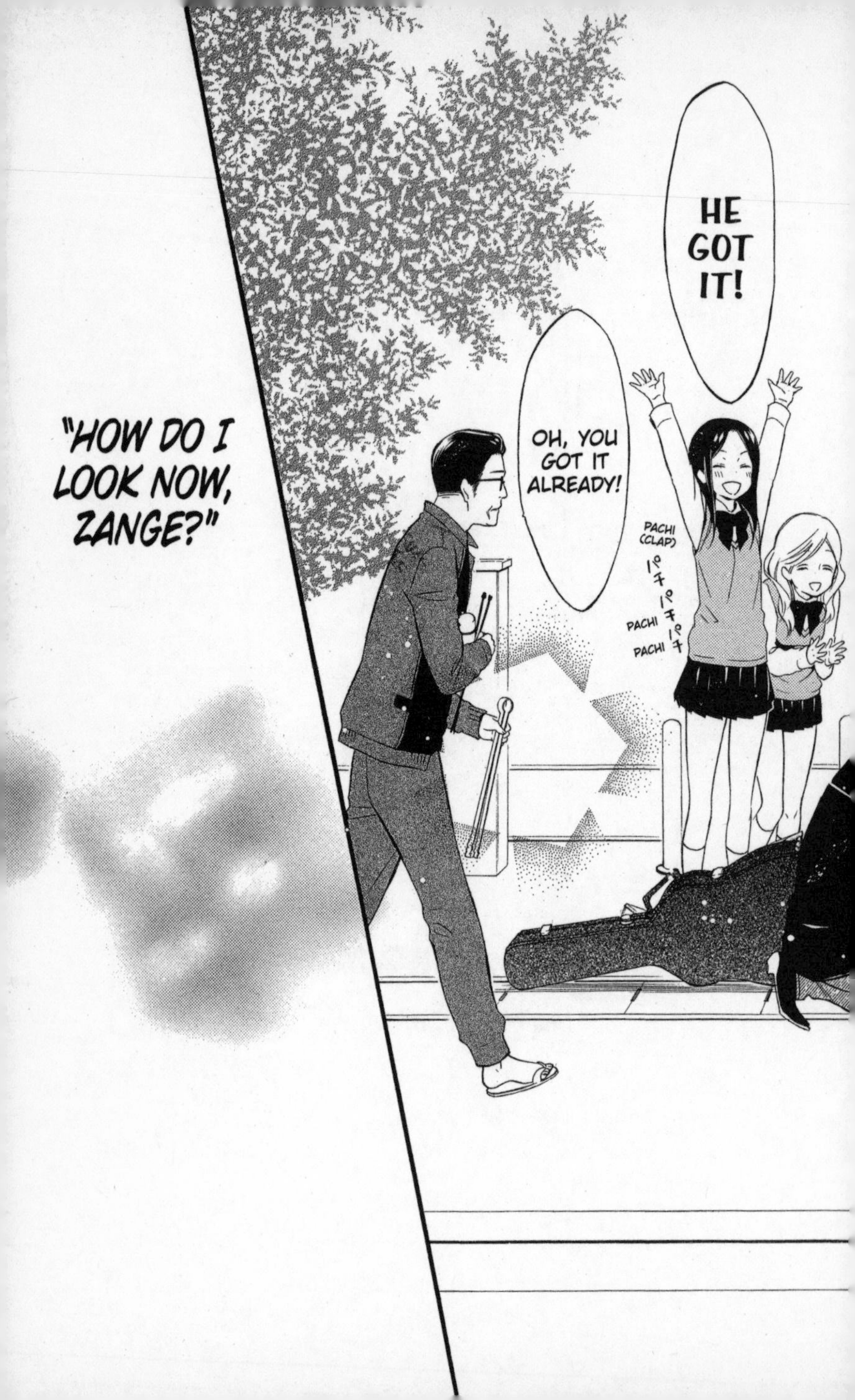
HE GOT IT!
OH, YOU GOT IT ALREADY!
PACHI (CLAP)
パチパチパチ
PACHI
PACHI
"HOW DO I LOOK NOW, ZANGE?"

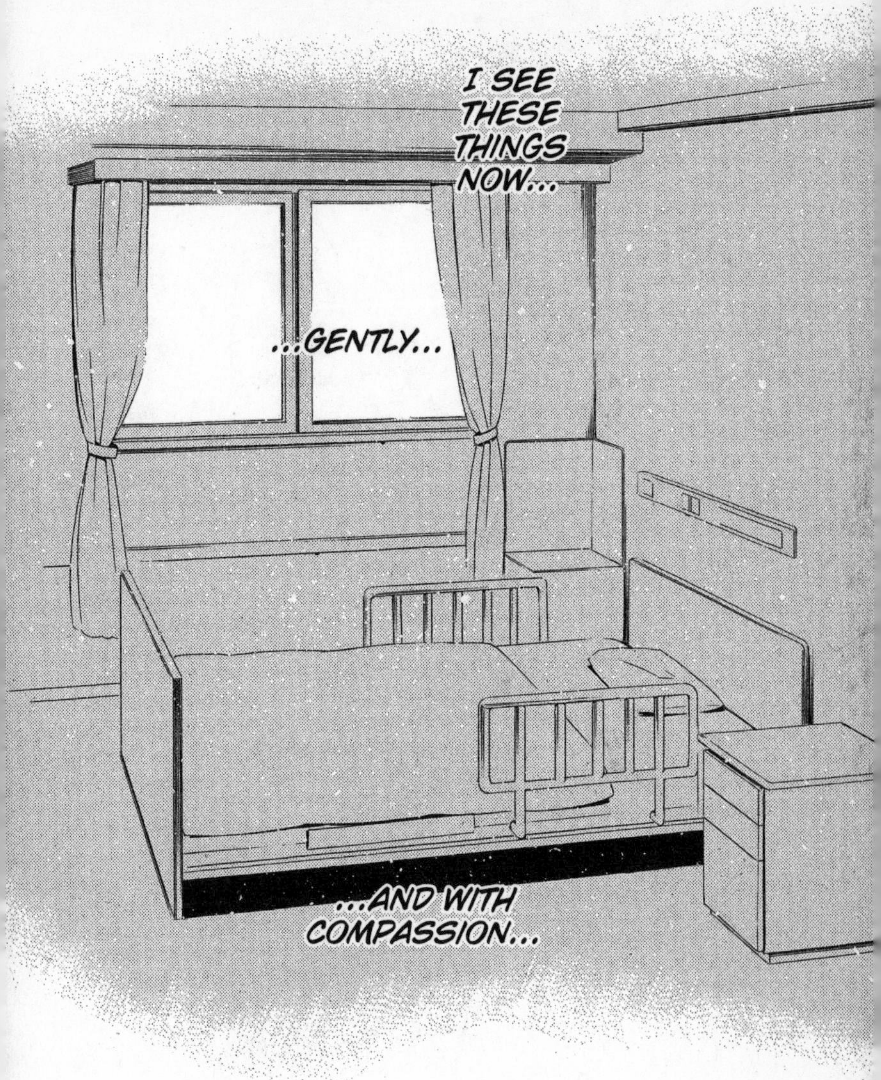
I SEE THESE THINGS NOW...
...GENTLY...
...AND WITH COMPASSION...

INU×BOKU SS

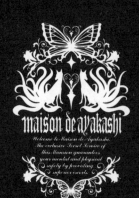

maison de ayakashi

Welcome to Maison de Ayakashi.
The exclusive Secret Service of
this Mansion guarantees
your mental and physical
safety by providing
superior escorts.

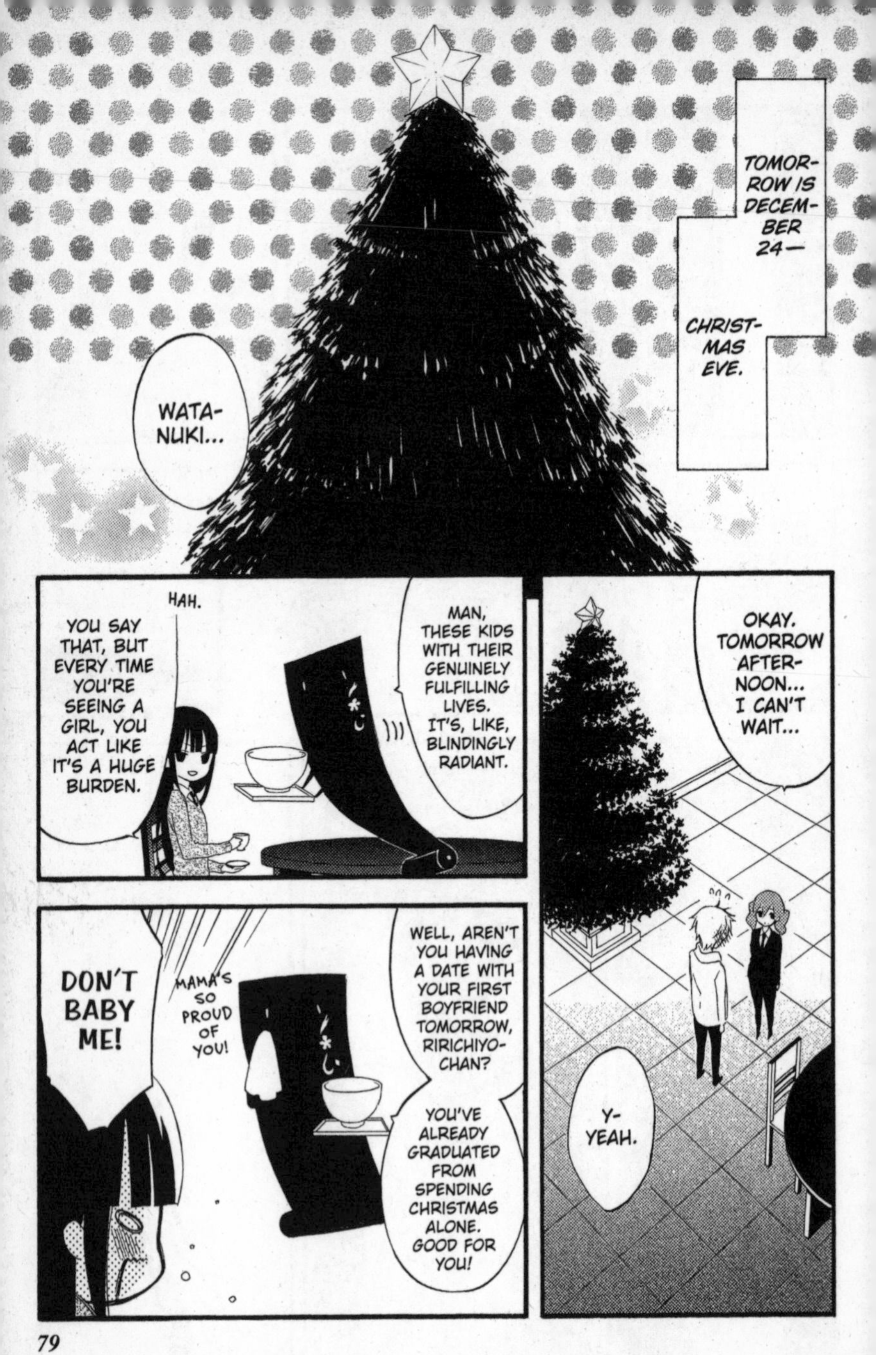
TOMORROW IS DECEMBER 24— CHRISTMAS EVE.
WATANUKI...
OKAY. TOMORROW AFTERNOON... I CAN'T WAIT...
Y-YEAH.
MAN, THESE KIDS WITH THEIR GENUINELY FULFILLING LIVES. IT'S, LIKE, BLINDINGLY RADIANT.
HAH.
YOU SAY THAT, BUT EVERY TIME YOU'RE SEEING A GIRL, YOU ACT LIKE IT'S A HUGE BURDEN.
WELL, AREN'T YOU HAVING A DATE WITH YOUR FIRST BOYFRIEND TOMORROW, RIRICHIYO-CHAN?
YOU'VE ALREADY GRADUATED FROM SPENDING CHRISTMAS ALONE. GOOD FOR YOU!
MAMA'S SO PROUD OF YOU!
DON'T BABY ME!

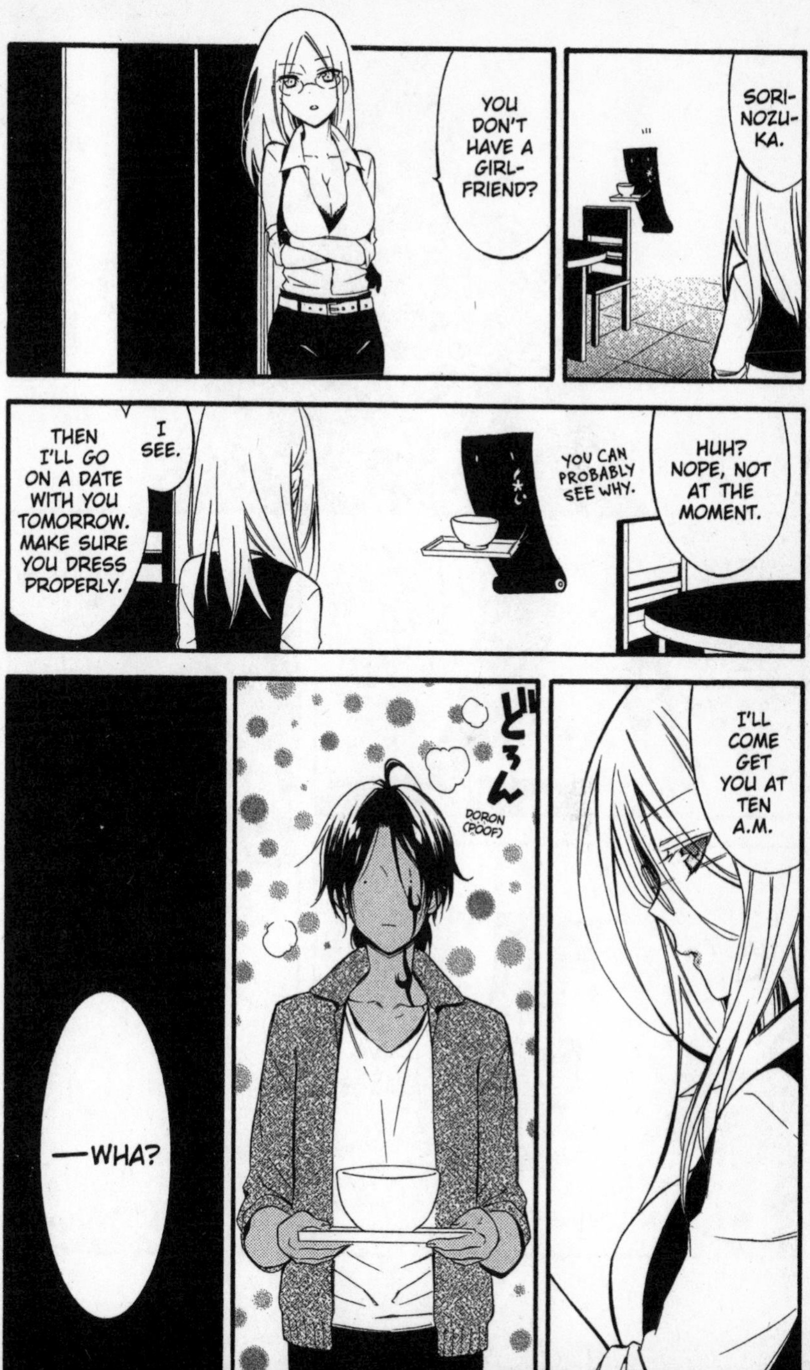
SORI-NOZU-KA.
YOU DON'T HAVE A GIRL-FRIEND?
HUH? NOPE, NOT AT THE MOMENT.
YOU CAN PROBABLY SEE WHY.
I SEE.
THEN I'LL GO ON A DATE WITH YOU TOMORROW. MAKE SURE YOU DRESS PROPERLY.
I'LL COME GET YOU AT TEN A.M.
どろん
DORON (POOF)
—WHA?

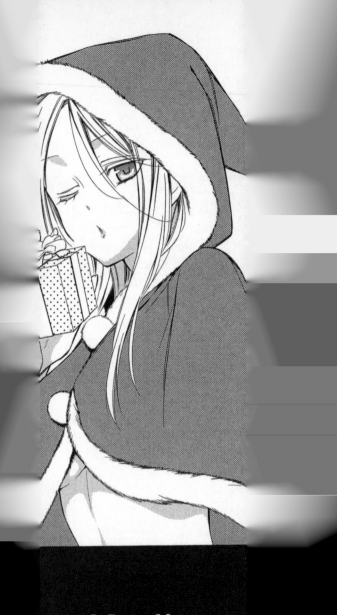

INTERLUDE **5**: SMEXY MOONLIGHTIN

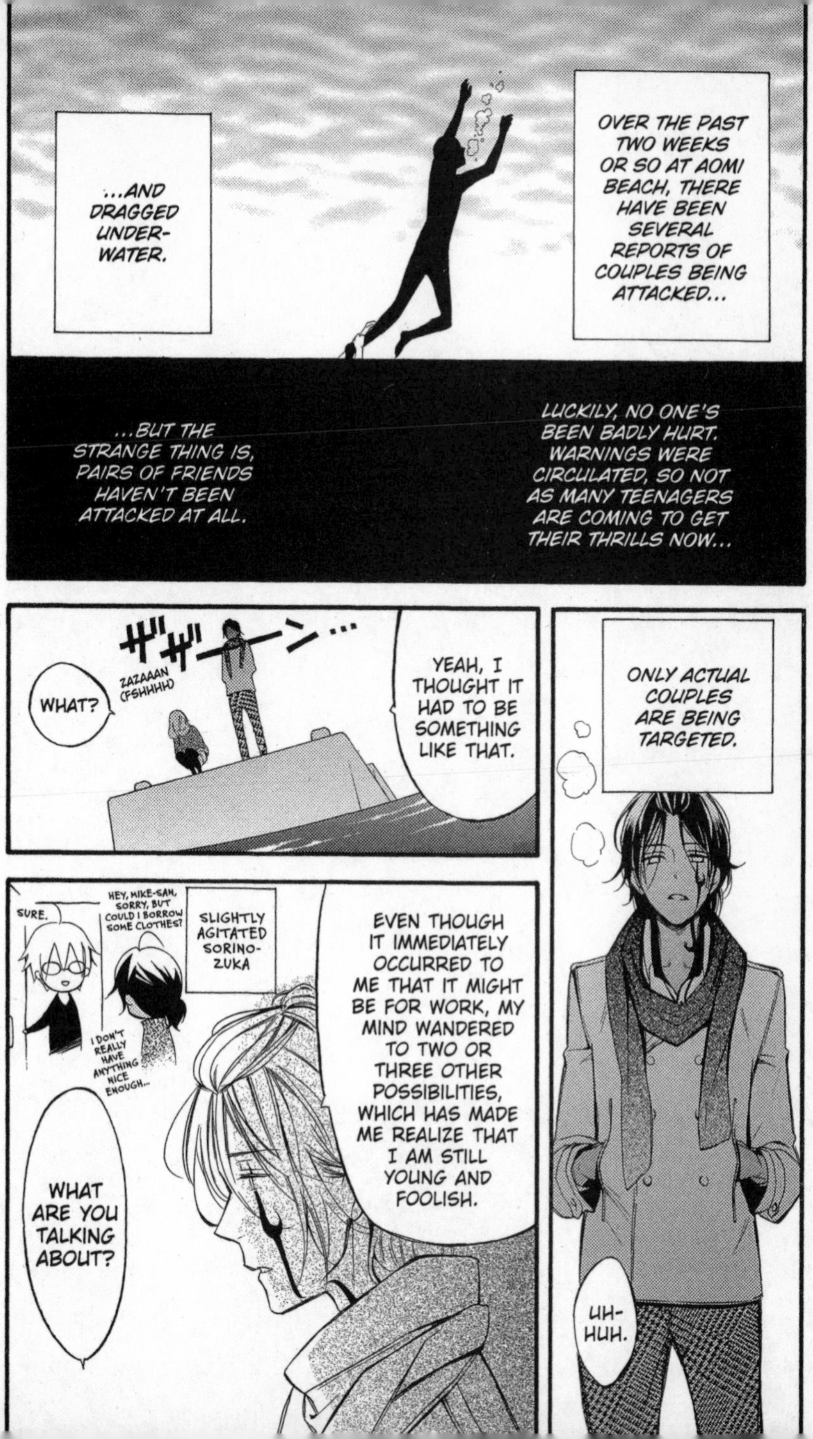

OVER THE PAST TWO WEEKS OR SO AT AOMI BEACH, THERE HAVE BEEN SEVERAL REPORTS OF COUPLES BEING ATTACKED...
...AND DRAGGED UNDER-WATER.
LUCKILY, NO ONE'S BEEN BADLY HURT. WARNINGS WERE CIRCULATED, SO NOT AS MANY TEENAGERS ARE COMING TO GET THEIR THRILLS NOW...
...BUT THE STRANGE THING IS, PAIRS OF FRIENDS HAVEN'T BEEN ATTACKED AT ALL.
ONLY ACTUAL COUPLES ARE BEING TARGETED.
UH-HUH.
YEAH, I THOUGHT IT HAD TO BE SOMETHING LIKE THAT.
ザザーン…
ZAZAAAN (FSHHHH)
WHAT?
EVEN THOUGH IT IMMEDIATELY OCCURRED TO ME THAT IT MIGHT BE FOR WORK, MY MIND WANDERED TO TWO OR THREE OTHER POSSIBILITIES, WHICH HAS MADE ME REALIZE THAT I AM STILL YOUNG AND FOOLISH.
SLIGHTLY AGITATED SORINO-ZUKA
HEY, MIKE-SAN, SORRY, BUT COULD I BORROW SOME CLOTHES?
SURE.
I DON'T REALLY HAVE ANYTHING NICE ENOUGH...
WHAT ARE YOU TALKING ABOUT?

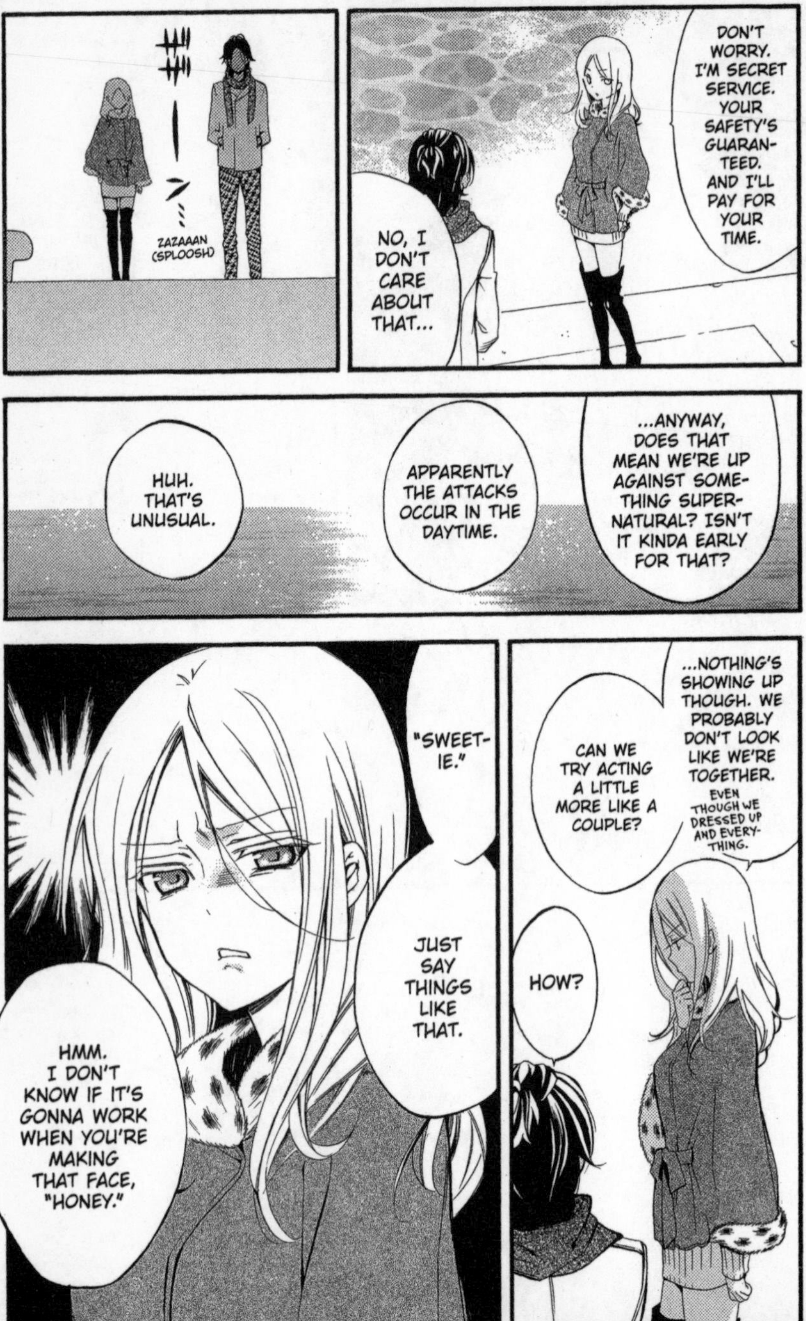
DON'T WORRY. I'M SECRET SERVICE. YOUR SAFETY'S GUARAN-TEED. AND I'LL PAY FOR YOUR TIME.
NO, I DON'T CARE ABOUT THAT...
ZAZAAAN (SPLOOSH)
...ANYWAY, DOES THAT MEAN WE'RE UP AGAINST SOME-THING SUPER-NATURAL? ISN'T IT KINDA EARLY FOR THAT?
APPARENTLY THE ATTACKS OCCUR IN THE DAYTIME.
HUH. THAT'S UNUSUAL.
...NOTHING'S SHOWING UP THOUGH. WE PROBABLY DON'T LOOK LIKE WE'RE TOGETHER.
EVEN THOUGH WE DRESSED UP AND EVERY-THING.
CAN WE TRY ACTING A LITTLE MORE LIKE A COUPLE?
HOW?
"SWEET-IE."
JUST SAY THINGS LIKE THAT.
HMM. I DON'T KNOW IF IT'S GONNA WORK WHEN YOU'RE MAKING THAT FACE, "HONEY."

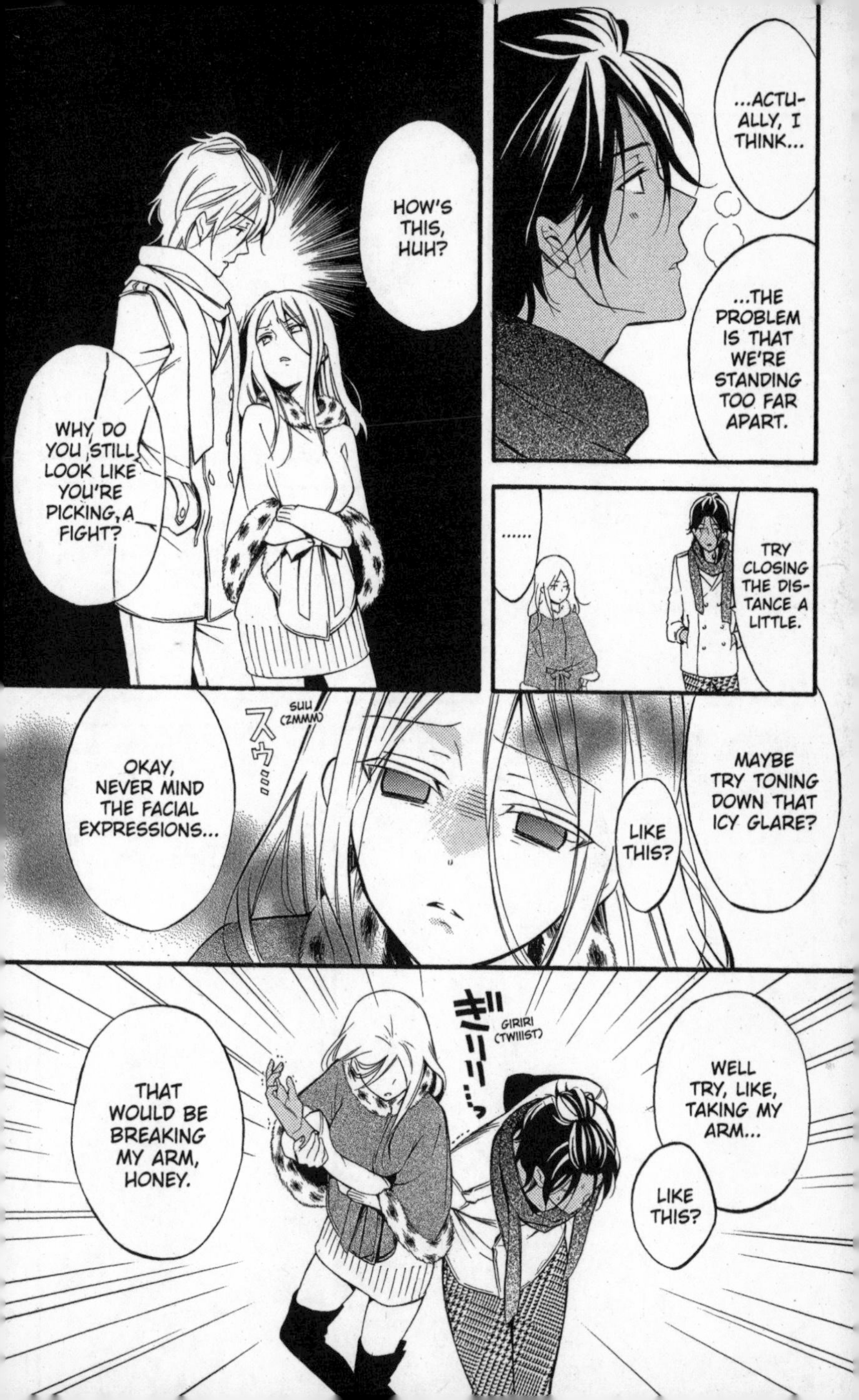
...ACTU-ALLY, I THINK...
...THE PROBLEM IS THAT WE'RE STANDING TOO FAR APART.
TRY CLOSING THE DIS-TANCE A LITTLE.
......
HOW'S THIS, HUH?
WHY DO YOU STILL LOOK LIKE YOU'RE PICKING A FIGHT?
MAYBE TRY TONING DOWN THAT ICY GLARE?
LIKE THIS?
スゥ…
SUU (ZMMMM)
OKAY, NEVER MIND THE FACIAL EXPRESSIONS...
WELL TRY, LIKE, TAKING MY ARM...
LIKE THIS?
ギリリ…
GIRIRI (TWIIIST)
THAT WOULD BE BREAKING MY ARM, HONEY.

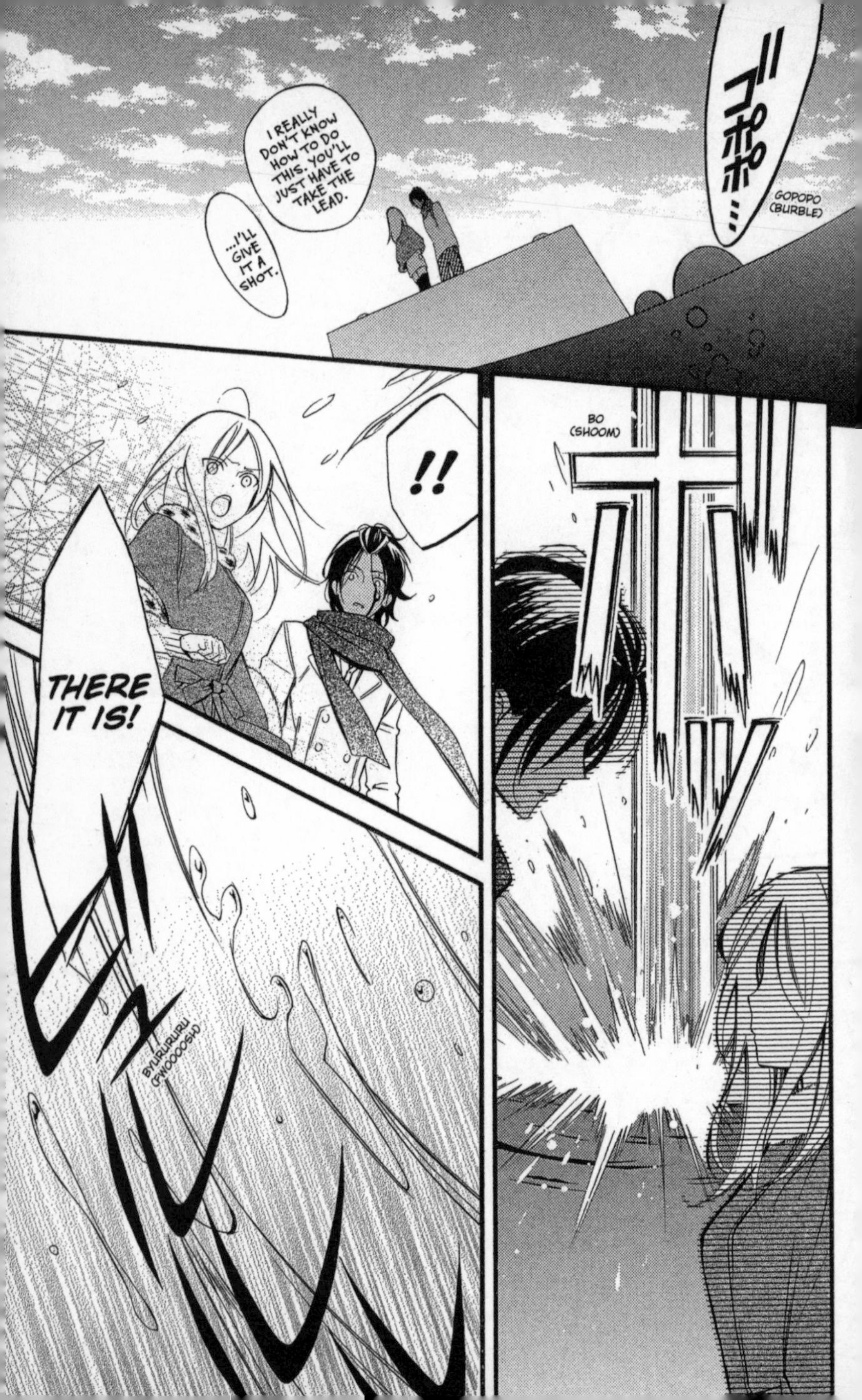
ゴポポ
GOPOPO (BURBLE)
I REALLY DON'T KNOW HOW TO DO THIS. YOU'LL JUST HAVE TO TAKE THE LEAD.
...I'LL GIVE IT A SHOT.
BO (SHOOM)
!!
THERE IT IS!
BYURURURU (FWOOOOSH)

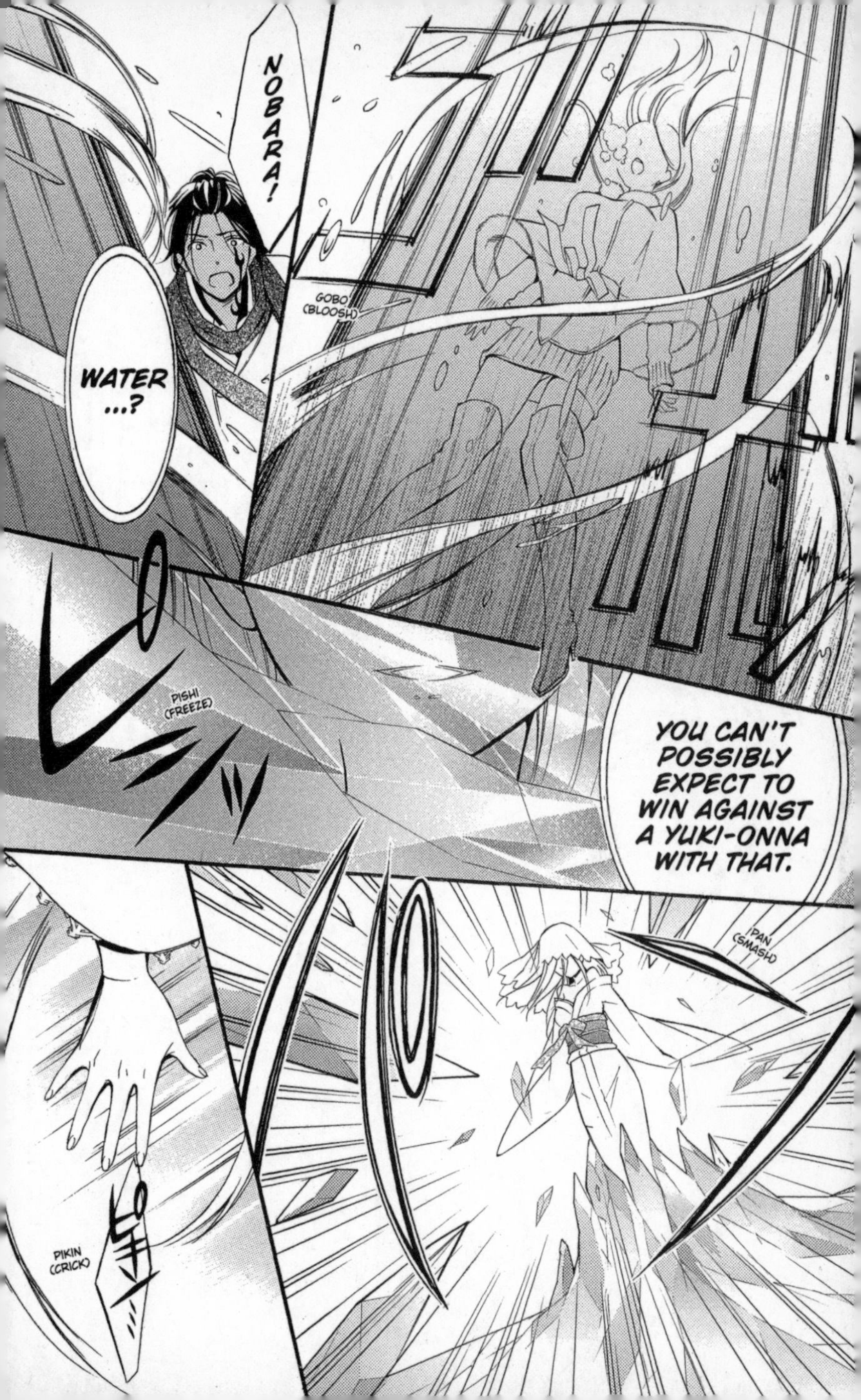
GOBO (BLOOSH)
NOBARA!
WATER ...?
YOU CAN'T POSSIBLY EXPECT TO WIN AGAINST A YUKI-ONNA WITH THAT.
PISHI (FREEZE)
PAN (SMASH)
PIKIN (CRICK)

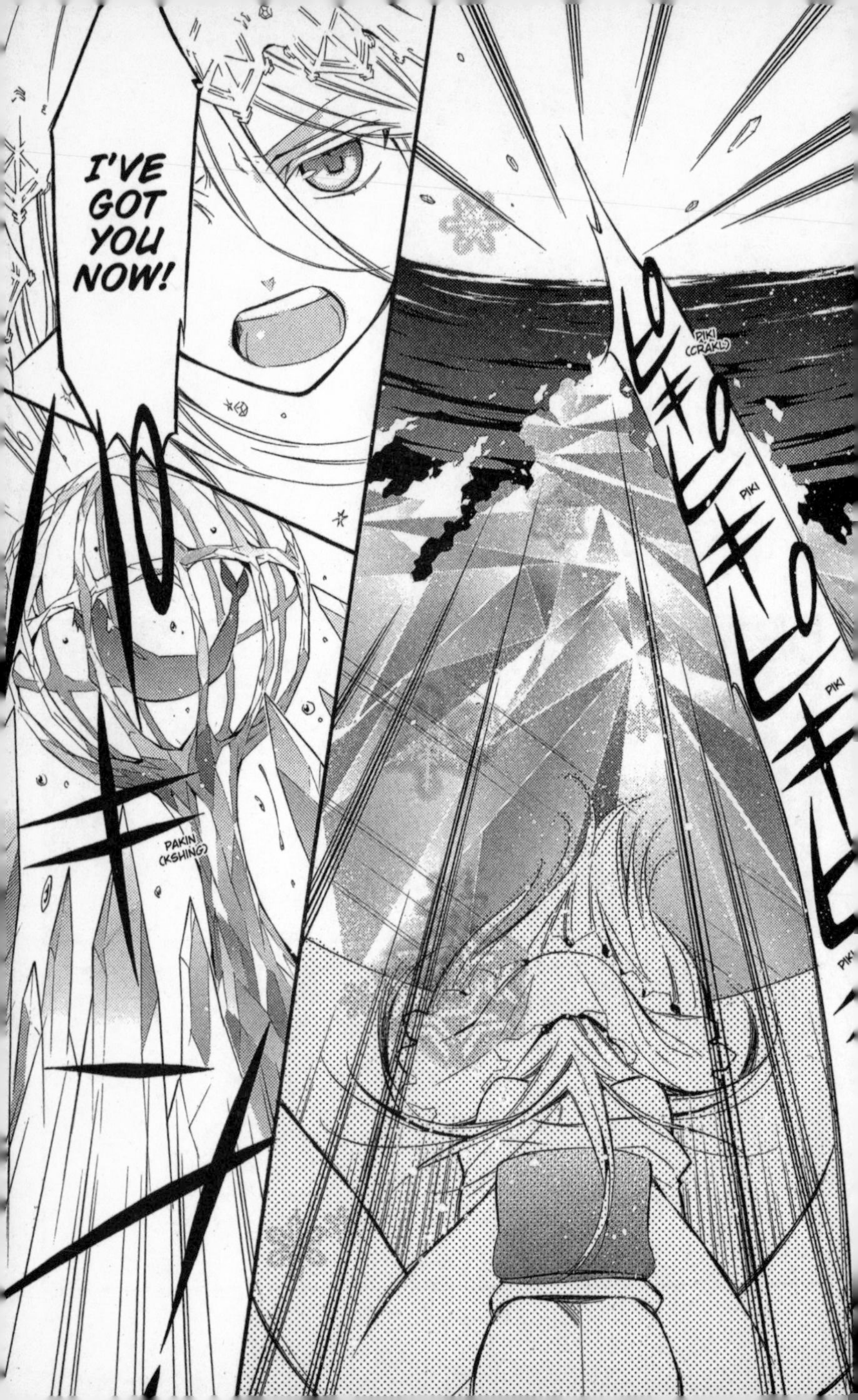
PIKI (CRAKL)
PIKI
PIKI
PIKI
I'VE GOT YOU NOW!
PAKIN (KSHING)

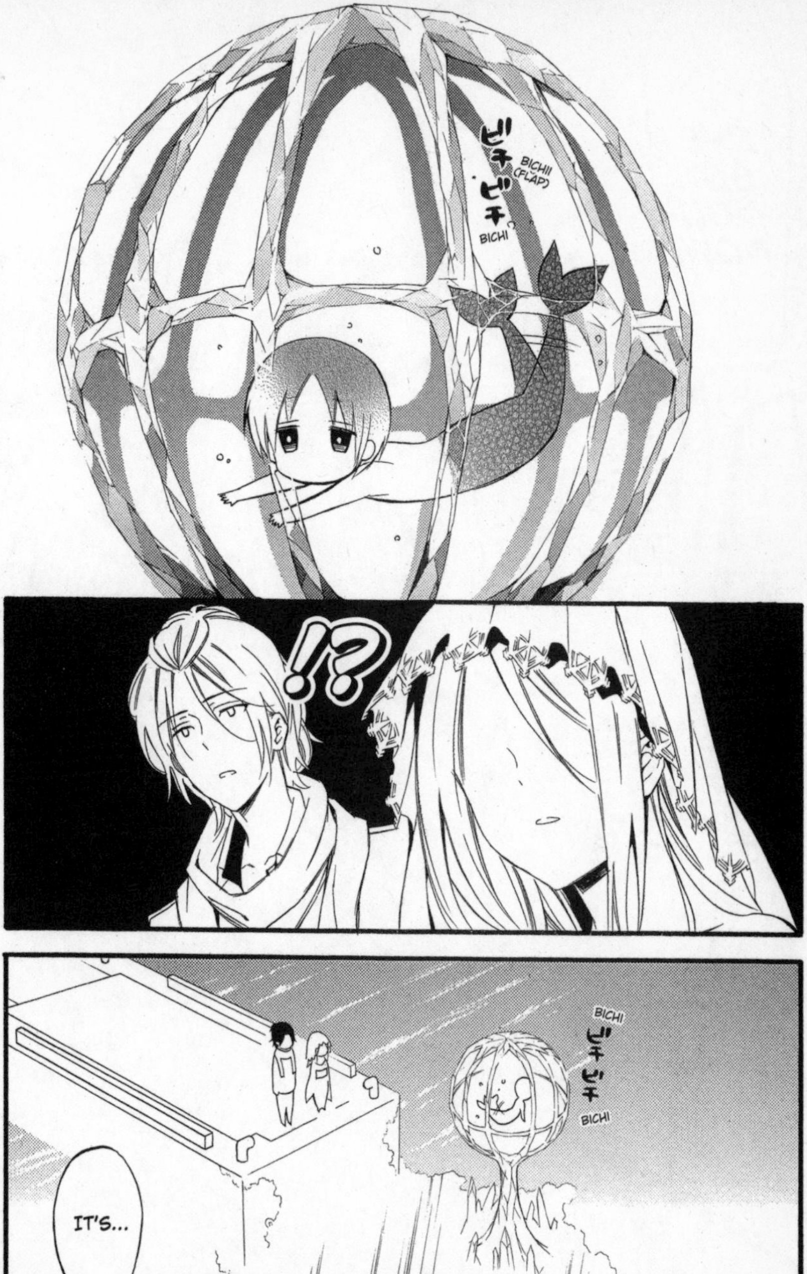

ビチ
BICHII (FLAP)
ビチ
BICHI
!?
BICHI
ビチ
ビチ
BICHI
IT'S...

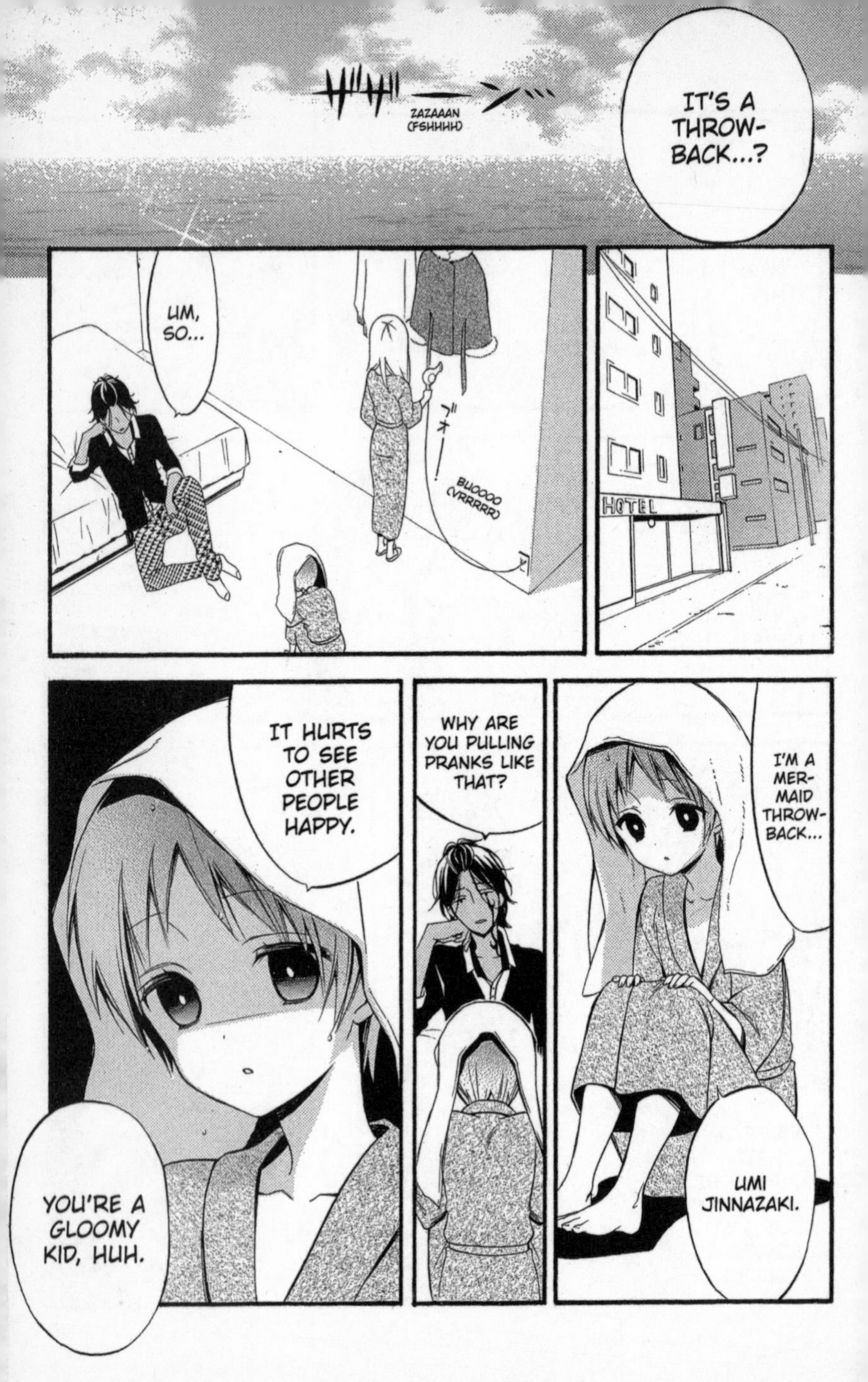
IT'S A THROW-BACK...?
ZAZAAAN (FSHHHH)
HOTEL
BUOOOO (VRRRRR)
UM, SO...
I'M A MER-MAID THROW-BACK...
UMI JINNAZAKI.
WHY ARE YOU PULLING PRANKS LIKE THAT?
IT HURTS TO SEE OTHER PEOPLE HAPPY.
YOU'RE A GLOOMY KID, HUH.

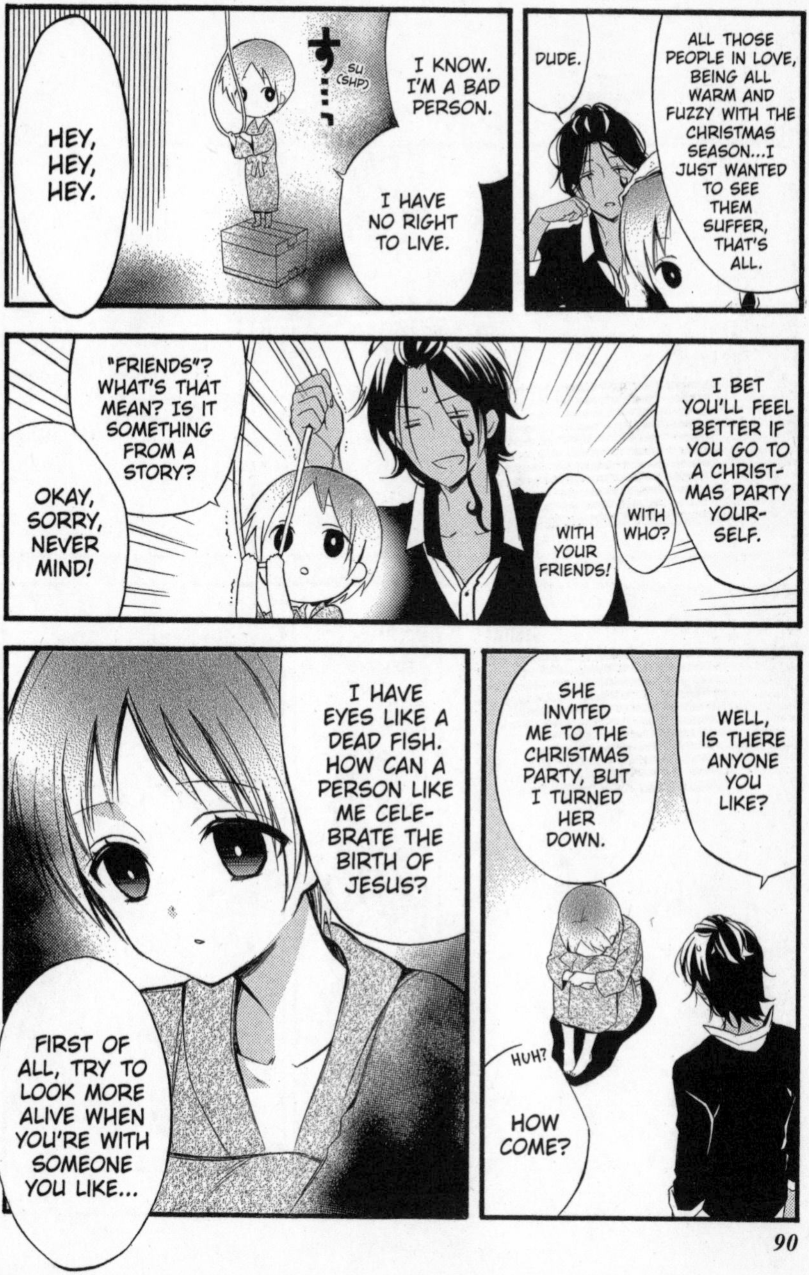
ALL THOSE PEOPLE IN LOVE, BEING ALL WARM AND FUZZY WITH THE CHRISTMAS SEASON...I JUST WANTED TO SEE THEM SUFFER, THAT'S ALL.
DUDE.
I KNOW. I'M A BAD PERSON.
す
SU (SHP)
I HAVE NO RIGHT TO LIVE.
HEY, HEY, HEY.
I BET YOU'LL FEEL BETTER IF YOU GO TO A CHRISTMAS PARTY YOURSELF.
WITH WHO?
WITH YOUR FRIENDS!
"FRIENDS"? WHAT'S THAT MEAN? IS IT SOMETHING FROM A STORY?
OKAY, SORRY, NEVER MIND!
WELL, IS THERE ANYONE YOU LIKE?
SHE INVITED ME TO THE CHRISTMAS PARTY, BUT I TURNED HER DOWN.
HUH?
HOW COME?
I HAVE EYES LIKE A DEAD FISH. HOW CAN A PERSON LIKE ME CELEBRATE THE BIRTH OF JESUS?
FIRST OF ALL, TRY TO LOOK MORE ALIVE WHEN YOU'RE WITH SOMEONE YOU LIKE...

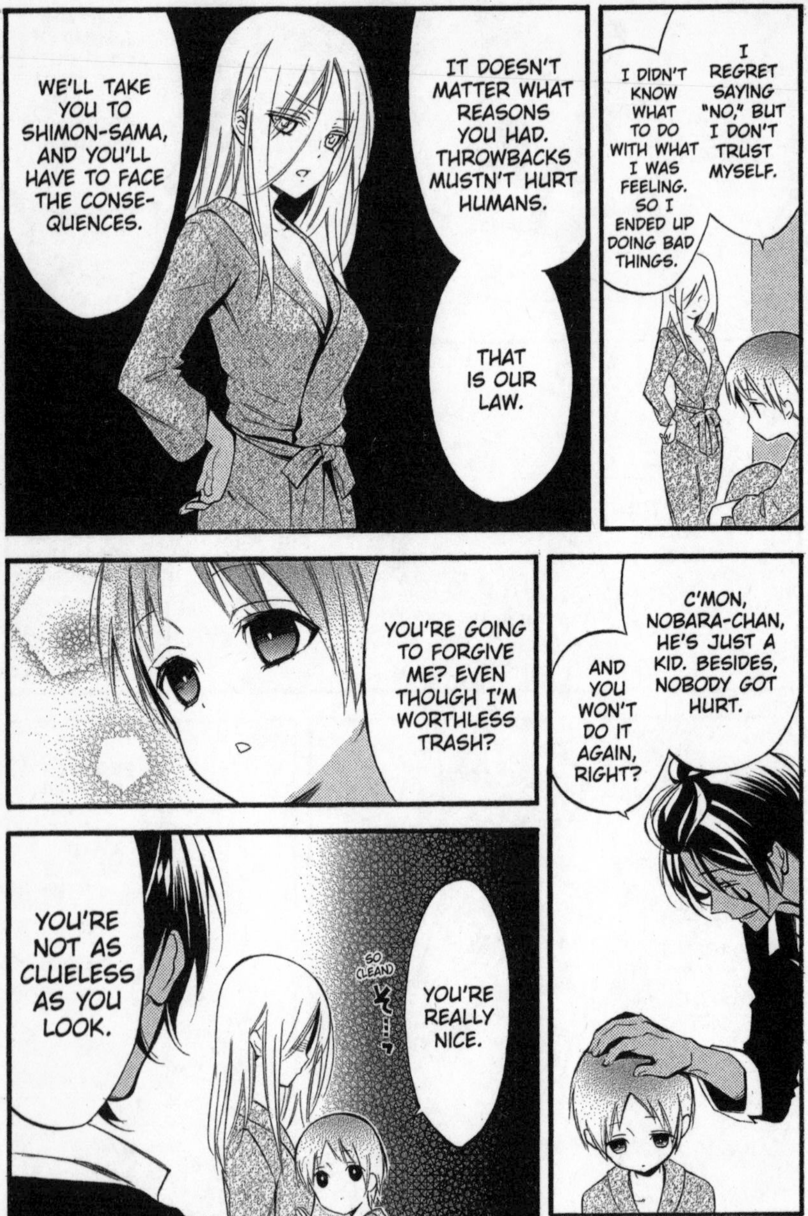
I REGRET SAYING "NO," BUT I DON'T TRUST MYSELF.
I DIDN'T KNOW WHAT TO DO WITH WHAT I WAS FEELING. SO I ENDED UP DOING BAD THINGS.
IT DOESN'T MATTER WHAT REASONS YOU HAD. THROWBACKS MUSTN'T HURT HUMANS.
THAT IS OUR LAW.
WE'LL TAKE YOU TO SHIMON-SAMA, AND YOU'LL HAVE TO FACE THE CONSE-QUENCES.
C'MON, NOBARA-CHAN, HE'S JUST A KID. BESIDES, NOBODY GOT HURT.
AND YOU WON'T DO IT AGAIN, RIGHT?
YOU'RE GOING TO FORGIVE ME? EVEN THOUGH I'M WORTHLESS TRASH?
YOU'RE REALLY NICE.
SO CLEAN
YOU'RE NOT AS CLUELESS AS YOU LOOK.

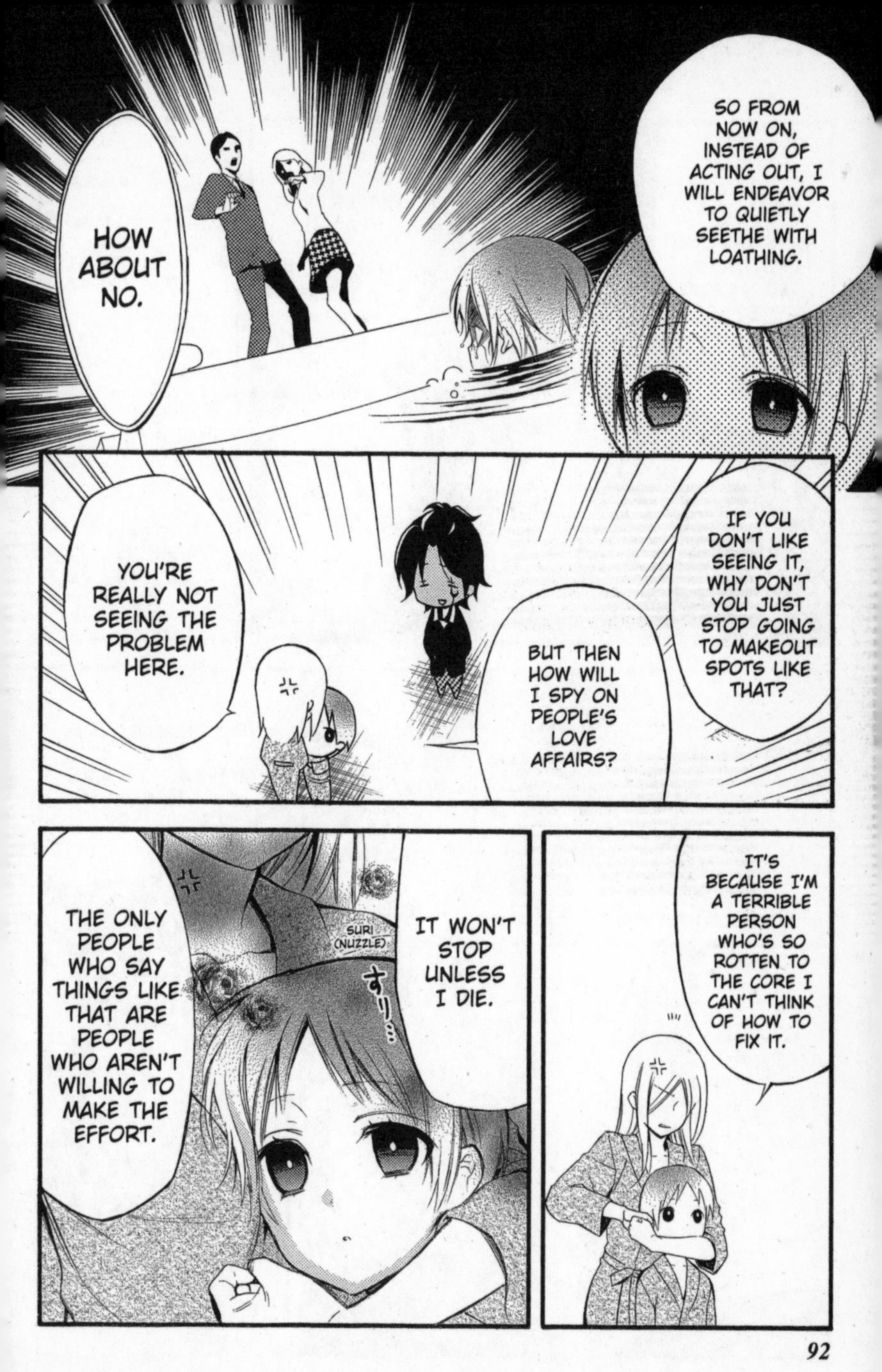
SO FROM NOW ON, INSTEAD OF ACTING OUT, I WILL ENDEAVOR TO QUIETLY SEETHE WITH LOATHING.
HOW ABOUT NO.
IF YOU DON'T LIKE SEEING IT, WHY DON'T YOU JUST STOP GOING TO MAKEOUT SPOTS LIKE THAT?
BUT THEN HOW WILL I SPY ON PEOPLE'S LOVE AFFAIRS?
YOU'RE REALLY NOT SEEING THE PROBLEM HERE.
IT'S BECAUSE I'M A TERRIBLE PERSON WHO'S SO ROTTEN TO THE CORE I CAN'T THINK OF HOW TO FIX IT.
IT WON'T STOP UNLESS I DIE.
SURI (NUZZLE)
すり…
THE ONLY PEOPLE WHO SAY THINGS LIKE THAT ARE PEOPLE WHO AREN'T WILLING TO MAKE THE EFFORT.

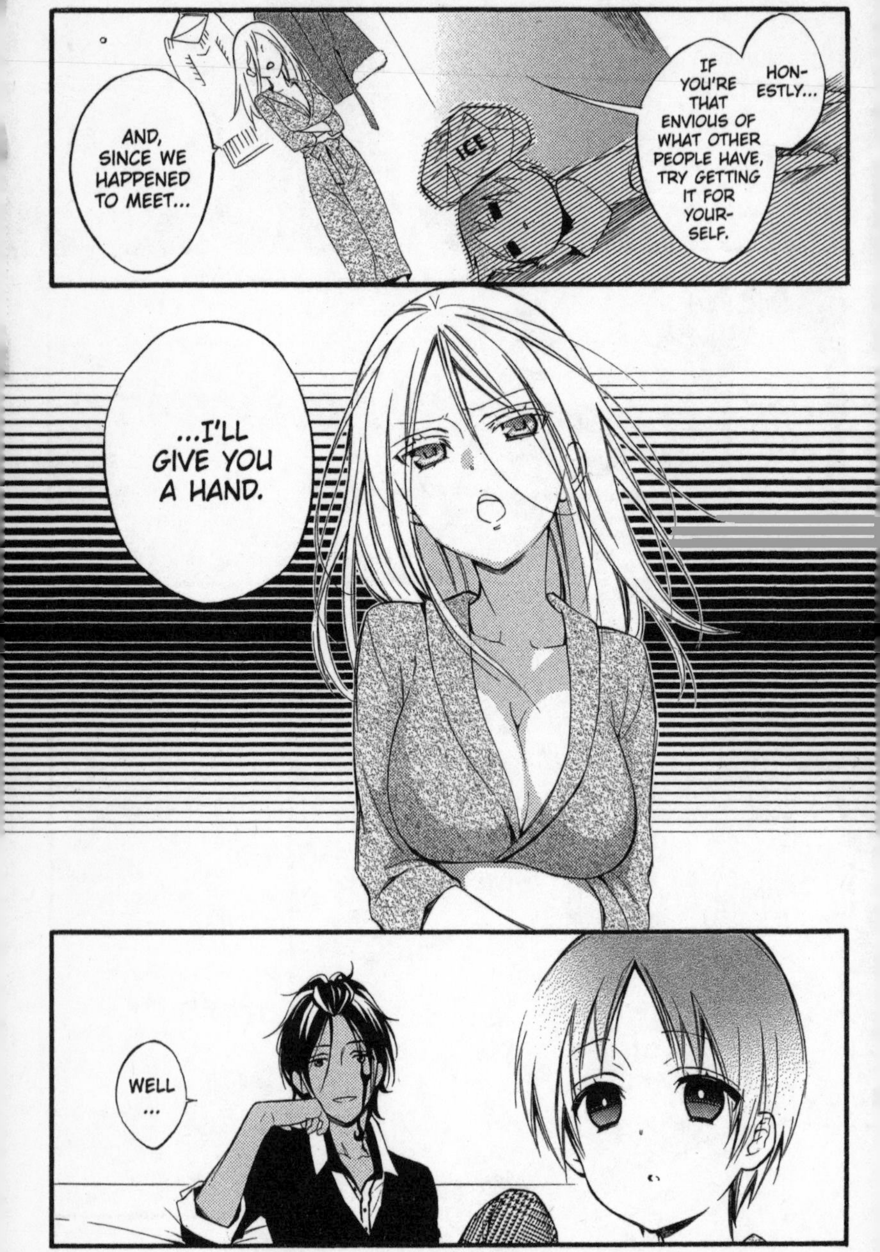
HON-ESTLY...
IF YOU'RE THAT ENVIOUS OF WHAT OTHER PEOPLE HAVE, TRY GETTING IT FOR YOUR-SELF.
AND, SINCE WE HAPPENED TO MEET...
...I'LL GIVE YOU A HAND.
WELL ...

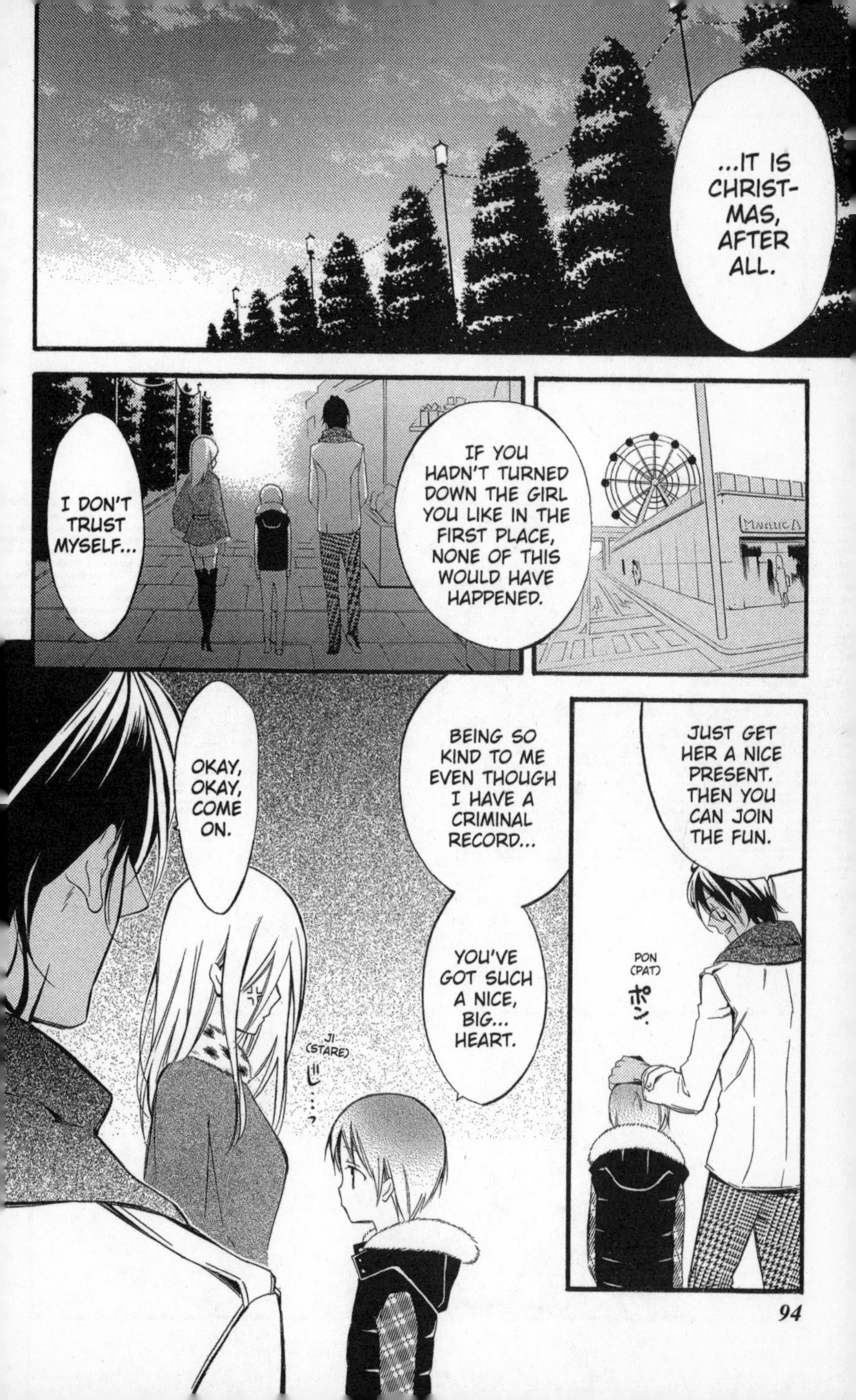
...IT IS CHRISTMAS, AFTER ALL.
IF YOU HADN'T TURNED DOWN THE GIRL YOU LIKE IN THE FIRST PLACE, NONE OF THIS WOULD HAVE HAPPENED.
I DON'T TRUST MYSELF...
JUST GET HER A NICE PRESENT. THEN YOU CAN JOIN THE FUN.
PON (PAT)
ポン
BEING SO KIND TO ME EVEN THOUGH I HAVE A CRIMINAL RECORD...
YOU'VE GOT SUCH A NICE, BIG... HEART.
OKAY, OKAY, COME ON.
JI (STARE)
じ…

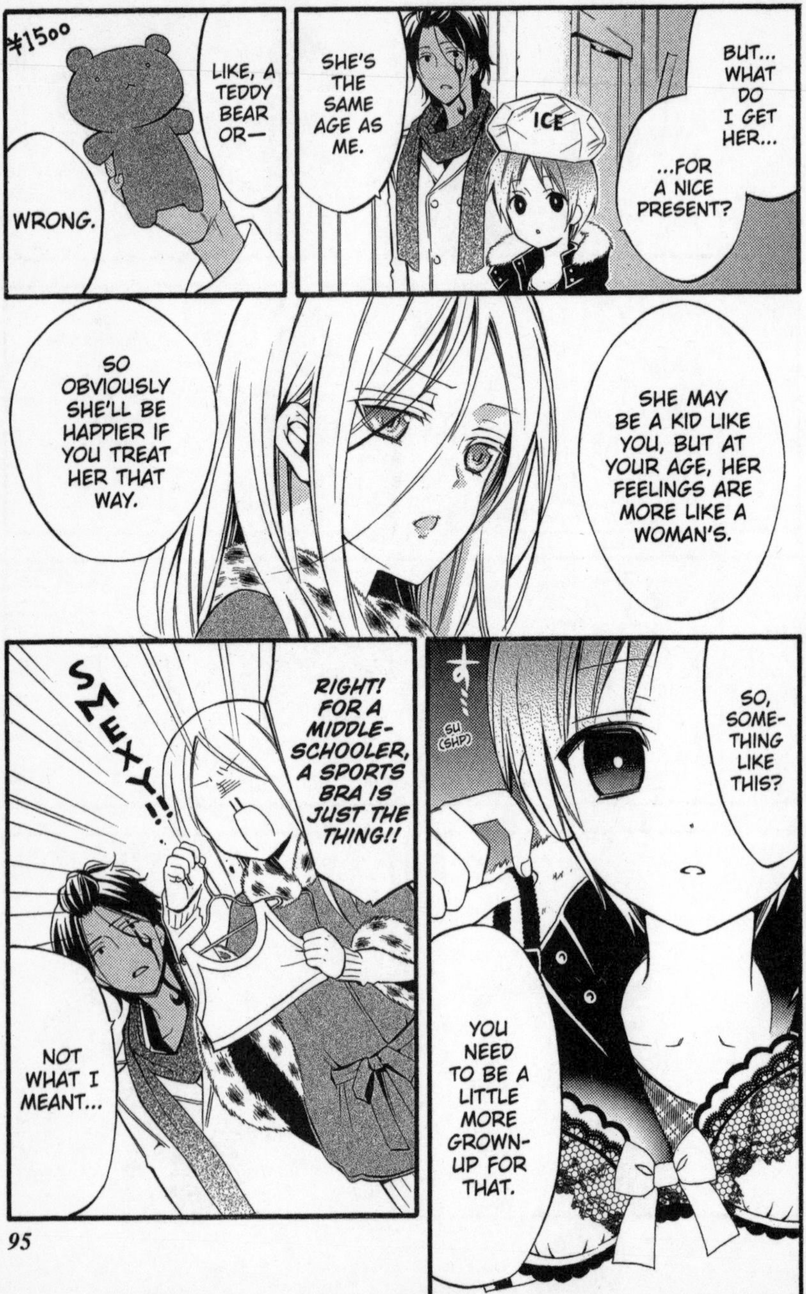
BUT... WHAT DO I GET HER...
...FOR A NICE PRESENT?
ICE
SHE'S THE SAME AGE AS ME.
¥1500
LIKE, A TEDDY BEAR OR—
WRONG.
SHE MAY BE A KID LIKE YOU, BUT AT YOUR AGE, HER FEELINGS ARE MORE LIKE A WOMAN'S.
SO OBVIOUSLY SHE'LL BE HAPPIER IF YOU TREAT HER THAT WAY.
SU (SHP)
SO, SOME-THING LIKE THIS?
YOU NEED TO BE A LITTLE MORE GROWN-UP FOR THAT.
RIGHT! FOR A MIDDLE-SCHOOLER, A SPORTS BRA IS JUST THE THING!!
SEXY!!
NOT WHAT I MEANT...

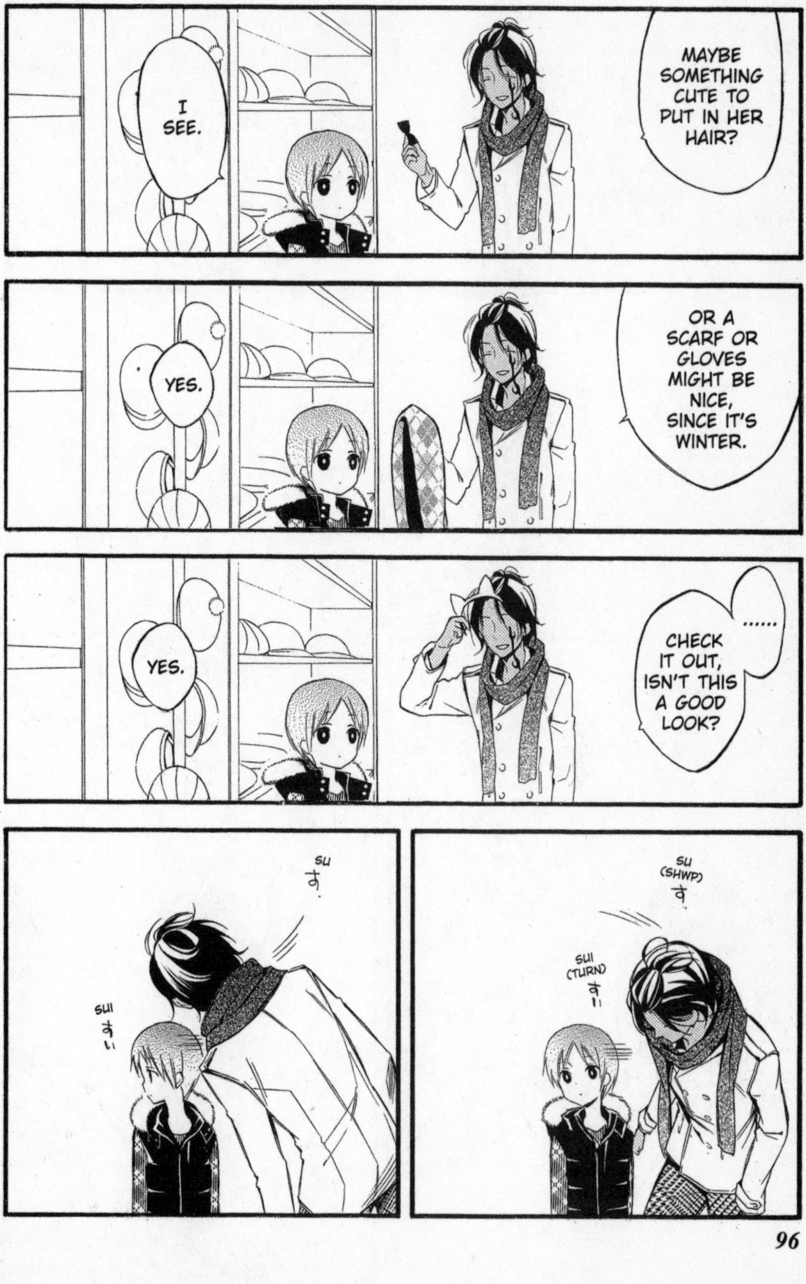
MAYBE SOMETHING CUTE TO PUT IN HER HAIR?
I SEE.
OR A SCARF OR GLOVES MIGHT BE NICE, SINCE IT'S WINTER.
YES.
......
CHECK IT OUT, ISN'T THIS A GOOD LOOK?
YES.
SU (SHWP) す
SUI (TURN) すい
SU す
SUI すい

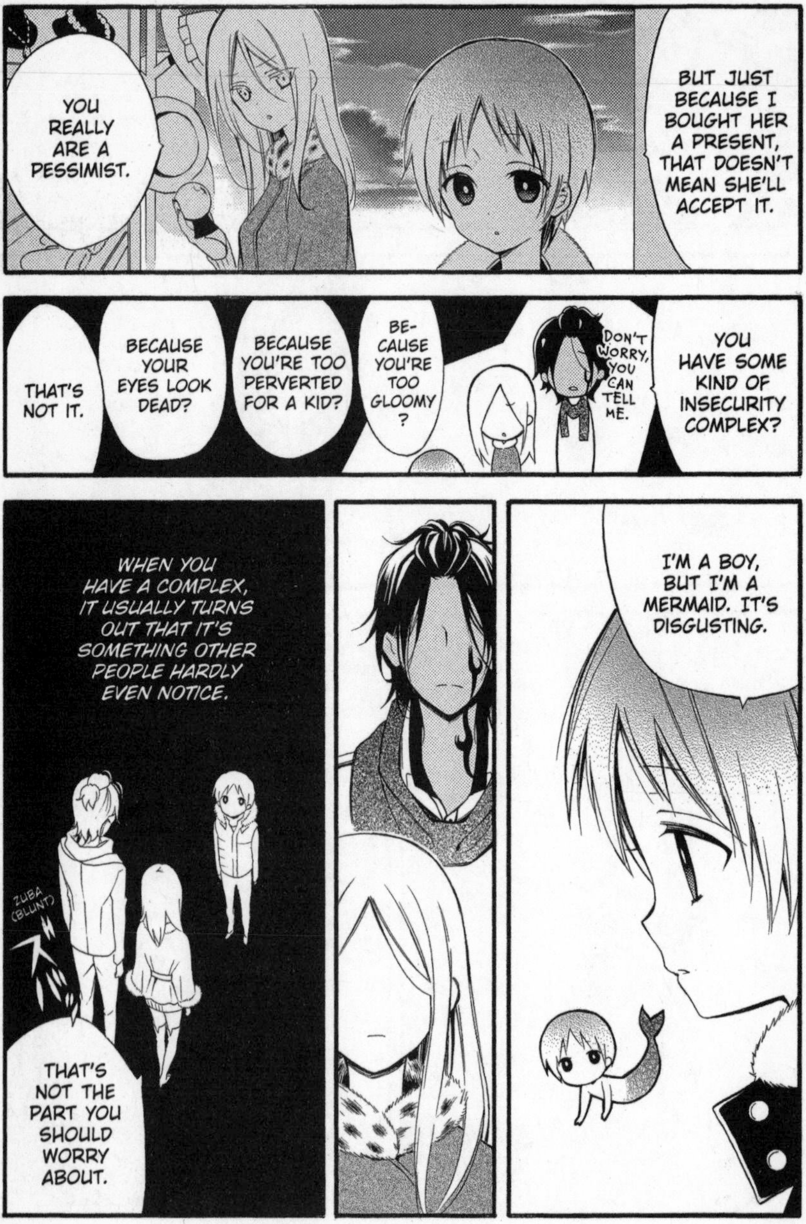
BUT JUST BECAUSE I BOUGHT HER A PRESENT, THAT DOESN'T MEAN SHE'LL ACCEPT IT.
YOU REALLY ARE A PESSIMIST.
YOU HAVE SOME KIND OF INSECURITY COMPLEX?
DON'T WORRY, YOU CAN TELL ME.
BE-CAUSE YOU'RE TOO GLOOMY?
BECAUSE YOU'RE TOO PERVERTED FOR A KID?
BECAUSE YOUR EYES LOOK DEAD?
THAT'S NOT IT.
I'M A BOY, BUT I'M A MERMAID. IT'S DISGUSTING.
WHEN YOU HAVE A COMPLEX, IT USUALLY TURNS OUT THAT IT'S SOMETHING OTHER PEOPLE HARDLY EVEN NOTICE.
ZUBA (BLUNT)
THAT'S NOT THE PART YOU SHOULD WORRY ABOUT.

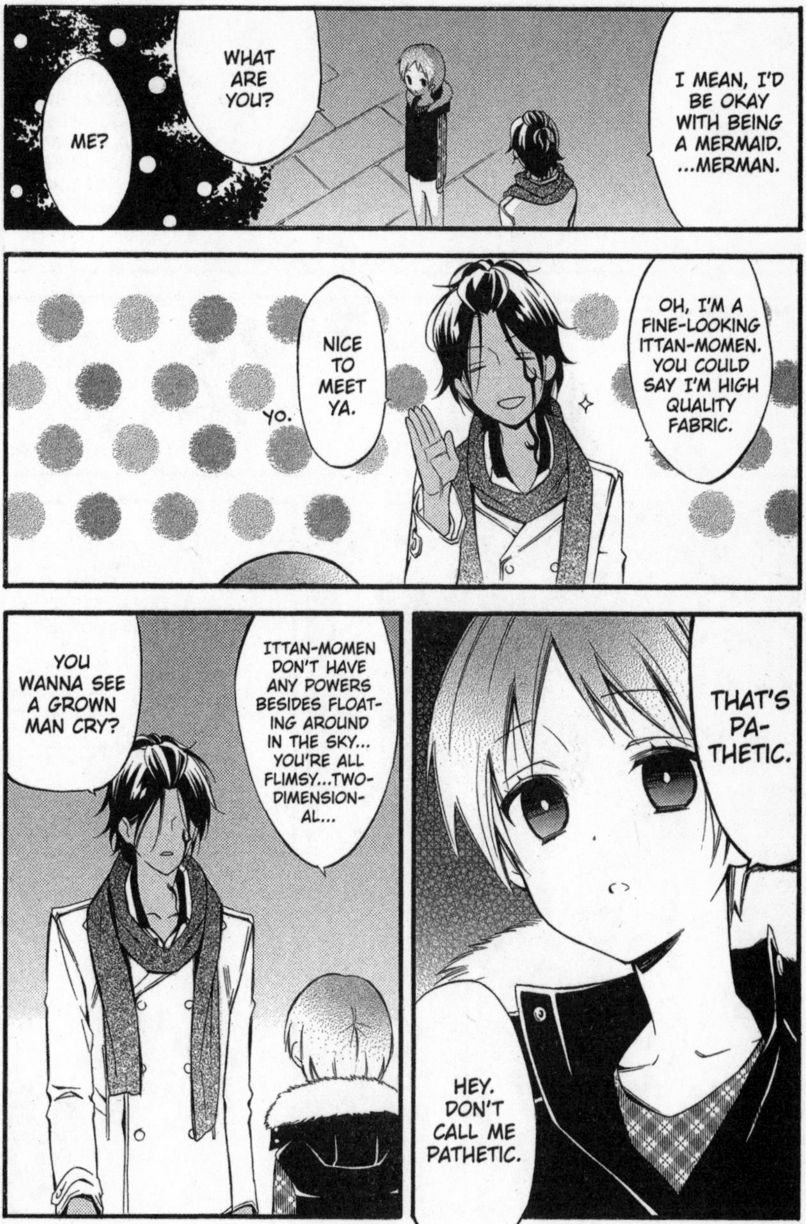
I MEAN, I'D BE OKAY WITH BEING A MERMAID. ...MERMAN.
WHAT ARE YOU?
ME?
OH, I'M A FINE-LOOKING ITTAN-MOMEN. YOU COULD SAY I'M HIGH QUALITY FABRIC.
NICE TO MEET YA.
YO.
THAT'S PA-THETIC.
HEY. DON'T CALL ME PATHETIC.
ITTAN-MOMEN DON'T HAVE ANY POWERS BESIDES FLOAT-ING AROUND IN THE SKY... YOU'RE ALL FLIMSY...TWO-DIMENSION-AL...
YOU WANNA SEE A GROWN MAN CRY?

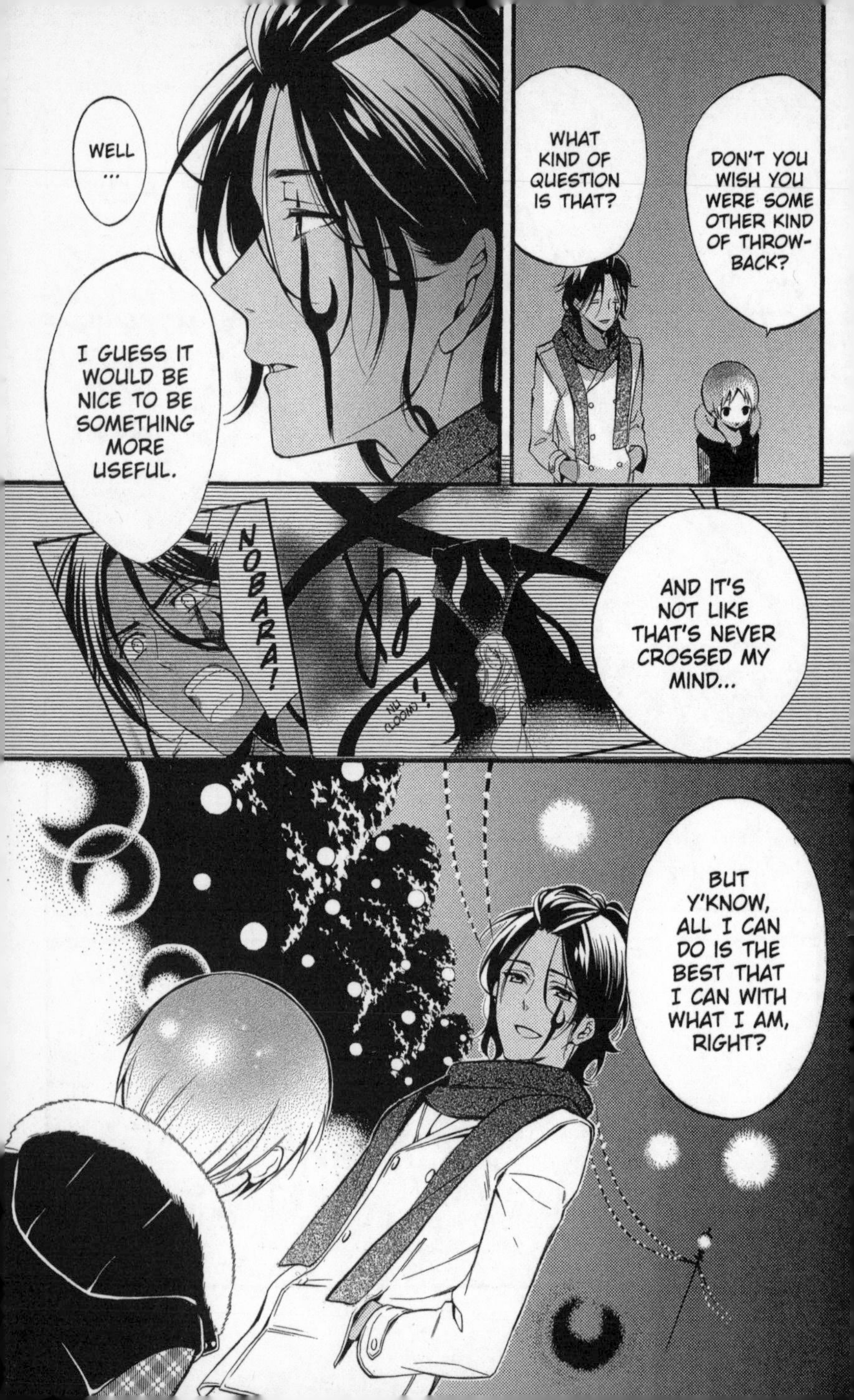
DON'T YOU WISH YOU WERE SOME OTHER KIND OF THROW-BACK?
WHAT KIND OF QUESTION IS THAT?
WELL ...
I GUESS IT WOULD BE NICE TO BE SOMETHING MORE USEFUL.
AND IT'S NOT LIKE THAT'S NEVER CROSSED MY MIND...
NOBARA!
NU (LOOM)
BUT Y'KNOW, ALL I CAN DO IS THE BEST THAT I CAN WITH WHAT I AM, RIGHT?

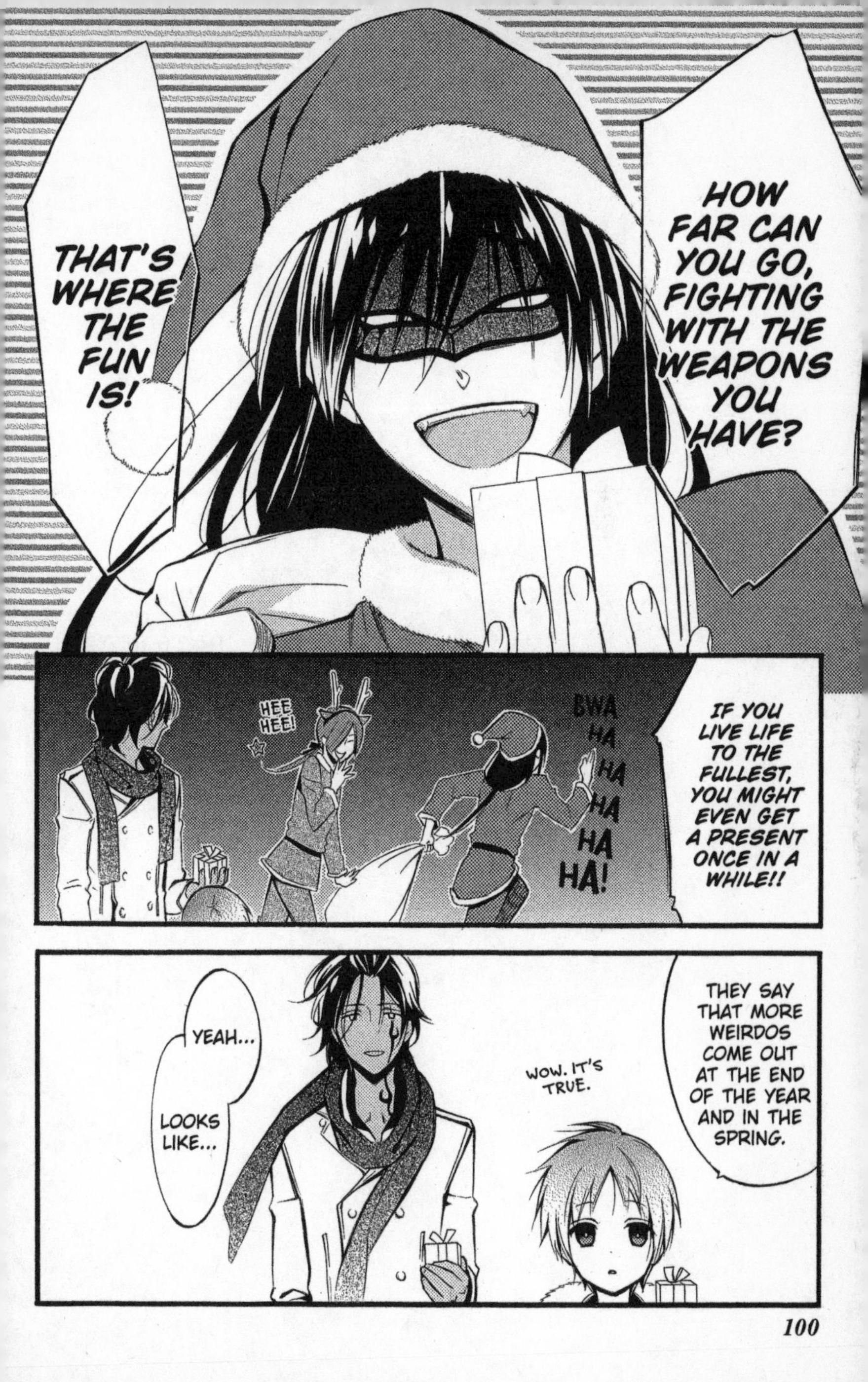
HOW FAR CAN YOU GO, FIGHTING WITH THE WEAPONS YOU HAVE?
THAT'S WHERE THE FUN IS!
IF YOU LIVE LIFE TO THE FULLEST, YOU MIGHT EVEN GET A PRESENT ONCE IN A WHILE!!
BWA HA HA HA HA HA!
HEE HEE!
THEY SAY THAT MORE WEIRDOS COME OUT AT THE END OF THE YEAR AND IN THE SPRING.
WOW. IT'S TRUE.
YEAH...
LOOKS LIKE...

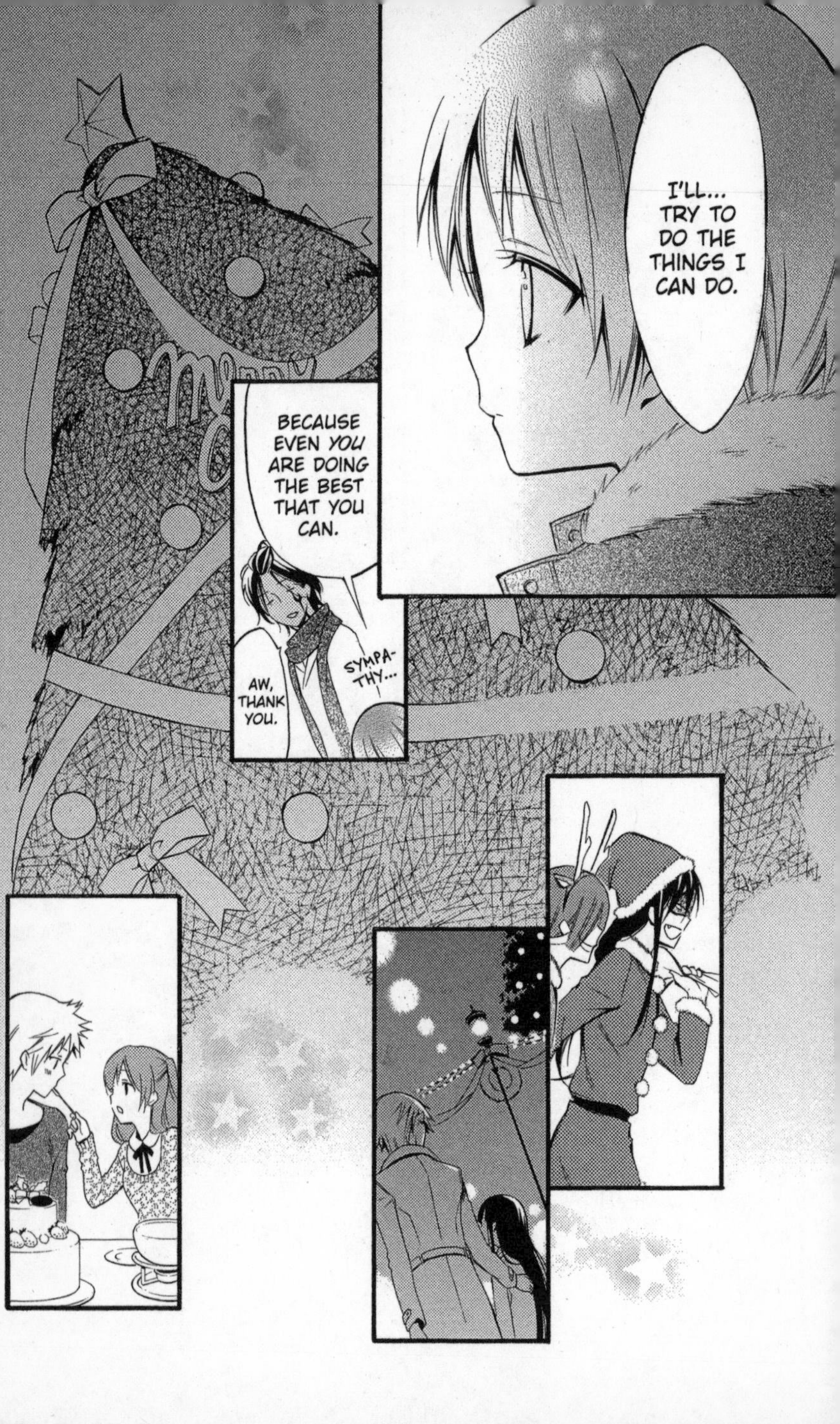
I'LL... TRY TO DO THE THINGS I CAN DO.
BECAUSE EVEN YOU ARE DOING THE BEST THAT YOU CAN.
SYMPA-THY...
AW, THANK YOU.

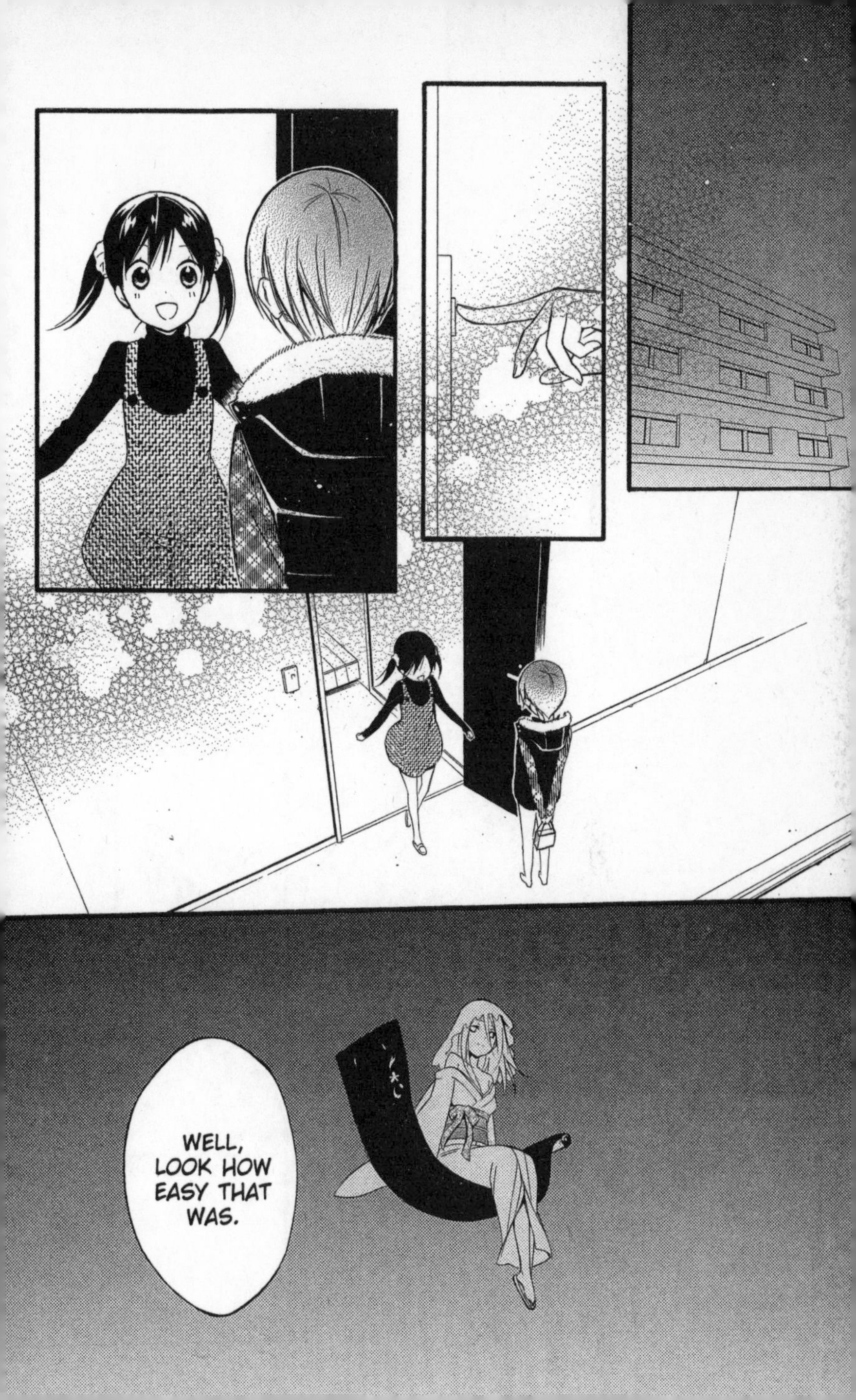
WELL, LOOK HOW EASY THAT WAS.

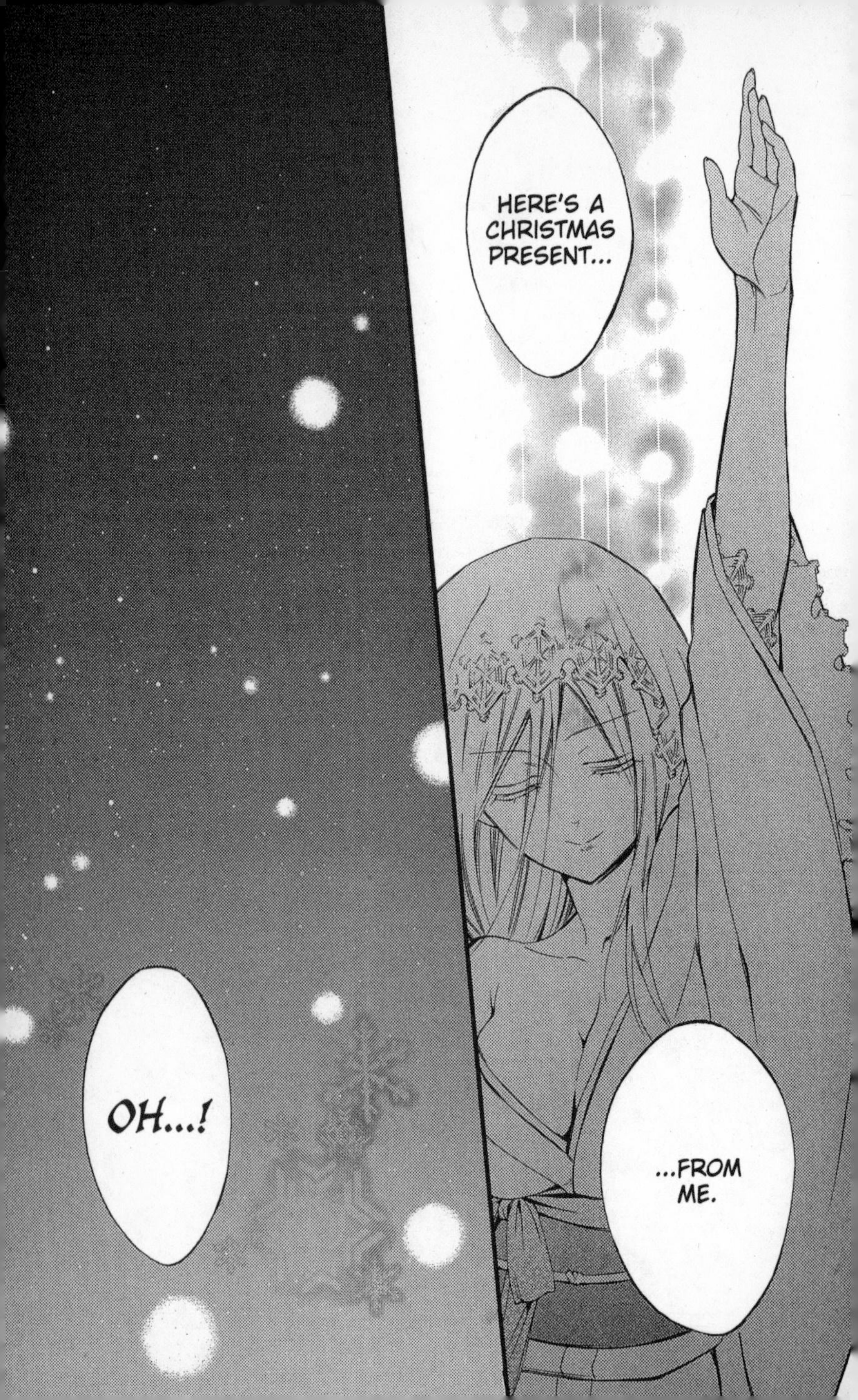
HERE'S A CHRISTMAS PRESENT...
...FROM ME.
OH...!

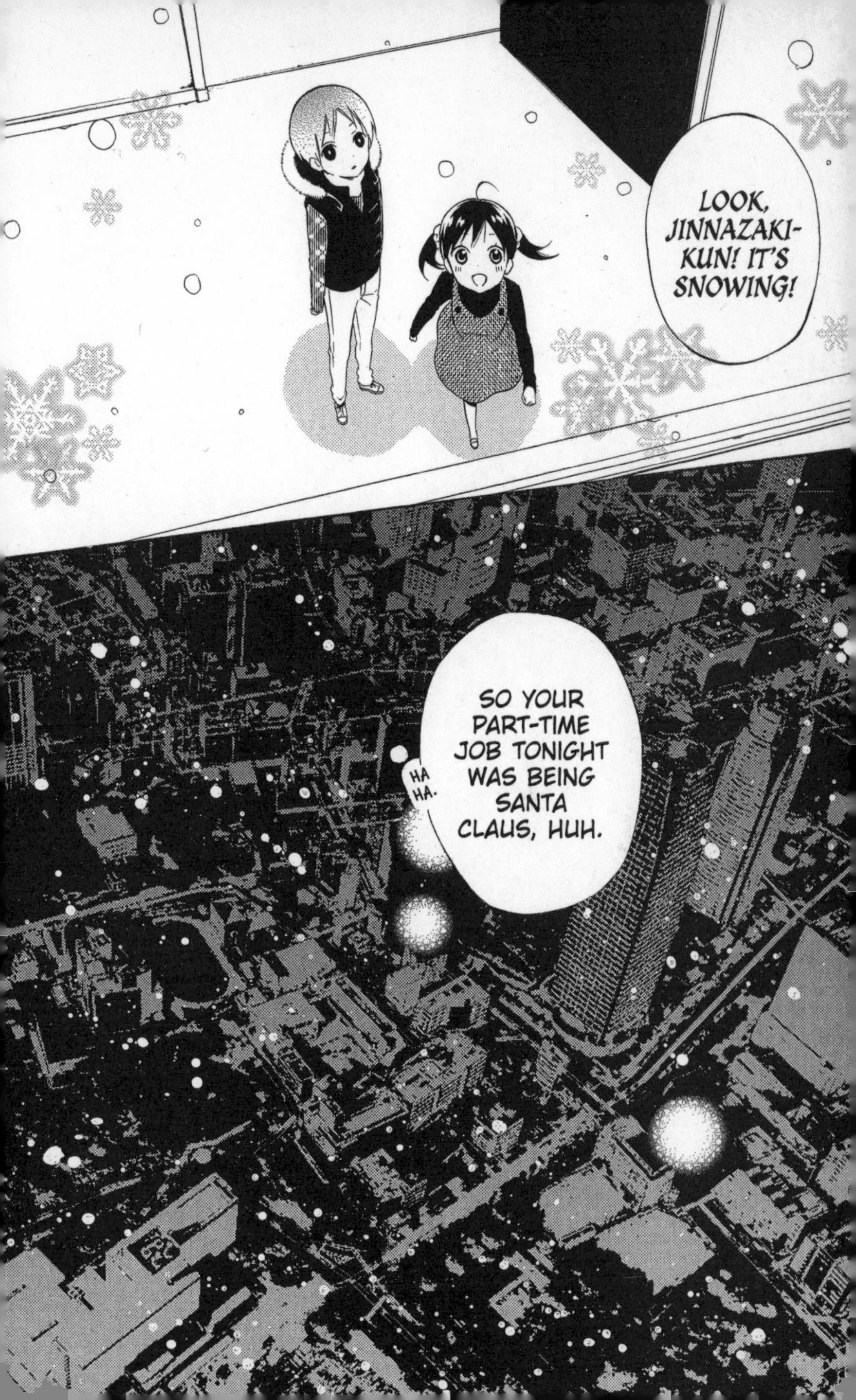
LOOK, JINNAZAKI-KUN! IT'S SNOWING!
SO YOUR PART-TIME JOB TONIGHT WAS BEING SANTA CLAUS, HUH.
HA HA.

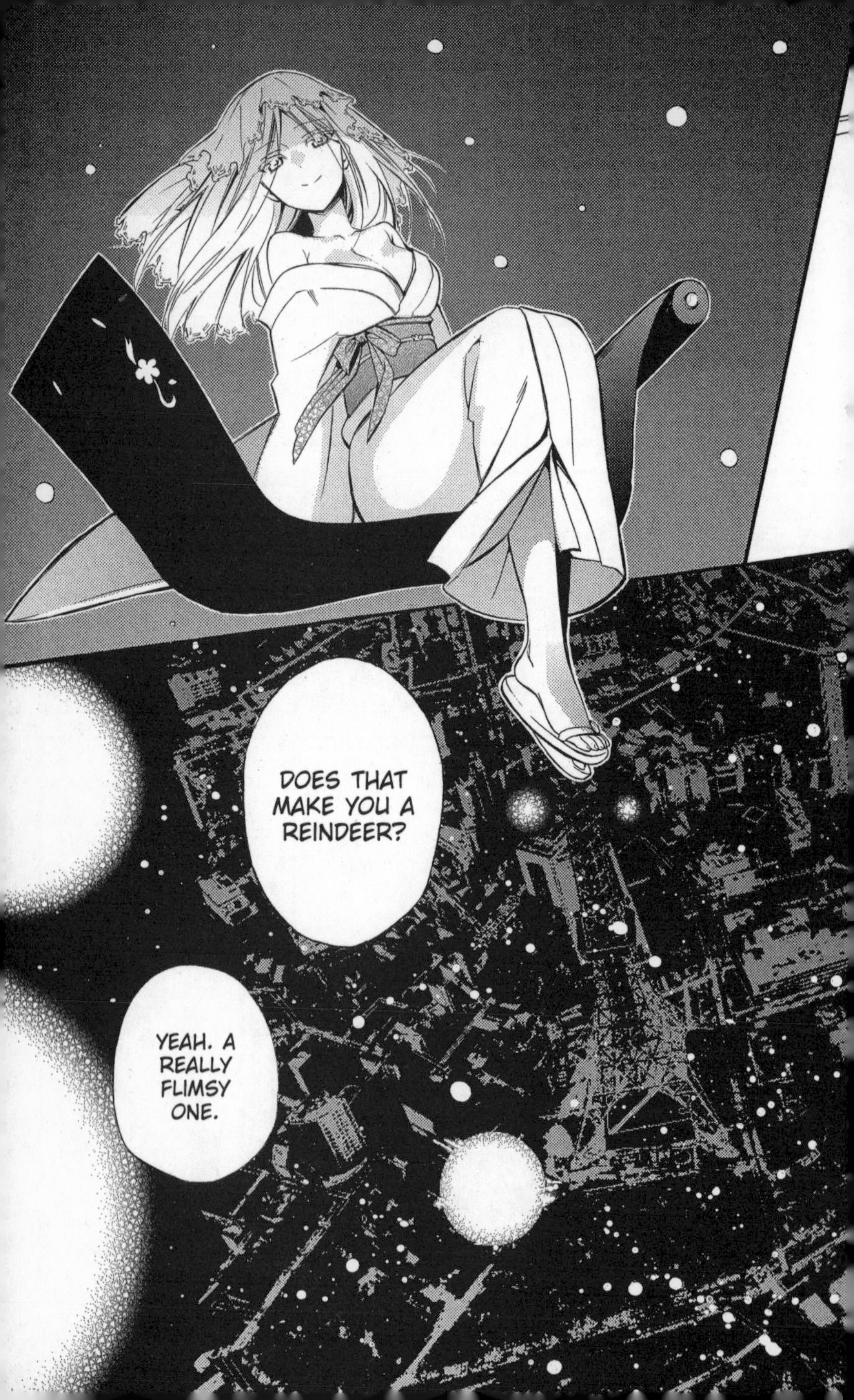
DOES THAT MAKE YOU A REINDEER?
YEAH. A REALLY FLIMSY ONE.

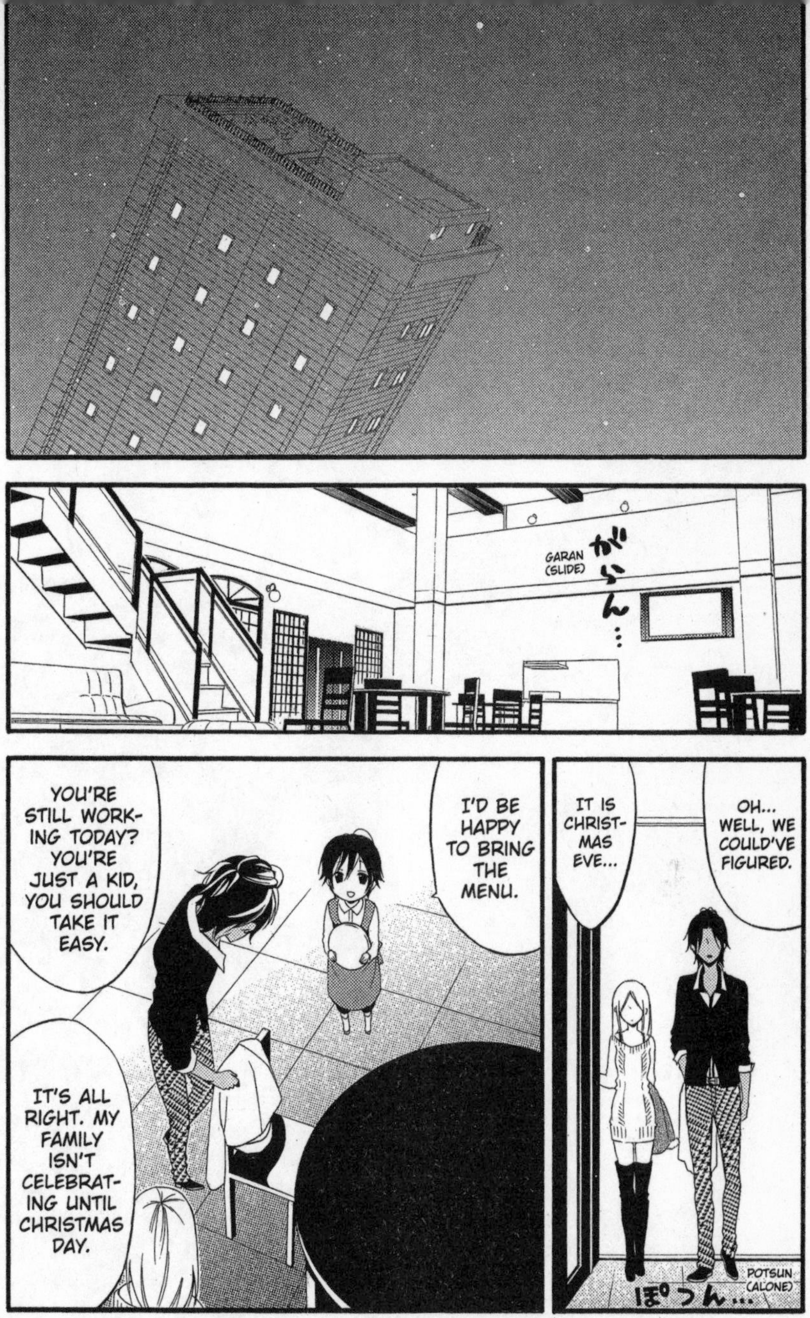
GARAN (SLIDE)
がらん…
OH... WELL, WE COULD'VE FIGURED.
IT IS CHRISTMAS EVE...
POTSUN (ALONE)
ぽつん…
I'D BE HAPPY TO BRING THE MENU.
YOU'RE STILL WORKING TODAY? YOU'RE JUST A KID, YOU SHOULD TAKE IT EASY.
IT'S ALL RIGHT. MY FAMILY ISN'T CELEBRATING UNTIL CHRISTMAS DAY.

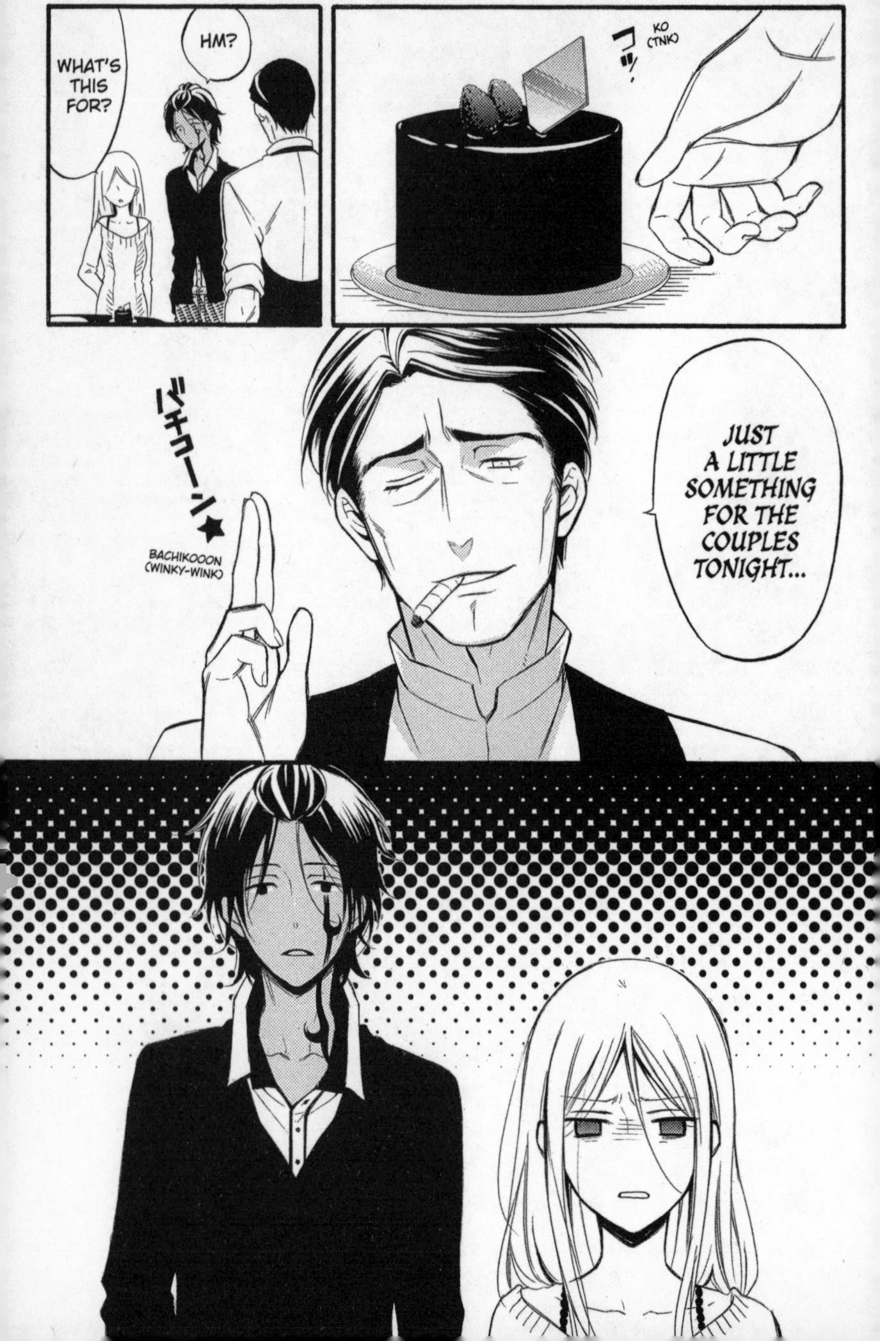
コッ
KO (TNK)
HM?
WHAT'S THIS FOR?
JUST A LITTLE SOMETHING FOR THE COUPLES TONIGHT...
バチコーン★
BACHIKOOON (WINKY-WINK)

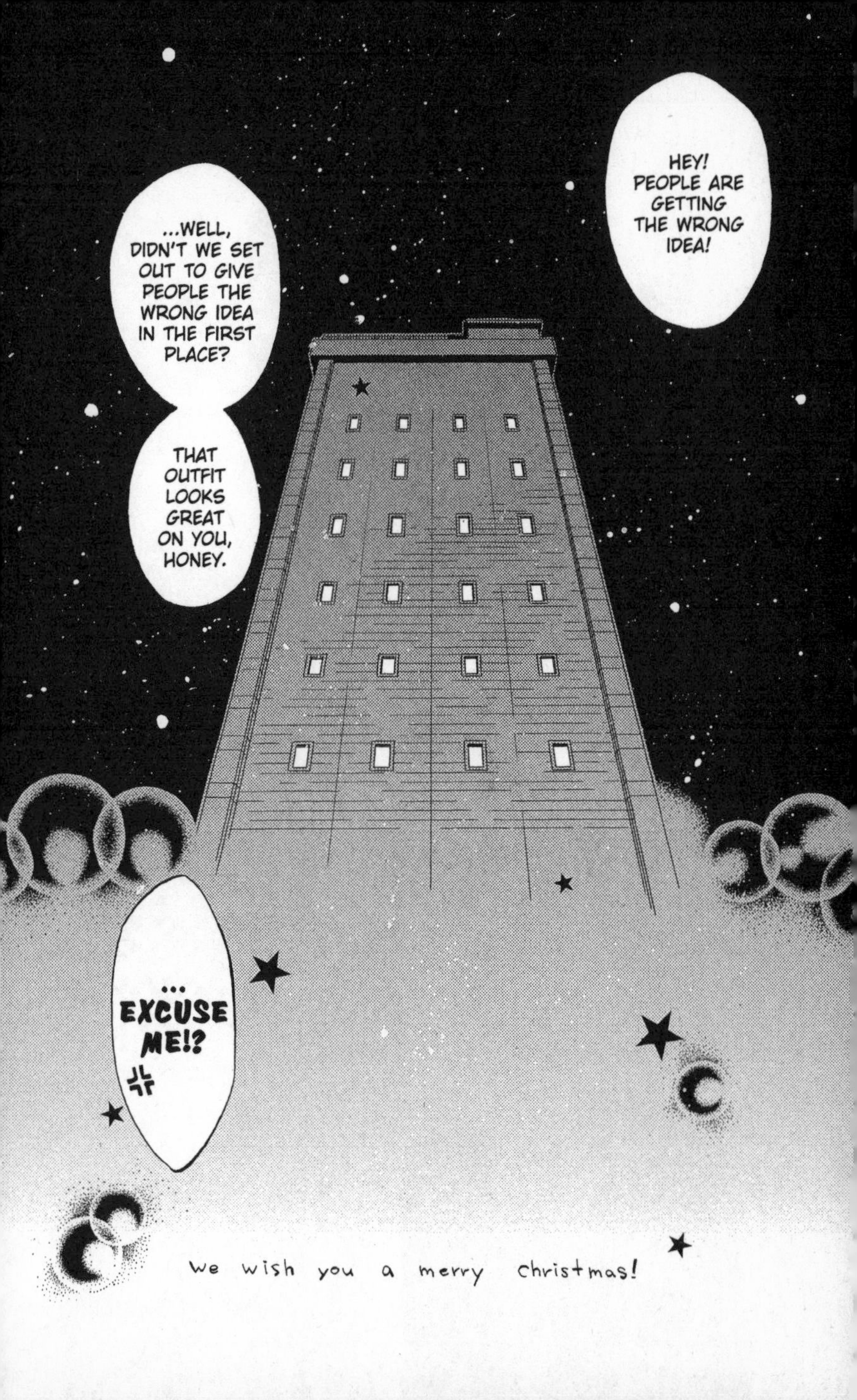
HEY! PEOPLE ARE GETTING THE WRONG IDEA!
...WELL, DIDN'T WE SET OUT TO GIVE PEOPLE THE WRONG IDEA IN THE FIRST PLACE?
THAT OUTFIT LOOKS GREAT ON YOU, HONEY.
...EXCUSE ME!?
we wish you a merry christmas!

INU×BOKU SS

INU×BOKU OUTLINE

THE NIGHT PARADE OF A HUNDRED DEMONS

Under the curse of another supernatural throwback, the mysterious Mikoto Inugami, other throwbacks lose self-awareness and go wild, wandering about in a pack called the Night Parade of a Hundred Demons. When this disaster struck the residents of Ayakashi Hall, nearly all of them lost their lives...

Soushi was cruelly struck down while protecting Ririchiyo... With his last breath, he expressed his gratitude to her...

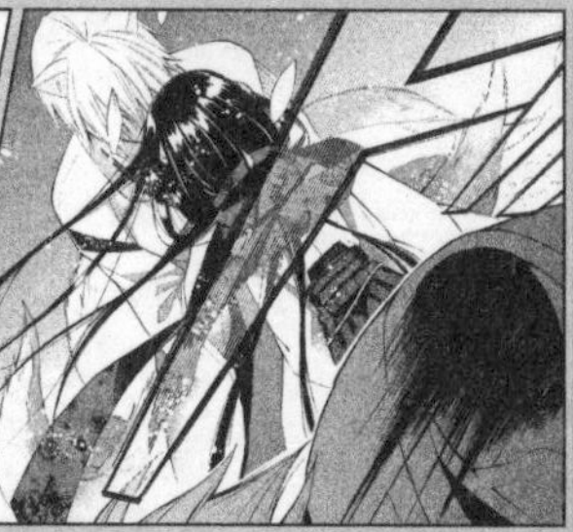

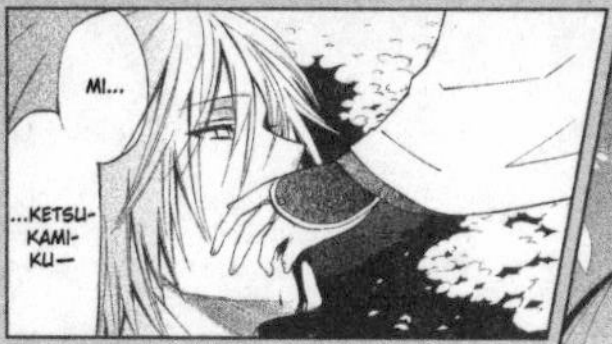
MI...
...KETSU-KAMI-KU—

Only Renshou survived the Night Parade. All the other residents of Ayakashi Hall and their bodyguards were killed.

AND THEN, 23 YEARS AFTER THOSE UNTIMELY DEATHS...

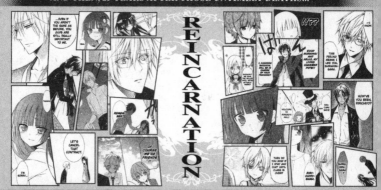

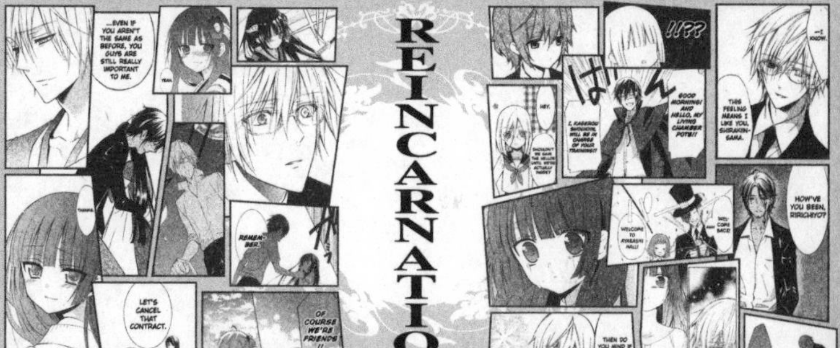
—I KNOW.
THIS FEELING MEANS I LIKE YOU, SHIRAKIN-SAMA.
!!??
GOOD MORNING! AND HELLO, MY LIVING CHAMBER POTS!!
I, KAGEROU SHOUKIIN, WILL BE IN CHARGE OF YOUR TRAINING!!
HEY.
HOW'VE YOU BEEN, RIRICHIYO?
WEL-COME BACK!
WELCOME TO AYAKASHI HALL!
SHIRA-KIIN-SAMA...?
RIRI-CHIYO-SAMA.
THEN DO YOU MIND IF I STAY AND CHAT UNTIL CLASS IS OVER?
REINCARNATION
...EVEN IF YOU AREN'T THE SAME AS BEFORE, YOU GUYS ARE STILL REALLY IMPORTANT TO ME.
REMEM-BER.
OF COURSE WE'RE FRIENDS!!
LET'S CANCEL THAT CONTRACT.
I'M SORRY...

Some things changed, some things didn't...
Ririchiyo and the others struggled to deal with their clashing feelings as their past lives collided with the present.

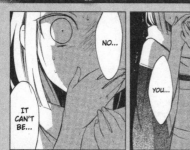

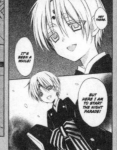

Then—Mikoto Inugami appeared again!

Will this be a reprise of the Night Parade...!?

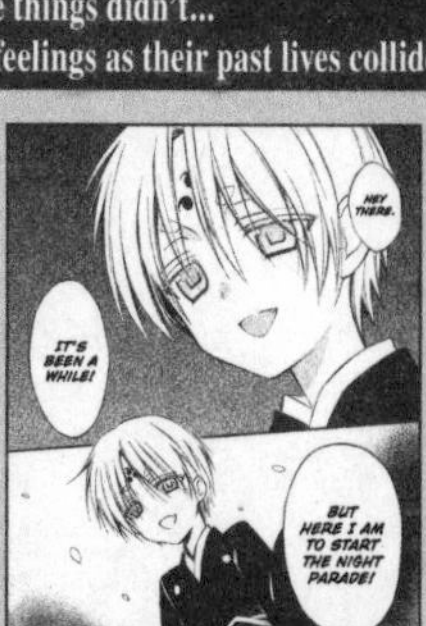
HEY THERE.
IT'S BEEN A WHILE!
BUT HERE I AM TO START THE NIGHT PARADE!

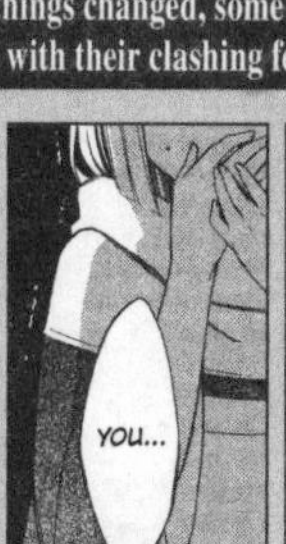
YOU...

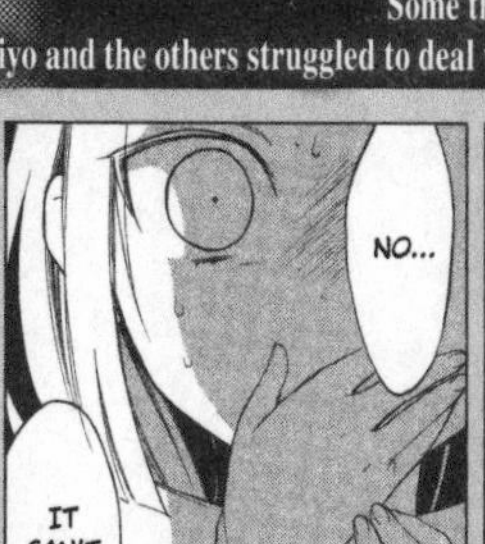
NO...
IT CAN'T BE...

Shimon realized Mikoto's true intent...which is...!

The Millennium Cherry Tree has the power to pull those with unresolved feelings back into the past...and Mikoto would use it to go back in time to 23 years ago and repeat the Night Parade of a Hundred Demons.

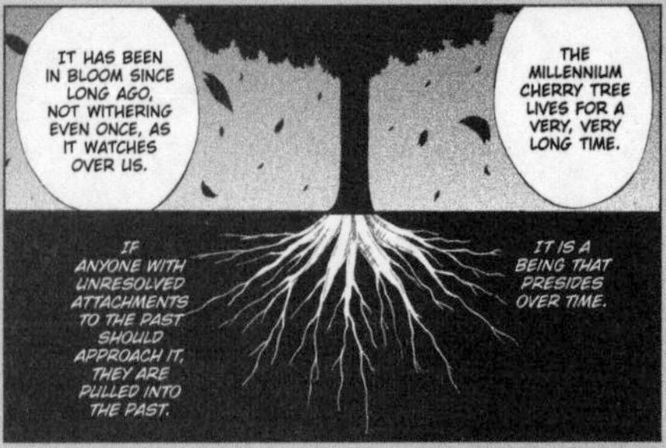
THE MILLENNIUM CHERRY TREE LIVES FOR A VERY, VERY LONG TIME.
IT HAS BEEN IN BLOOM SINCE LONG AGO, NOT WITHERING EVEN ONCE, AS IT WATCHES OVER US.
IT IS A BEING THAT PRESIDES OVER TIME.
IF ANYONE WITH UNRESOLVED ATTACHMENTS TO THE PAST SHOULD APPROACH IT, THEY ARE PULLED INTO THE PAST.

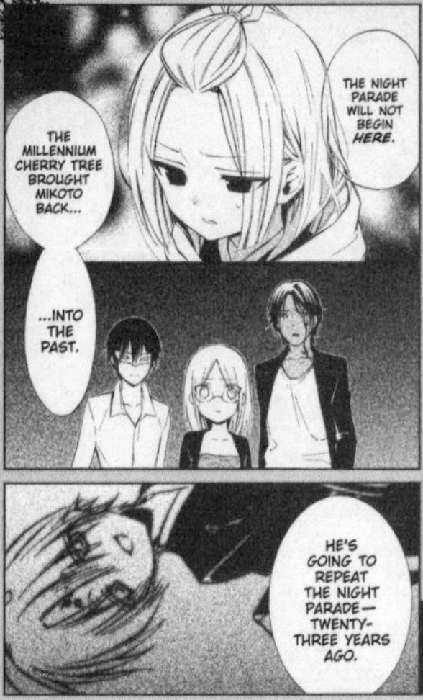
THE NIGHT PARADE WILL NOT BEGIN *HERE*.
THE MILLENNIUM CHERRY TREE BROUGHT MIKOTO BACK...
...INTO THE PAST.
HE'S GOING TO REPEAT THE NIGHT PARADE—TWENTY-THREE YEARS AGO.

The Night Parade will only begin again!
How can they warn the past...!?

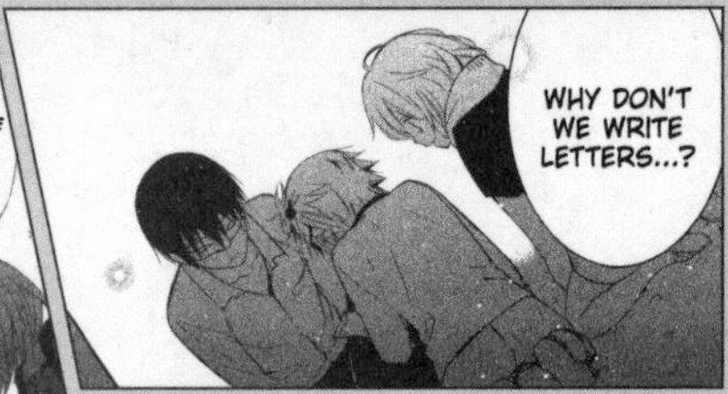
WHY DON'T WE WRITE LETTERS...?

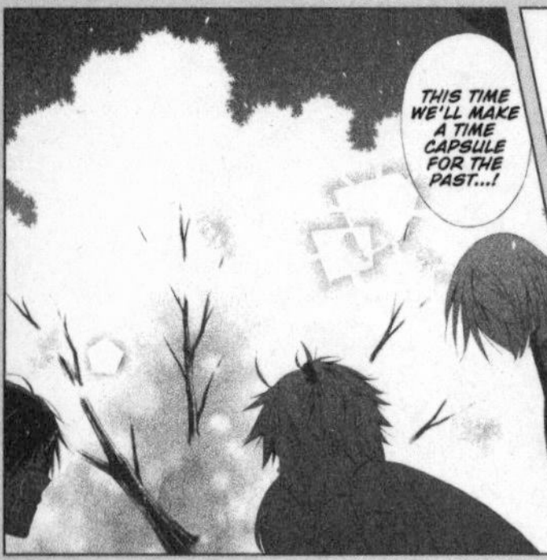
THIS TIME WE'LL MAKE A TIME CAPSULE FOR THE PAST...!

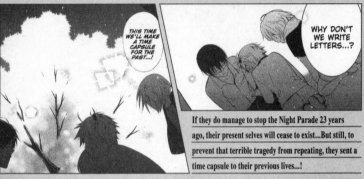

If they do manage to stop the Night Parade 23 years ago, their present selves will cease to exist...But still, to prevent that terrible tragedy from repeating, they sent a time capsule to their previous lives...!

And 23 years in the past...

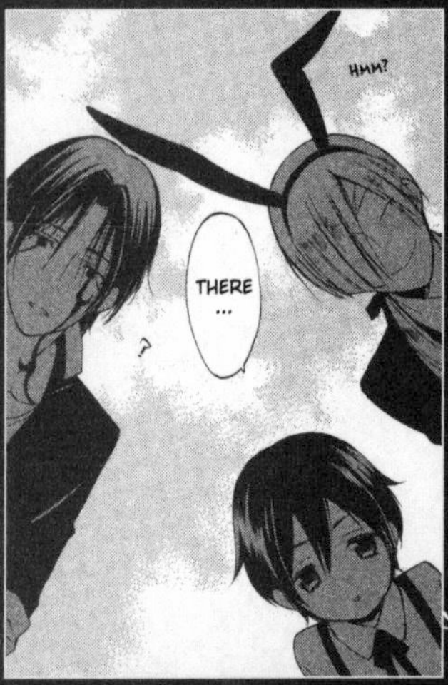
HMM?
THERE...

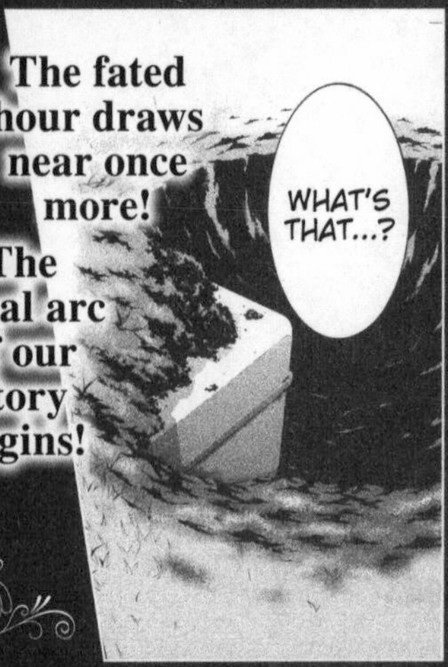
WHAT'S THAT...?

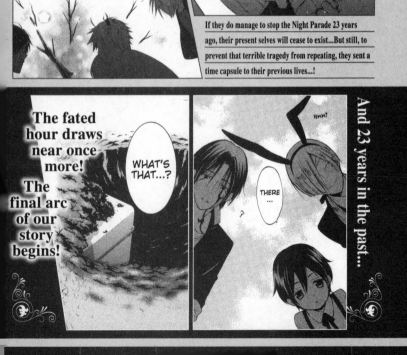

The fated hour draws near once more!
The final arc of our story begins!

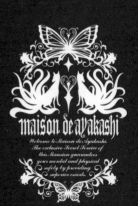

maison de ayakashi

Welcome to Maison de Ayakashi.
The exclusive Secret Service of
this Mansion guarantees
your mental and physical
safety by providing
superior escorts.

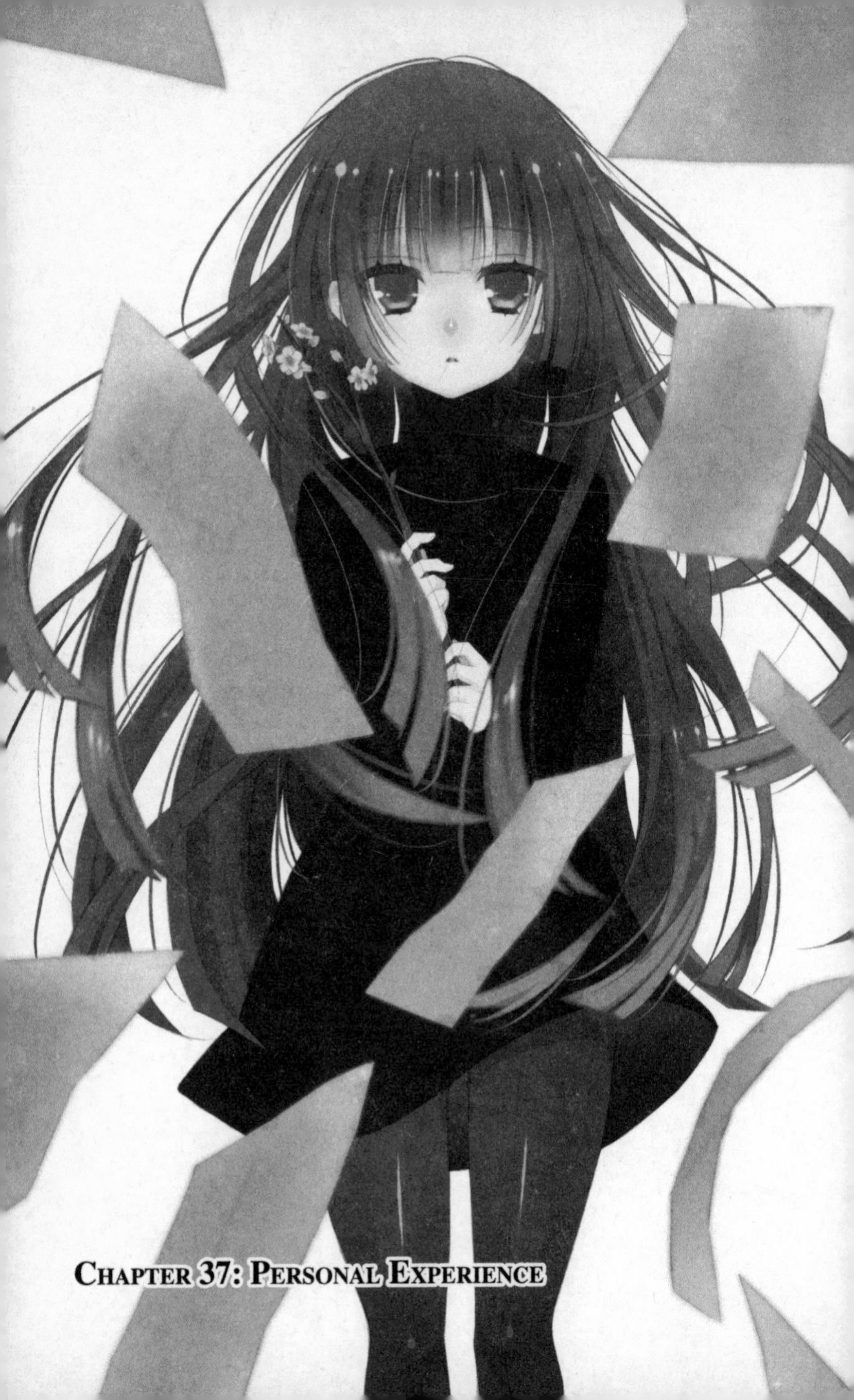

Chapter 37: Personal Experience

INU✕BOKU SS

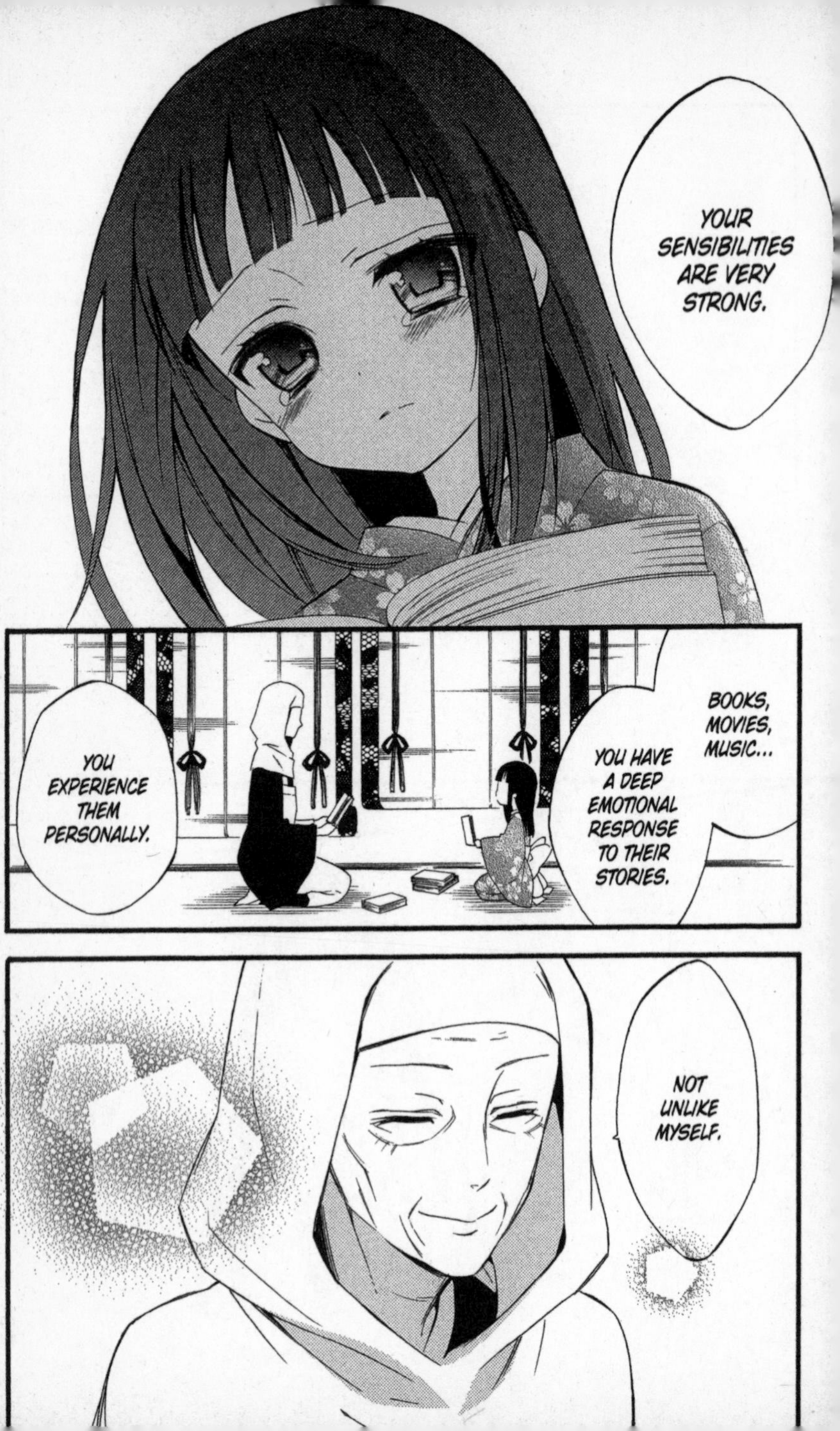
YOUR SENSIBILITIES ARE VERY STRONG.
BOOKS, MOVIES, MUSIC...
YOU HAVE A DEEP EMOTIONAL RESPONSE TO THEIR STORIES.
YOU EXPERIENCE THEM PERSONALLY.
NOT UNLIKE MYSELF.

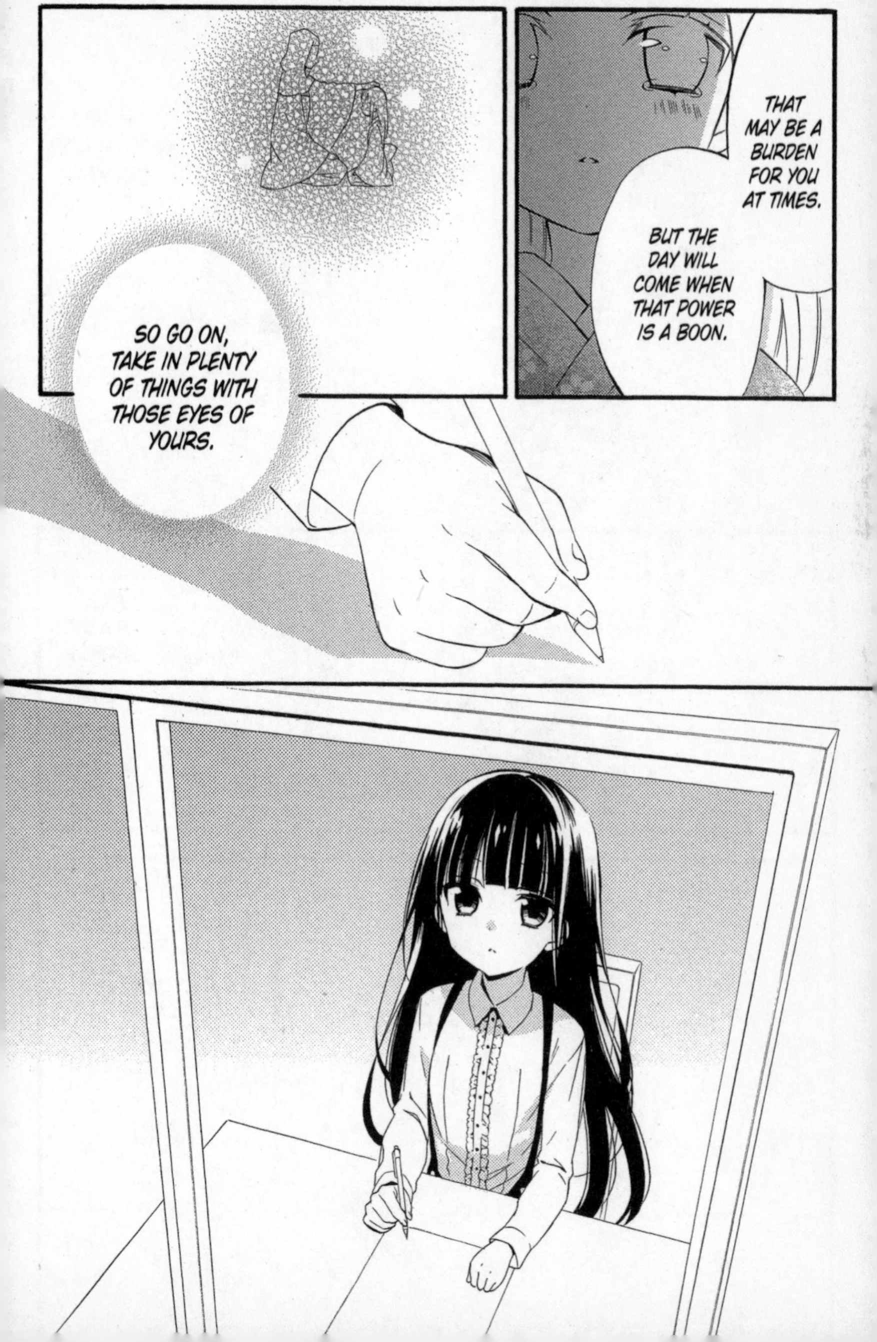
THAT MAY BE A BURDEN FOR YOU AT TIMES.
BUT THE DAY WILL COME WHEN THAT POWER IS A BOON.
SO GO ON, TAKE IN PLENTY OF THINGS WITH THOSE EYES OF YOURS.

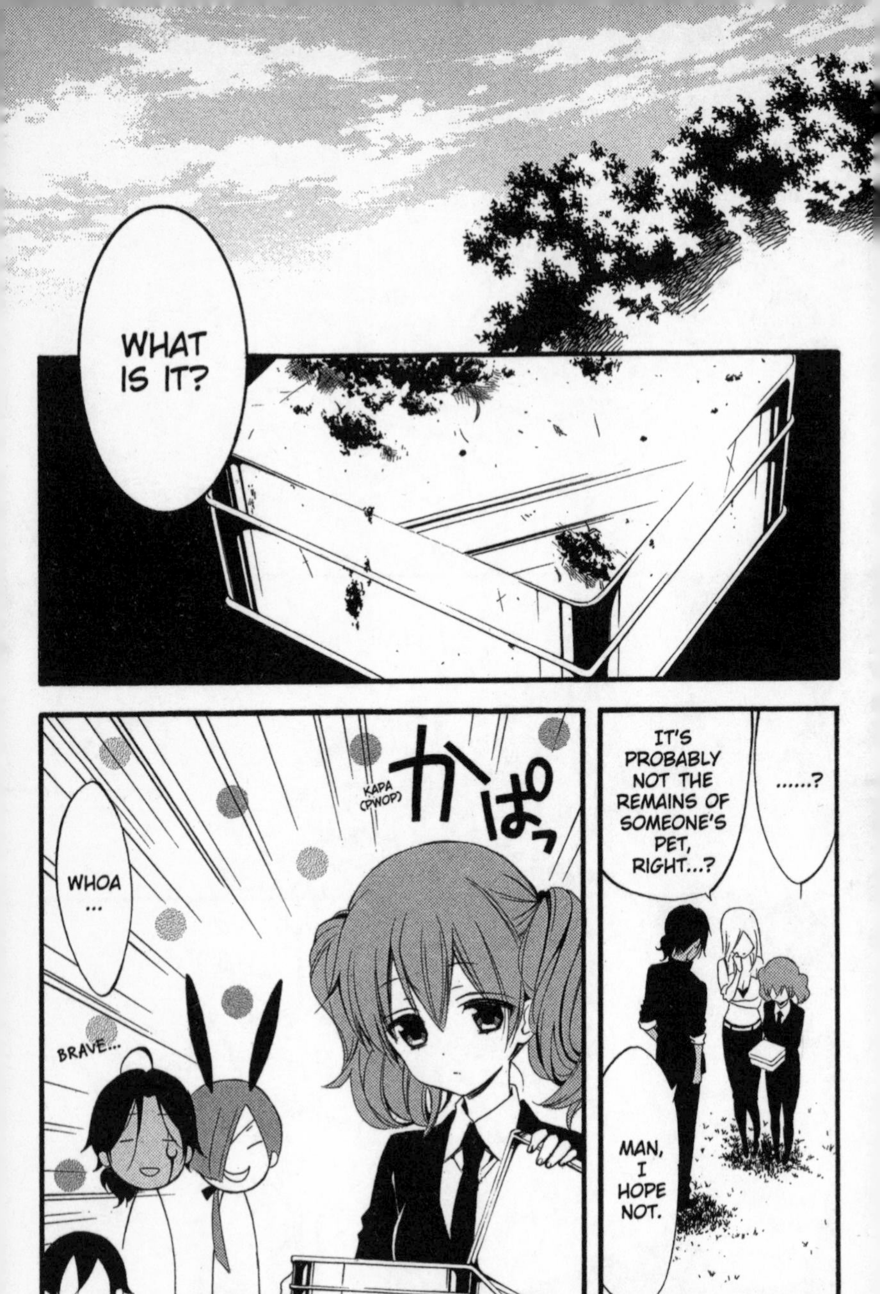
WHAT IS IT?
......?
IT'S PROBABLY NOT THE REMAINS OF SOMEONE'S PET, RIGHT...?
MAN, I HOPE NOT.
かぱっ
KAPA (PWOP)
WHOA ...
BRAVE...

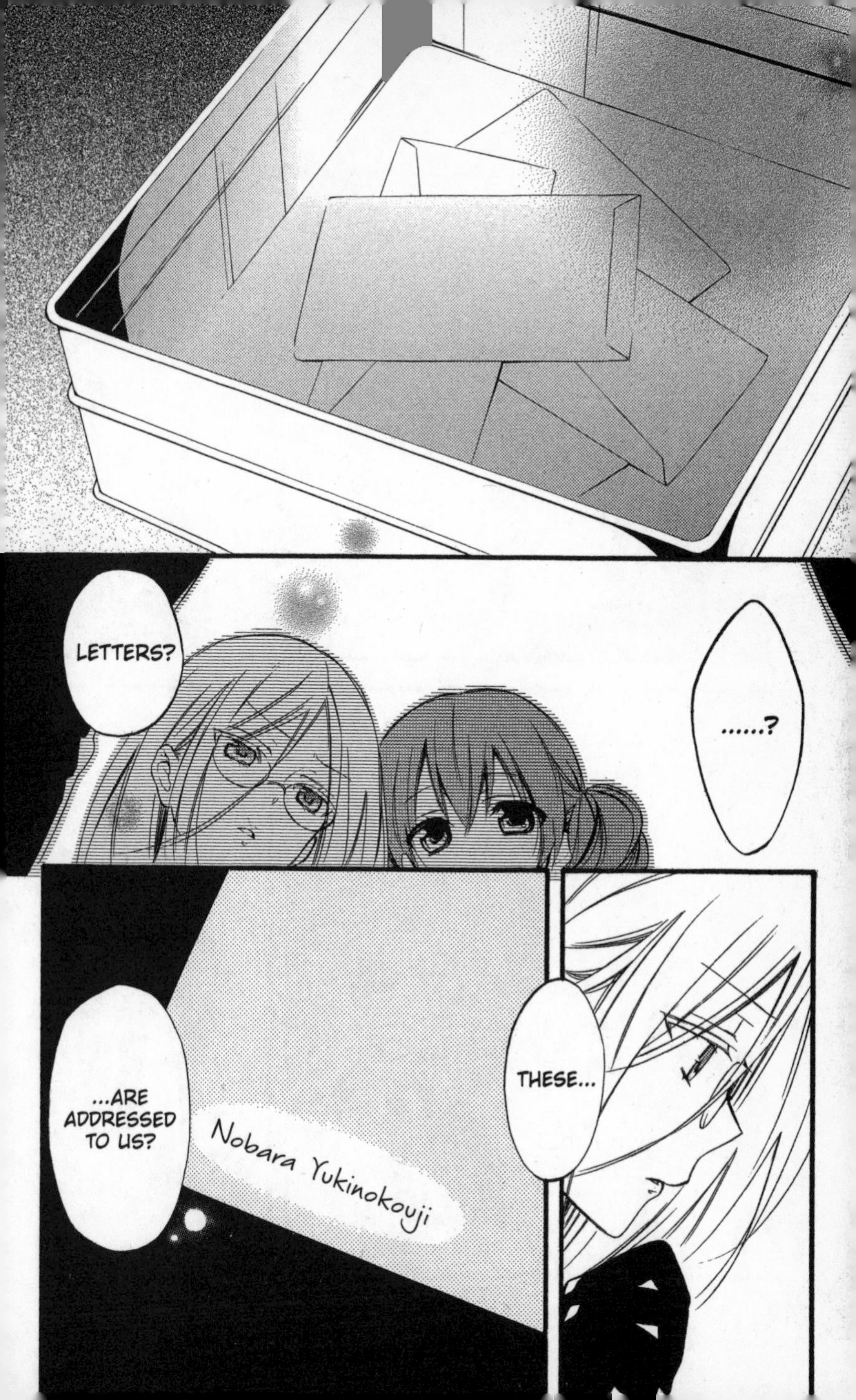
......?
LETTERS?
THESE...
...ARE ADDRESSED TO US?
Nobara Yukinokouji

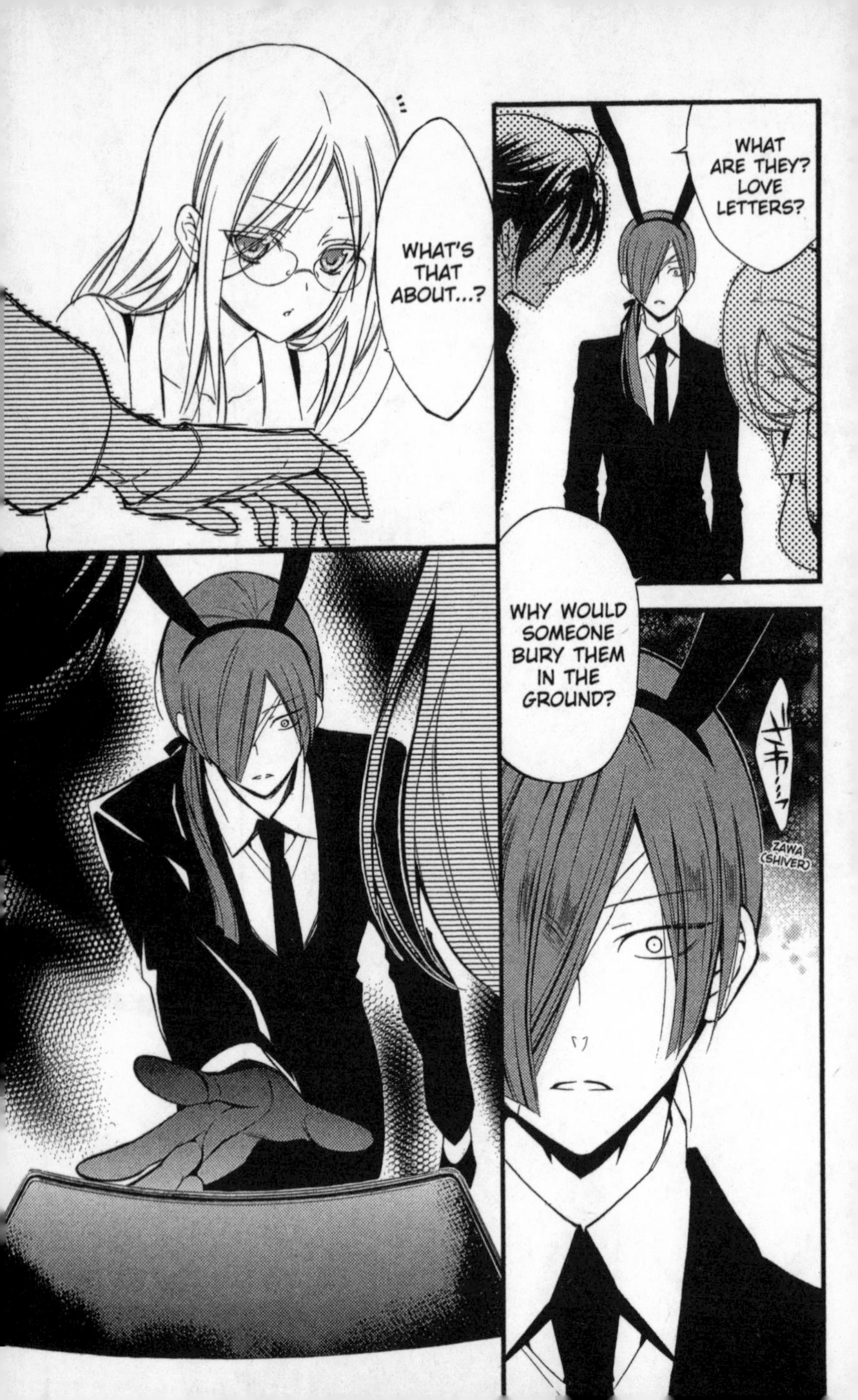
WHAT ARE THEY? LOVE LETTERS?
...
WHAT'S THAT ABOUT...?
WHY WOULD SOMEONE BURY THEM IN THE GROUND?
ZAWA (SHIVER)

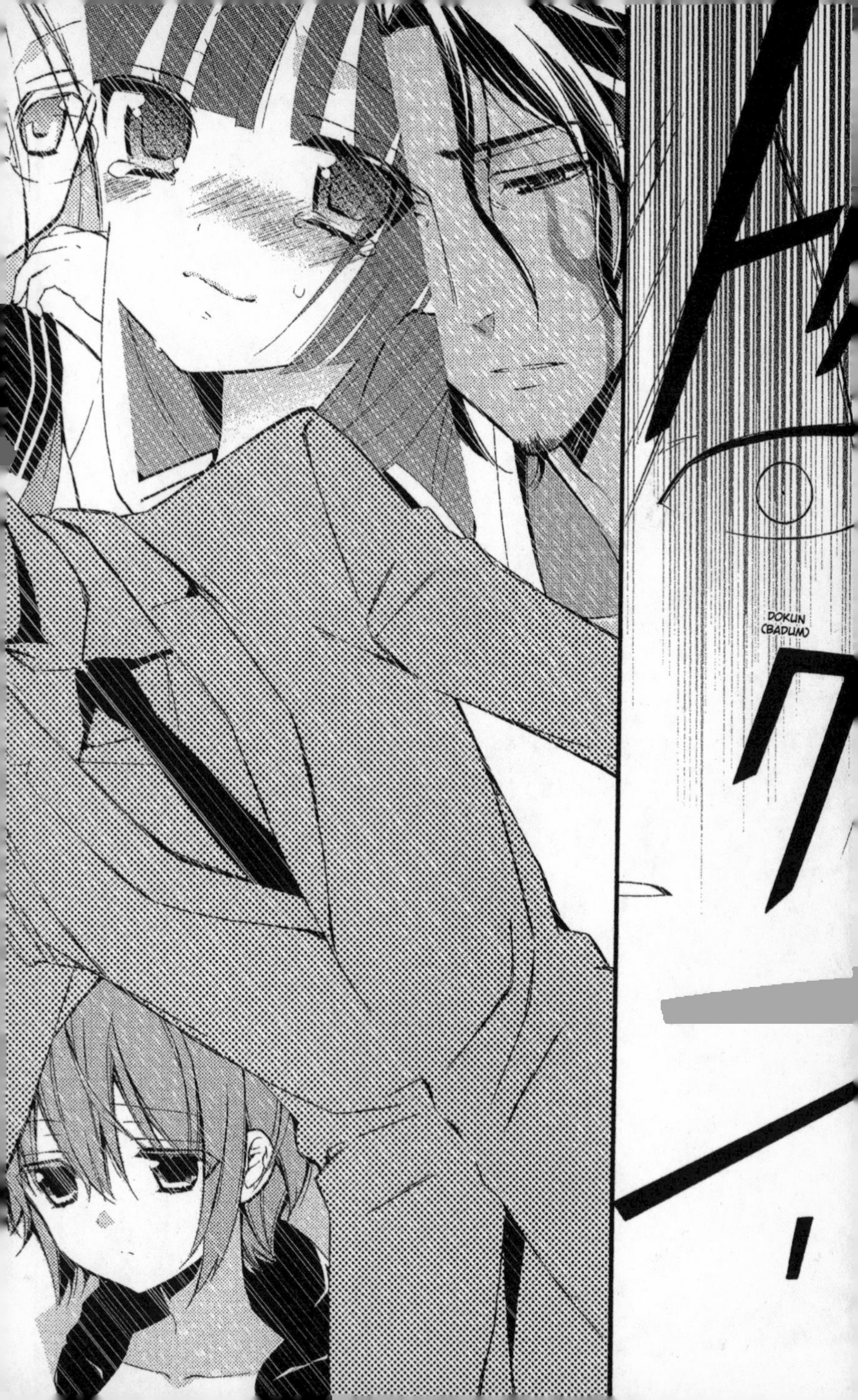
DOKUN
(BADUM)

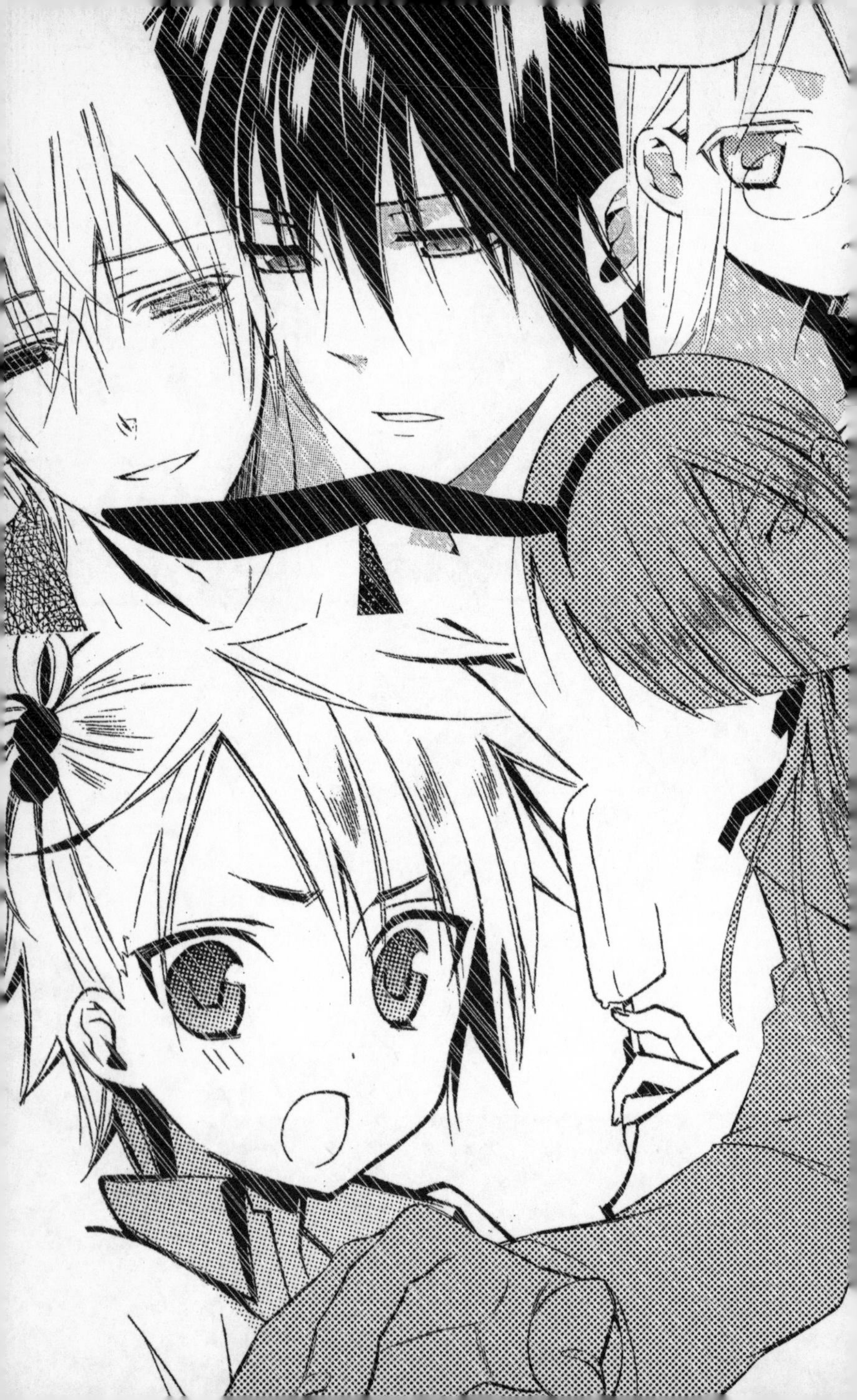

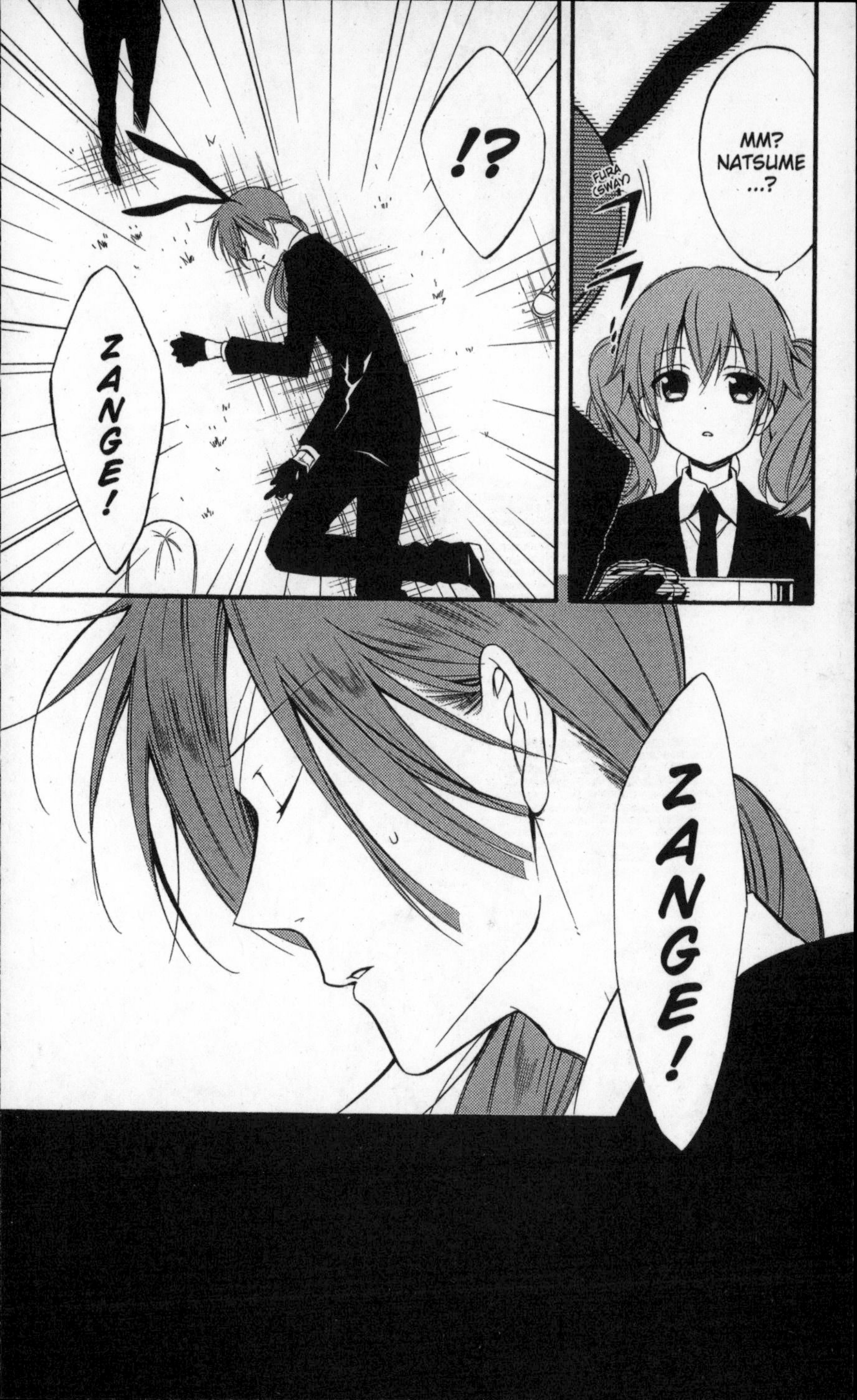
MM? NATSUME ...?
FURA (SWAY)
!?
ZANGE!
ZANGE!

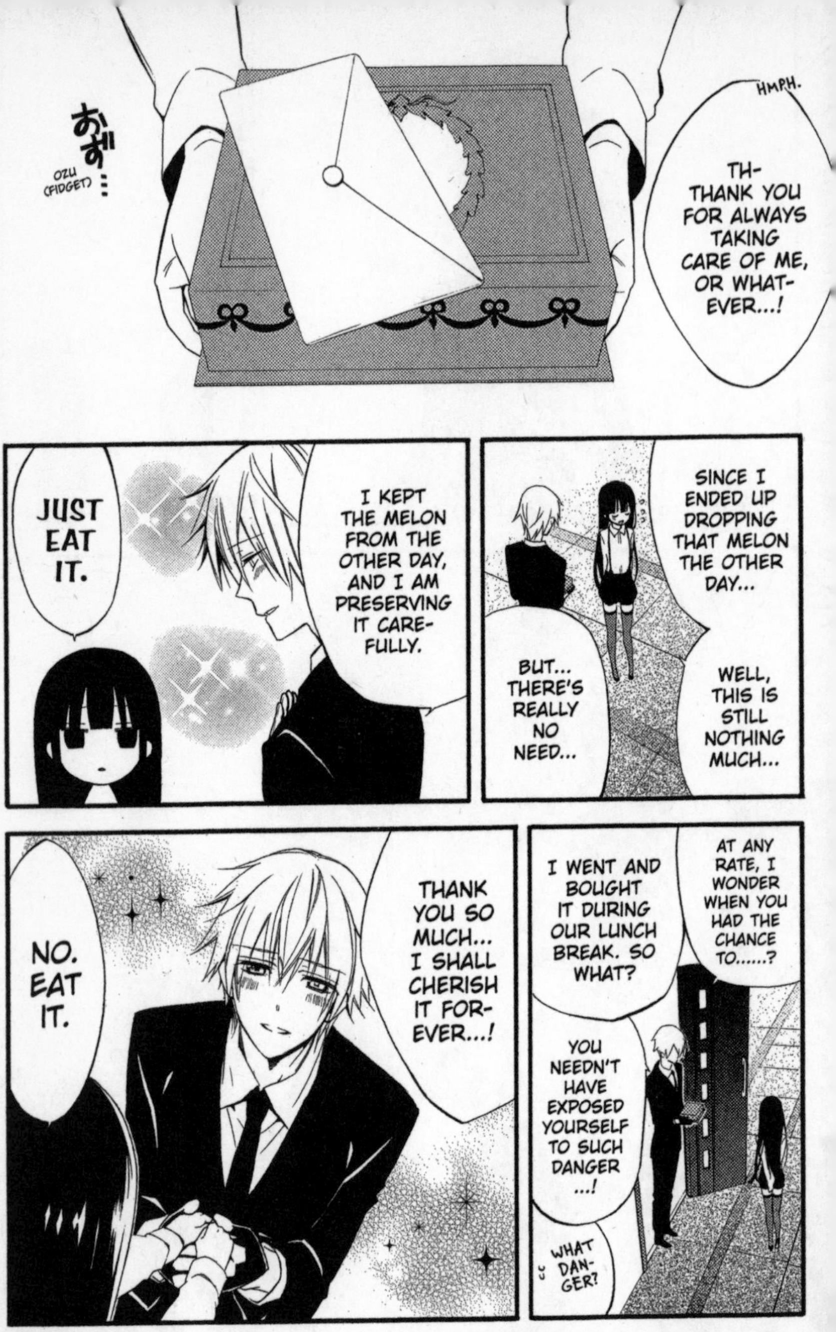
HMPH.
TH- THANK YOU FOR ALWAYS TAKING CARE OF ME, OR WHAT-EVER...!
おず…
OZU (FIDGET)
SINCE I ENDED UP DROPPING THAT MELON THE OTHER DAY...
WELL, THIS IS STILL NOTHING MUCH...
BUT... THERE'S REALLY NO NEED...
I KEPT THE MELON FROM THE OTHER DAY, AND I AM PRESERVING IT CARE-FULLY.
JUST EAT IT.
AT ANY RATE, I WONDER WHEN YOU HAD THE CHANCE TO......?
I WENT AND BOUGHT IT DURING OUR LUNCH BREAK. SO WHAT?
YOU NEEDN'T HAVE EXPOSED YOURSELF TO SUCH DANGER...!
WHAT DAN-GER?
THANK YOU SO MUCH... I SHALL CHERISH IT FOR-EVER...!
NO. EAT IT.

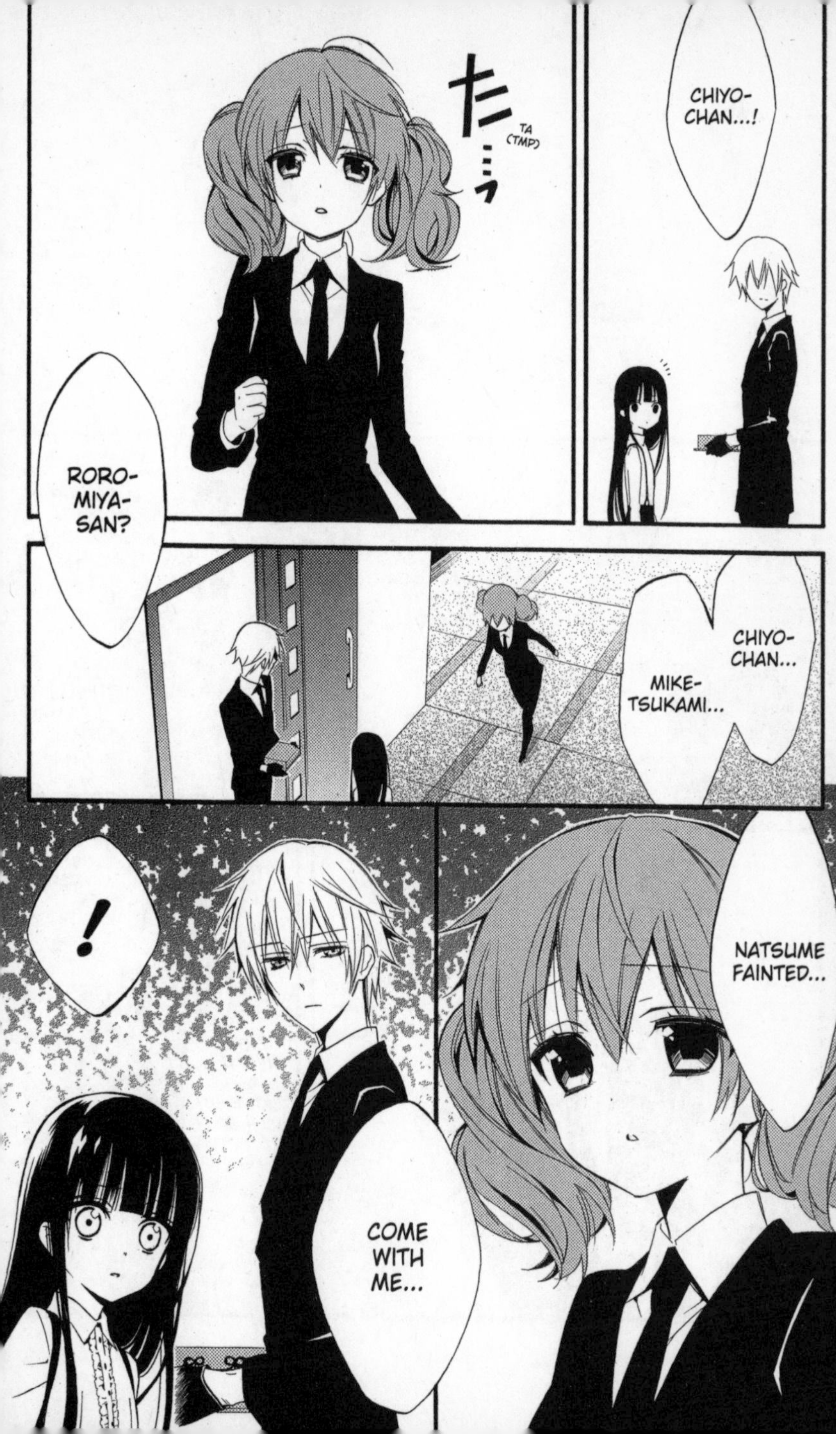
CHIYO-CHAN...!
TA (TMP)
RORO-MIYA-SAN?
CHIYO-CHAN...
MIKE-TSUKAMI...
NATSUME FAINTED...
!
COME WITH ME...

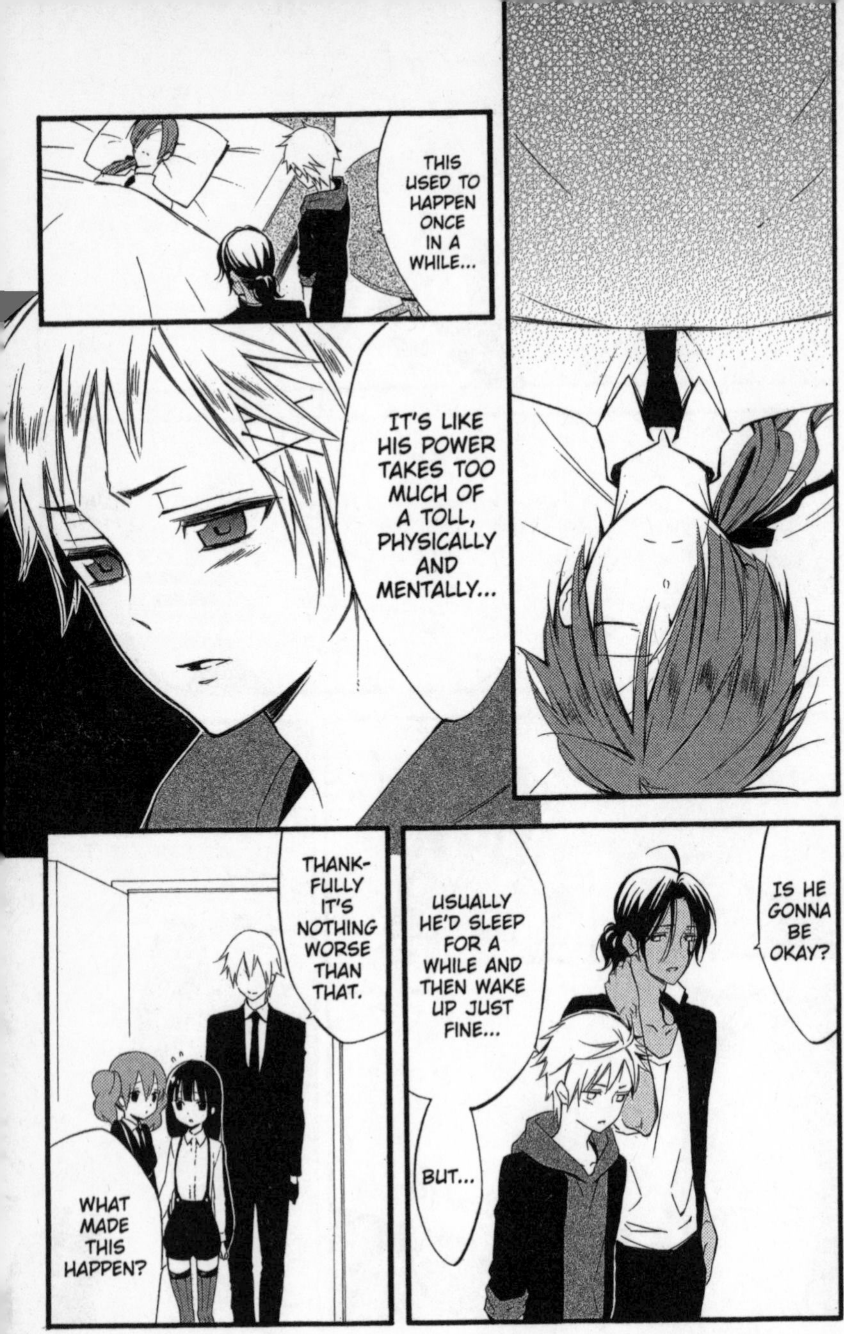
THIS USED TO HAPPEN ONCE IN A WHILE...
IT'S LIKE HIS POWER TAKES TOO MUCH OF A TOLL, PHYSICALLY AND MENTALLY...
IS HE GONNA BE OKAY?
USUALLY HE'D SLEEP FOR A WHILE AND THEN WAKE UP JUST FINE...
BUT...
THANKFULLY IT'S NOTHING WORSE THAN THAT.
WHAT MADE THIS HAPPEN?

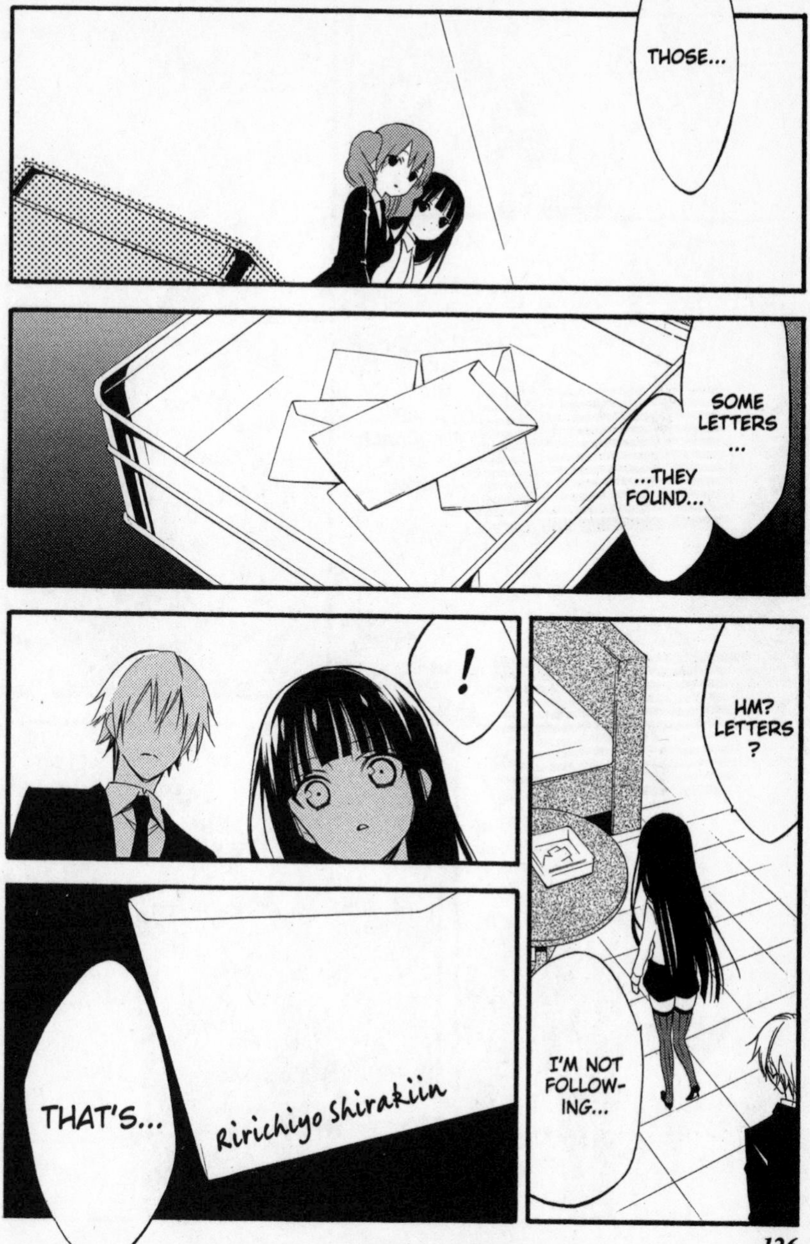
THOSE...
SOME LETTERS ...
...THEY FOUND...
HM? LETTERS ?
I'M NOT FOLLOW-ING...
!
THAT'S...
Ririchiyo Shirakiin

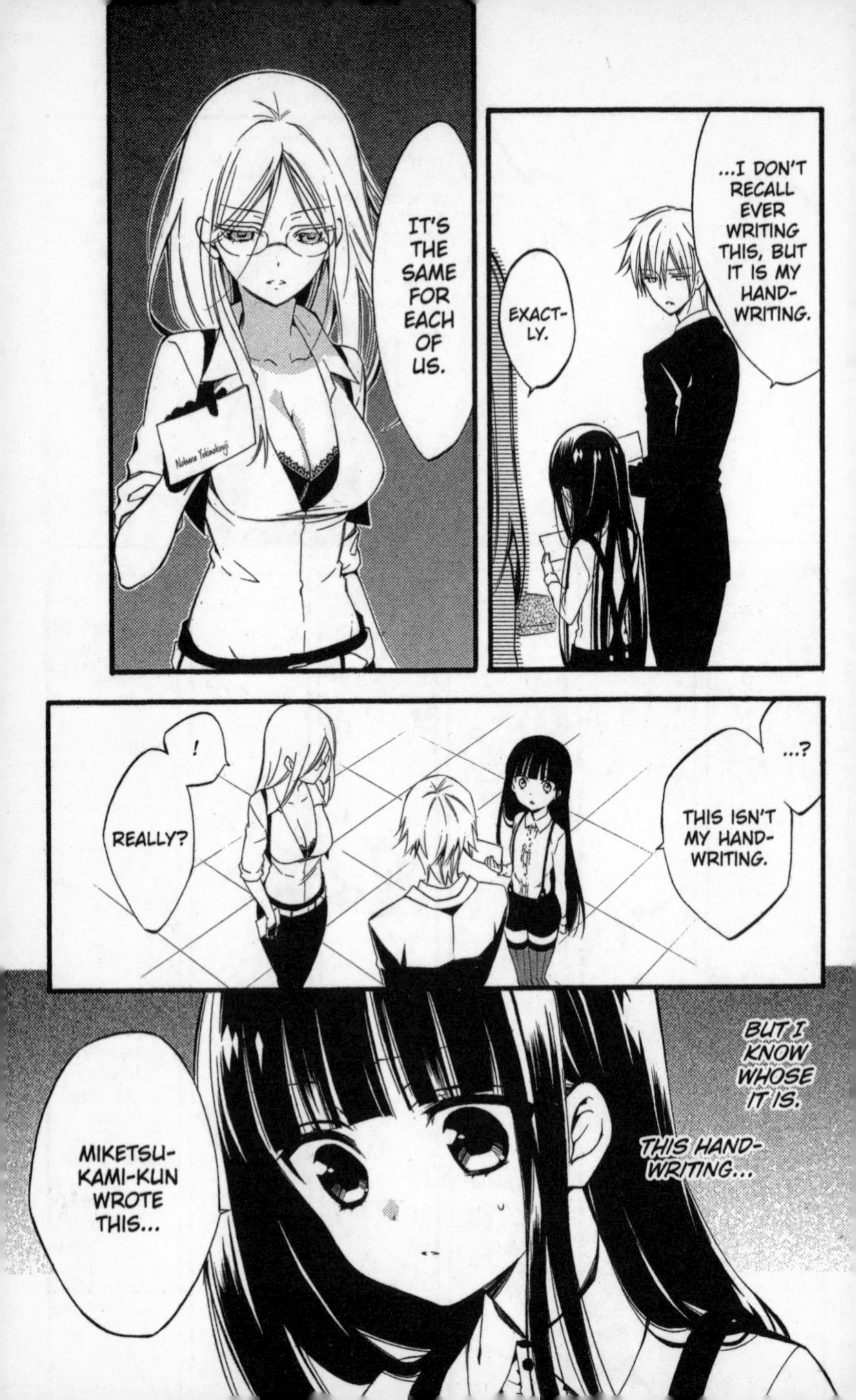
...I DON'T RECALL EVER WRITING THIS, BUT IT IS MY HAND-WRITING.
EXACTLY.
IT'S THE SAME FOR EACH OF US.
...?
THIS ISN'T MY HAND-WRITING.
!
REALLY?
BUT I KNOW WHOSE IT IS.
THIS HAND-WRITING...
MIKETSU-KAMI-KUN WROTE THIS...

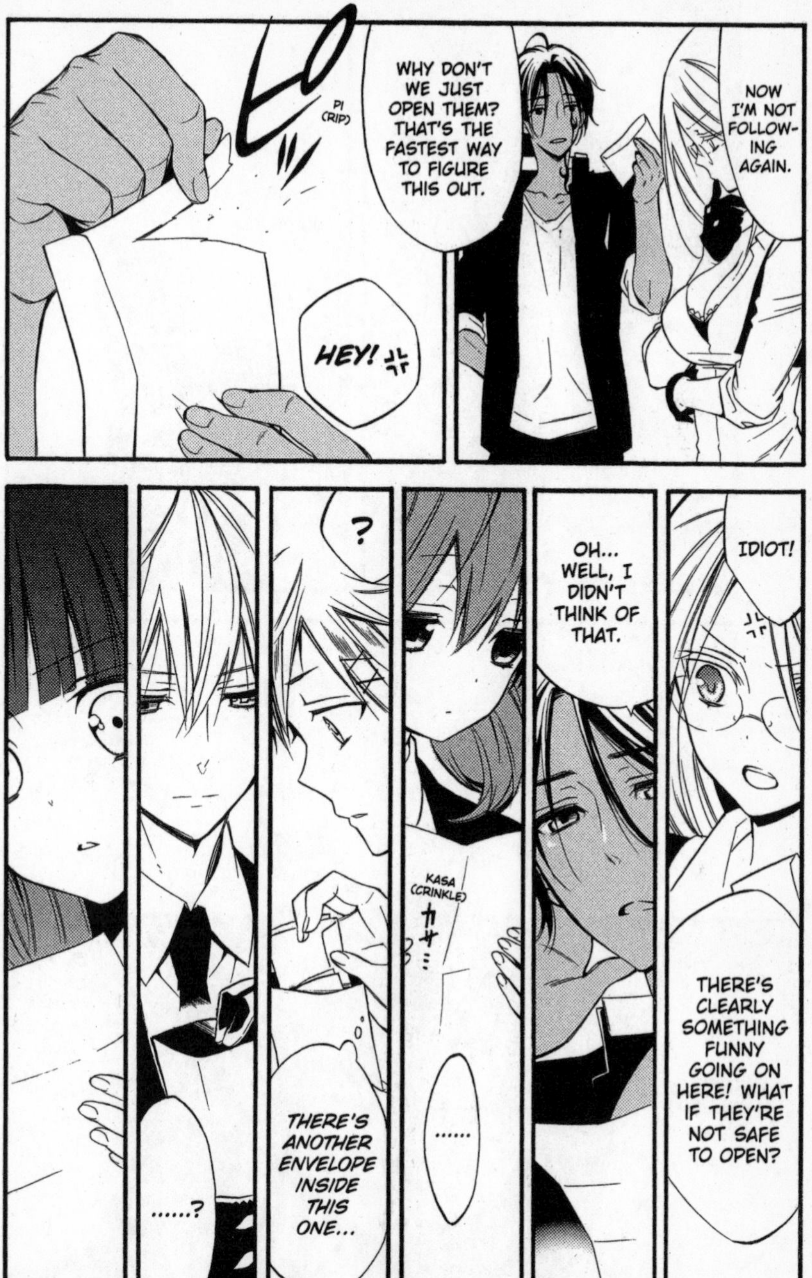
NOW I'M NOT FOLLOWING AGAIN.
WHY DON'T WE JUST OPEN THEM? THAT'S THE FASTEST WAY TO FIGURE THIS OUT.
PI (RIP)
HEY!
IDIOT!
THERE'S CLEARLY SOMETHING FUNNY GOING ON HERE! WHAT IF THEY'RE NOT SAFE TO OPEN?
OH... WELL, I DIDN'T THINK OF THAT.
KASA (CRINKLE)
......
?
THERE'S ANOTHER ENVELOPE INSIDE THIS ONE...
......?

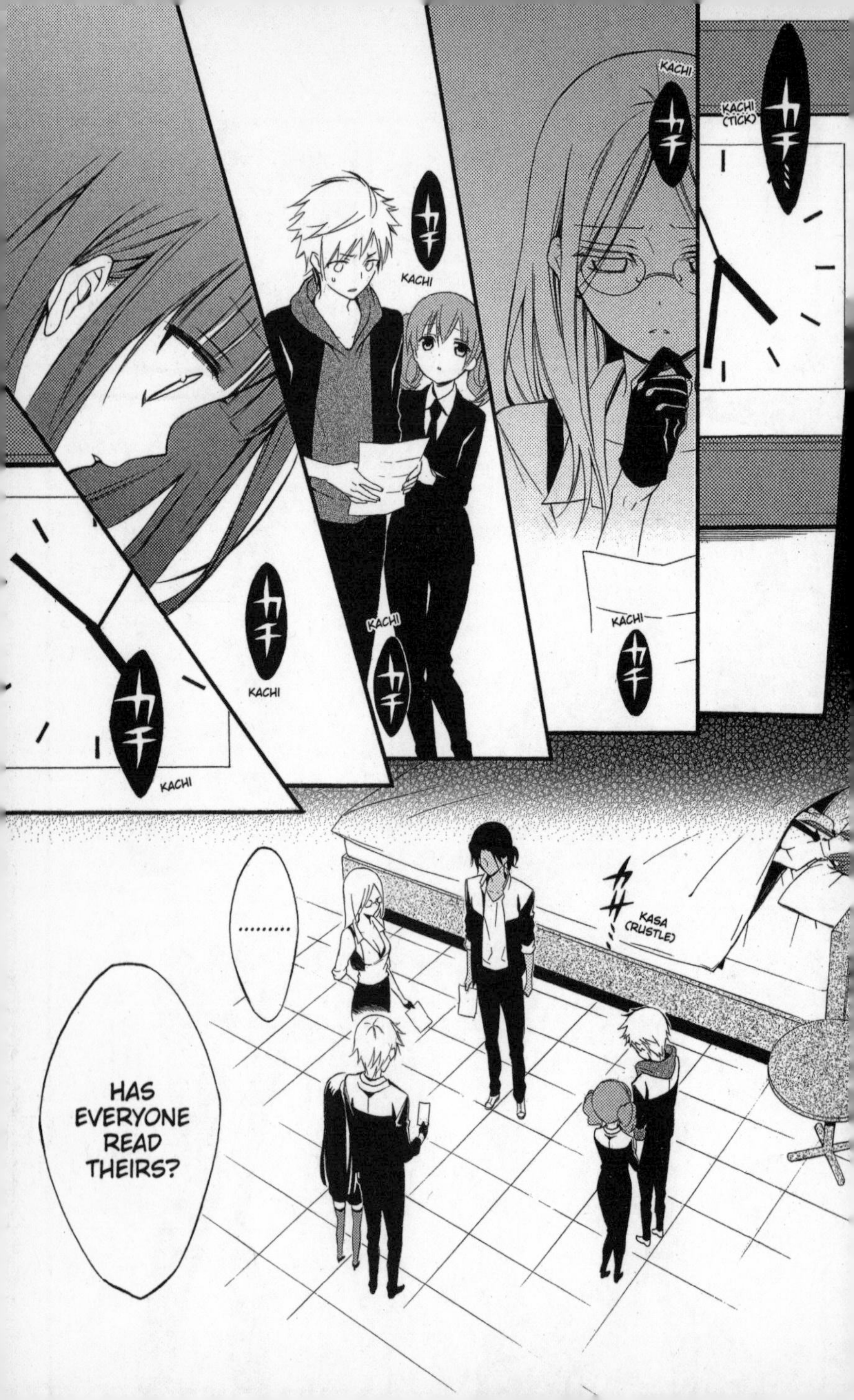
KACHI (TICK)
KACHI
KACHI
KACHI
KACHI
KACHI
KACHI
KACHI
KASA (RUSTLE)
....
HAS EVERYONE READ THEIRS?

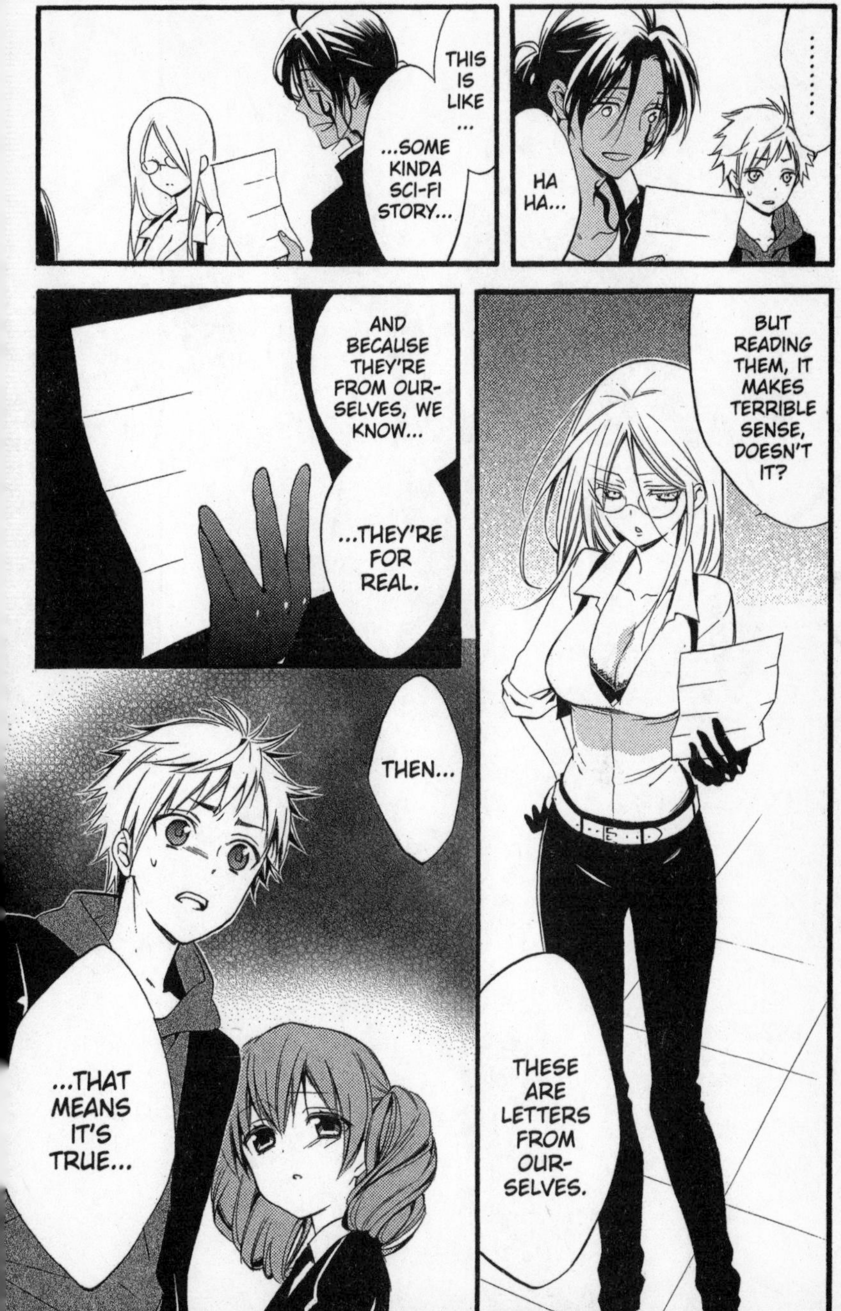
......
HA HA...
THIS IS LIKE ...
...SOME KINDA SCI-FI STORY...
BUT READING THEM, IT MAKES TERRIBLE SENSE, DOESN'T IT?
THESE ARE LETTERS FROM OURSELVES.
AND BECAUSE THEY'RE FROM OURSELVES, WE KNOW...
...THEY'RE FOR REAL.
THEN...
...THAT MEANS IT'S TRUE...

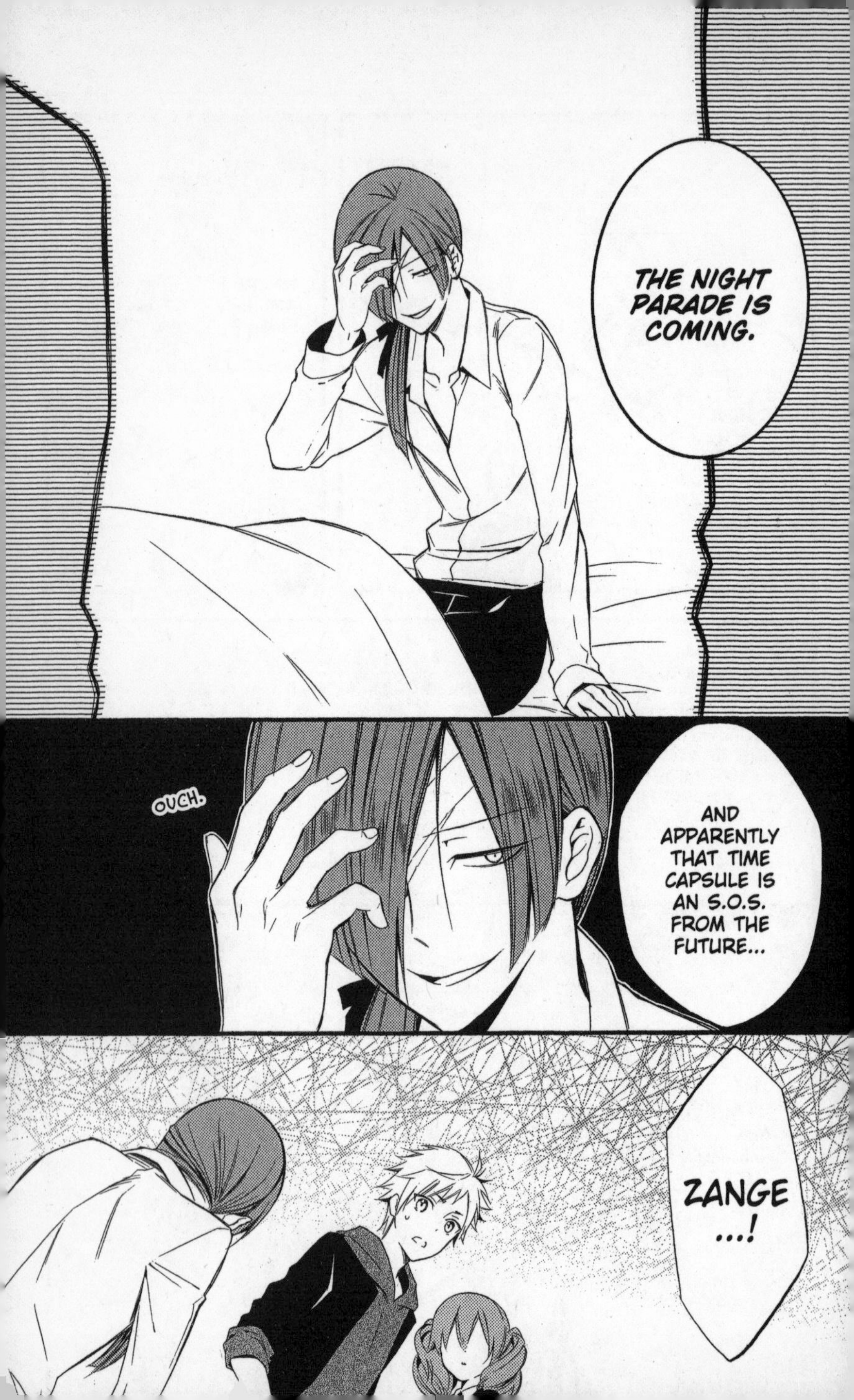
THE NIGHT PARADE IS COMING.
AND APPARENTLY THAT TIME CAPSULE IS AN S.O.S. FROM THE FUTURE...
OUCH.
ZANGE ...!

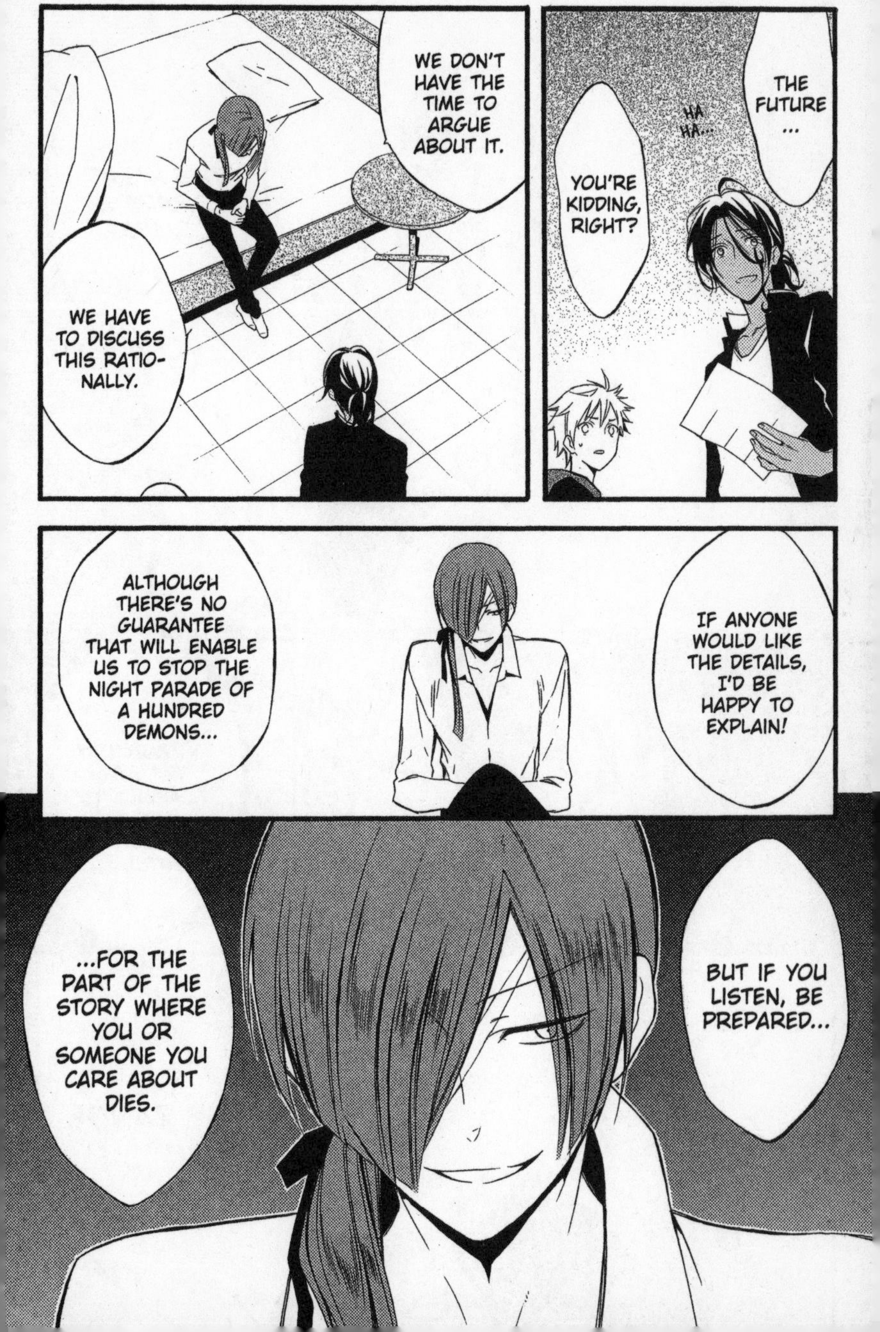
THE FUTURE ...
HA HA...
YOU'RE KIDDING, RIGHT?
WE DON'T HAVE THE TIME TO ARGUE ABOUT IT.
WE HAVE TO DISCUSS THIS RATIONALLY.
IF ANYONE WOULD LIKE THE DETAILS, I'D BE HAPPY TO EXPLAIN!
ALTHOUGH THERE'S NO GUARANTEE THAT WILL ENABLE US TO STOP THE NIGHT PARADE OF A HUNDRED DEMONS...
BUT IF YOU LISTEN, BE PREPARED...
...FOR THE PART OF THE STORY WHERE YOU OR SOMEONE YOU CARE ABOUT DIES.

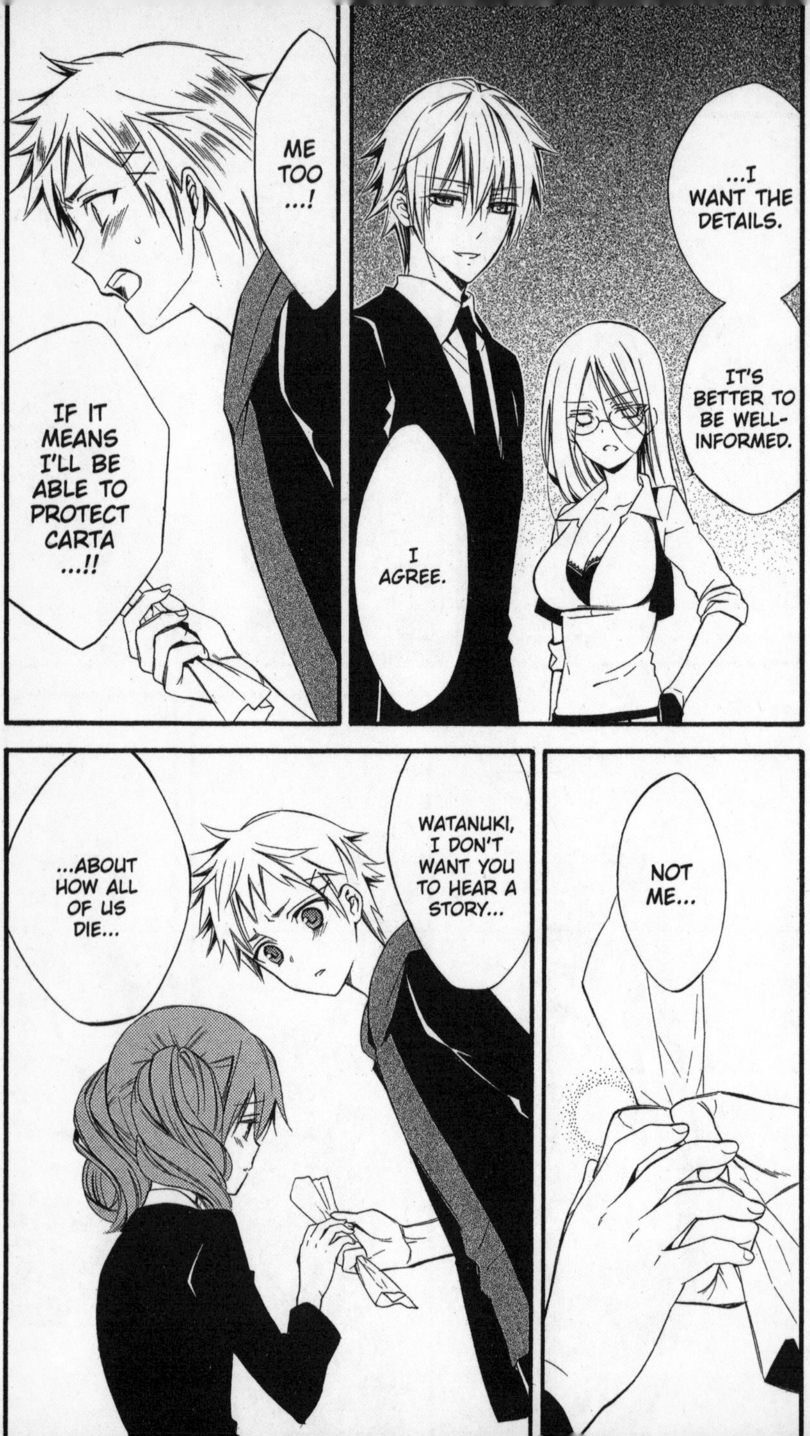
...I WANT THE DETAILS.
IT'S BETTER TO BE WELL-INFORMED.
I AGREE.
ME TOO ...!
IF IT MEANS I'LL BE ABLE TO PROTECT CARTA ...!!
NOT ME...
WATANUKI, I DON'T WANT YOU TO HEAR A STORY...
...ABOUT HOW ALL OF US DIE...

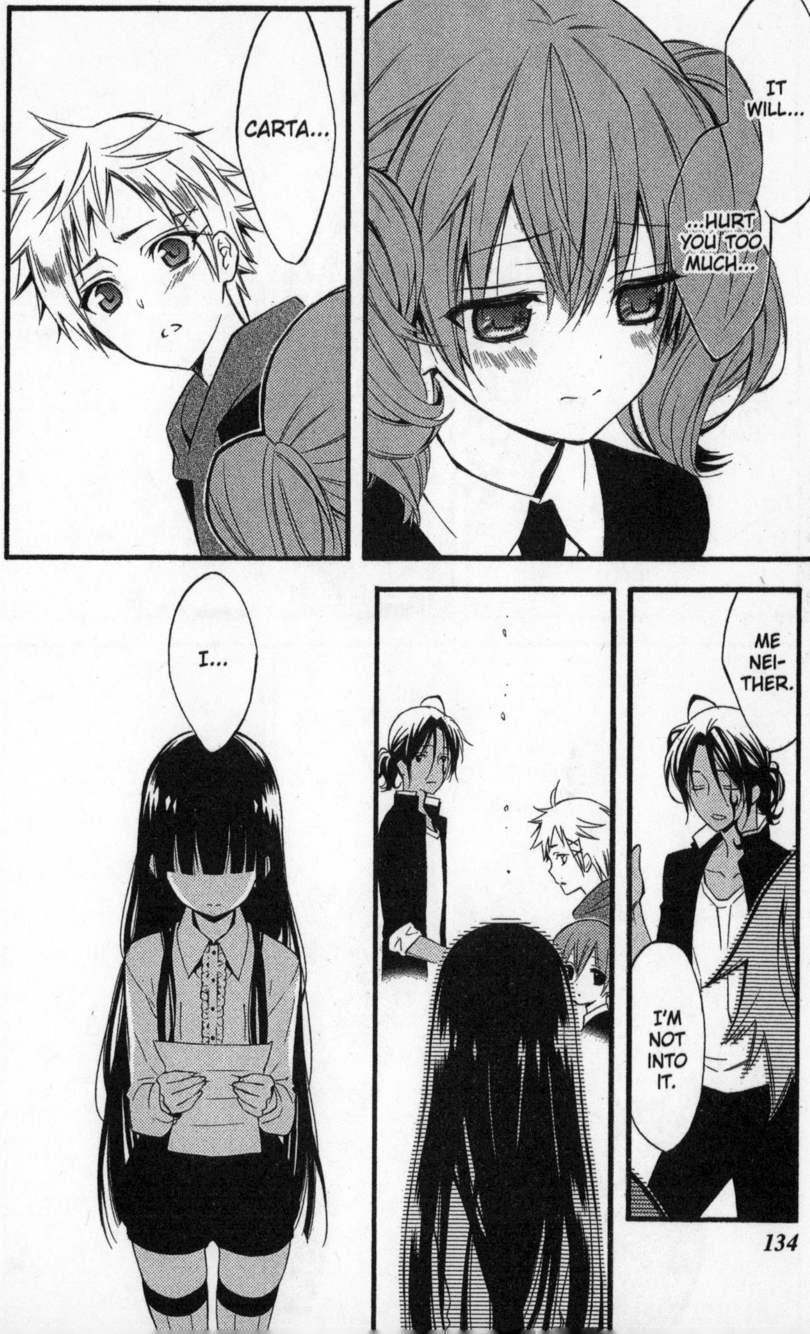
IT WILL...
...HURT YOU TOO MUCH...
CARTA...
ME NEI-THER.
I'M NOT INTO IT.
...
I...

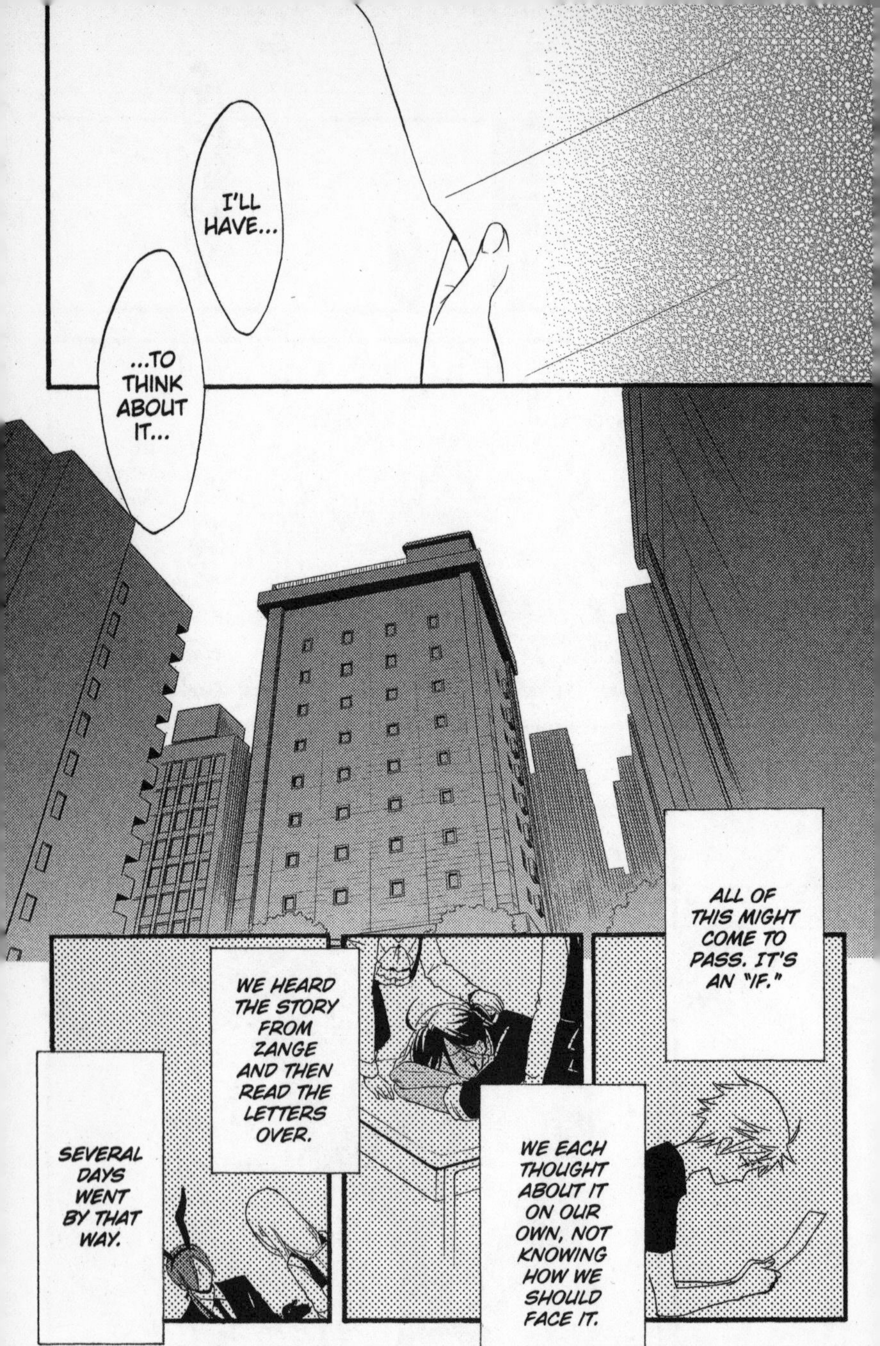
I'LL HAVE...
...TO THINK ABOUT IT...
ALL OF THIS MIGHT COME TO PASS. IT'S AN "IF."
WE EACH THOUGHT ABOUT IT ON OUR OWN, NOT KNOWING HOW WE SHOULD FACE IT.
WE HEARD THE STORY FROM ZANGE AND THEN READ THE LETTERS OVER.
SEVERAL DAYS WENT BY THAT WAY.

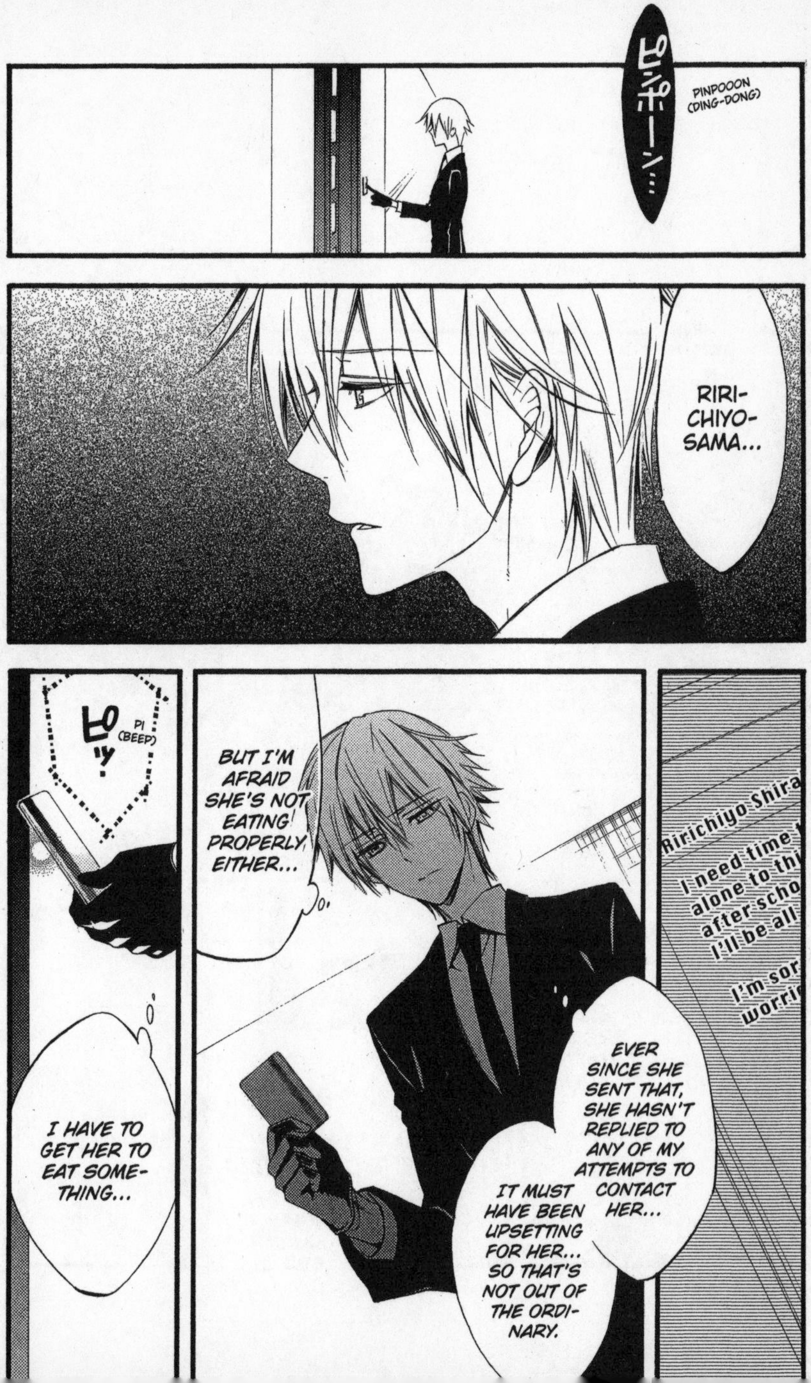
ピンポーン…
PINPOOON (DING-DONG)
RIRI-CHIYO-SAMA...
Ririchiyo Shira
I need time
alone to th
after scho
I'll be all
I'm sor
worri
EVER SINCE SHE SENT THAT, SHE HASN'T REPLIED TO ANY OF MY ATTEMPTS TO CONTACT HER...
IT MUST HAVE BEEN UPSETTING FOR HER... SO THAT'S NOT OUT OF THE ORDINARY.
BUT I'M AFRAID SHE'S NOT EATING PROPERLY EITHER...
ピッ
PI (BEEP)
I HAVE TO GET HER TO EAT SOME-THING...

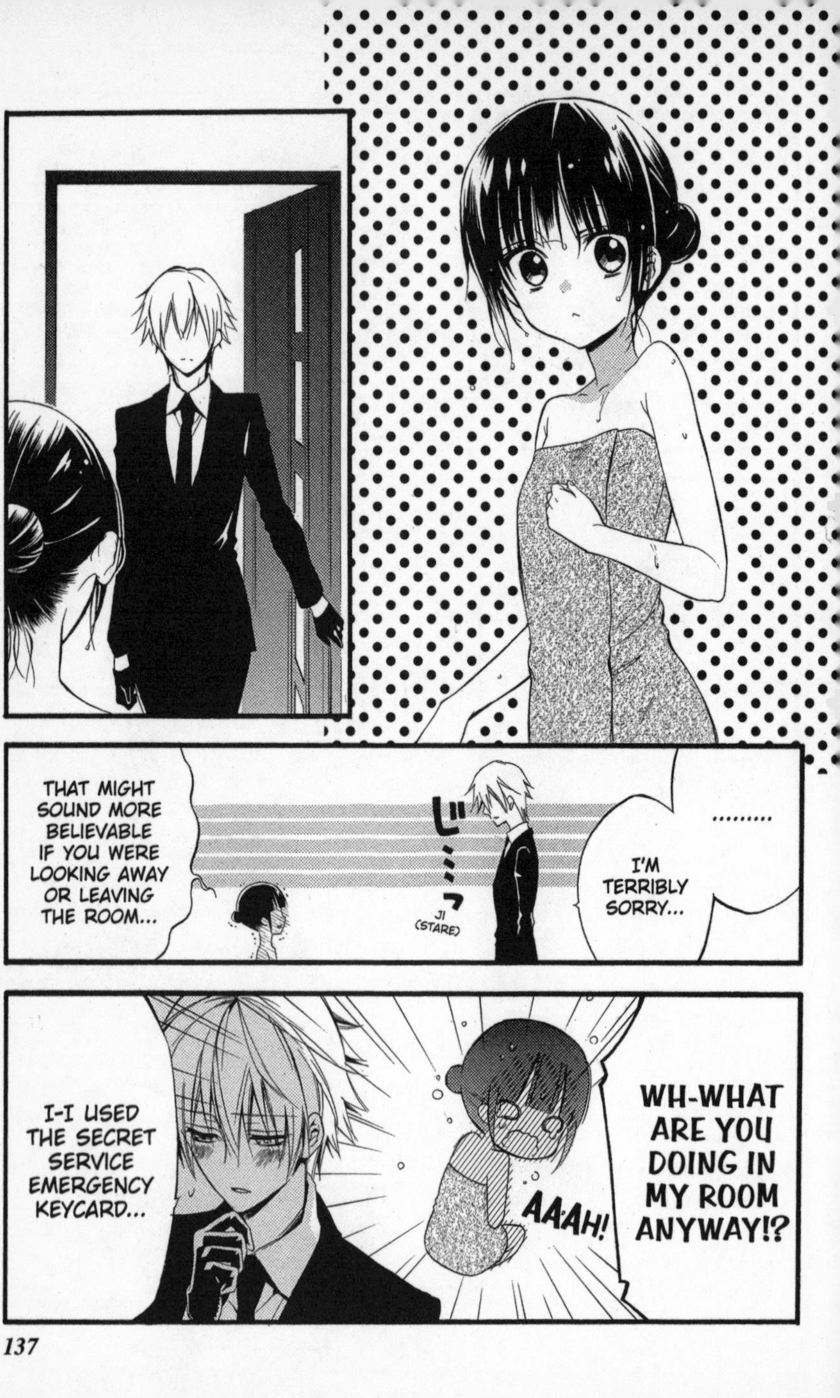
....
I'M TERRIBLY SORRY...
JI (STARE)
THAT MIGHT SOUND MORE BELIEVABLE IF YOU WERE LOOKING AWAY OR LEAVING THE ROOM...
WH-WHAT ARE YOU DOING IN MY ROOM ANYWAY!?
AAAH!
I-I USED THE SECRET SERVICE EMERGENCY KEYCARD...

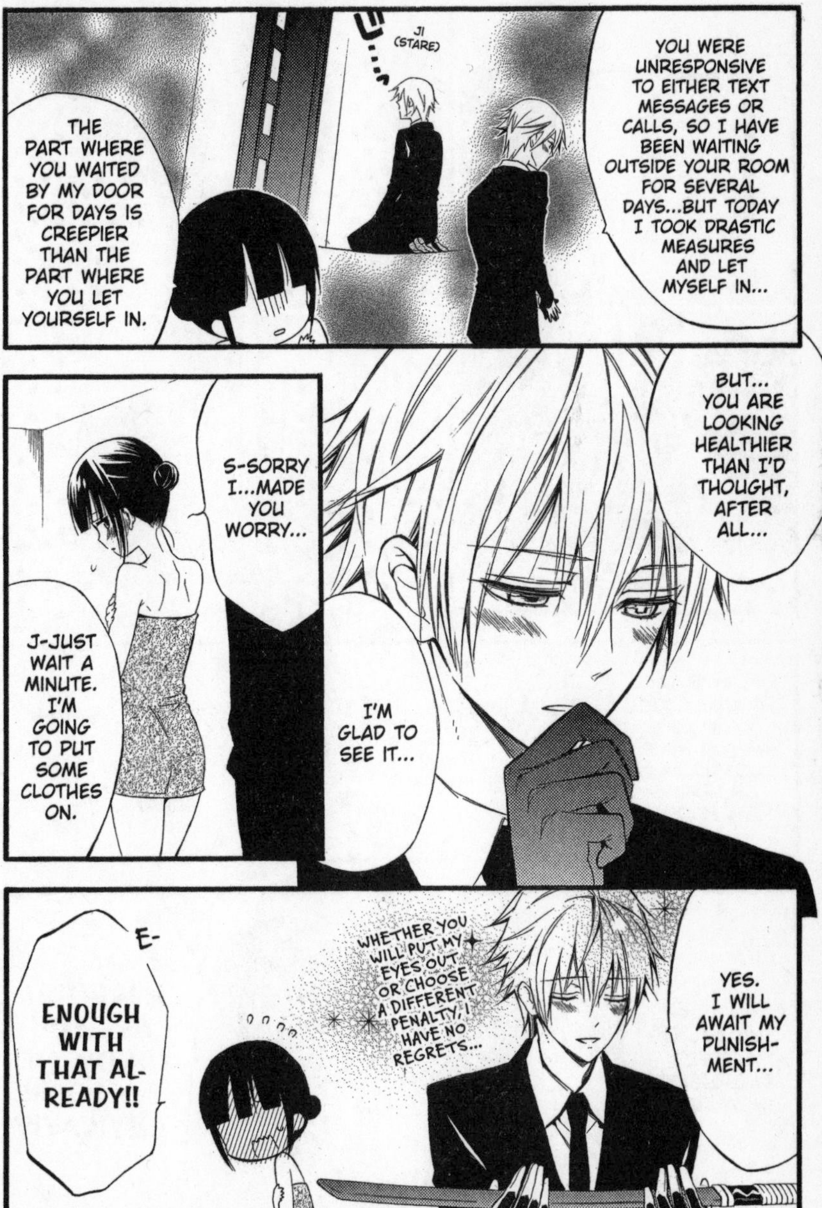
YOU WERE UNRESPONSIVE TO EITHER TEXT MESSAGES OR CALLS, SO I HAVE BEEN WAITING OUTSIDE YOUR ROOM FOR SEVERAL DAYS...BUT TODAY I TOOK DRASTIC MEASURES AND LET MYSELF IN...
JI (STARE)
THE PART WHERE YOU WAITED BY MY DOOR FOR DAYS IS CREEPIER THAN THE PART WHERE YOU LET YOURSELF IN.
BUT... YOU ARE LOOKING HEALTHIER THAN I'D THOUGHT, AFTER ALL...
I'M GLAD TO SEE IT...
S-SORRY I...MADE YOU WORRY...
J-JUST WAIT A MINUTE. I'M GOING TO PUT SOME CLOTHES ON.
YES. I WILL AWAIT MY PUNISHMENT...
WHETHER YOU WILL PUT MY EYES OUT OR CHOOSE A DIFFERENT PENALTY, I HAVE NO REGRETS...
E-
ENOUGH WITH THAT AL-READY!!

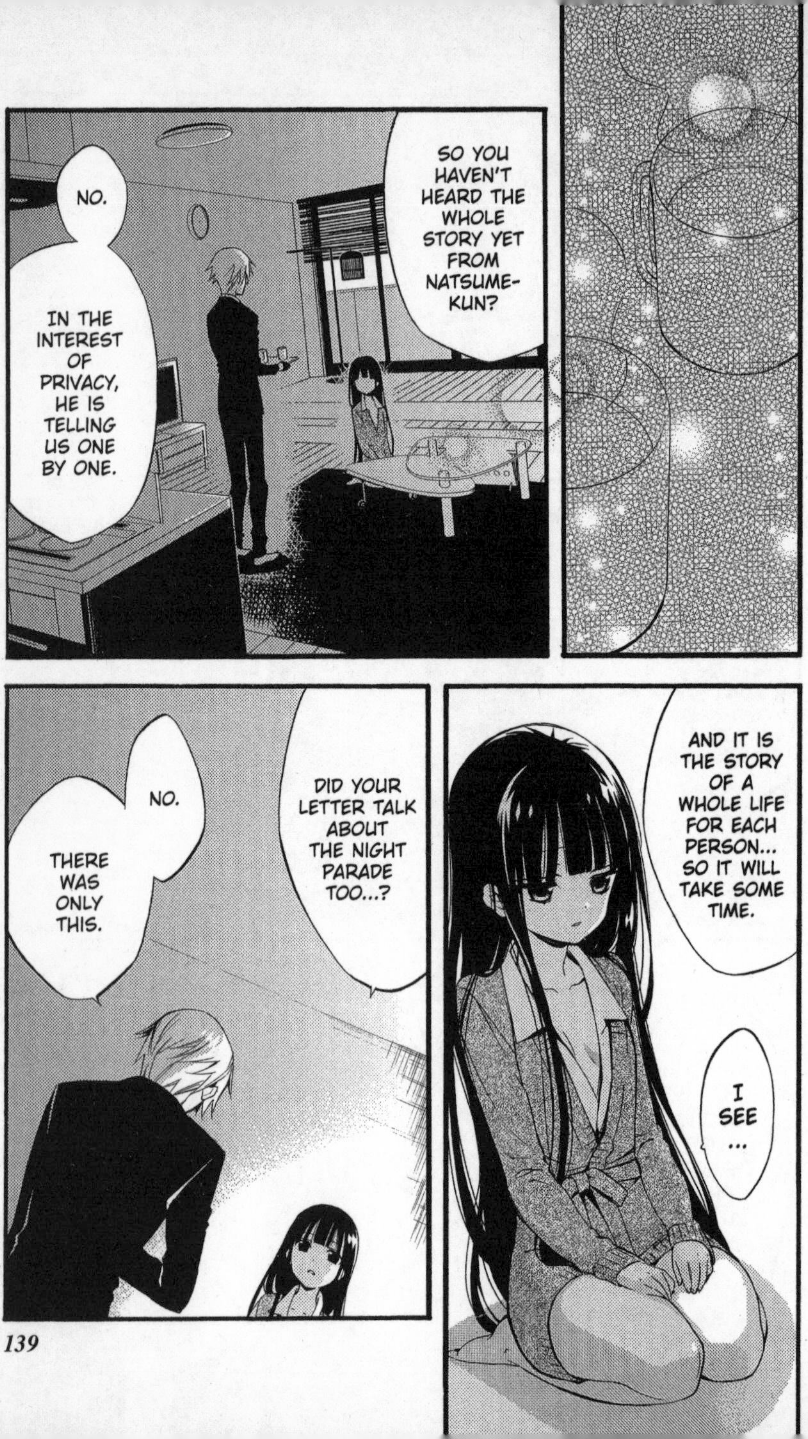
SO YOU HAVEN'T HEARD THE WHOLE STORY YET FROM NATSUME-KUN?
NO.
IN THE INTEREST OF PRIVACY, HE IS TELLING US ONE BY ONE.
AND IT IS THE STORY OF A WHOLE LIFE FOR EACH PERSON... SO IT WILL TAKE SOME TIME.
I SEE...
DID YOUR LETTER TALK ABOUT THE NIGHT PARADE TOO...?
NO.
THERE WAS ONLY THIS.

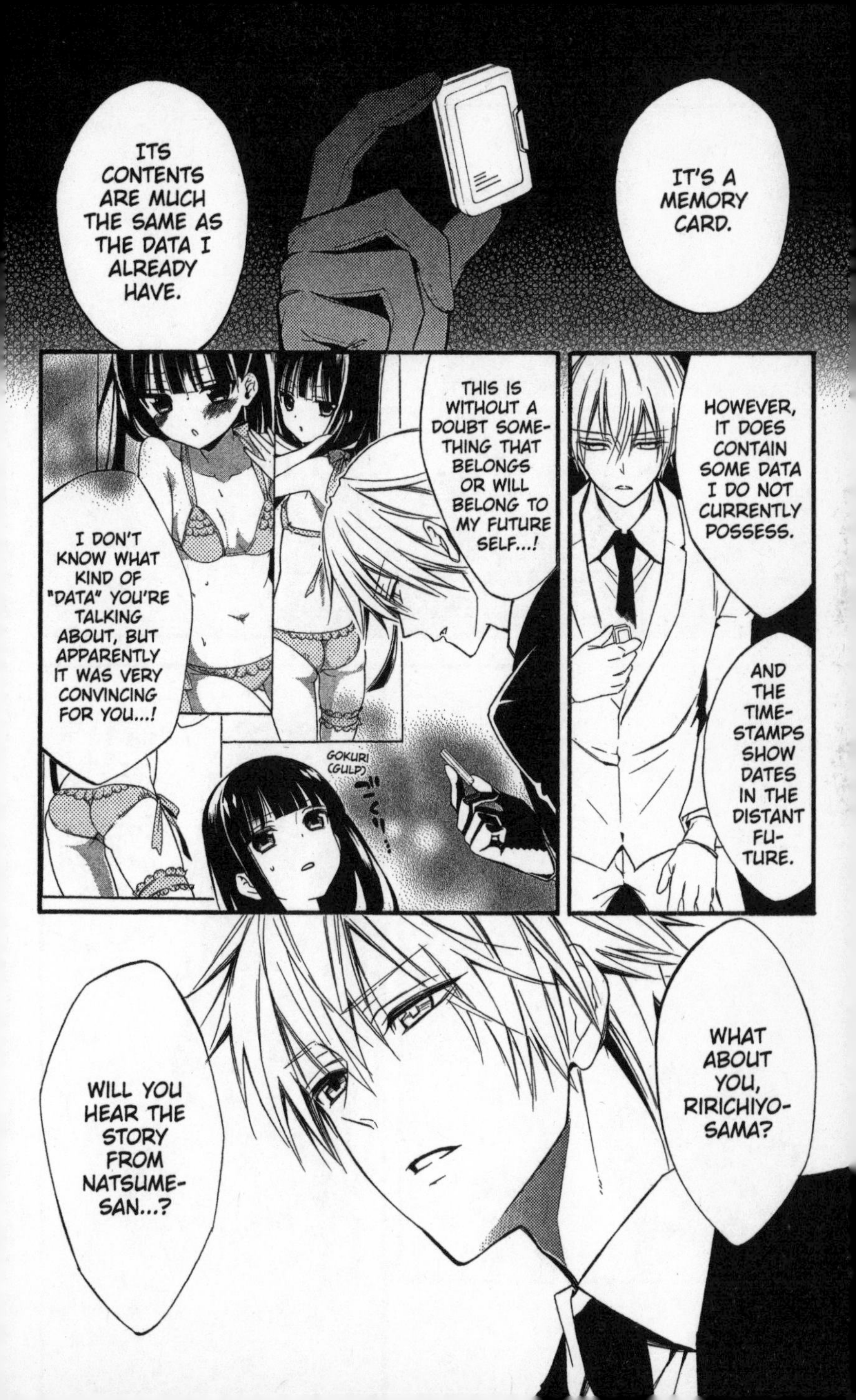
IT'S A MEMORY CARD.
ITS CONTENTS ARE MUCH THE SAME AS THE DATA I ALREADY HAVE.
HOWEVER, IT DOES CONTAIN SOME DATA I DO NOT CURRENTLY POSSESS.
AND THE TIME-STAMPS SHOW DATES IN THE DISTANT FUTURE.
THIS IS WITHOUT A DOUBT SOMETHING THAT BELONGS OR WILL BELONG TO MY FUTURE SELF...!
I DON'T KNOW WHAT KIND OF "DATA" YOU'RE TALKING ABOUT, BUT APPARENTLY IT WAS VERY CONVINCING FOR YOU...!
GOKURI (GULP)
WHAT ABOUT YOU, RIRICHIYO-SAMA?
WILL YOU HEAR THE STORY FROM NATSUME-SAN...?

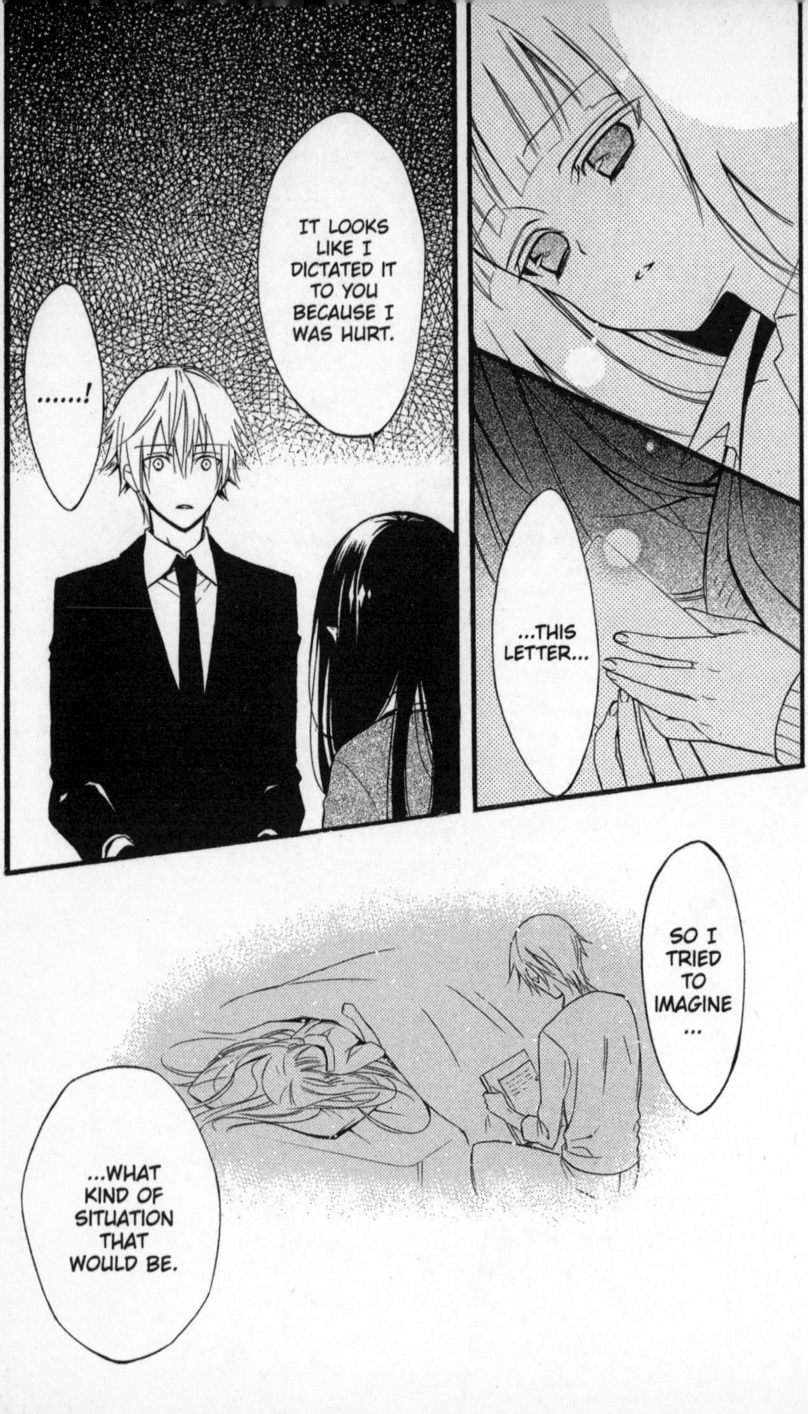
...THIS LETTER...
IT LOOKS LIKE I DICTATED IT TO YOU BECAUSE I WAS HURT.
......!
SO I TRIED TO IMAGINE ...
...WHAT KIND OF SITUATION THAT WOULD BE.

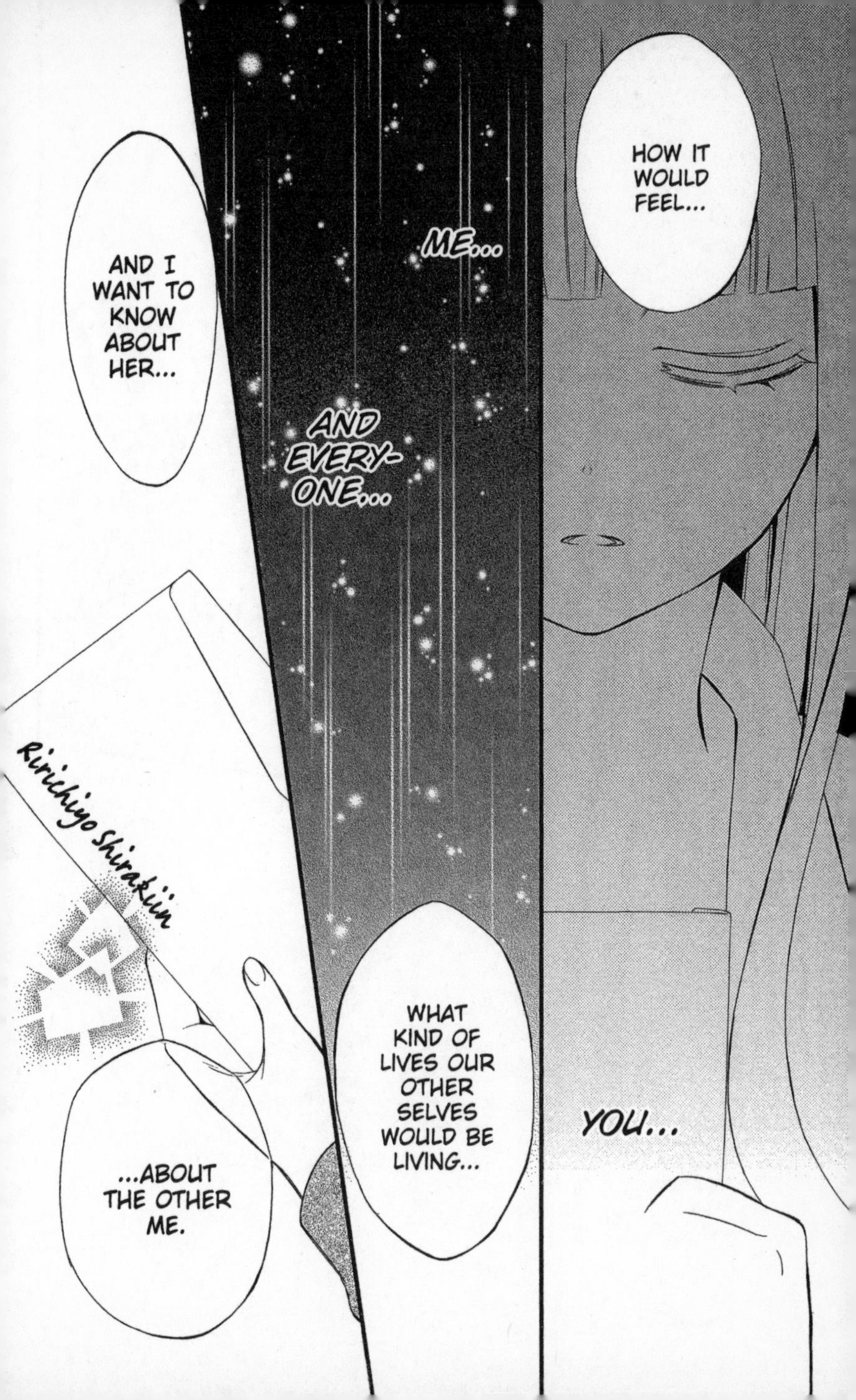
HOW IT WOULD FEEL...
YOU...
ME...
AND EVERY-ONE...
WHAT KIND OF LIVES OUR OTHER SELVES WOULD BE LIVING...
AND I WANT TO KNOW ABOUT HER...
Ririchiyo Shirakiin
...ABOUT THE OTHER ME.

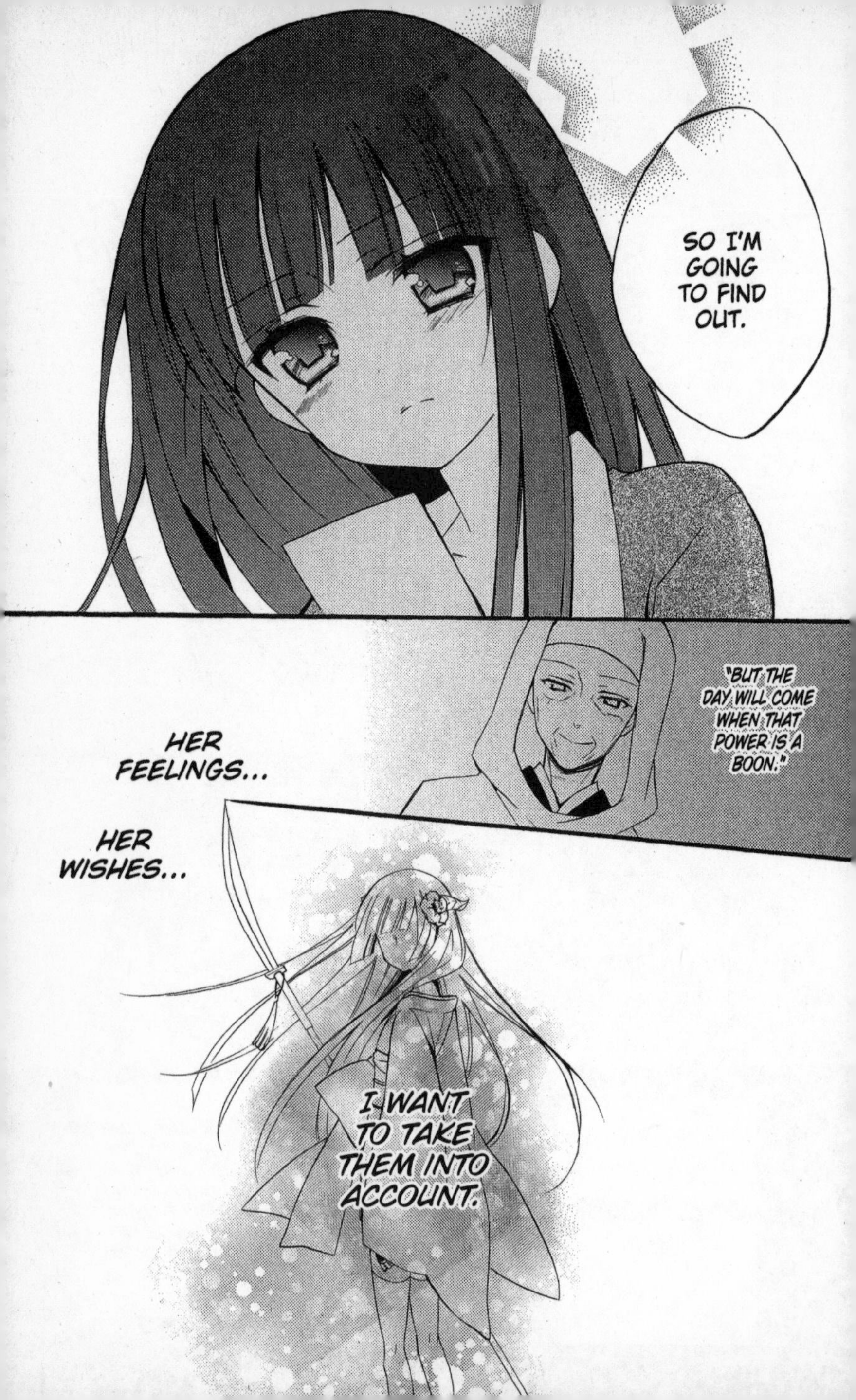
SO I'M GOING TO FIND OUT.
"BUT THE DAY WILL COME WHEN THAT POWER IS A BOON."
HER FEELINGS...
HER WISHES...
I WANT TO TAKE THEM INTO ACCOUNT.

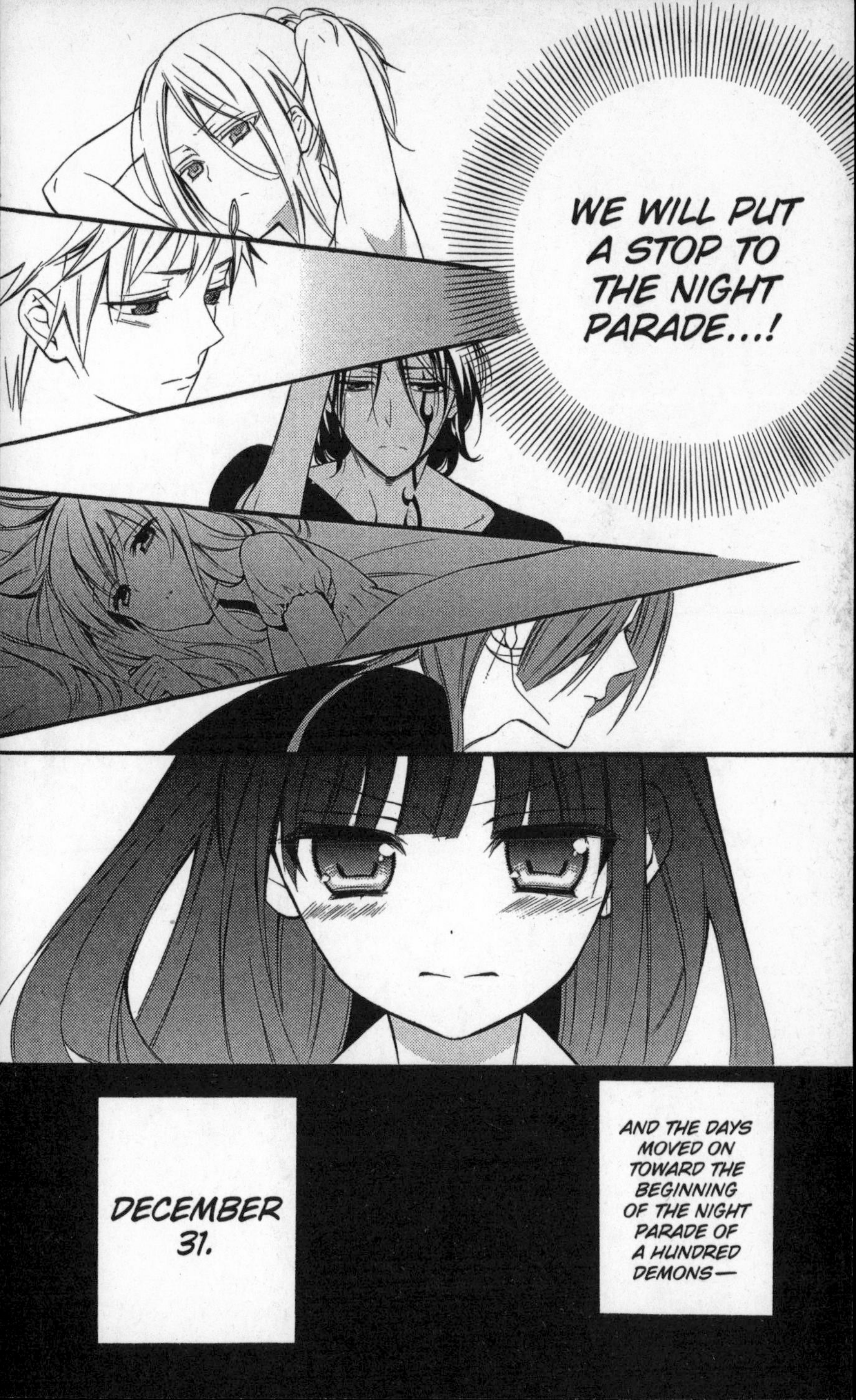
WE WILL PUT A STOP TO THE NIGHT PARADE...!
AND THE DAYS MOVED ON TOWARD THE BEGINNING OF THE NIGHT PARADE OF A HUNDRED DEMONS—
DECEMBER 31.

INU╳BOKU SS

THE FINAL ARC:
"AWAKENING TO SPRING"

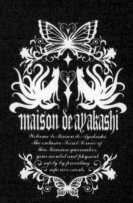

maison de ayakashi

Welcome to Maison de Ayakashi.
The exclusive Secret Service of
this Mansion guarantees
your mental and physical
safety by providing
superior escorts.

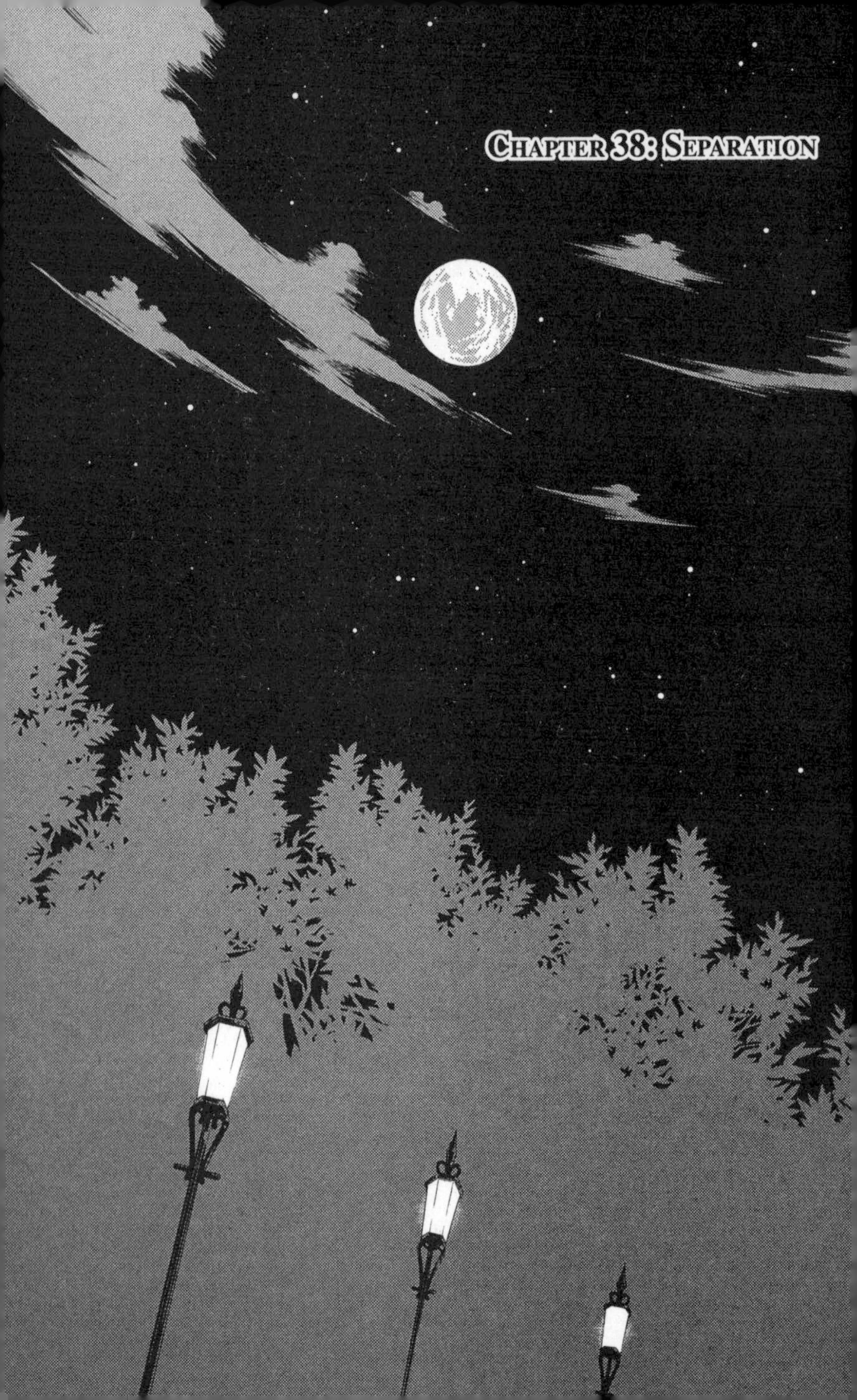
Chapter 38: Separation

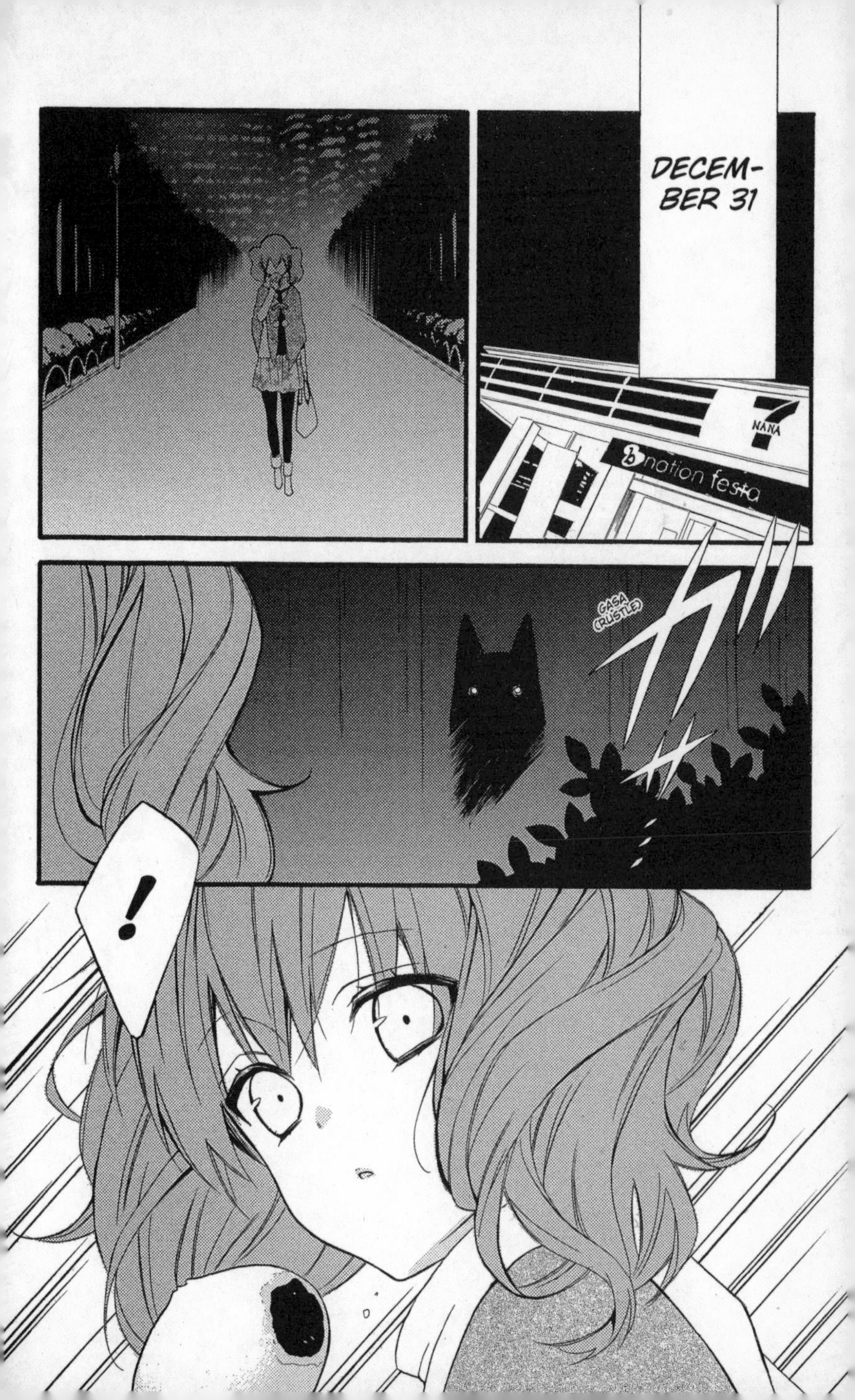
DECEM- BER 31
NANA
nation festa
GASA (RUSTLE)
!

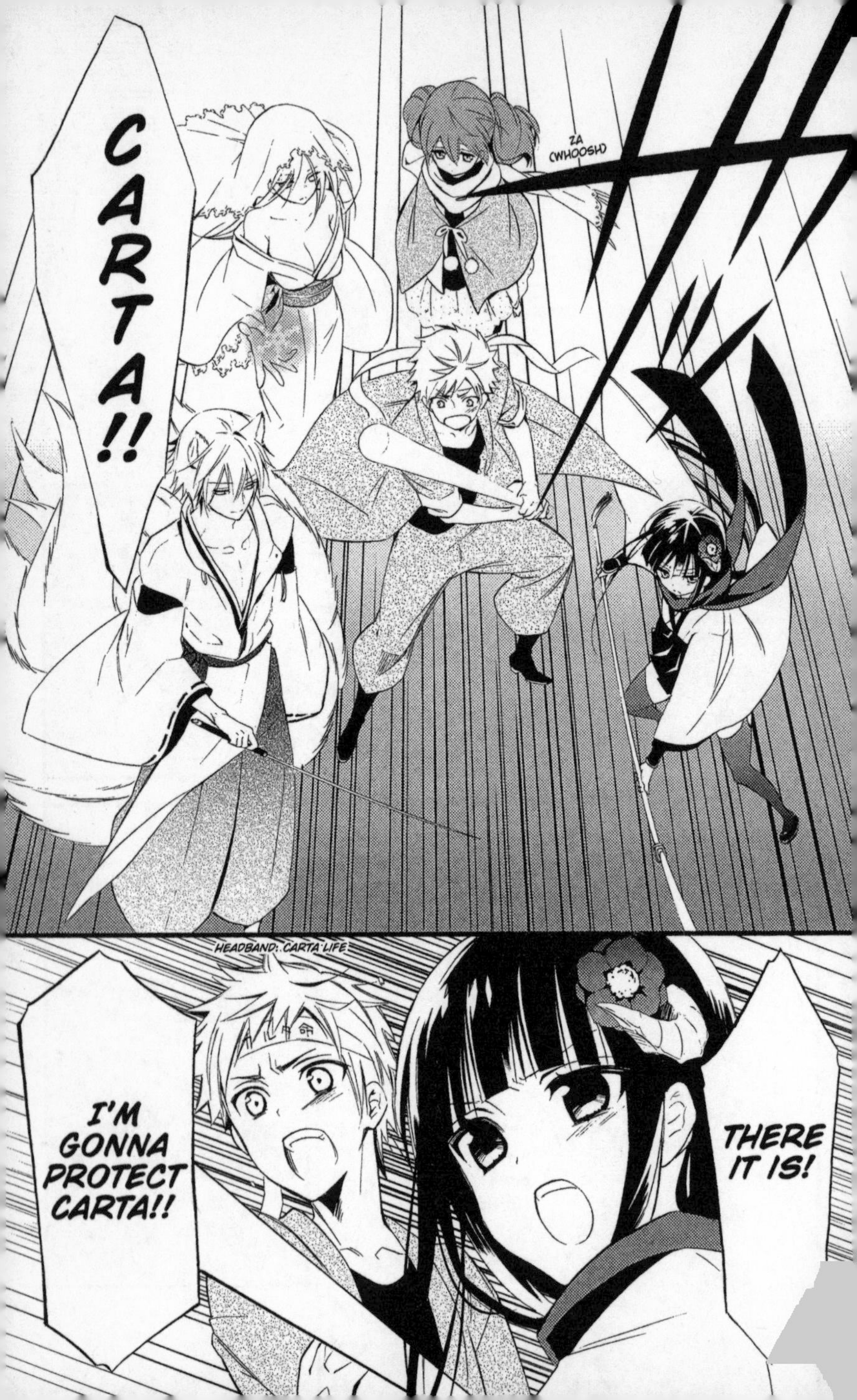
ZA (WHOOSH)
CARTA!!
THERE IT IS!
HEADBAND: CARTA LIFE
I'M GONNA PROTECT CARTA!!

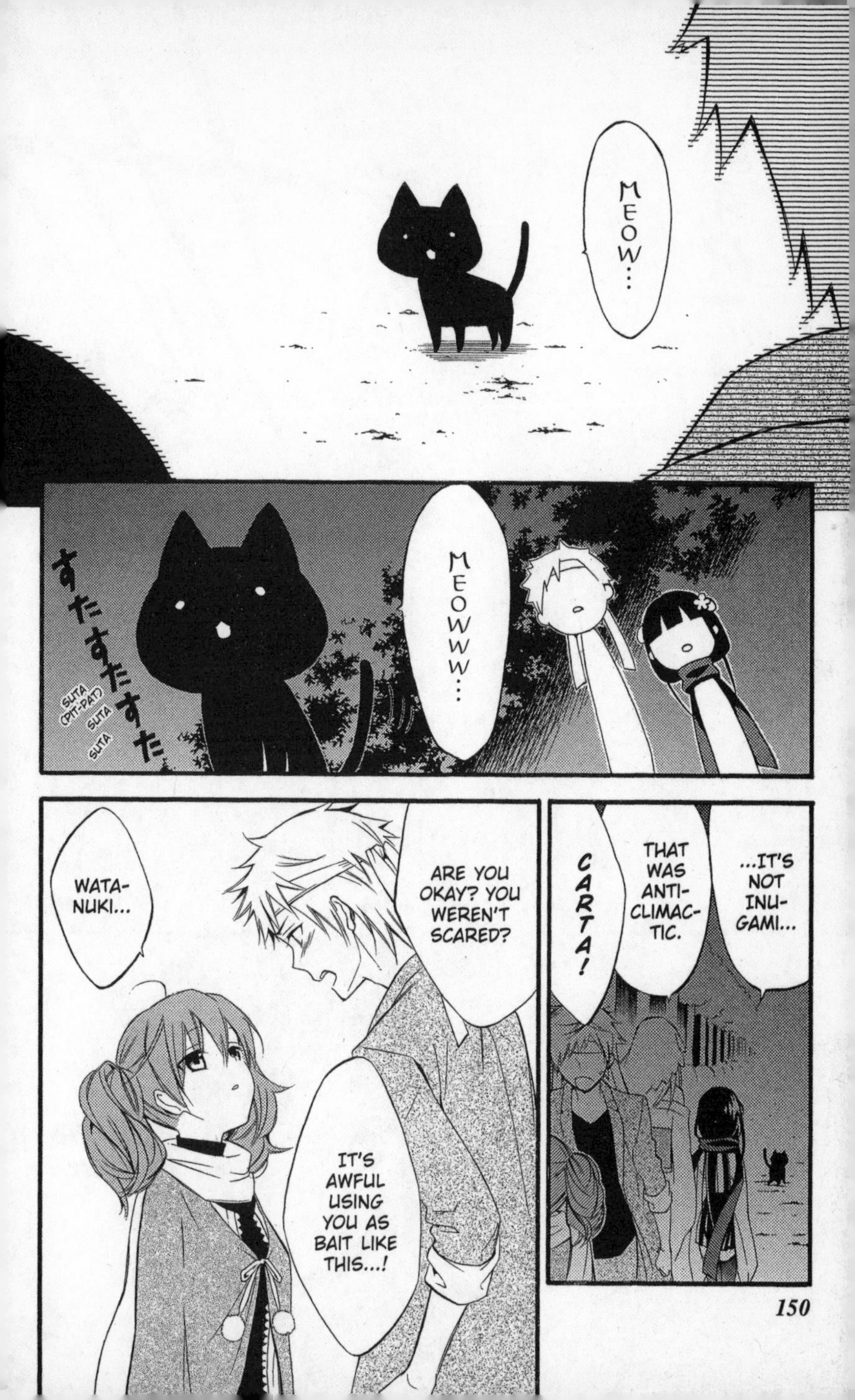
MEOW...
MEOWWW...
すたすたすた
SUTA (PIT-PAT) SUTA SUTA
...IT'S NOT INUGAMI...
THAT WAS ANTI-CLIMACTIC.
CARTA!
ARE YOU OKAY? YOU WEREN'T SCARED?
WATA-NUKI...
IT'S AWFUL USING YOU AS BAIT LIKE THIS...!

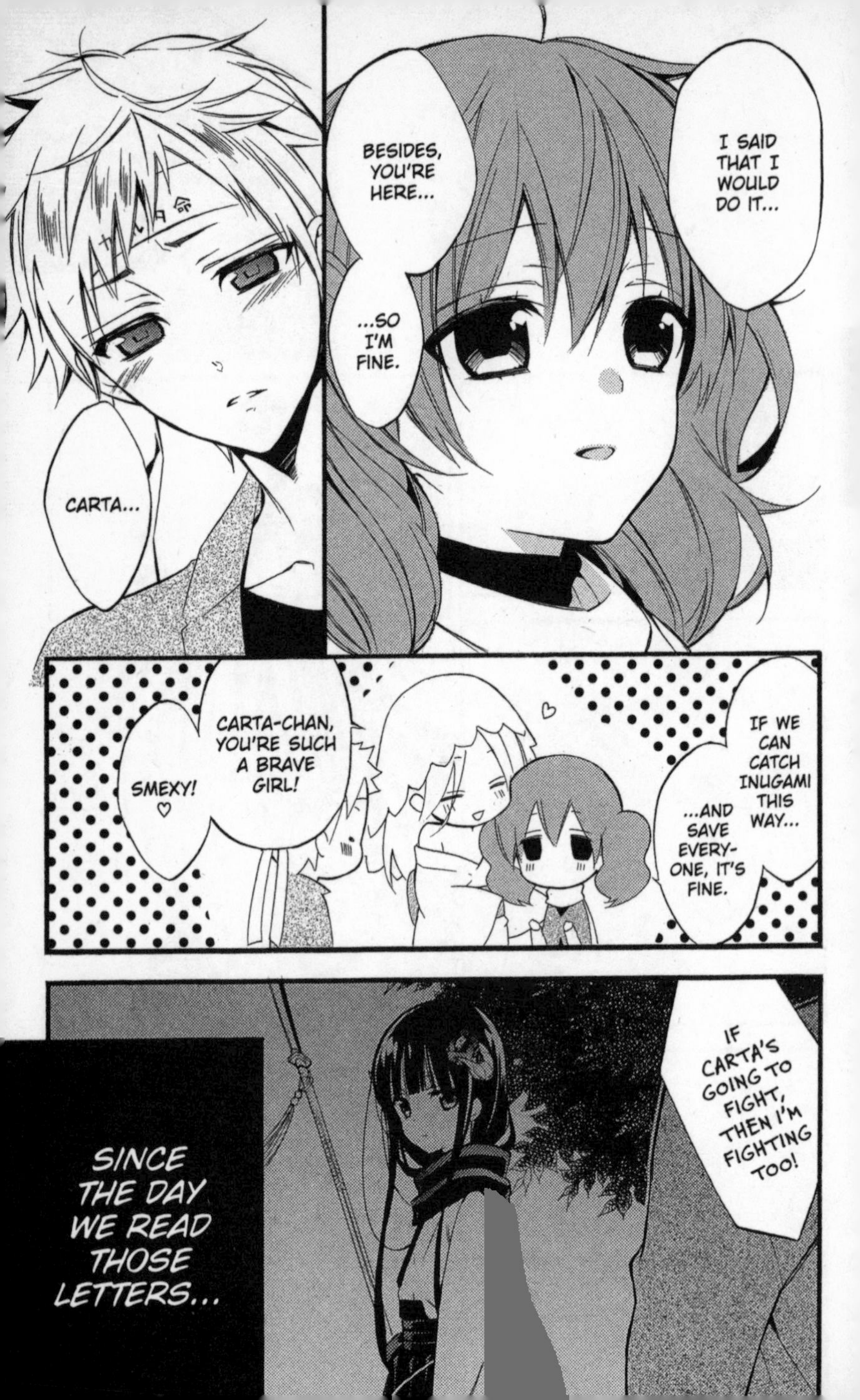
I SAID THAT I WOULD DO IT...
BESIDES, YOU'RE HERE...
...SO I'M FINE.
CARTA...
IF WE CAN CATCH INUGAMI THIS WAY...
...AND SAVE EVERY-ONE, IT'S FINE.
CARTA-CHAN, YOU'RE SUCH A BRAVE GIRL!
SMEXY! ♡
IF CARTA'S GOING TO FIGHT, THEN I'M FIGHTING TOO!
SINCE THE DAY WE READ THOSE LETTERS...

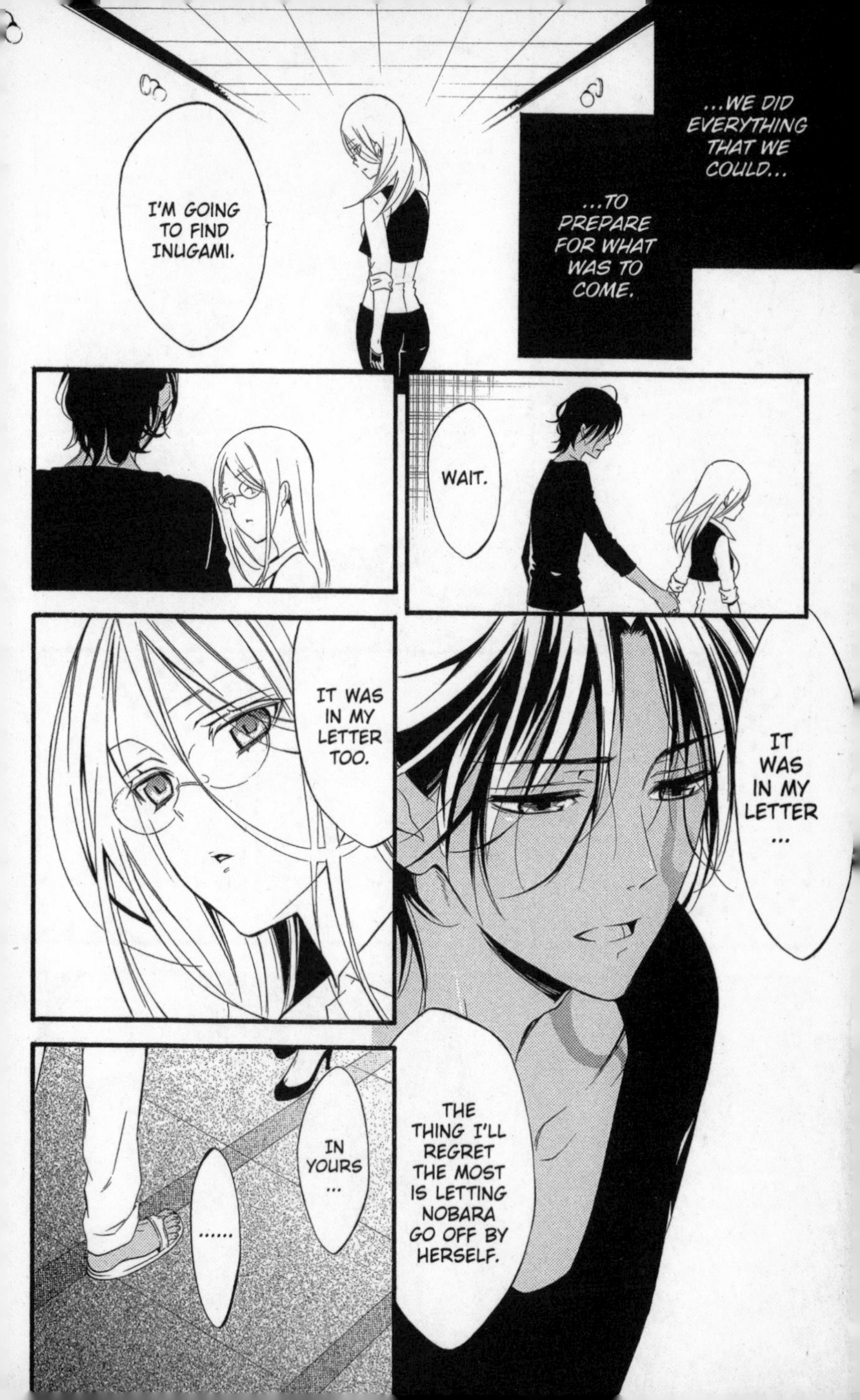
...WE DID EVERYTHING THAT WE COULD...
...TO PREPARE FOR WHAT WAS TO COME.
I'M GOING TO FIND INUGAMI.
WAIT.
IT WAS IN MY LETTER ...
IT WAS IN MY LETTER TOO.
THE THING I'LL REGRET THE MOST IS LETTING NOBARA GO OFF BY HERSELF.
IN YOURS ...
......

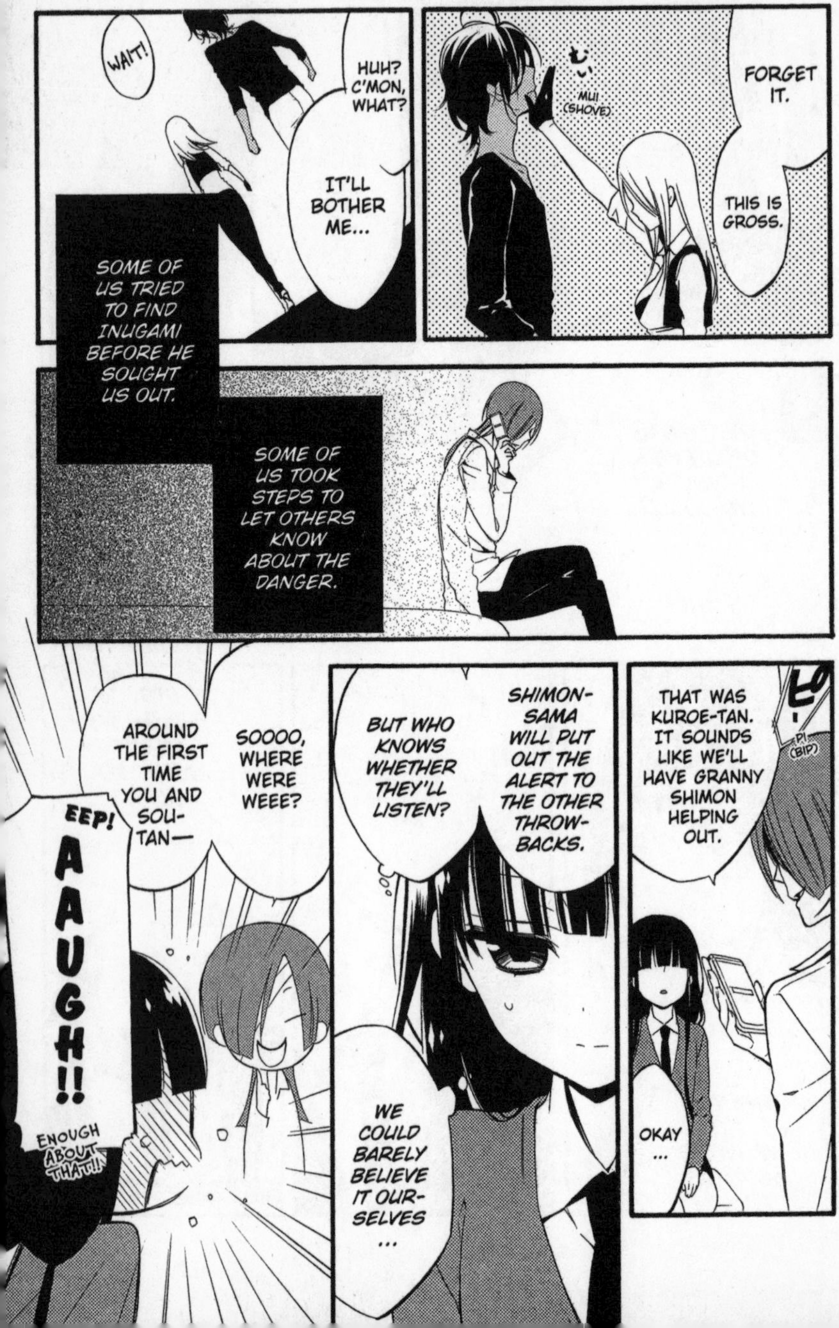
MUI (SHOVE)
FORGET IT.
THIS IS GROSS.
HUH? C'MON, WHAT?
IT'LL BOTHER ME...
WAIT!
SOME OF US TRIED TO FIND INUGAMI BEFORE HE SOUGHT US OUT.
SOME OF US TOOK STEPS TO LET OTHERS KNOW ABOUT THE DANGER.
PI (BIP)
THAT WAS KUROE-TAN. IT SOUNDS LIKE WE'LL HAVE GRANNY SHIMON HELPING OUT.
OKAY ...
SHIMON-SAMA WILL PUT OUT THE ALERT TO THE OTHER THROW-BACKS.
BUT WHO KNOWS WHETHER THEY'LL LISTEN?
WE COULD BARELY BELIEVE IT OURSELVES ...
SOOOO, WHERE WERE WEEE?
AROUND THE FIRST TIME YOU AND SOU-TAN—
EEP!
AAUGH!!
ENOUGH ABOUT THAT!!

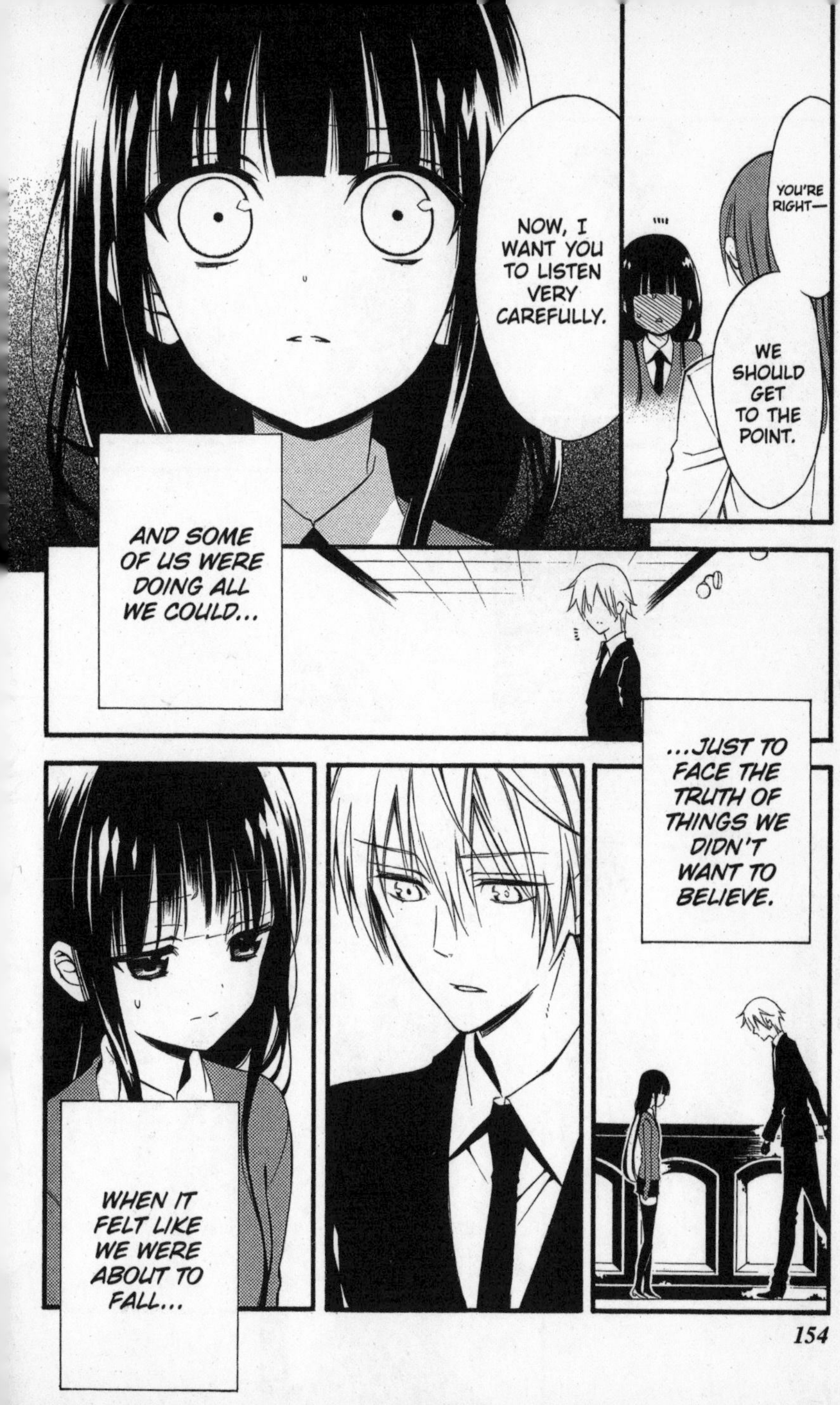
YOU'RE RIGHT—
WE SHOULD GET TO THE POINT.
NOW, I WANT YOU TO LISTEN VERY CAREFULLY.
AND SOME OF US WERE DOING ALL WE COULD...
...JUST TO FACE THE TRUTH OF THINGS WE DIDN'T WANT TO BELIEVE.
WHEN IT FELT LIKE WE WERE ABOUT TO FALL...

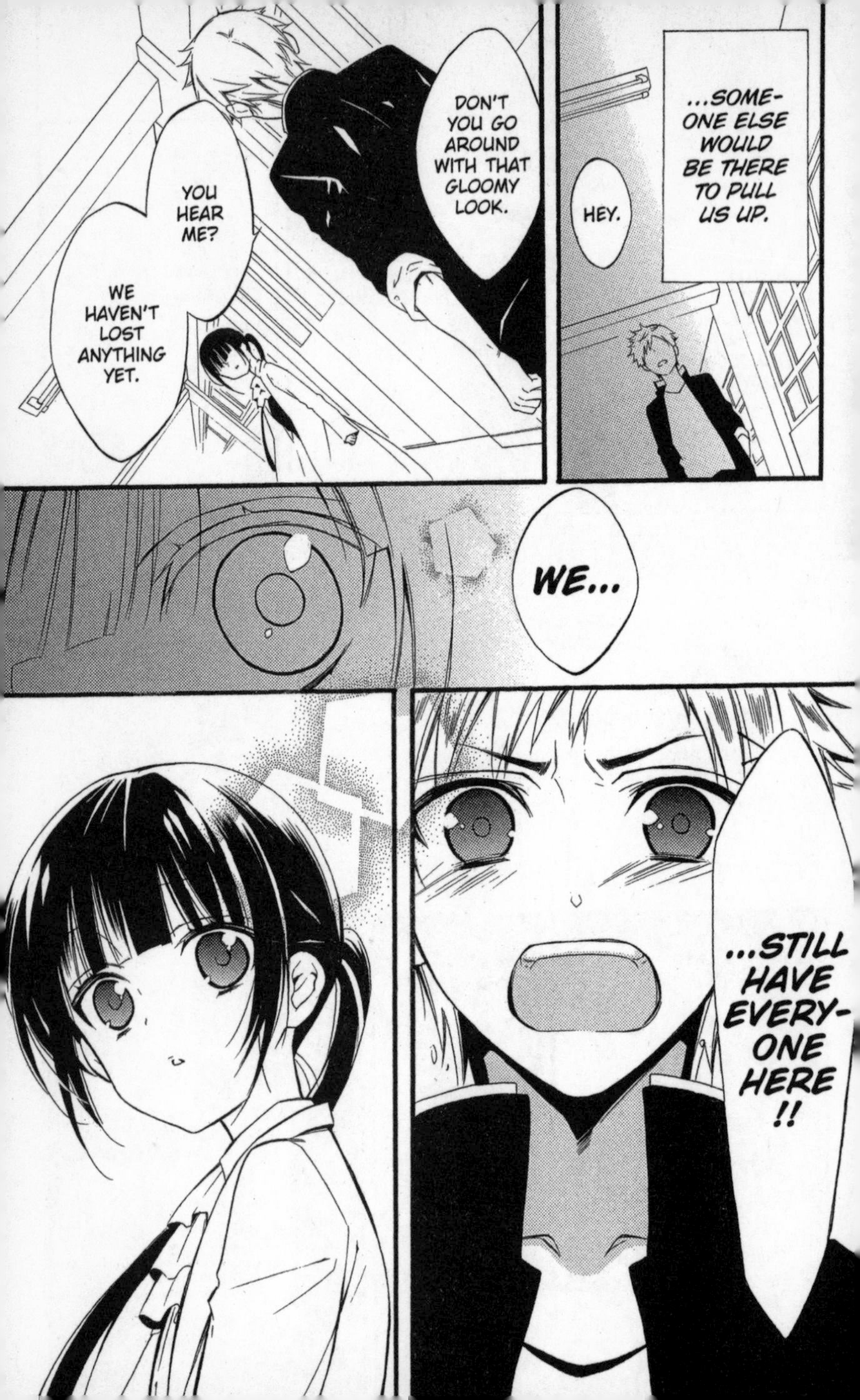
...SOME-ONE ELSE WOULD BE THERE TO PULL US UP.
HEY.
DON'T YOU GO AROUND WITH THAT GLOOMY LOOK.
YOU HEAR ME?
WE HAVEN'T LOST ANYTHING YET.
WE...
...STILL HAVE EVERY-ONE HERE!!

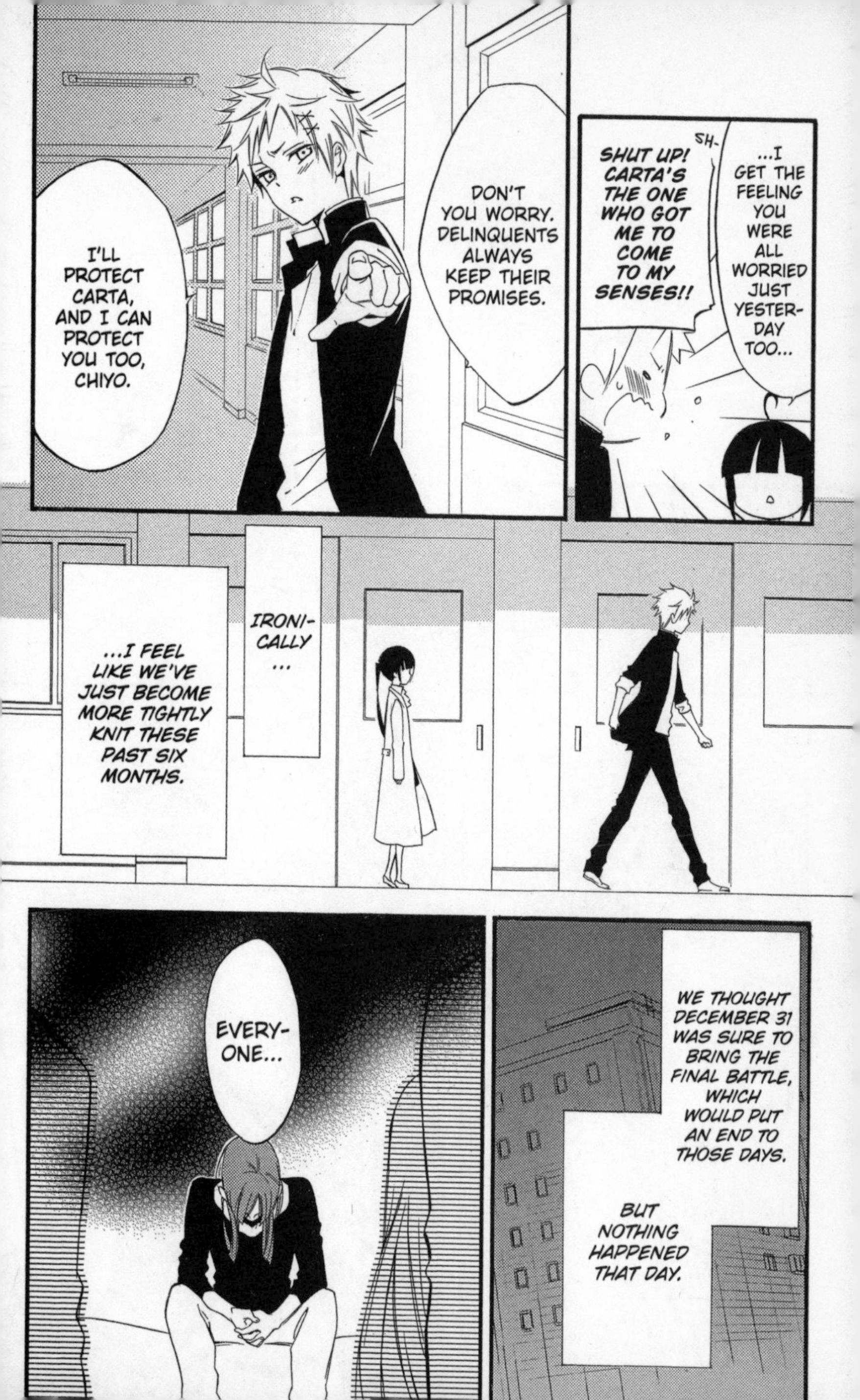
...I GET THE FEELING YOU WERE ALL WORRIED JUST YESTER-DAY TOO...
SH-
SHUT UP! CARTA'S THE ONE WHO GOT ME TO COME TO MY SENSES!!
DON'T YOU WORRY. DELINQUENTS ALWAYS KEEP THEIR PROMISES.
I'LL PROTECT CARTA, AND I CAN PROTECT YOU TOO, CHIYO.
IRONI-CALLY...
...I FEEL LIKE WE'VE JUST BECOME MORE TIGHTLY KNIT THESE PAST SIX MONTHS.
WE THOUGHT DECEMBER 31 WAS SURE TO BRING THE FINAL BATTLE, WHICH WOULD PUT AN END TO THOSE DAYS.
BUT NOTHING HAPPENED THAT DAY.
EVERY-ONE...

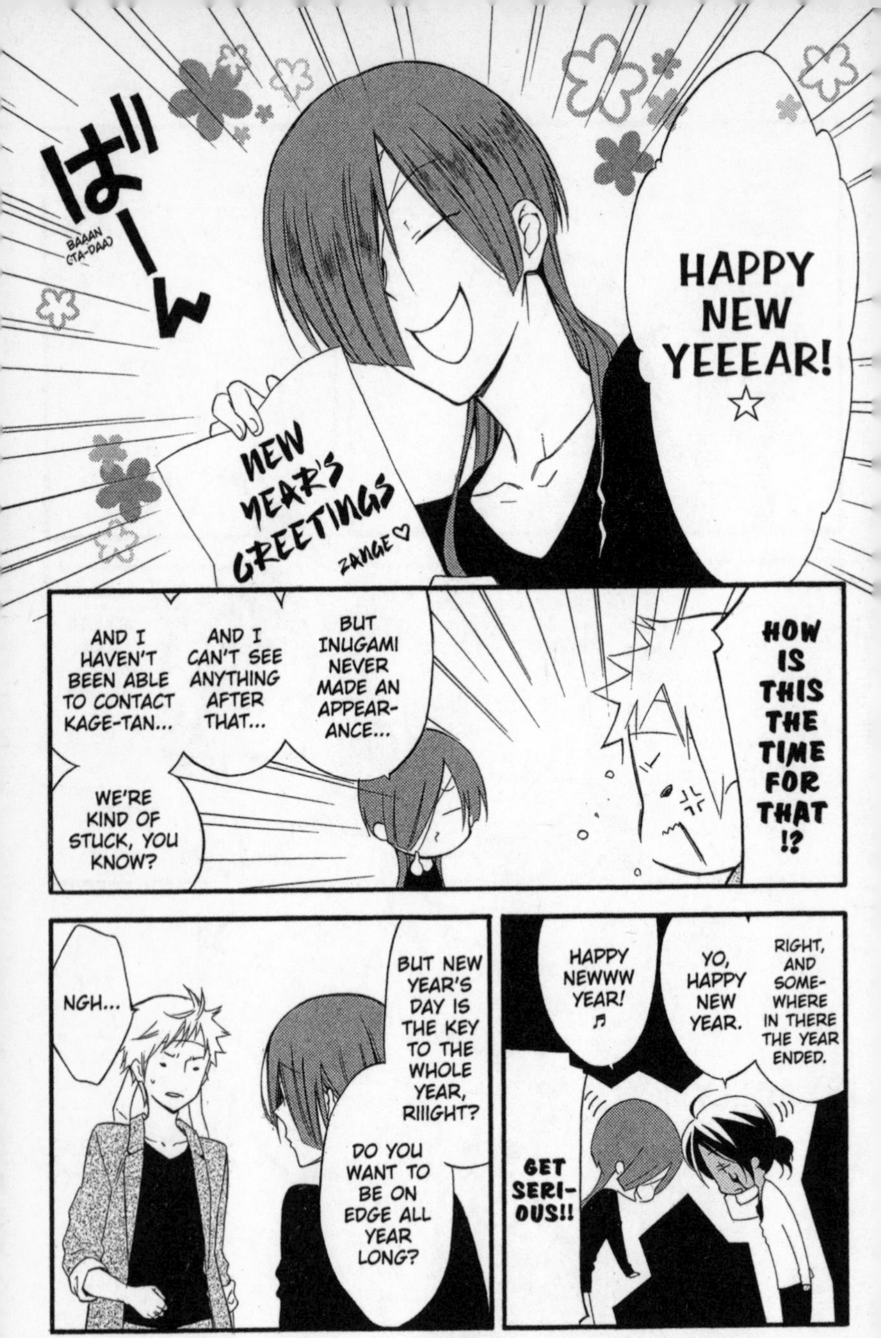
HAPPY NEW YEEEAR! ☆
NEW YEAR'S GREETINGS
ZANGE♡
ぱーん
BAAAN (TA-DAA)
HOW IS THIS THE TIME FOR THAT!?
BUT INUGAMI NEVER MADE AN APPEARANCE...
AND I CAN'T SEE ANYTHING AFTER THAT...
AND I HAVEN'T BEEN ABLE TO CONTACT KAGE-TAN...
WE'RE KIND OF STUCK, YOU KNOW?
RIGHT, AND SOMEWHERE IN THERE THE YEAR ENDED.
YO, HAPPY NEW YEAR.
HAPPY NEWWW YEAR! ♫
GET SERIOUS!!
BUT NEW YEAR'S DAY IS THE KEY TO THE WHOLE YEAR, RIIIGHT?
DO YOU WANT TO BE ON EDGE ALL YEAR LONG?
NGH...

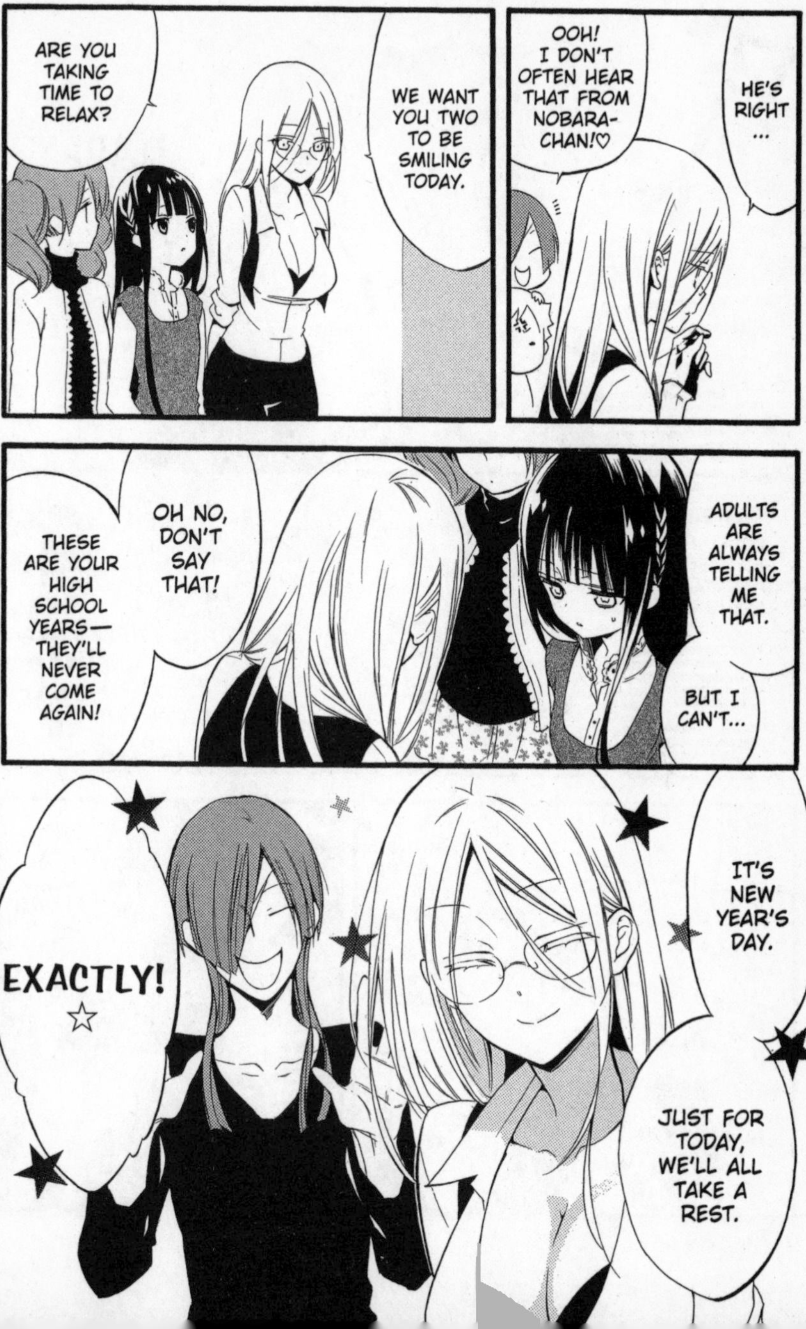
HE'S RIGHT ...
OOH! I DON'T OFTEN HEAR THAT FROM NOBARA-CHAN!♡
WE WANT YOU TWO TO BE SMILING TODAY.
ARE YOU TAKING TIME TO RELAX?
ADULTS ARE ALWAYS TELLING ME THAT.
BUT I CAN'T...
OH NO, DON'T SAY THAT!
THESE ARE YOUR HIGH SCHOOL YEARS—THEY'LL NEVER COME AGAIN!
IT'S NEW YEAR'S DAY.
JUST FOR TODAY, WE'LL ALL TAKE A REST.
EXACTLY! ☆

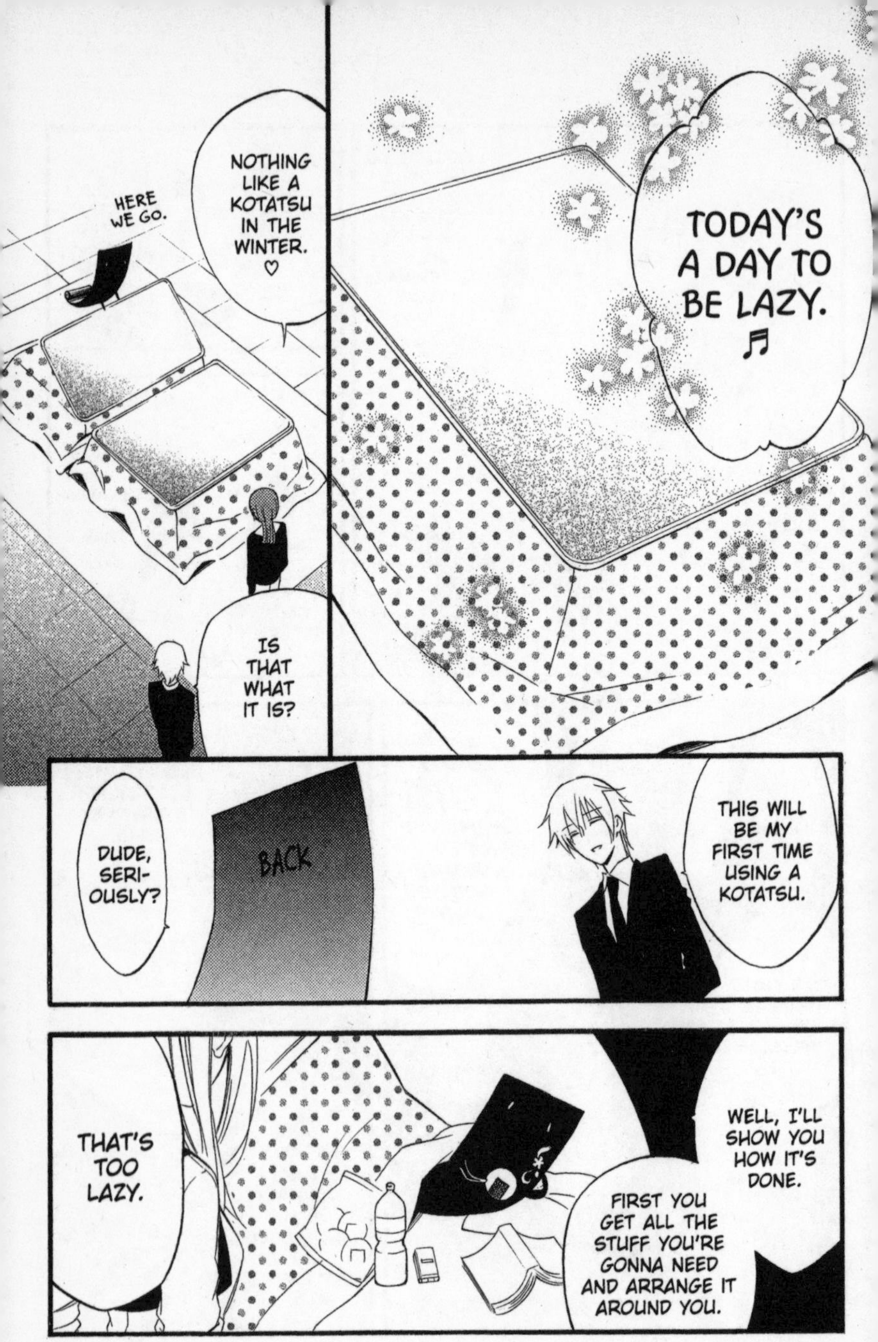
TODAY'S A DAY TO BE LAZY. ♫
NOTHING LIKE A KOTATSU IN THE WINTER. ♡
HERE WE GO.
IS THAT WHAT IT IS?
THIS WILL BE MY FIRST TIME USING A KOTATSU.
BACK
DUDE, SERI-OUSLY?
WELL, I'LL SHOW YOU HOW IT'S DONE.
FIRST YOU GET ALL THE STUFF YOU'RE GONNA NEED AND ARRANGE IT AROUND YOU.
THAT'S TOO LAZY.

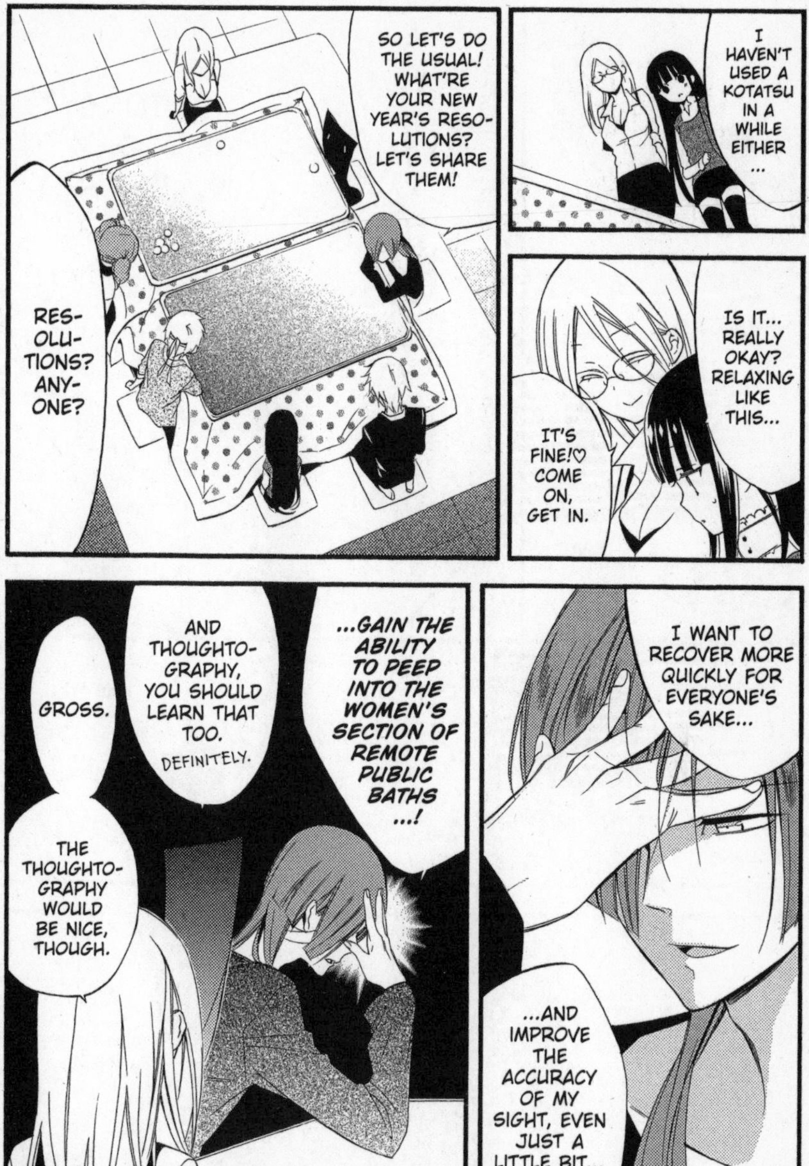
I HAVEN'T USED A KOTATSU IN A WHILE EITHER ...
IS IT... REALLY OKAY? RELAXING LIKE THIS...
IT'S FINE!♡ COME ON, GET IN.
SO LET'S DO THE USUAL! WHAT'RE YOUR NEW YEAR'S RESOLUTIONS? LET'S SHARE THEM!
RESOLUTIONS? ANYONE?
I WANT TO RECOVER MORE QUICKLY FOR EVERYONE'S SAKE...
...AND IMPROVE THE ACCURACY OF MY SIGHT, EVEN JUST A LITTLE BIT... AND...
...GAIN THE ABILITY TO PEEP INTO THE WOMEN'S SECTION OF REMOTE PUBLIC BATHS ...!
AND THOUGHTOGRAPHY, YOU SHOULD LEARN THAT TOO.
DEFINITELY.
GROSS.
THE THOUGHTOGRAPHY WOULD BE NICE, THOUGH.

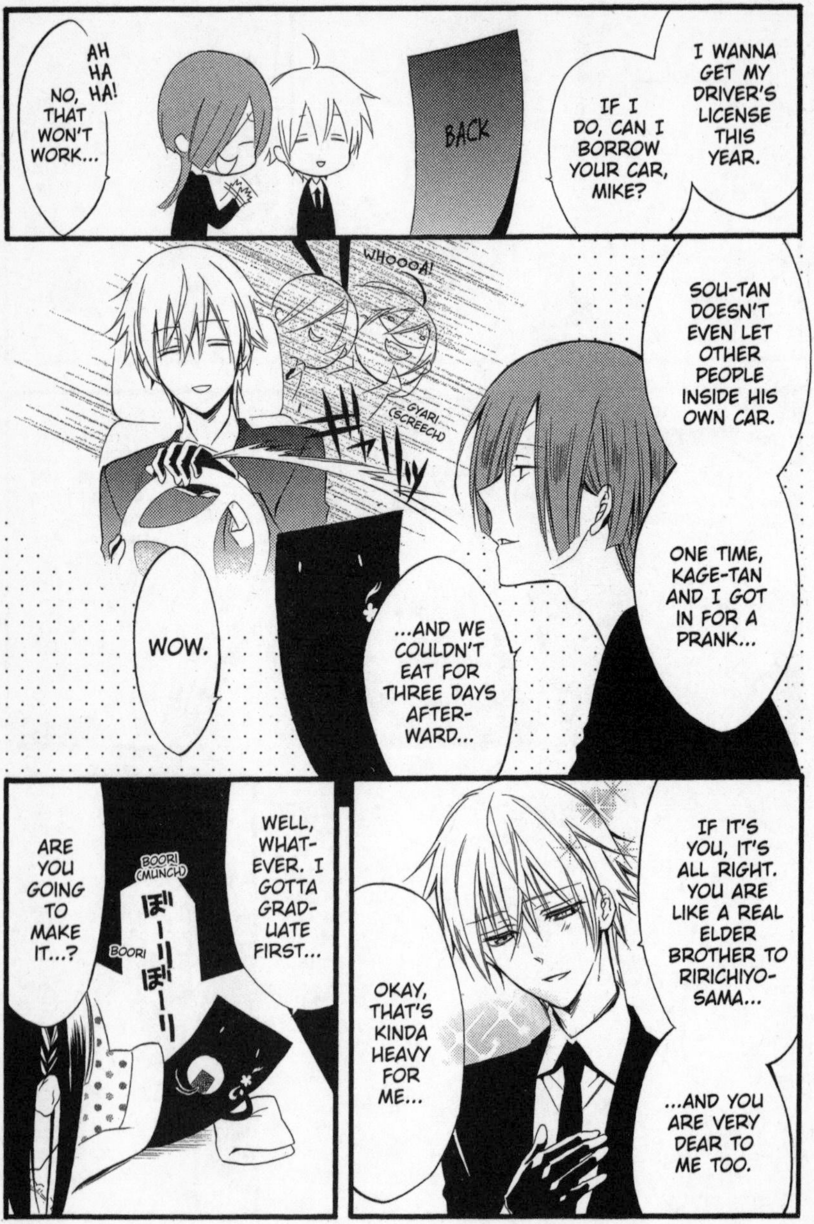
I WANNA GET MY DRIVER'S LICENSE THIS YEAR.
IF I DO, CAN I BORROW YOUR CAR, MIKE?
BACK
AH HA HA! NO, THAT WON'T WORK...
SOU-TAN DOESN'T EVEN LET OTHER PEOPLE INSIDE HIS OWN CAR.
ONE TIME, KAGE-TAN AND I GOT IN FOR A PRANK...
...AND WE COULDN'T EAT FOR THREE DAYS AFTERWARD...
WHOOOA!
GYARI (SCREECH)
WOW.
IF IT'S YOU, IT'S ALL RIGHT. YOU ARE LIKE A REAL ELDER BROTHER TO RIRICHIYO-SAMA...
...AND YOU ARE VERY DEAR TO ME TOO.
OKAY, THAT'S KINDA HEAVY FOR ME...
WELL, WHATEVER. I GOTTA GRADUATE FIRST...
BOORI (MUNCH)
BOORI
ARE YOU GOING TO MAKE IT...?

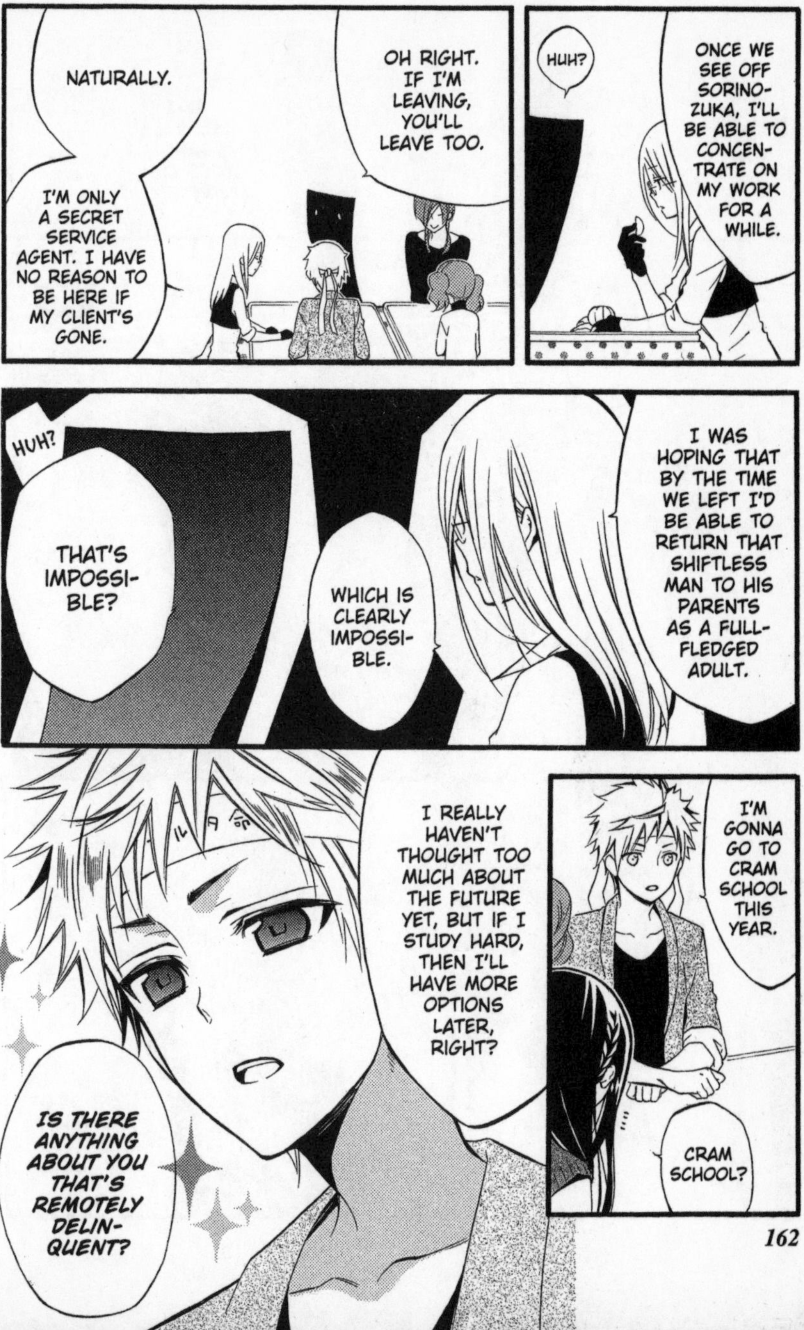
ONCE WE SEE OFF SORINO-ZUKA, I'LL BE ABLE TO CONCEN-TRATE ON MY WORK FOR A WHILE.
HUH?
OH RIGHT. IF I'M LEAVING, YOU'LL LEAVE TOO.
NATURALLY.
I'M ONLY A SECRET SERVICE AGENT. I HAVE NO REASON TO BE HERE IF MY CLIENT'S GONE.
I WAS HOPING THAT BY THE TIME WE LEFT I'D BE ABLE TO RETURN THAT SHIFTLESS MAN TO HIS PARENTS AS A FULL-FLEDGED ADULT.
WHICH IS CLEARLY IMPOSSI-BLE.
HUH?
THAT'S IMPOSSI-BLE?
I'M GONNA GO TO CRAM SCHOOL THIS YEAR.
...
CRAM SCHOOL?
I REALLY HAVEN'T THOUGHT TOO MUCH ABOUT THE FUTURE YET, BUT IF I STUDY HARD, THEN I'LL HAVE MORE OPTIONS LATER, RIGHT?
IS THERE ANYTHING ABOUT YOU THAT'S REMOTELY DELIN-QUENT?

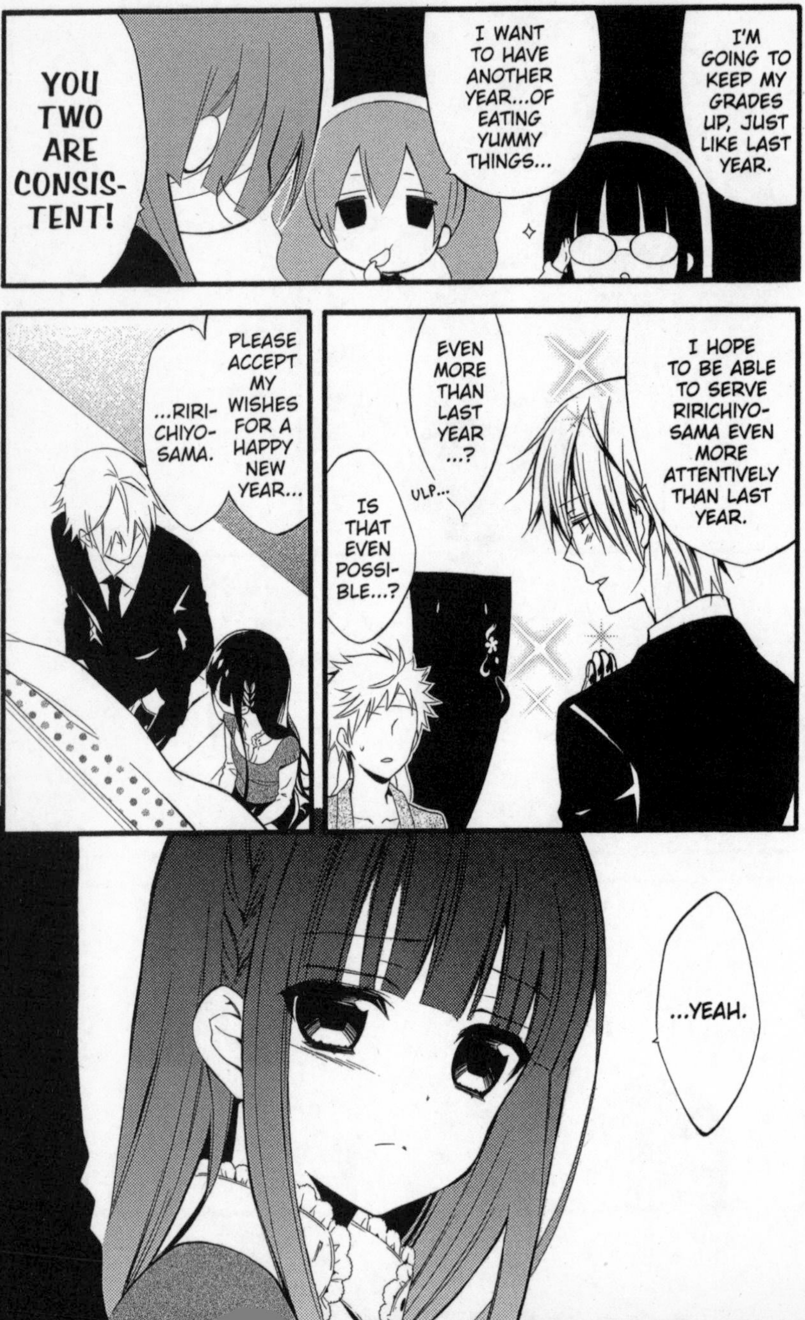
I'M GOING TO KEEP MY GRADES UP, JUST LIKE LAST YEAR.
I WANT TO HAVE ANOTHER YEAR...OF EATING YUMMY THINGS...
YOU TWO ARE CONSIS-TENT!
I HOPE TO BE ABLE TO SERVE RIRICHIYO-SAMA EVEN MORE ATTENTIVELY THAN LAST YEAR.
EVEN MORE THAN LAST YEAR ...?
ULP...
IS THAT EVEN POSSI-BLE...?
PLEASE ACCEPT MY WISHES FOR A HAPPY NEW YEAR...
...RIRI-CHIYO-SAMA.
...YEAH.

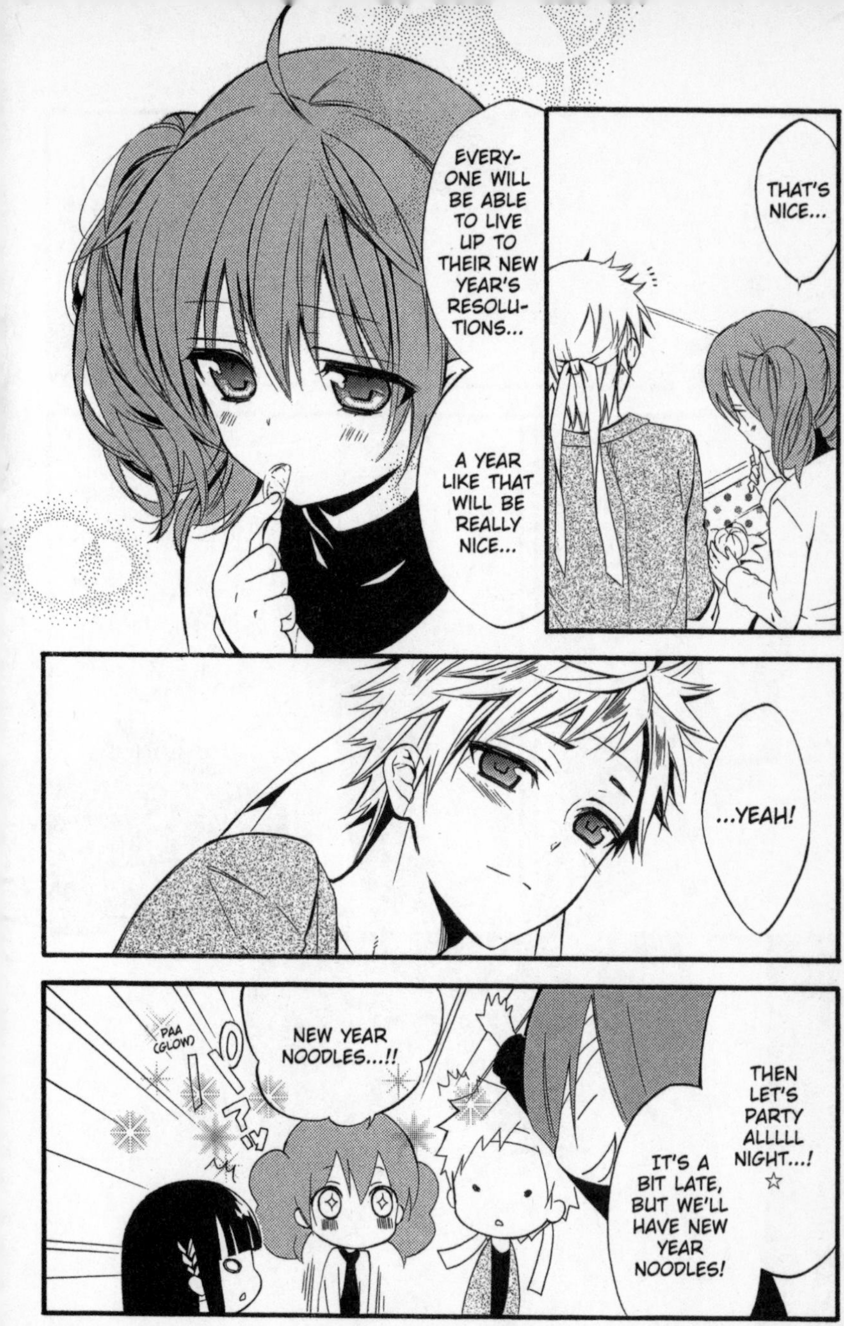
THAT'S NICE...
EVERY-ONE WILL BE ABLE TO LIVE UP TO THEIR NEW YEAR'S RESOLU-TIONS...
A YEAR LIKE THAT WILL BE REALLY NICE...
...YEAH!
THEN LET'S PARTY ALLLLL NIGHT...! ☆
IT'S A BIT LATE, BUT WE'LL HAVE NEW YEAR NOODLES!
NEW YEAR NOODLES...!!
PAA (GLOW)

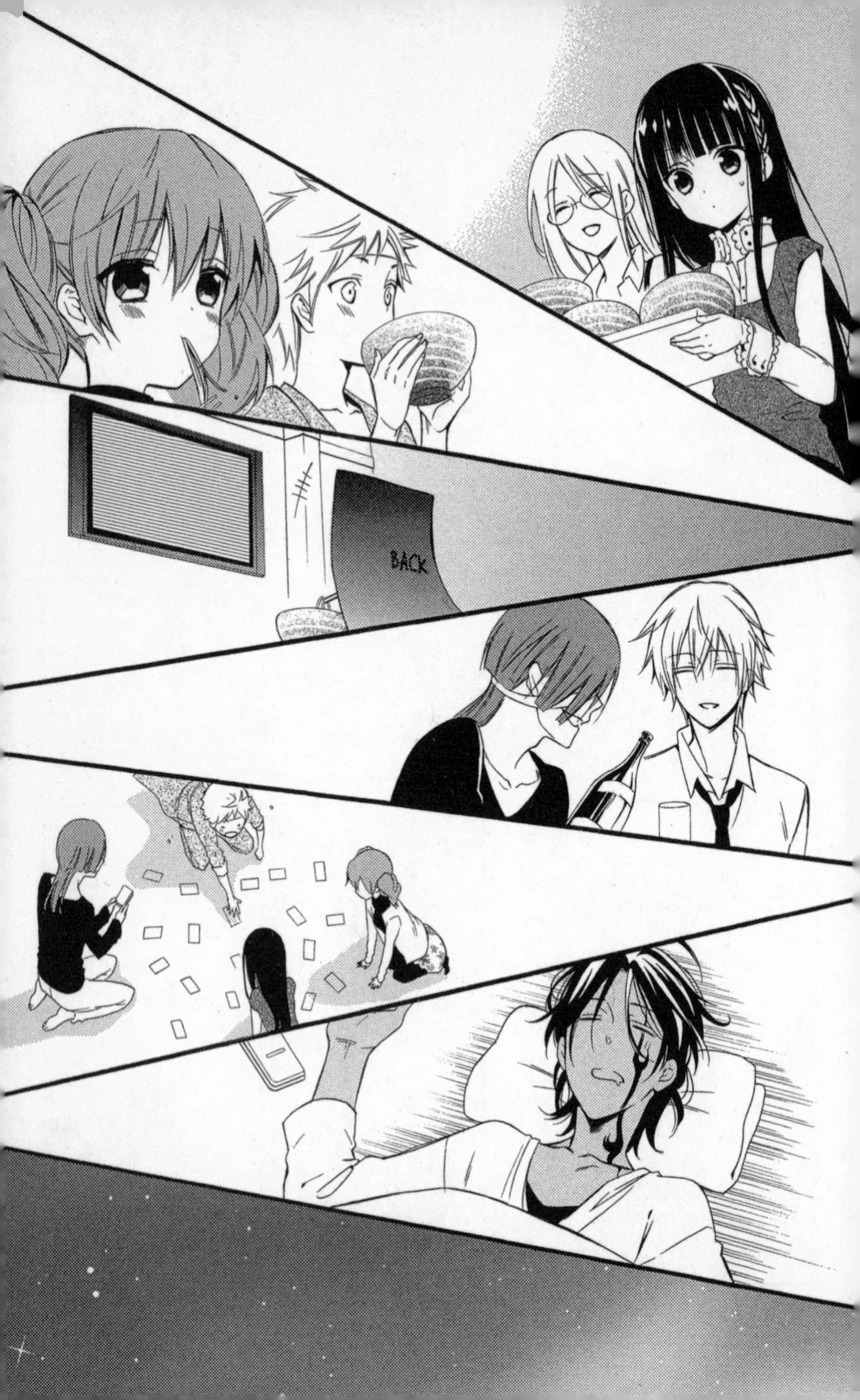
BACK

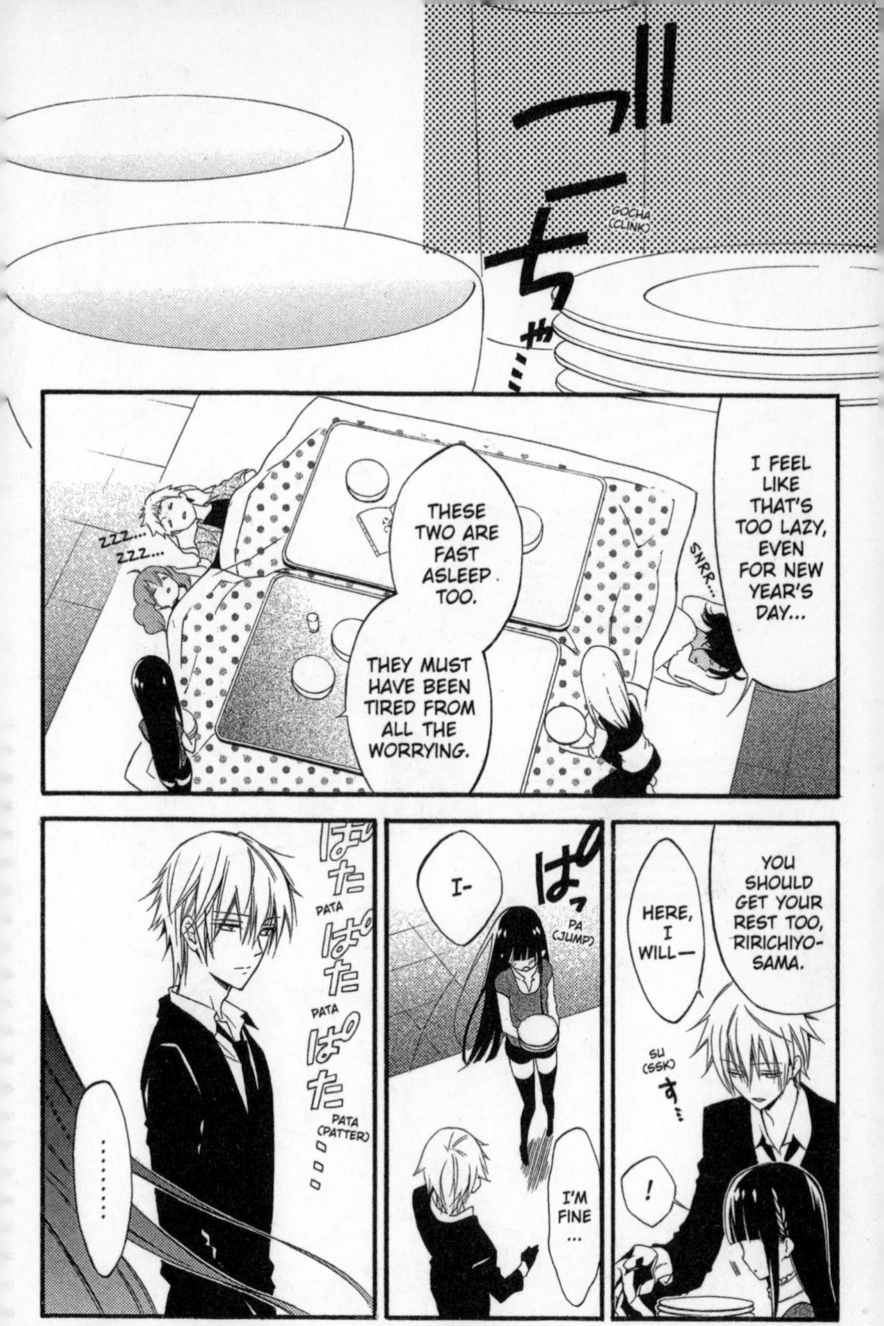
GOCHA (CLINK)
I FEEL LIKE THAT'S TOO LAZY, EVEN FOR NEW YEAR'S DAY...
SNRR...
THESE TWO ARE FAST ASLEEP TOO.
THEY MUST HAVE BEEN TIRED FROM ALL THE WORRYING.
ZZZ... ZZZ...
YOU SHOULD GET YOUR REST TOO, RIRICHIYO-SAMA.
HERE, I WILL—
SU (SSK)
!
PA (JUMP)
I-
I'M FINE ...
PATA PATA PATA (PATTER)
......

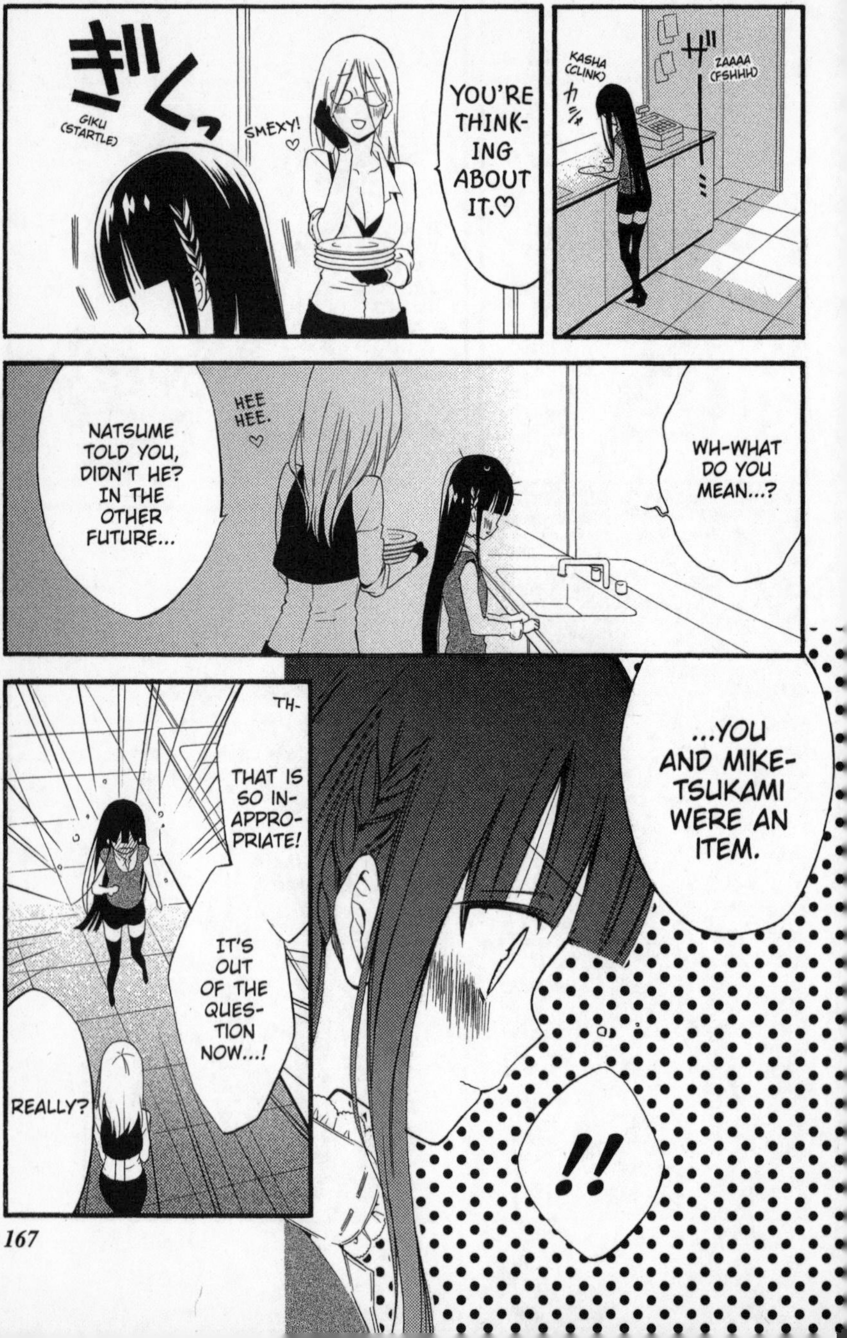
KASHA (CLINK)
ZAAAA (FSHHH)
YOU'RE THINKING ABOUT IT.♡
SMEXY! ♡
ぎくっ
GIKU (STARTLE)
WH-WHAT DO YOU MEAN...?
HEE HEE. ♡
NATSUME TOLD YOU, DIDN'T HE? IN THE OTHER FUTURE...
...YOU AND MIKETSUKAMI WERE AN ITEM.
!!
TH-
THAT IS SO INAPPROPRIATE!
IT'S OUT OF THE QUESTION NOW...!
REALLY?

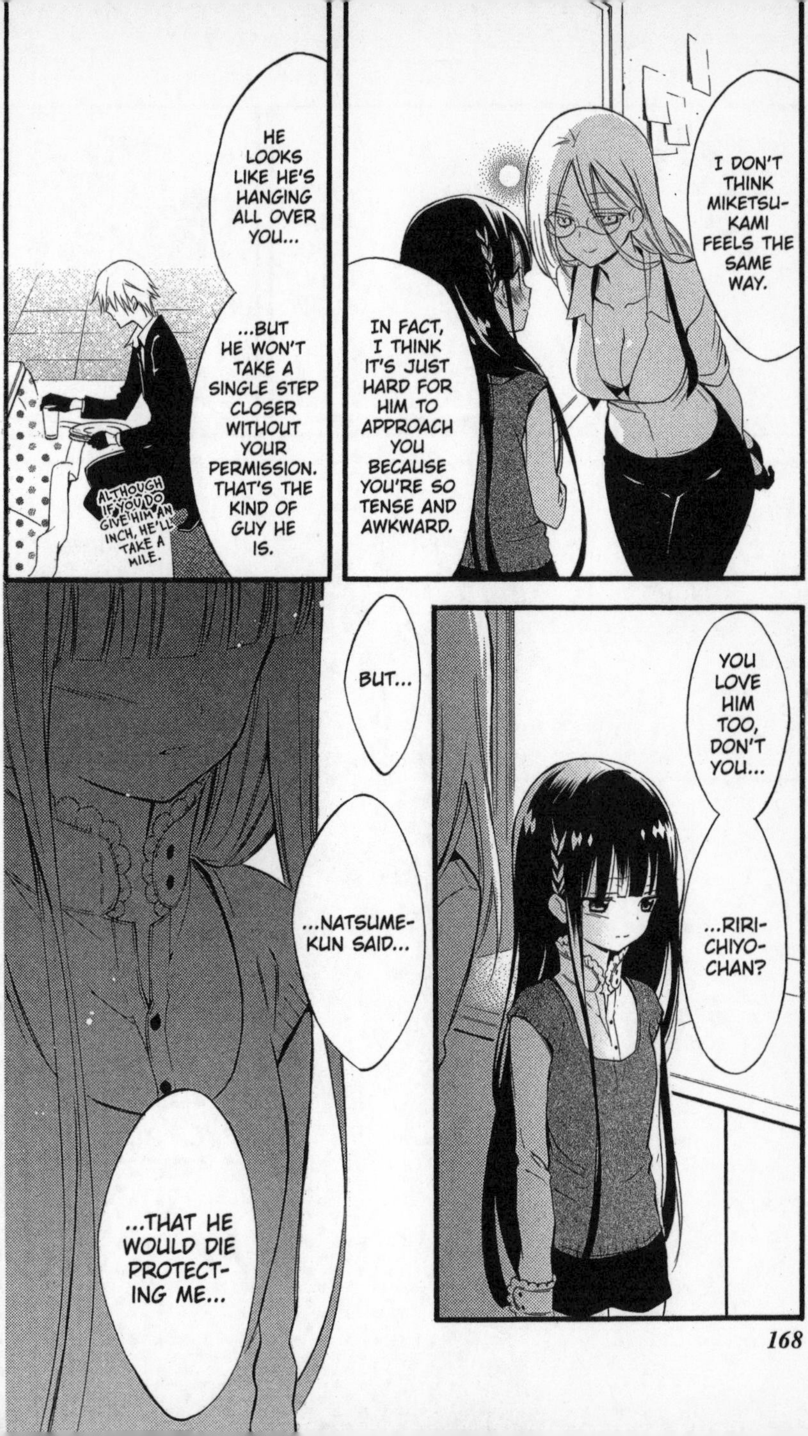
I DON'T THINK MIKETSU-KAMI FEELS THE SAME WAY.
IN FACT, I THINK IT'S JUST HARD FOR HIM TO APPROACH YOU BECAUSE YOU'RE SO TENSE AND AWKWARD.
HE LOOKS LIKE HE'S HANGING ALL OVER YOU...
...BUT HE WON'T TAKE A SINGLE STEP CLOSER WITHOUT YOUR PERMISSION. THAT'S THE KIND OF GUY HE IS.
ALTHOUGH IF YOU DO GIVE HIM AN INCH, HE'LL TAKE A MILE.
YOU LOVE HIM TOO, DON'T YOU...
...RIRI-CHIYO-CHAN?
BUT...
...NATSUME-KUN SAID...
...THAT HE WOULD DIE PROTECT-ING ME...

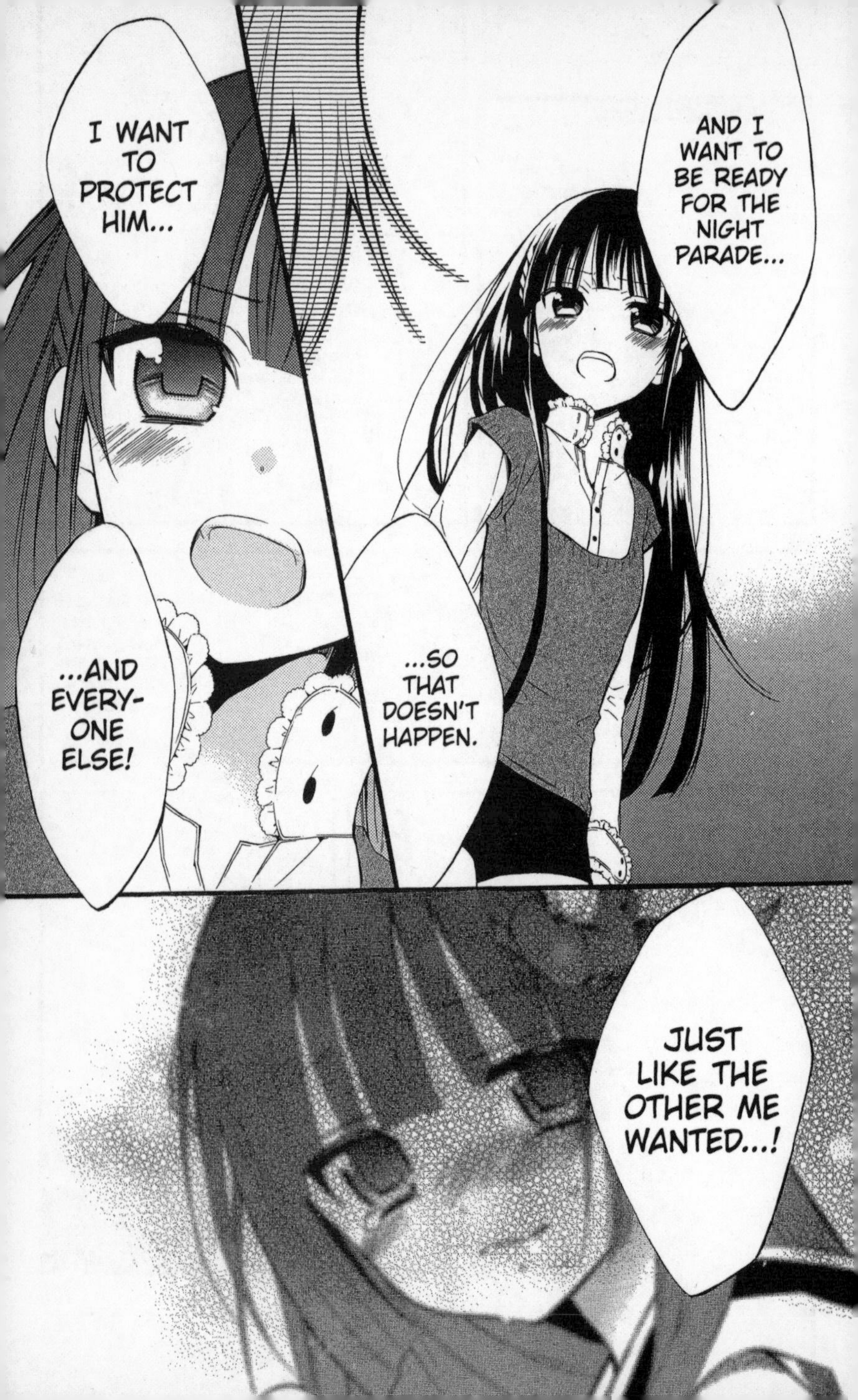
AND I WANT TO BE READY FOR THE NIGHT PARADE...
...SO THAT DOESN'T HAPPEN.
I WANT TO PROTECT HIM...
...AND EVERY-ONE ELSE!
JUST LIKE THE OTHER ME WANTED...!

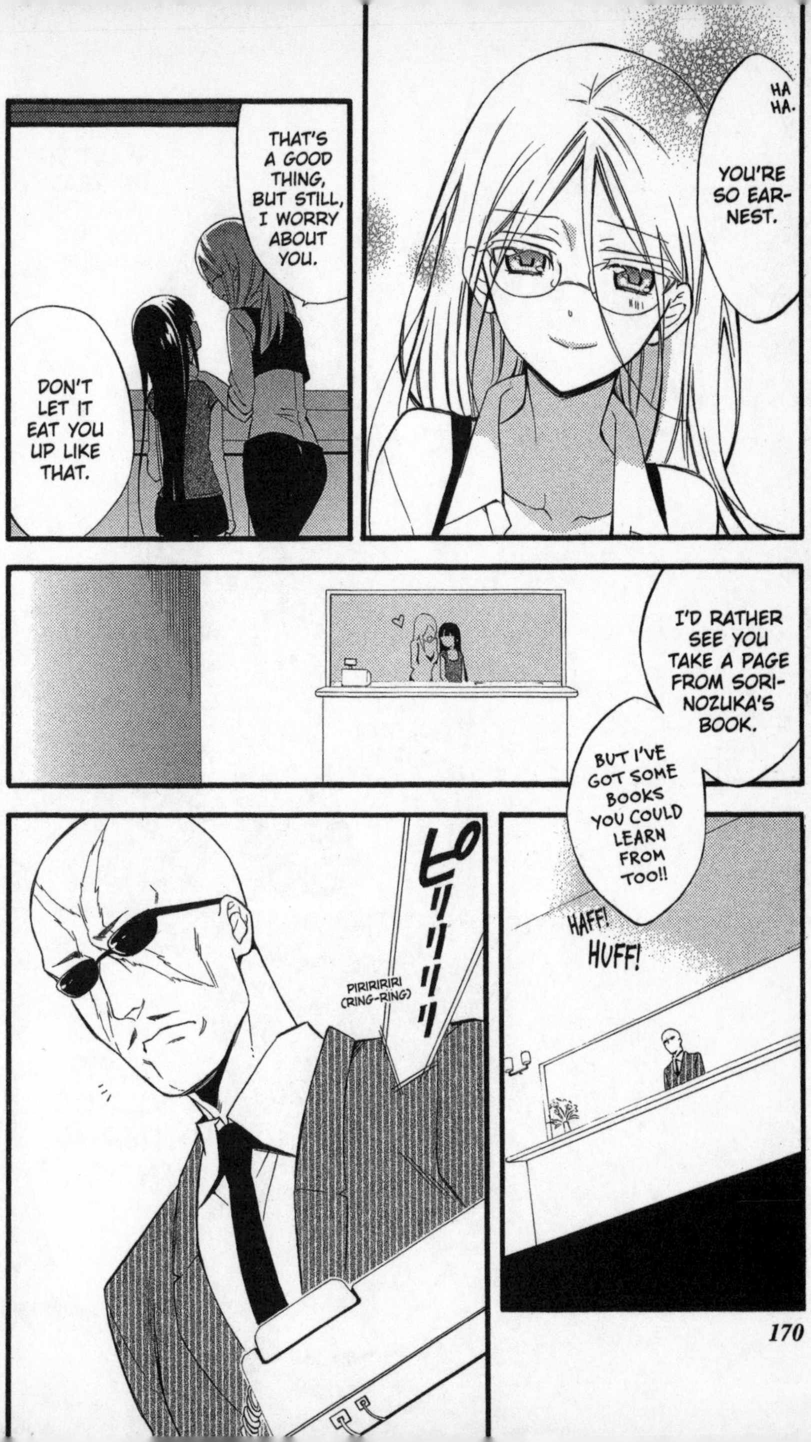
HA HA.
YOU'RE SO EARNEST.
THAT'S A GOOD THING, BUT STILL, I WORRY ABOUT YOU.
DON'T LET IT EAT YOU UP LIKE THAT.
I'D RATHER SEE YOU TAKE A PAGE FROM SORI-NOZUKA'S BOOK.
BUT I'VE GOT SOME BOOKS YOU COULD LEARN FROM TOO!!
HAFF! HUFF!
PIRIRIRIRI (RING-RING)

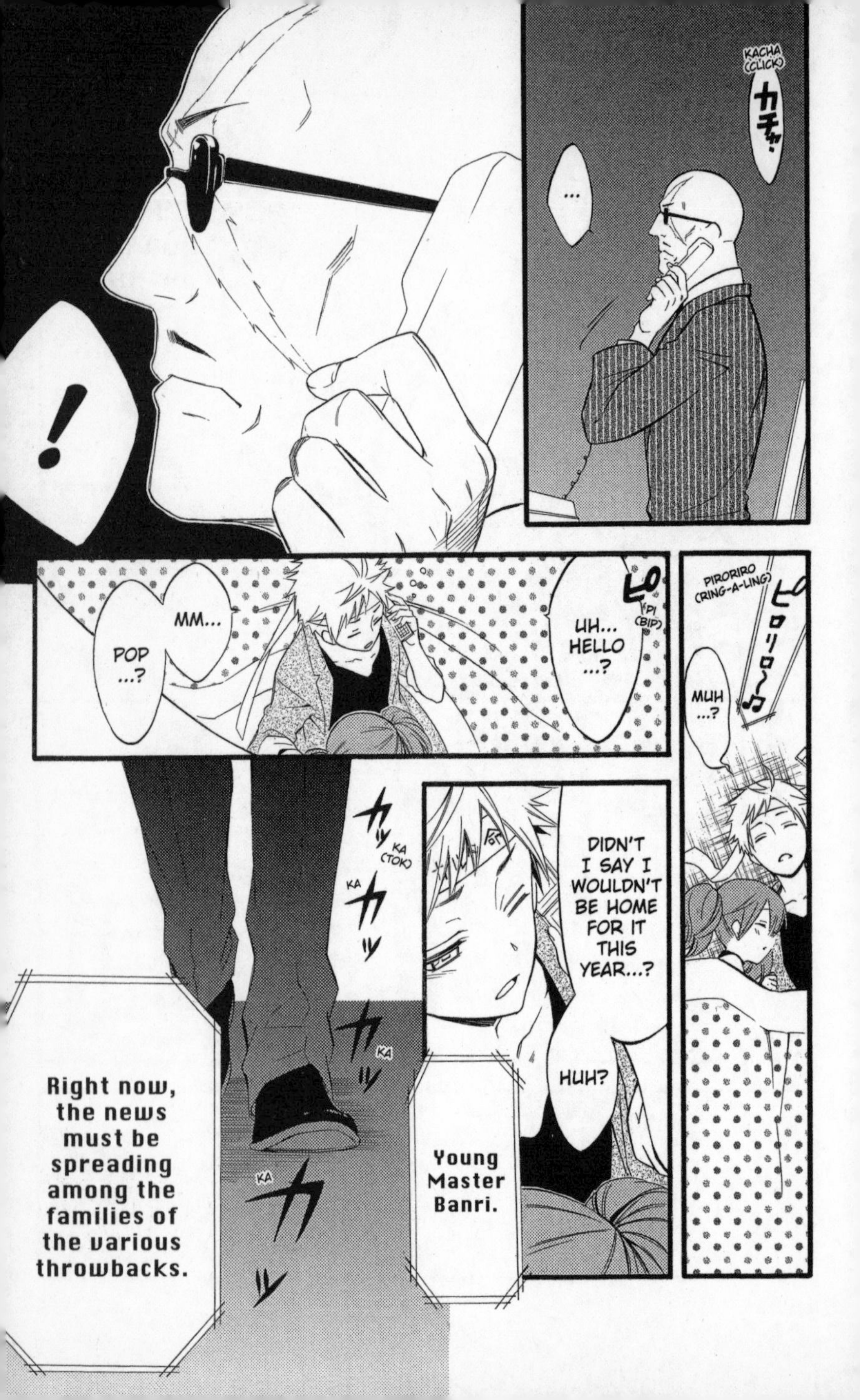
KACHA (CLICK)
カチャ
...
!
PIRORIRO (RING-A-LING)
ピロリロ〜♫
MUH ...?
ピ
PI (BIP)
UH... HELLO ...?
MM...
POP ...?
DIDN'T I SAY I WOULDN'T BE HOME FOR IT THIS YEAR...?
HUH?
Young Master Banri.
カッ
KA (TOK)
KA
カッ
カッ
KA
KA
カッ
Right now, the news must be spreading among the families of the various throwbacks.

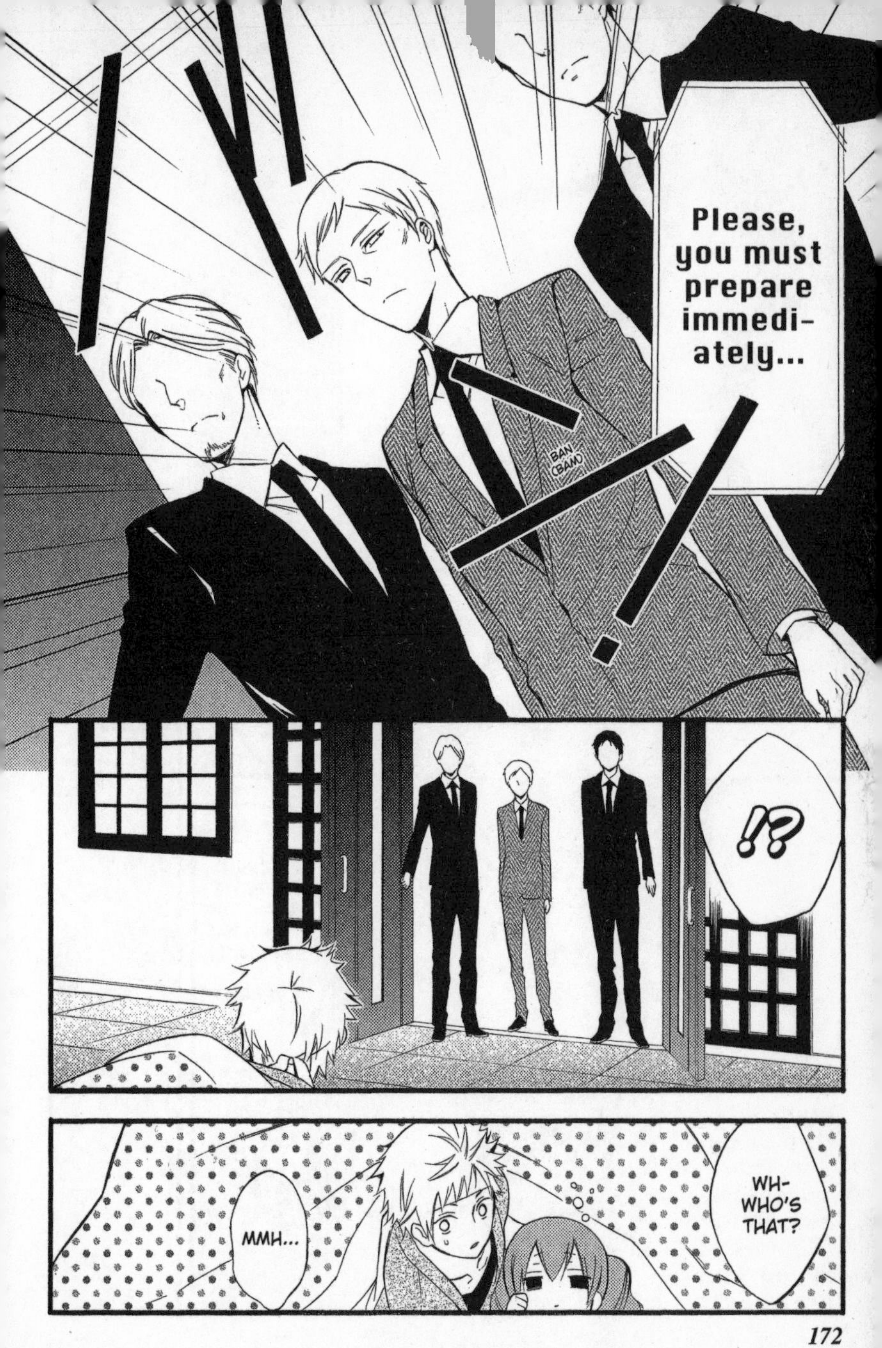
Please, you must prepare immedi-ately...
BAN (BAM)
!?
WH- WHO'S THAT?
MMH...

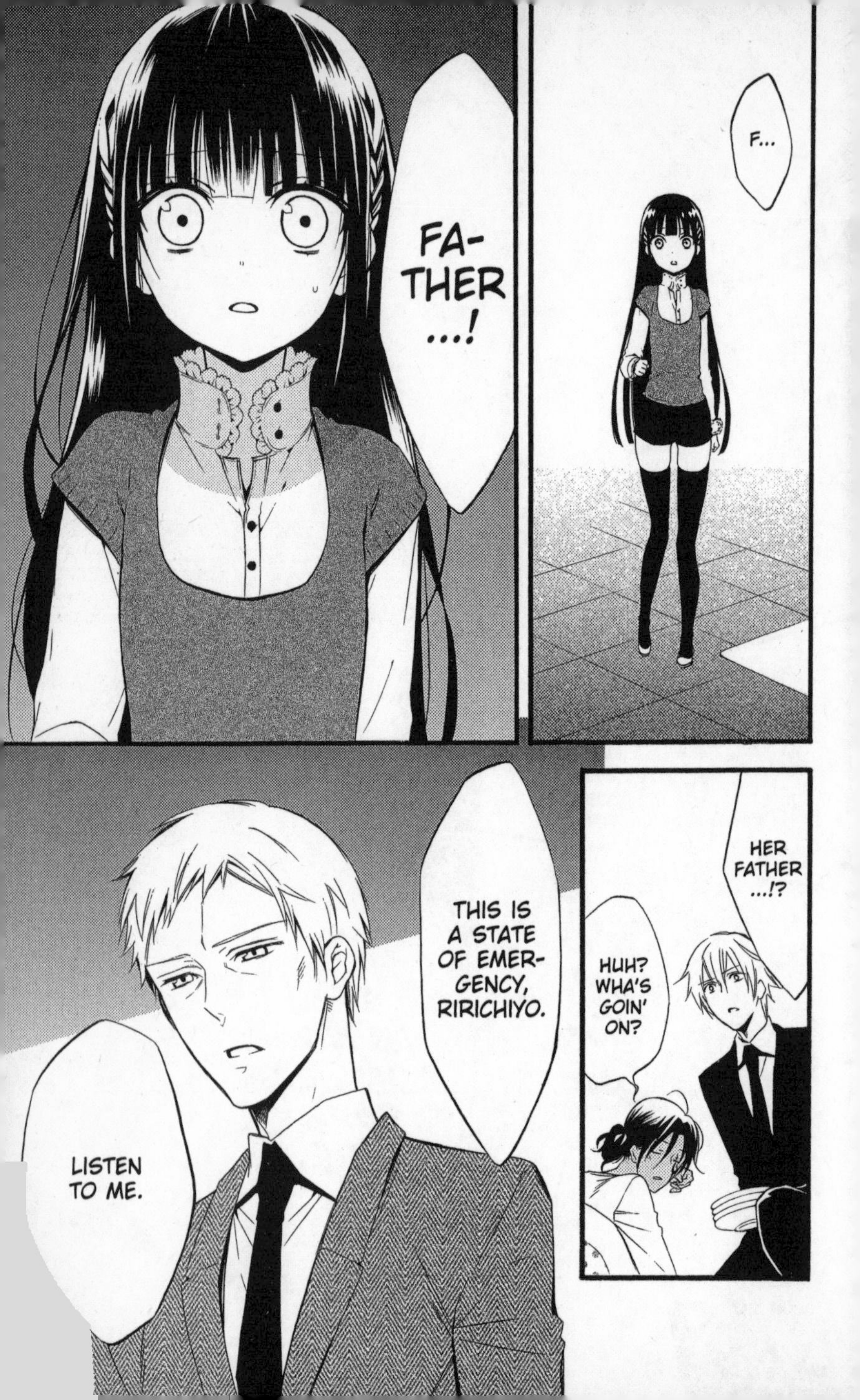
F...
FA-THER...!
HER FATHER...!?
HUH? WHA'S GOIN' ON?
THIS IS A STATE OF EMERGENCY, RIRICHIYO.
LISTEN TO ME.

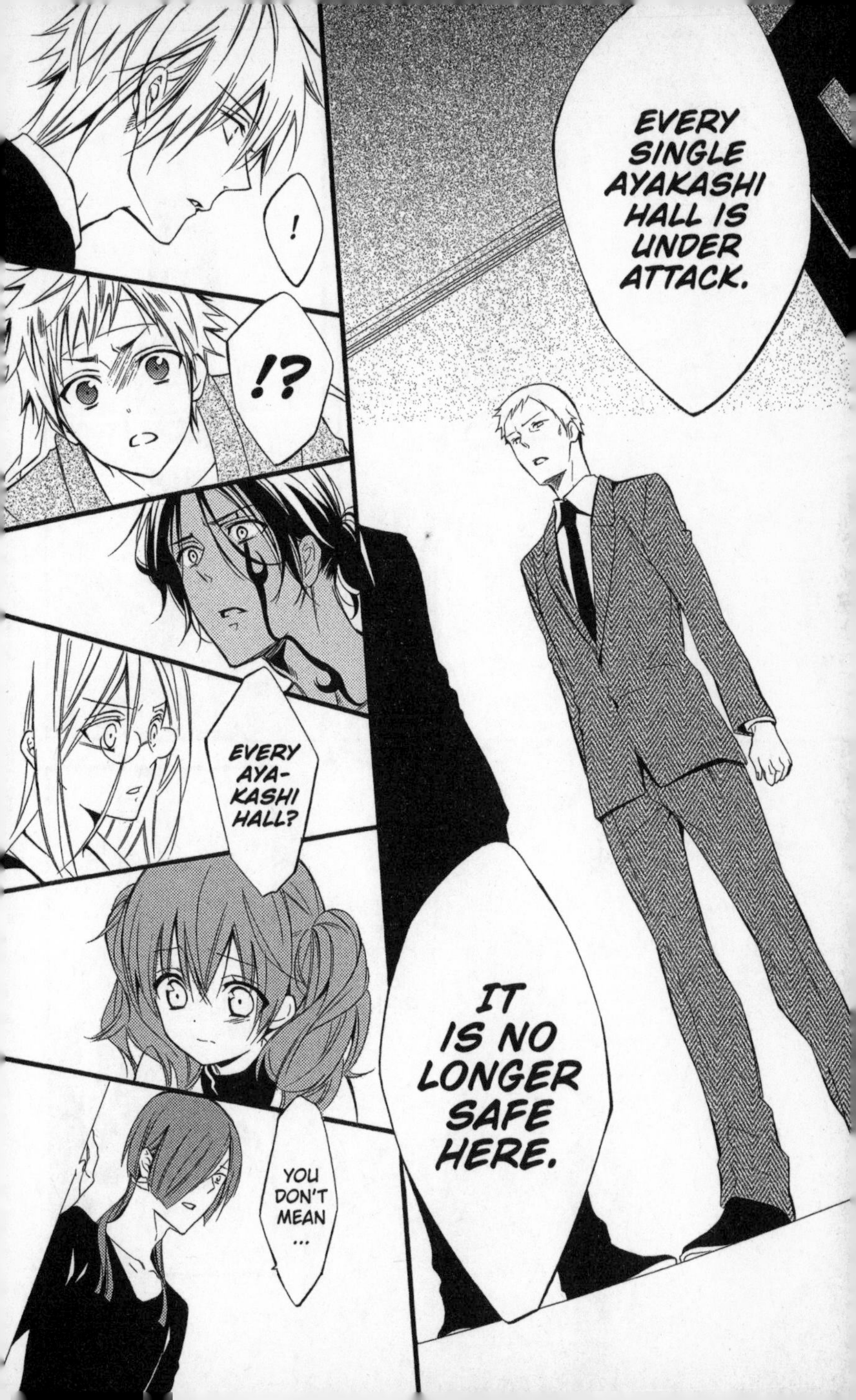
EVERY SINGLE AYAKASHI HALL IS UNDER ATTACK.
IT IS NO LONGER SAFE HERE.
!
!?
EVERY AYA-KASHI HALL?
YOU DON'T MEAN ...

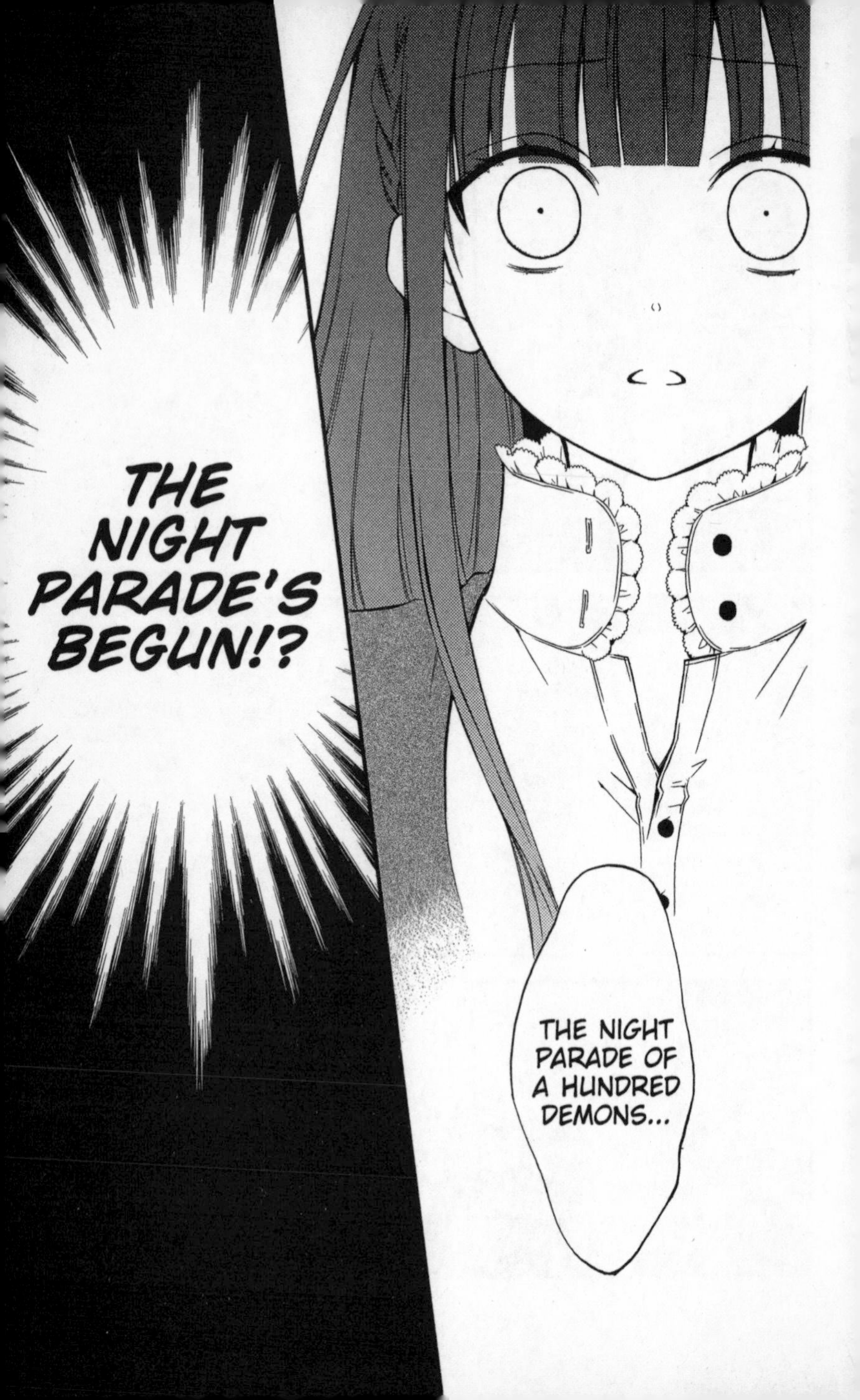
THE NIGHT PARADE OF A HUNDRED DEMONS...
THE NIGHT PARADE'S BEGUN!?

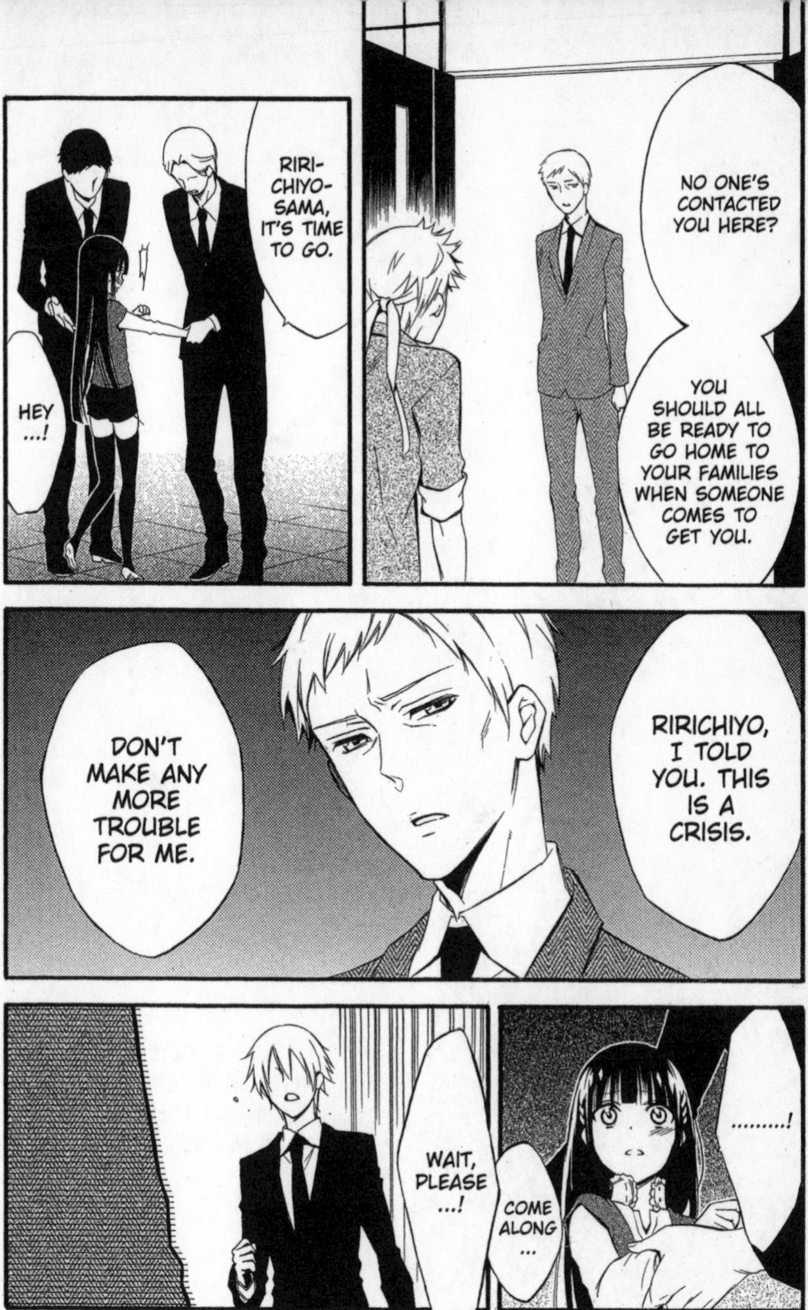
NO ONE'S CONTACTED YOU HERE?
YOU SHOULD ALL BE READY TO GO HOME TO YOUR FAMILIES WHEN SOMEONE COMES TO GET YOU.
RIRI-CHIYO-SAMA, IT'S TIME TO GO.
HEY ...!
RIRICHIYO, I TOLD YOU. THIS IS A CRISIS.
DON'T MAKE ANY MORE TROUBLE FOR ME.
.........!
COME ALONG ...
WAIT, PLEASE ...!

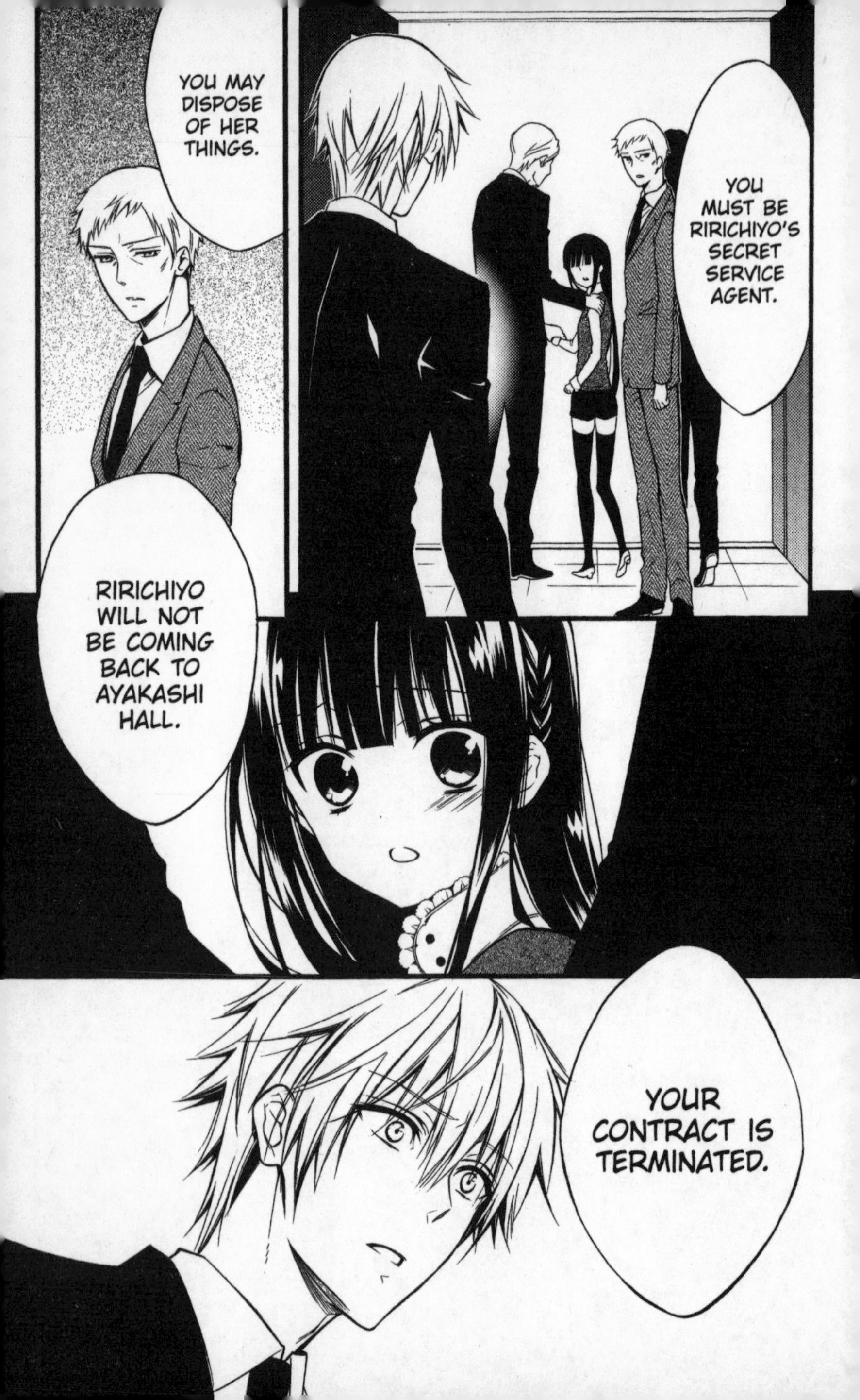
YOU MUST BE RIRICHIYO'S SECRET SERVICE AGENT.
YOU MAY DISPOSE OF HER THINGS.
RIRICHIYO WILL NOT BE COMING BACK TO AYAKASHI HALL.
YOUR CONTRACT IS TERMINATED.

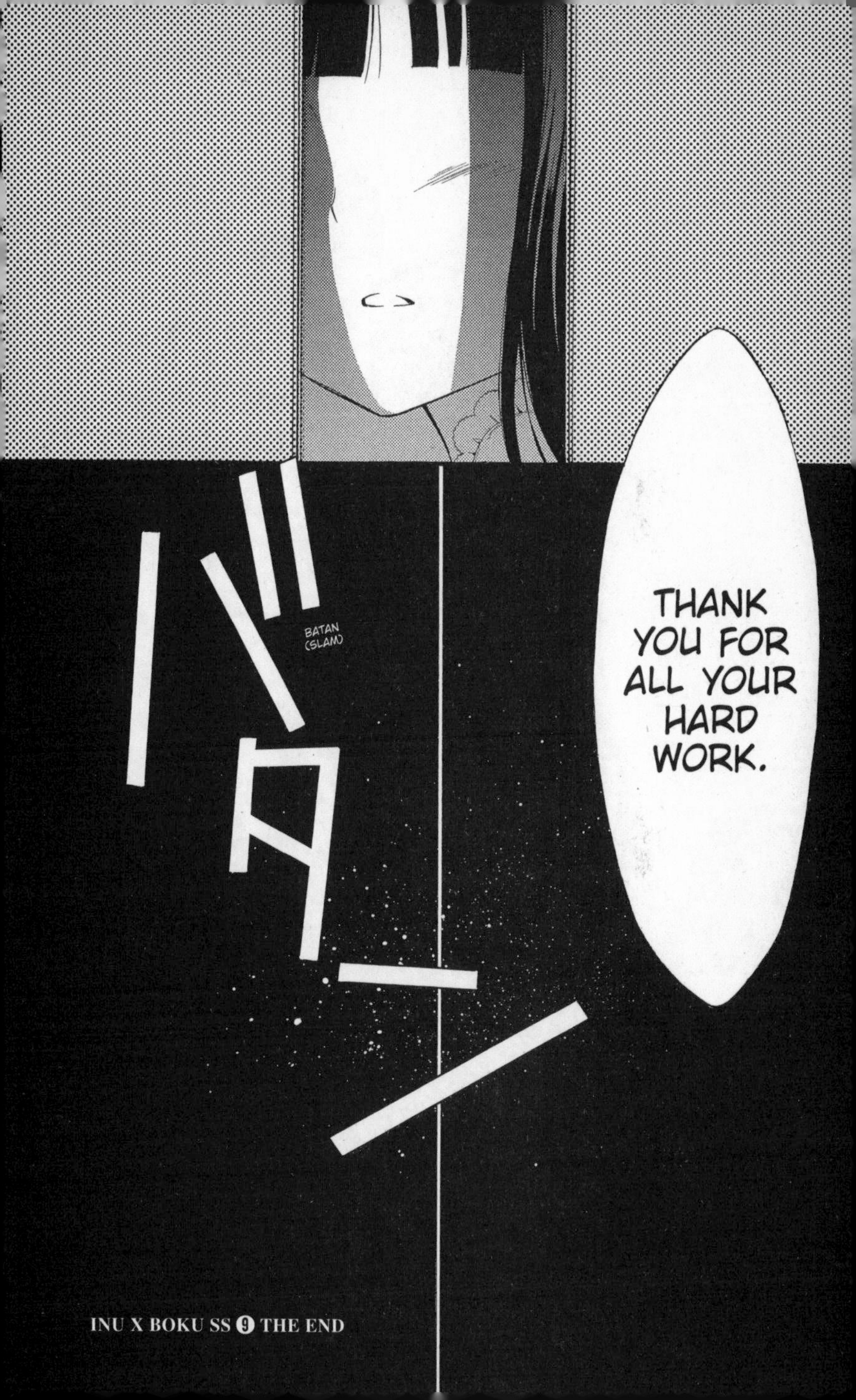
THANK YOU FOR ALL YOUR HARD WORK.
BATAN (SLAM)
INU X BOKU SS 9 THE END

TRANSLATION NOTES

COMMON HONORIFICS

no honorific: Indicates familiarity or closeness; if used without permission or reason, addressing someone in this manner would be an insult.

-san: The Japanese equivalent of Mr./Mrs./Miss. If a situation calls for politeness, this is the fail-safe honorific.

-sama: Conveys great respect; may also indicate that the social status of the speaker is lower than that of the addressee.

-kun: Used most often when referring to boys, this indicates affection or familiarity. Occasionally used by older men among their peers, but it may also be used by anyone referring to a person of lower standing.

-chan, -tan: An affectionate honorific indicating familiarity used mostly in reference to girls; also used in reference to cute persons or animals of either gender.

Used throughout the original text, **youkai** and **ayakashi** are umbrella terms for ghosts, monsters, haunted objects, mythical animals, and all sorts of uncanny things from Japanese folklore.

PAGE 17

Photograph of Paradise (Rakuen no Photograph) is the second ending theme of the anime and is actually performed by Soushi's voice actor. It's, well…not super upbeat.

PAGE 18

"Graduating from their control" is a line from *Graduation (Sotsugyou)*, a 1985 song by Yutaka Ozaki.

PAGE 79

Due to the influence of ad campaigns over the past few decades, **Christmas** has taken on the image of a romantic holiday in Japan, and Christmas Eve is traditionally spent with a significant other…like we in the West (hope to) do on Valentine's Day.

PAGE 157

Why are they **bowing** when they say, "Happy New Year"? It's a more traditional holiday in Japan and new year's greetings are quite formal—even though these two are informally abbreviating the traditional set phrases. And the usual formality of the new year's greeting is being used for a gag here…

PAGE 159

A *kotatsu* is a low table covered by a blanket with a little space heater under it. Nice and cozy.

PAGE 164

New Year noodles, or *toshikoshi soba* (literally "year-crossing buckwheat noodles"), are supposed to be eaten at midnight on the New Year, the same hour when Americans are supposed to find someone to kiss. So on the night of New Year's Day is a day late…

INU✕BOKU SS

WATANUKI'S LETTER 1

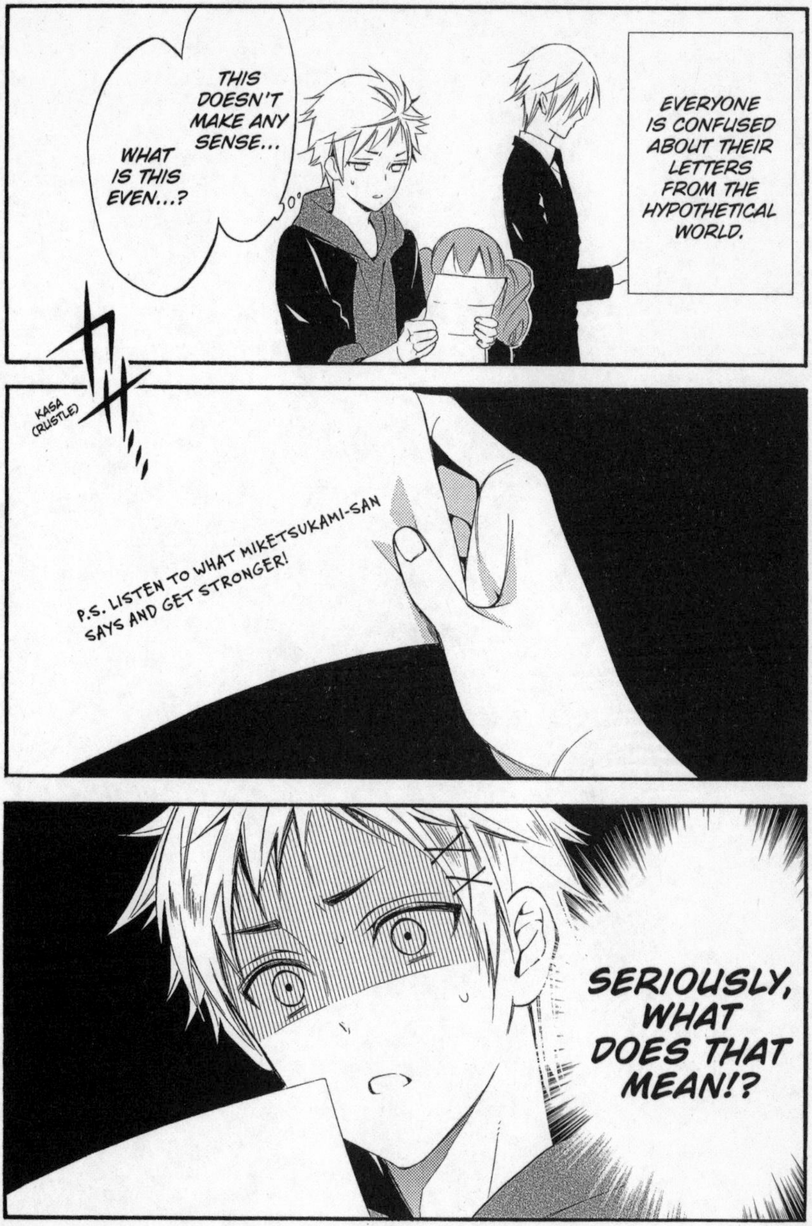
EVERYONE IS CONFUSED ABOUT THEIR LETTERS FROM THE HYPOTHETICAL WORLD.
THIS DOESN'T MAKE ANY SENSE...
WHAT IS THIS EVEN...?
KASA (RUSTLE)
P.S. LISTEN TO WHAT MIKETSUKAMI-SAN SAYS AND GET STRONGER!
SERIOUSLY, WHAT DOES THAT MEAN!?

WATANUKI'S LETTER 2

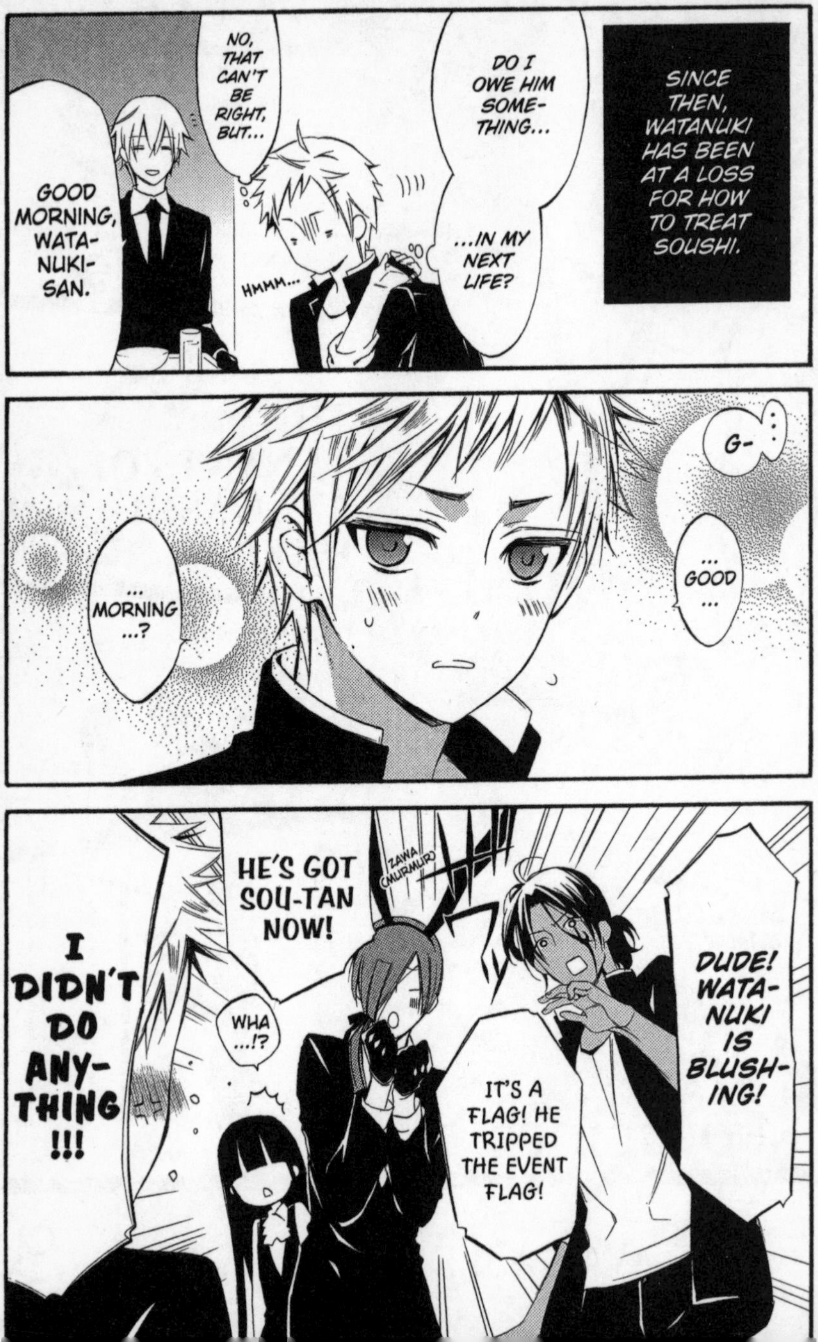
SINCE THEN, WATANUKI HAS BEEN AT A LOSS FOR HOW TO TREAT SOUSHI.
DO I OWE HIM SOMETHING...
...IN MY NEXT LIFE?
NO, THAT CAN'T BE RIGHT, BUT...
HMMM...
GOOD MORNING, WATANUKI-SAN.
G-
...GOOD...
...MORNING...?
DUDE! WATANUKI IS BLUSHING!
IT'S A FLAG! HE TRIPPED THE EVENT FLAG!
ZAWA (MURMUR)
HE'S GOT SOU-TAN NOW!
WHA...!?
I DIDN'T DO ANYTHING!!!

NEXT VOLUME PREVIEW

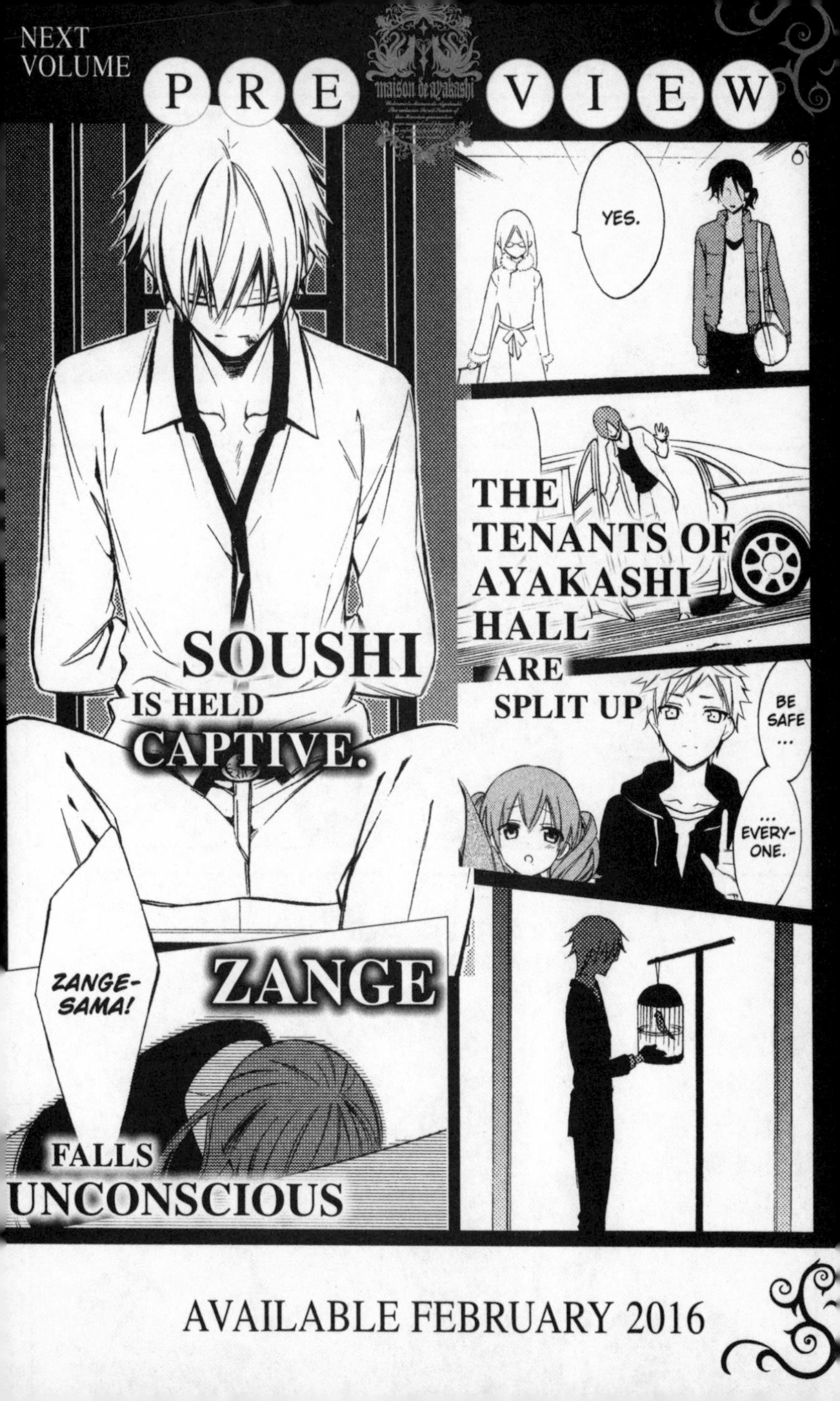
YES.
THE TENANTS OF AYAKASHI HALL ARE SPLIT UP
BE SAFE ...
... EVERY-ONE.
SOUSHI IS HELD CAPTIVE.
ZANGE-SAMA!
ZANGE FALLS UNCONSCIOUS

AVAILABLE FEBRUARY 2016

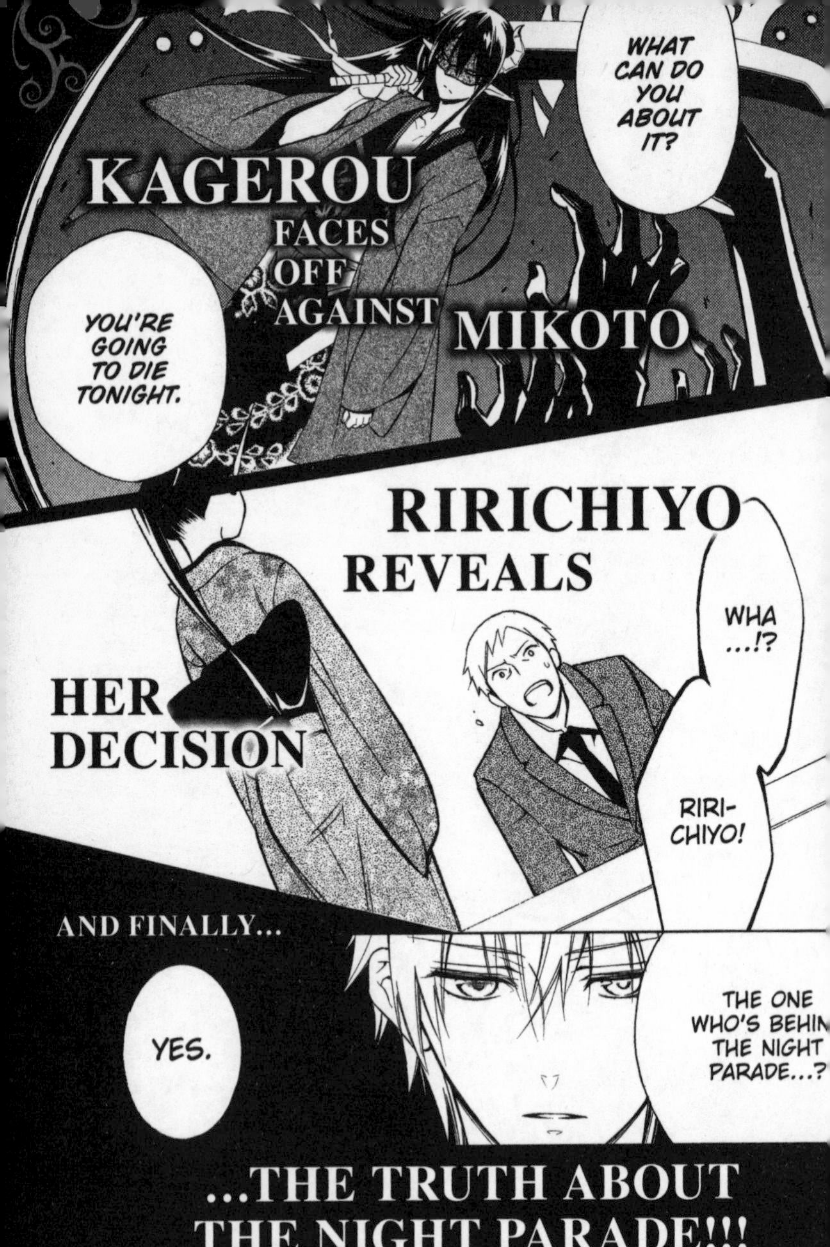
WHAT CAN DO YOU ABOUT IT?
KAGEROU FACES OFF AGAINST MIKOTO
YOU'RE GOING TO DIE TONIGHT.
RIRICHIYO REVEALS HER DECISION
WHA ...!?
RIRI-CHIYO!
AND FINALLY...
THE ONE WHO'S BEHIN THE NIGHT PARADE...?
YES.
...THE TRUTH ABOUT THE NIGHT PARADE!!!

INU×BOKU SS ⑩

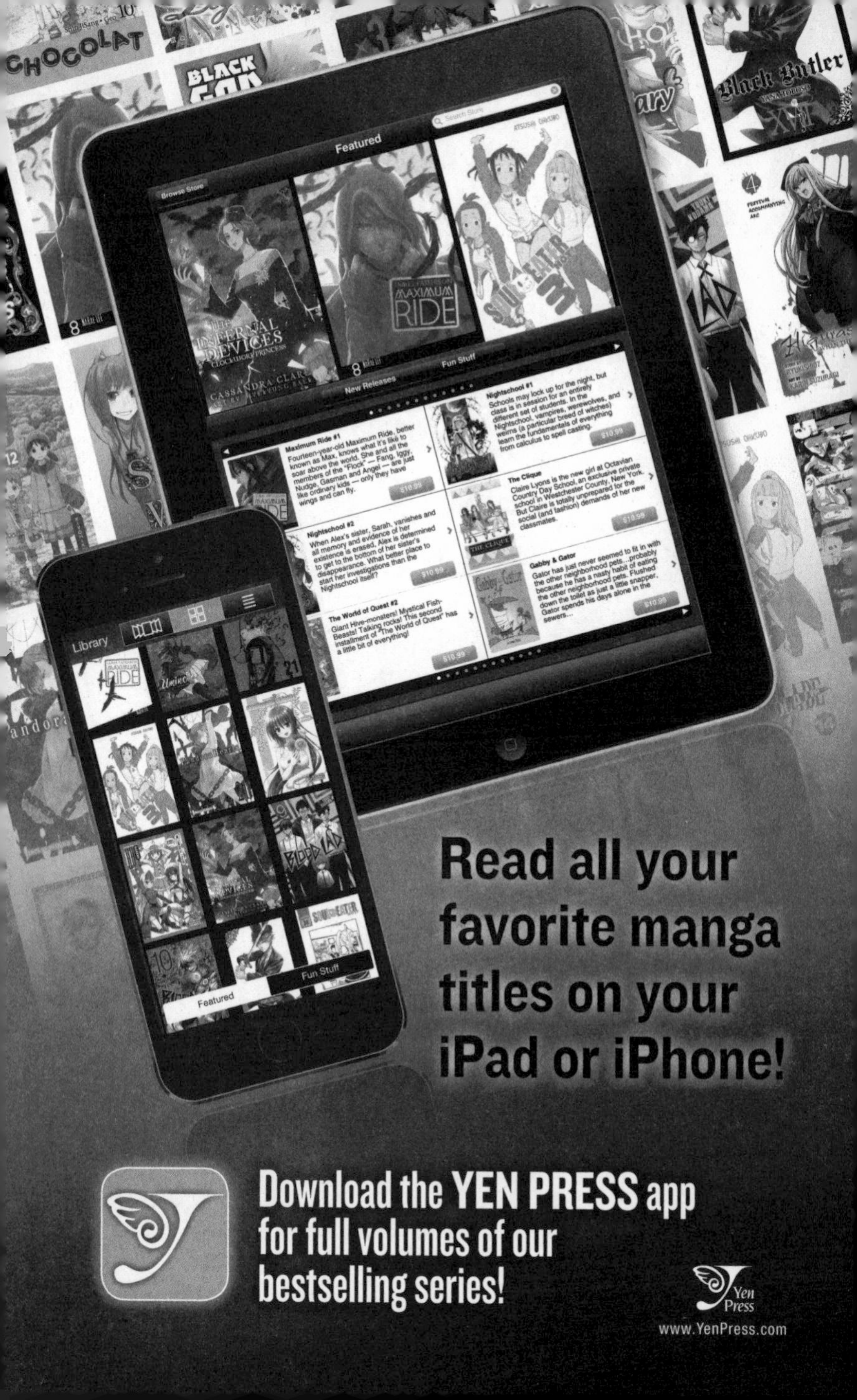
Read all your favorite manga titles on your iPad or iPhone!
Download the YEN PRESS app for full volumes of our bestselling series!
Yen Press
www.YenPress.com

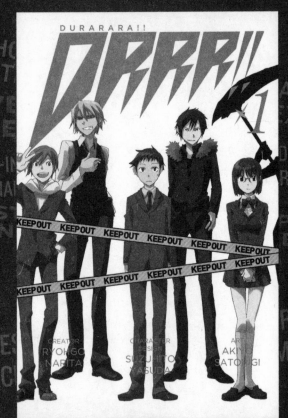

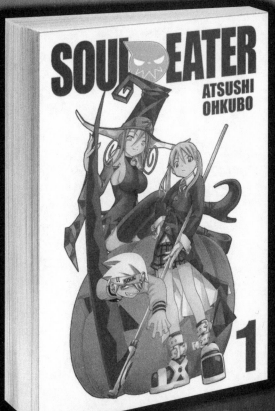

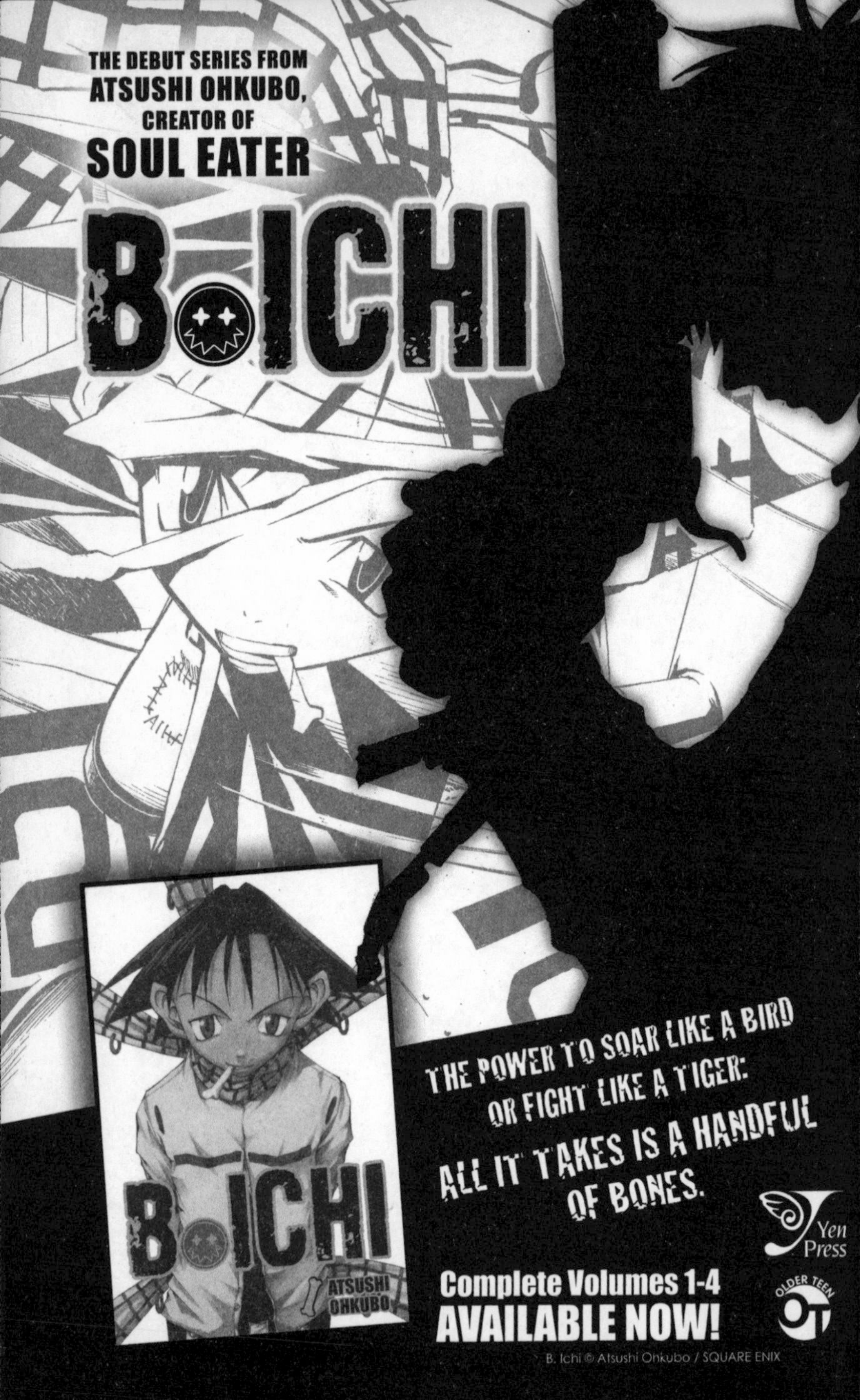
THE DEBUT SERIES FROM
ATSUSHI OHKUBO,
CREATOR OF
SOUL EATER
B. ICHI
B. ICHI
ATSUSHI OHKUBO
THE POWER TO SOAR LIKE A BIRD
OR FIGHT LIKE A TIGER:
ALL IT TAKES IS A HANDFUL
OF BONES.
Yen Press
Complete Volumes 1-4
AVAILABLE NOW!
OLDER TEEN
OT
B. Ichi © Atsushi Ohkubo / SQUARE ENIX

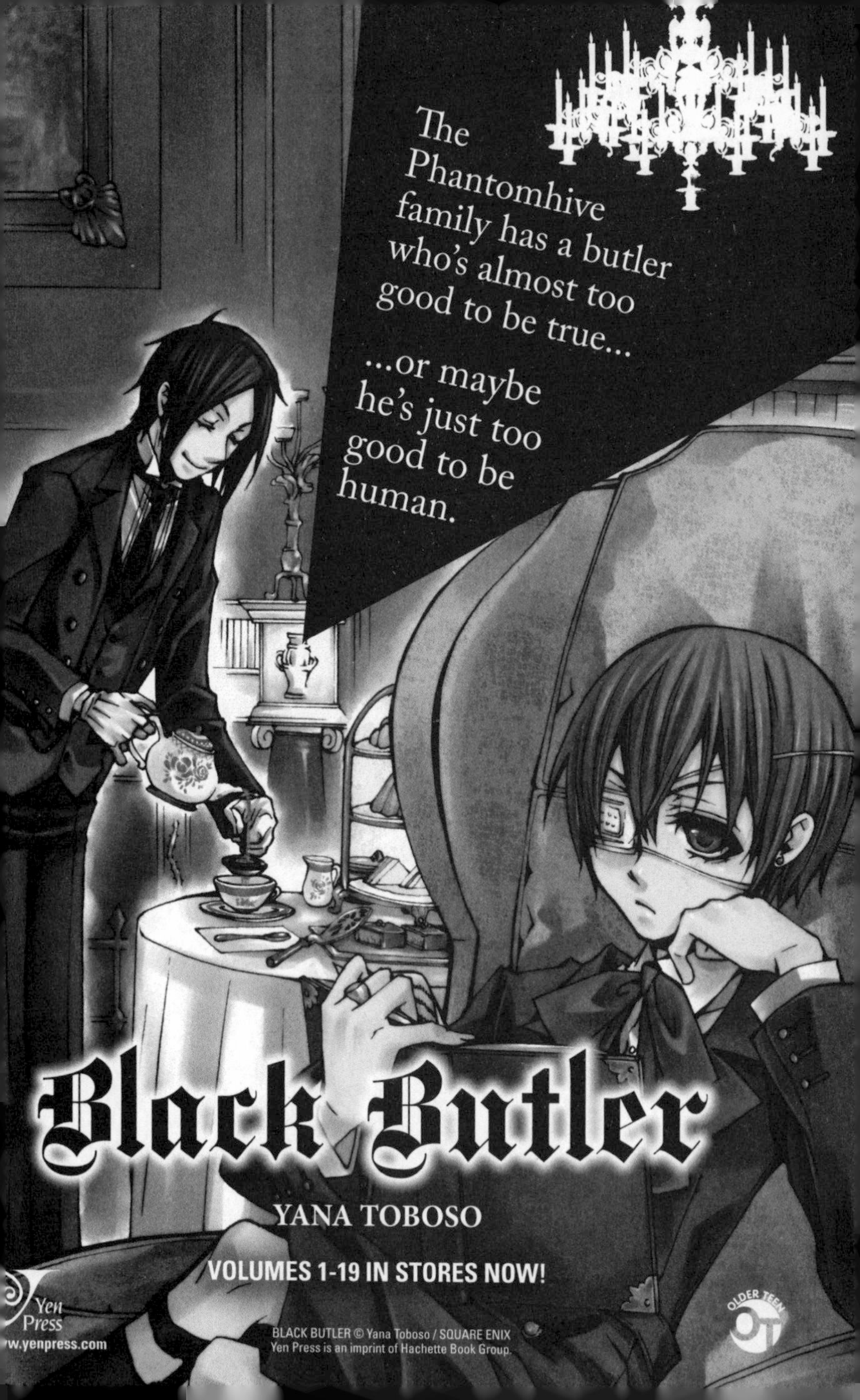

The Phantomhive family has a butler who's almost too good to be true...
...or maybe he's just too good to be human.
Black Butler
YANA TOBOSO
VOLUMES 1-19 IN STORES NOW!
Yen Press
w.yenpress.com
BLACK BUTLER © Yana Toboso / SQUARE ENIX
Yen Press is an imprint of Hachette Book Group.
OLDER TEEN
OT

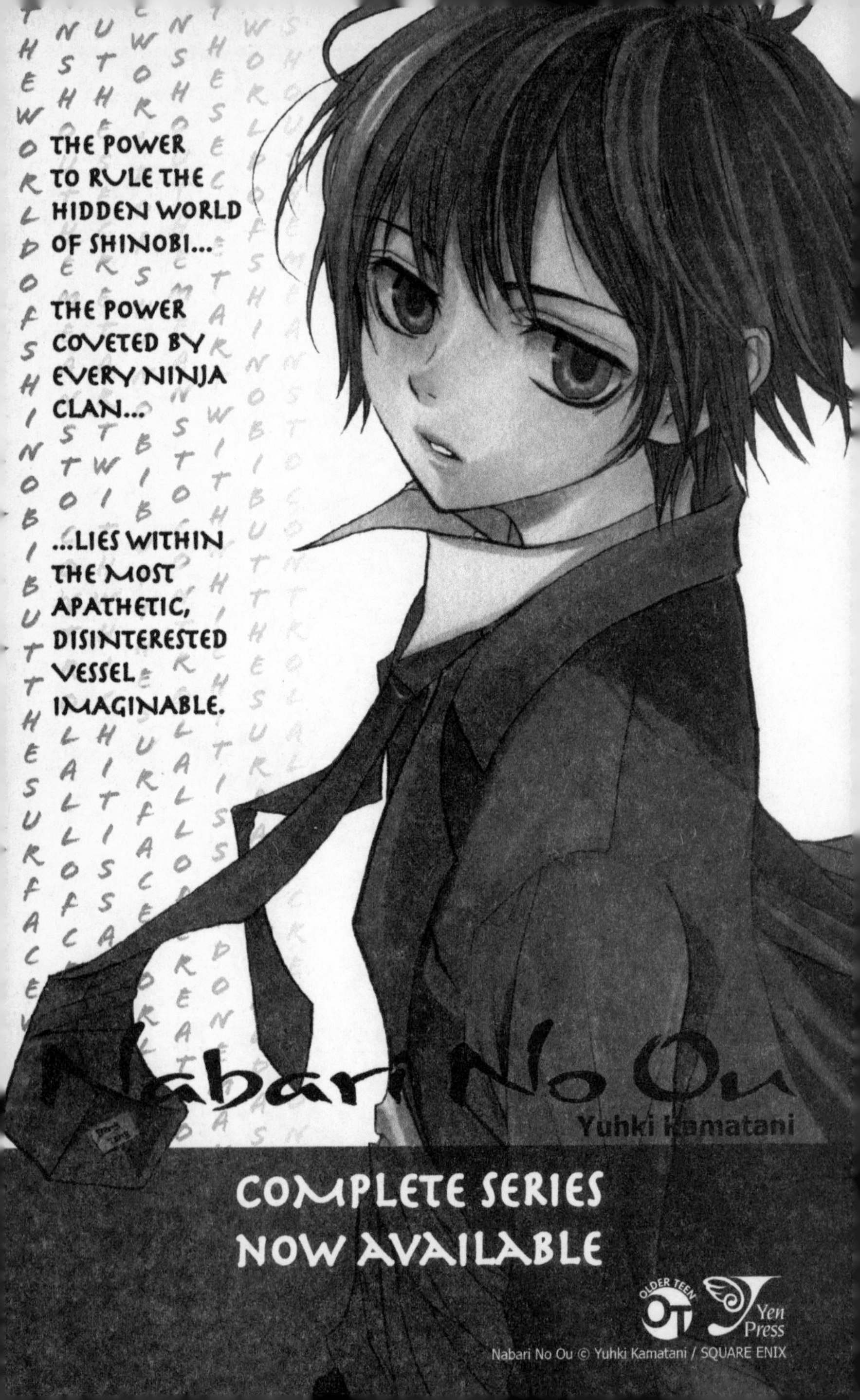

THE POWER TO RULE THE HIDDEN WORLD OF SHINOBI...
THE POWER COVETED BY EVERY NINJA CLAN...
...LIES WITHIN THE MOST APATHETIC, DISINTERESTED VESSEL IMAGINABLE.
Nabari No Ou
Yuhki Kamatani
COMPLETE SERIES NOW AVAILABLE
OLDER TEEN OT
Yen Press
Nabari No Ou © Yuhki Kamatani / SQUARE ENIX

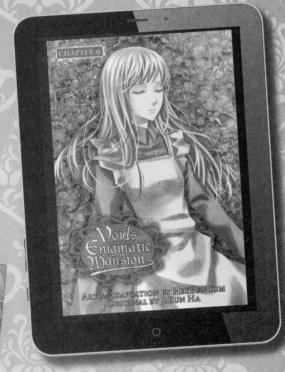

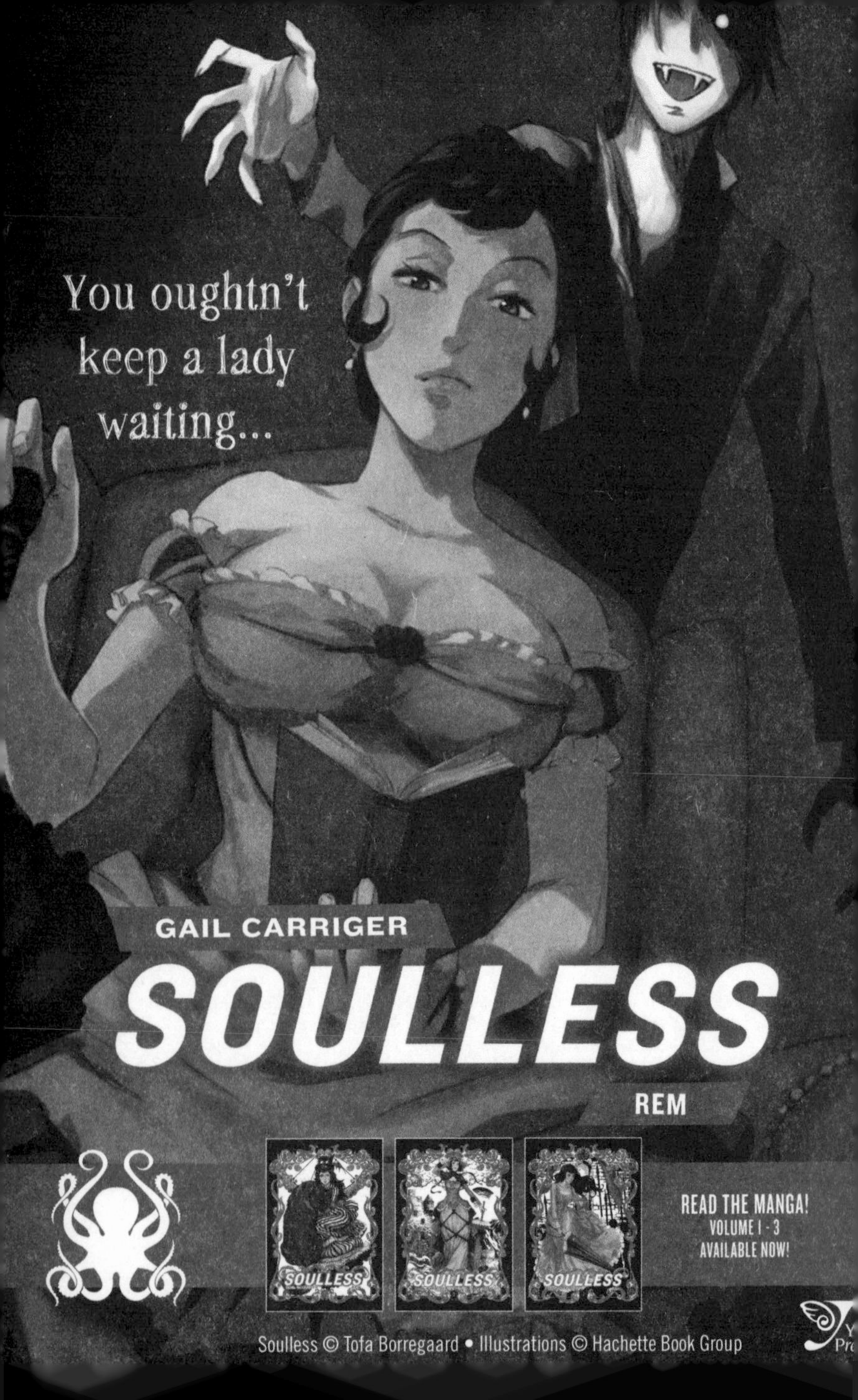
You oughtn't keep a lady waiting...
GAIL CARRIGER
SOULLESS
REM
SOULLESS
SOULLESS
SOULLESS
READ THE MANGA!
VOLUME 1 - 3
AVAILABLE NOW!
Soulless © Tofa Borregaard • Illustrations © Hachette Book Group

INU X BOKU SS 9

COCOA FUJIWARA

Translation: Melissa Tanaka • Lettering: Abigail Blackman

INUBOKU SECRET SERVICE Vol. 9 © 2013 Cocoa Fujiwara / SQUARE ENIX CO., LTD. First published in Japan in 2013 by SQUARE ENIX CO., LTD. English translation rights arranged with SQUARE ENIX CO., LTD. and Hachette Book Group through Tuttle-Mori Agency, Inc., Tokyo.

Translation © 2015 by SQUARE ENIX CO., LTD.

Yen Press
Hachette Book Group
1290 Avenue of the Americas
New York, NY 10104

www.HachetteBookGroup.com
www.YenPress.com

Yen Press is an imprint of Hachette Book Group, Inc. The Yen Press name and logo are trademarks of Hachette Book Group, Inc.

The publisher is not responsible for websites (or their contents) that are not owned by the publisher.

First Yen Press Edition: November 2015

ISBN: 978-0-316-35211-6

10 9 8 7 6 5 4 3 2 1

BVG

Printed in the United States of America